Jungian Shakespeare

Jungian Shakespeare is an original work of Jungian literary criticism, examining the psychological expression within three plays from different times in Shakespeare's career through a Jungian framework.

The book focuses on *King John*, *Cymbeline*, and *Twelfth Night*. Each play is explored both as a dramatic work meant to be fully realized onstage and as an expression of deep psychological processes. The eternal boy archetype and its relationships with father, mother, and trickster are examined through *King John*; *Twelfth Night* helps to unpack performance and the histrionic personality, while Jungian personality typology illuminates *Cymbeline*'s remarkable psychological wholeness. Rather than merely applying theory to text, the analysis reveals what Shakespeare's works inherently understand about psyche. The two fields—Shakespearean and Jungian—are brought together in a way that not only keeps the work of art intact but attempts to enrich both art and psychology.

This interdisciplinary work appeals to Jungian analysts, psychotherapists, theatre practitioners, Shakespeare scholars, and enthusiasts of literature and theatre, as well as anyone interested in the connections between Jungian psychology and Shakespeare.

Joel Crichton, BFA, MPS, is a Jungian Analyst and theatre professional with a Diploma in Analytical Psychology from the C.G. Jung-Institut in Zürich and a Master of Psychotherapy and Spirituality from St. Stephen's College. He has worked in the performing arts for over twenty years.

'A captivating book that manages to bridge the distance between theory and practice in a carefully studied and personal reading of three of Shakespeare's most enigmatic plays. Crichton's application of Jungian analysis offers the reader many neglected entry points into the texts, as well as into their value beyond the stage. *Jungian Shakespeare* is a thoughtful reminder that these works reveal their meaning reluctantly. I shall welcome this book to my own library and certainly recommend it to my students—it provides so many untouched keys to meaning and power in a play we know a little about, another we know quite well, and a third we hardly know at all. It rewards anyone dedicated to thinking about Shakespeare in new ways, and exploring their potency through their mystery.'

Peter Hinton-Davis, O.C., *is a stage director and educator. Since 1985 he has directed over 250 productions of classical and contemporary work. In 2009 he was made an officer of the Order of Canada*

'Joel Crichton constructs from Shakespeare's opus a trilogy of plays and writes a commentary that illuminates the plays and the Jungian notion of individuation as incarnating archetypes in the here and now. The argument consists in part in wonderful story-telling, also in an evocative gathering of associations and amplifications, and in hard-won brilliant insights about grounding light in darkness, embodying idealism into sensibility, and rendering what functions demonically into forms that can nourish a just society.'

Craig E. Stephenson, *author of* Possession, Anteros: A Forgotten Myth, *and* Ages of Anxiety

'As a playwright, this immensely readable book gave me new tools for approaching Shakespeare's text; it also provided insight into how a play may be considered a character itself: a complex psychology that is, through its structure and action, engaged in the messy struggles of being human. Beyond its obvious value to Shakespearean and Jungian scholars alike, this is a tremendous resource for theatre practitioners—especially directors and actors—who are tackling the challenging works of *King John*, *Twelfth Night* or *Cymbeline*. But the insights provided here may reframe an artist's approach to any of Shakespeare's plays, transforming perceived "bugs" in any play's structure, narrative or formal devices into "features" that can hint at the play's own internal psychology.'

Kevin Kerr, *University of Victoria; Playwright and Co-Founder of the Electric Company Theatre*

'With a witty and multifaceted grasp of the complexities of marrying two jealously different endeavours, Crichton offers a stunningly compelling way into Shakespeare's most enigmatic plays while redeeming the lenses provided by the heritage of Jungian depth psychology.'

Susan Rowland, PhD, *Pacifica Graduate Institute, author of* Jungian Literary Criticism

Jungian Shakespeare

Coming Down to Earth in *King John*, *Twelfth Night*, and *Cymbeline*

Joel Crichton

Routledge
Taylor & Francis Group

LONDON AND NEW YORK

Designed cover image: Getty Images

First published 2026
by Routledge
4 Park Square, Milton Park, Abingdon, Oxon OX14 4RN

and by Routledge
605 Third Avenue, New York, NY 10158

Routledge is an imprint of the Taylor & Francis Group, an informa business

© 2026 Joel Crichton

British Library Cataloguing-in-Publication Data
A catalogue record for this book is available from the British Library

Library of Congress Cataloging-in-Publication Data
Names: Crichton, Joel author
Title: Jungian Shakespeare : coming down to earth in King John, Twelfth night, and Cymbeline / Joel Crichton.
Description: London ; New York : Routledge, 2026. | Includes bibliographical references and index.
Identifiers: LCCN 2025029804 (print) | LCCN 2025029805 (ebook) | ISBN 9781032980850 hardback | ISBN 9781032980836 paperback | ISBN 9781003596967 ebook
Subjects: LCSH: Shakespeare, William, 1564–1616–Knowledge and learning | Jung, C. G. (Carl Gustav), 1875–1961 | Shakespeare, William, 1564–1616. King John | Shakespeare, William, 1564–1616. Twelfth night | Shakespeare, William, 1564–1616. Cymbeline | English drama–Early modern and Elizabethan, 1500–1600–History and criticism | Psychoanalysis and literature–England | Drama–Psychological aspects | Archetype (Psychology) in literature
Classification: LCC PR3065 .C75 2026 (print) | LCC PR3065 (ebook)
LC record available at https://lccn.loc.gov/2025029804
LC ebook record available at https://lccn.loc.gov/2025029805

ISBN: 978-1-032-98085-0 (hbk)
ISBN: 978-1-032-98083-6 (pbk)
ISBN: 978-1-003-59696-7 (ebk)

DOI: 10.4324/9781003596967

Typeset in Times New Roman
by Apex CoVantage, LLC

For Imo, naturally.

Contents

Foreword   *x*
by John Beebe

Introduction: Coming Down to Earth   1

1   "A strange beginning": Introduction to *King John*   22

2   The Faithless Eros of *King John*   32

3   "Smiling at grief": Introduction to *Twelfth Night, or What
     You Will*   78

4   The Histrionic Pattern in *Twelfth Night*   88

5   "But what's the matter?": Introduction to *Cymbeline*   142

6   The Achievement of Normality in *Cymbeline*   164

7   Postlude: Good (Enough) Ground   240

     Acknowledgments   *242*
     Bibliography   *244*
     Index   *256*

Foreword

A number of readers who have found their way to this book are here because they have already found the idea of a Jungian Shakespeare attractive. Others may enter with scepticism, resenting the idea that Shakespeare will once again have to be turned into something else to be understood. Even Jan Kott's happy title, *Shakespeare Our Contemporary*, can offend, since Shakespeare seems quite at home being one of his *own* contemporaries, having come to treasure *his* place and time: England, "This precious stone set in the silver sea" (*RII* 2.1.46), in the last half of the 16th century and his sliver of the 17th century before the Civil War, a time when the idea of the New World had found ground and origin in Renaissance England as a setting where good and evil could still be individually reconciled. Fortunately, that is the ground that this book is able to come to via its use of a Jungian understanding of what Shakespeare himself was intending to individuate.

Why, then, entice Shakespeare into modern psychological dress when he graced his Globe with souls set free to make meaning of their *own* time? Why imply that the Bard's effort was anachronistically determined by its future in a world gone Jungian? Shakespeare was guided not by Jung but by Ovid, who had made Augustan Rome a place to celebrate myth. I believe that Shakespeare took heart from Ovid's example and believed that as an English poet, he could make the Elizabethan environment equally mythic ground.

As a Jungian analyst who has found concepts like 'complex', 'psychological type', and 'archetype' to be useful ways to see Shakespeare's method of outlining what the actors on his stage would bring to psychological life, I'm moved to call attention to a statement of Jung's from his *Aion*, defending his rather histrionic way of animating psyches:

> . . . in describing the living process of the psyche, I deliberately and consciously give preference to a dramatic, mythological way of thinking and speaking, because this is not only more expressive but also more exact than an abstract scientific terminology.[1]

Jung comes close to saying here that a psyche is naturally dramatic. Elsewhere, he makes clear that the most theatrical of his own concepts, archetype, is not intended to make one think of a characteristic *figure*, but rather of a typical *situation* in which character gets a chance to emerge. Crichton helps us to understand this by saying that Shakespeare's understanding of dramatic situations is that they are not archetypes but 'archetypal,' which is a Jungian way of realizing that situations find their mythic resonance through the transcendent quality of the patterns of behaviour they permit.

Recognizing the supraordinate power of situations led Jung to state in his work on synchronicity, which he began to publish in 1951, "I turned my attention to the intuitive technique of *grasping the total situation* which is so characteristic of China, namely the *I Ching* or *Book of Changes*."[2] It should not surprise the reader that Crichton in the present work has also turned to the *I Ching* to amplify the kinds of situations Shakespeare dramatizes. That is because it is a situation that summons the psyches of the players in a Shakespeare play, however preposterous the situation, to worry about whether they are managing their part in it wisely. And this is what keeps Shakespeare so relevant, because this same moral anxiety is the usual tension of our own lives.

Psyches, as both Jung and Shakespeare understood, come to life in situations that call for consciousness, and in their own particularity for the types of psychological consciousness Jung discovered, with the now-famous categories of extraverted and introverted as applied to the faculties of thinking, feeling, sensation, and intuition that he deemed the basis of consciousness itself. What Jung turned to the *I Ching* to amplify was his insight that finding the appropriate consciousness for a difficult situation is how a will can become wise. In Shakespeare's plays this insight is enunciated, often unexpectedly, by many of his characters (however minor) who in pausing to become oracular make us realize that anyone can for a moment become as objective as a Greek chorus.

That Shakespeare, centuries before Jung, had recognized that consciousness emerges out of complexity only when pressed into service by what has dramatically emerged in archetypal form suggests that Shakespeare had already come to what Jung was to call the reality of the psyche and what Crichton in this book calls 'ground.' Joel Crichton was an actor who has now become an analyst, and there is a great deal to enjoy here in his performance as a hermeneutic appreciator of psychological design in the plays he has chosen to analyse. Unlocking the meaning and purpose of some of Shakespeare's most extreme dramatizations of personal and political perplexity in three of his most flagrantly complex but undeniably archetypal plays, Crichton, with impressive command of a Jungian critical vocabulary, has in these pages given shape, nuance, and critical size to the signature concepts of Jungian thought, allowing them to become keys to the royal chambers in which—as Shakespeare famously intuited—the drama of the psyche is actually situated. Knowingly employing the rigorous logos of performance and the playful eros of depth-psychological inquiry allows Crichton to unlock our experience of Shakespeare's psychological mind in the way it seems to have been designed to be unlocked, in turn allowing us all to enter a mystery that involves coming to a cultural consciousness which is bracing as well as renewing to share.

John Beebe

Notes

1 Jung (CW 9ii, 25)
2 Jung (CW 8, 863)

Introduction

Coming Down to Earth

You have to love Shakespeare in order to understand him. This is one half of the proposition made by the editors of the First Folio of his complete works, who exhort the "great Variety of Readers" to read the works "againe and againe: And if then you doe not like him, surely you are in some manifest danger not to understand him."

The other way to read that statement is something like: read him again and again, and then if you *still* do not like him, surely you are in some manifest danger not to *have understood* him. In other words, if there's anything you don't like about Shakespeare, it's probably just because you haven't yet understood it. That one may be true as well. Like the most unyielding of dreams, Shakespeare's works take months, years, decades—even centuries—to 'get'. Nevertheless, they abound in the feeling that there *is* always something *to* get, and it seems that at odd intervals in the studying or production of a play, a scene, line, or word previously thought to be impenetrable or superfluous suddenly reveals its necessity.

I begin this book with love because the union of psychoanalysis with Shakespeare has not always been a marriage of true minds. First of all, the psychoanalyst has a natural tendency, and indeed a vocational prerogative, to *analyse* psychological phenomena, including works of art, and analysis is as often as not a process of reduction and cutting to pieces. Psychology tends to reduce everything else to psychological data—not without good reason—however, the work of art, and especially its *overall effect as itself, on its own terms,* frequently dies on the table during this procedure. Second, I suspect there is a distinct and unconscious animosity among psychoanalysts toward Shakespeare in particular, because among all the wonderful insights of Freud and Jung, it so often seems that Shakespeare got there first. This is understandably narcissistically wounding, and evokes a natural resentment: that an "upstart crow" should have pre-empted our field;[1] and indeed Shakespeare has been credited more than once with the invention of psychoanalysis.[2]

One of the axioms of this book is that a human being's encounter with art follows the same logic as the meeting of two personalities, which Jung likens to "the contact of two chemical substances. If there is any reaction, both are transformed."[3] With this in mind, my intention here is not to write a Jungian psychoanalytic book *per se*, but rather to write a Jungian-Shakespearean literary criticism that

DOI: 10.4324/9781003596967-1

transforms (and benefits) both partners symbiotically, and which moreover stands up in terms of scholarship in both the Jungian and Shakespearean fields. I hope that what I write enhances the experience of the work of art through psychological understanding, and I hope that through my approach the work is allowed to reveal some of the significant psychological insight that it holds. New knowledge for both sides—with any luck.

The book is written with a broad, non-specialist audience in mind. It will, naturally, be most easily read by those familiar with both Jungian concepts and Shakespeare. However, it should be of interest to readers who are familiar with only one or neither, but who would like to know both better. I hope that it will be of use to theatre practitioners; I used to be one, and this infuses my writing. I have kept the unconscious use of technical jargon, Jungian or otherwise, to an absolute minimum. The key Jungian concepts will be covered later in this introduction.

The plays on which I focus in this book are *King John, Twelfth Night,* and *Cymbeline.* One is among Shakespeare's most produced works to this day, and two are virtually unknown to most audiences. The reader who does not know *King John* or *Cymbeline,* therefore, may take comfort that they are not alone. These three plays were not, at first, chosen with any conscious agenda in mind, but rather intuitively; I later found that they formed an unexpected triptych on the subject of this book's title: Coming Down to Earth. By this I mean many things: the movement from youth to adulthood, or from ideal to real, or from extraordinary to normal. The book is about the confrontation with reality—the difficult, often torturous, and necessary psychological work of grounding oneself, if one is ever going to live one's real life.

This is also what Jung's psychology is about. Jungian psychoanalysis must contend with the burden of its own wealth, insofar as it boasts many attractive yet easily misconstruable concepts—archetypes, anima/animus, collective unconscious, shadow, etc.—but fundamentally the field is aimed at living one's own true life. Perhaps this book can help to make that clearer.

The three chapters are individually organized, albeit loosely, around different Jungian concepts. But the play comes first, and the theory comes second; the tail does not wag the dog. I do not wish to provide Shakespearean proofs for Jungian theories; I want to get in touch with the heart of these plays, and along the way have *found* that Jungian concepts have helped to illuminate aspects of them which would otherwise have remained murky to me.

The chapter on *King John* has the tightest focus, being primarily about the archetypal pattern called the puer aeternus, or eternal boy. The puer, who in some sense is the background protagonist of this entire book, has to do with creative, childlike, and childish energies, which exist in every personality, but which can become one-sided and pathological. It is the puer who is most in need of coming down to earth.

The chapter on *Twelfth Night* deals with motifs of performance and authenticity. The play serves as a wealth of insight on the histrionic personality structure, which describes the character of a person given to theatricality and illusion.

The chapter on *Cymbeline* attempts to come to grips with the play *as a whole*, something that has often been avoided due to its long-standing (and totally unjust) reputation of "unresisting imbecility".[4] Jungian typological theory is mobilized to inquire into the unconscious structure of the play.

Each main chapter has its own introductory chapter, which contains a synopsis of the play, information on its origin, a few thoughts to orient the main discussion, and some critical history. I should emphasize the word *some*: it will be understood that these introductions cannot possibly provide a comprehensive overview of these plays' histories, but can only address selections. Their purpose is less to dialogue with the current scholarship, and more to prepare the reader for the following chapter. The reader interested in *more* is heartily encouraged to seek out the much fuller and more capable introductions which are published in many editions of the plays themselves. (As will be evident from my citations, I am personally partial to the Arden series.)

One idea from the work of scholar Michael Goldman informs my approach to these plays. I have taken to calling it the Goldmanian Centre. His view is that each play has been 'washed in its own water' (this alchemical phrase is my usage, not his). His own words propose that "the [actors] here must solve a problem parallel to those wrestled with both by the characters . . . and the audience."[5] This means not only that each play has its own style and energy, which is obvious, but that it has its own deep wholeness, a level at which all of the (at times apparently disparate) elements of the play connect, relating to and enriching one another. I consider each play in terms of these three levels—actors, character, and audience—and this orients each discussion. There is a quality—perhaps an archetype—at the heart of each play, which pulsates through every aspect of the play in some form, the way a real heart sends blood throughout the body. This concept, though technically posing the risk of engendering a myopic view of the play which assimilates everything to one single point, will prove very helpful in finding what seems (to me) to be its heart, and its essential expression throughout.

So much for hearts and love, for now.

A Man with a View

By *View,* I mean to evoke the 20th hexagram of *I Ching, or The Book of Changes*, which describes an ethical stance that I feel is common to both Jung and Shakespeare. *I Ching* (or *Yi Jing, Zhou Yi,* or 易经) is an ancient Chinese text with both Taoist and Confucian connections. Its main text is a sequence of 64 situation-images, each broken down into several parts, which purport to contain everything in the world. 'Hexagram' is the name for these situation-images, as they are each comprised of six lines, broken or unbroken. The name of the 20th—觀, *Guān*—is translated as "Contemplation (View)".[6] The six-line image is thought to evoke an ancient watchtower, situated on a hill, where one could watch and observe for miles around:

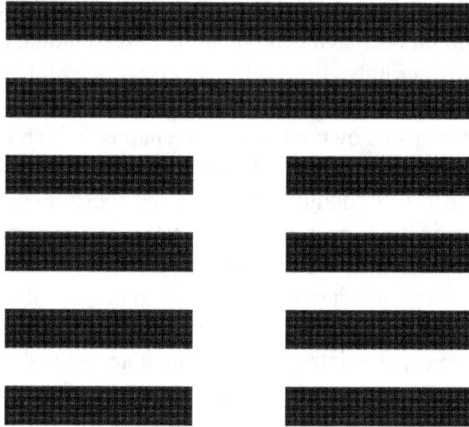

That Shakespeare has such a View of the world is undoubtable. His vision anticipates the psychoanalysts of the 20th century, as well as nearly every other writer in
the English language. Wherever you go, there Shakespeare is already. The transla-
tor Richard Wilhelm adds the following commentary to *Guān*:

> in making regular journeys the ruler could, in the first place, survey his realm and
> make certain that none of the existing usages of the people escaped notice . . .
> such a man will have a view of the real sentiments of the great mass of humanity
> and therefore cannot be deceived.[7]

This man brings to my mind Prince Hal, who can "drink with any tinker in his own
language" (*1HIV* 2.4.18–9), a statement which I suspect to be true of Shakespeare
as well. Having likely been familiar with the Roman Terence, Shakespeare also
seems to have comprehended the ethical motto that Jung would later repeat: *nil
humanum a me alienum esse*—nothing human is alien to me.[8] Jung gave some
advice, now well-known:

> [A]nyone who wants to know the human psyche . . . would be better advised
> to [abandon exact science] put away his scholar's gown, bid farewell to his
> study, and wander with human heart through the world. There, in the horrors
> of prisons, lunatic asylums and hospitals, in drab suburban pubs, in brothels
> and gambling-hells, in the salons of the elegant, the Stock Exchanges, Socialist
> meetings, churches, revivalist gatherings and ecstatic sects, through love and
> hate, through the experience of passion in every form in his own body, he would
> reap richer stores of knowledge than text-books a foot thick could give him, and
> he will know how to doctor the sick with real knowledge of the human soul.[9]

I consider Jung's advice to be consistent with Shakespeare's own ethic.[10] Shakespeare's characters consistently give the impression of full human beings, indeed so

much that they have often been the subject of psychological case studies. In addition to rivalling the Freudian perspicacity in observation of the human, all-too-human, Shakespeare also has a facility with the greater movements of psyche itself, which belong more to the Jungian View—here I allude to the 'archetypal'.

Shakespeare's characters do not flatten. All, great and small, are likewise both great *and* small at the same time; strong and weak, honourable and ruthless; to paraphrase Solzhenitsyn, the "line dividing good from evil" cuts through all of their hearts.[11] In this way, they evince what Jung would later identify as the *tension of opposites*, the fundamental psychological dynamic without which there would be no psychic energy.[12] Jung—another man with a View—developed a psychology that is attuned to this tension of opposites, as well as to their underlying identity, and therefore to the presence of paradox in the psyche; Jung's psychology is therefore uniquely suited to Shakespearean study.

Ben Kingsley speaks to the tensions in these characters, and the importance, for playing them, of *staying* with them. Regarding *Julius Caesar*'s Brutus, he said that

> He seems to be fraught with contradictions . . . Brutus' inconsistencies are only a microcosm of the whole play. If you try and iron out these inconsistencies in order to make the part playable, you will in fact anesthetize the energy within the lines. The energy of the character and the predicament of the character are only available to the audience if the tension between the opposing forces is observed, relished, and played.[13]

John Barton offered the simple summary, "In a way, the contradictions *are* the character." Kingsley's words provide an analogy to what is probably the prime criticism that Jung and his followers have of every other psychology: that the aim of other methods is to iron out the inconsistencies in the person to make the part playable, that is, to make the life more liveable. Of course a more liveable life is a legitimate aim of all psychotherapy, *but*, analyst and analysand alike must take great care not to anesthetize the energy within the life.

The Third: Life

In the matter of positioning this book academically, I have come to see that 'Jungian-Shakespearean literary criticism' is a subtle misdefinition. My focus is not Jung, nor Jung's writings, nor even Jung's concepts, though all of these form a completely invaluable and irreplaceable part of my foundation. Nor is it *quite* correct to identify the focus as Shakespeare. Really, the focus is life. Fundamentally, my interest is in better understanding *that*. As my inclusion of *I Ching* may intimate, an aspect of my focus is toward the ineffable laws which seem to govern existence, or at least the human experience of existence—the archetypal situations that make up life. The Jungian approach, or my version of it, is the best way I know to relate to this level of reality. To me, an interest in the archetypal is best satisfied through cultivation of a distinct interest in individual people and their circumstances, real or fictive: I am interested in *character*, and for me that includes the character of analysands, early modern writers, and most certainly the characters who exist on the Shakespearean page and come to life on the theatrical stage.

To me, the 'point' of all this—and the point of Jungian Psychology too—is, ultimately, to live better life, though naturally I leave the precise definition of that to the individuating 'liver'. Jung, near the end of his time, said:

> I aimed, after all, at *this* world and *this* life. No matter how deeply absorbed or how blown about I was, I always knew that everything I was experiencing was ultimately directed at this real life of mine. I meant to meet its obligations and fulfill its meanings.[14]

Shakespeare's works unite the verisimilitude of everyday-life-as-experienced-by-people with the archetypal resonances of myth and dream. The content of his work is big enough to retain some of the universal quality of myth, while also being small enough for one to be able to reliably encounter, in the phrase given us by Freud, "some character-types met with in psycho-analytic work"[15]—i.e., *people.* Shakespeare gives us the archetypal situation in manifestation, and let's us see it play out: speak, act, breathe, live, as a relation between human beings, from one moment to the next, expressed in text, to be embodied by actors. These plays are like a stepping-stone on the spectrum from personal to universal that runs anecdote-story-legend-fairytale-myth-archetype; one could slot them in between legend and fairytale, except that they also seem, at times, to run the gamut of the entire spectrum.

My former theatre career probably colours my understanding of a dramatic text in ways of which I am still unconscious. One thing of which I am conscious is that I know from experience that a play—especially one of Shakespeare's—can bear many, many different interpretations. In this respect, Shakespeare has been unbelievably generous, giving scripts that every individual reader or artist can find their own individual way through. Consider, as a representative point, the stage directions: unlike, say, G. B. Shaw, whose stage directions could clog a firehose, Shakespeare provides few, if any—most of those we have are given by editors. Very significantly, he does not explicitly tell us where he thinks the actors should *pause*, and therefore he does not telegraph where the most important emotional moments are. That alone makes all the difference to a production, without even yet taking into account the influence of different actors, directors, designers, *audience members*... Not only will every one of these have a different interpretation of a play, but difference and variation is the lifeblood of theatre, for every night of a play's performance is necessarily different, somewhat new, both reborn and dying in the moment it is performed, constantly phoenix-like.

"Almost anything can be projected into Shakespeare" wrote Ted Hughes,[16] and I would add that almost anything can *work.* This is my way of acknowledging that I cannot consider my interpretations of these plays authoritative or final in any sense—nor would I want that. We don't want to 'solve' a Shakespeare play;

we want to play with it. It is a great wonder that his work can survive this kaleidoscopic scrutiny. This is very like a dream: give the same dream to 100 analysts, and you will receive 100 different interpretations, and all of them will pick up on something true. Hamlet uses this principle to bedevil Polonius:

HAMLET: Do you see yonder cloud that's almost in shape of a camel?
POLONIUS: By th' mass and 'tis like a camel indeed.
HAMLET: Methinks it is backed like a weasel.
POLONIUS: It is backed like a weasel.
HAMLET: Or like a whale?
POLONIUS: Very like a whale.

(*Ham.* 3.2.367–72)

Key Jungian Concepts

It would be beyond the scope of this book to re-teach Jungian Psychology from the ground up. I feel parsimony to be more appropriate, and so here I restrict myself to identifying what appear to me to be the most relevant aspects of the approach to reading *this book specifically*. The concepts I include here are: part-psyche; the unconscious; archetypes; amplification; the finalistic perspective; individuation; and shadow. I try to explain them in a focused way, in terms of what I think will be useful to the reader. This means that the definitions are technically incomplete, but I am confident that the *best* way for me to define these concepts is by using them in context, as they become necessary. That will be the business of the rest of this book.

Part-Psyche

The most important Jungian concept to my approach is that I occasionally view characters in plays as part-psyches, or what Jung sometimes called "splinter psyches".[17] When looking in this way, I take a play as a metaphor for a whole psyche— a person, basically, who has shown up for psychoanalysis, and whose characters express different parts, energies, or functions within them, in much the same way as we might interpret a person's dream-characters as expressing different parts of a real person's psyche.

The Unconscious

The theory of the unconscious proposes that there are more things going on within our psyches than we can be aware of at any one time. This might include thoughts, sense-perceptions, intuitions, feelings, emotions, but it might just as well include the influence of unconscious part-psyches. The most easily-graspable example of this would be when we catch ourselves having an argument, in our minds, with somebody who is not there—until the moment we noticed ourselves doing it, it was unconscious.

Often in this work I will attribute an unconscious quality to phenomena that appear in a play. What I might mean depends on the context, but it is probably either that (a) I am proposing inner processes for a character, of which they are not conscious at the moment in question, or that (b) I am proposing that Shakespeare may have been unconscious of certain ideas which come across in his plays. I find the unconscious *per se* to be a necessary proposition where Shakespeare is concerned, because otherwise we have to propose that he was *consciously aware* of all the substance of all the millions of pages of interpretation that have been written on his work. For this to be true, he would have not only needed to be a God, but a completely obsessive-compulsive one, absolutely cramming his work with seemingly infinite levels of meaning. I find it much simpler to accept that the unconscious participated with Shakespeare's conscious personality in the writing process; in part this is because I, too, have been a playwright whose plays concealed far more than I had been consciously aware of. I also find this proposal much easier to accept than theories of alternate (or multiple) authors, although these theories are clearly *symbolically* true, if not literally, given the evidence of writerly collaboration and cross-pollination in Shakespeare's time,[18] not to mention generations of editors, critics, and theatre artists whose interpretations become definitive. (As one small example of the latter: when I read Falstaff's part, I cannot tell if I am reading Shakespeare or remembering Antony Sher.)

Archetypes

One major thing that I see the Jungian View offering Shakespeare is the concept of the archetypal. However, archetype is an infamously difficult thing to define, which is all the more troublesome since it is the concept at the absolute centre of Jungian Psychology.

It may be best to explain by comparison. In Janet Adelman's very well-argued and very Freudian *Suffocating Mothers*,[19] we may read a great deal about Shakespeare's personal mother complex. This is fine—the book is truly formidable—but I would argue that Shakespeare's writing *matters* because it is not solely about 'his' mother complex, but that it often has to do with the mother complex *as such*, and therefore with the mother *archetype*. Of course Shakespeare's work must, on some level, be as unconsciously autobiographical as the next artist's. But we pay attention to it not primarily because it tells us something about William's relationship with his mother Mary, or father John, or his marriage to Anne, or his fatherhood to children Hamnet, Judith, and Susanna, but rather because it transcends personalistic psychology and moves toward something deeply rooted in the human psyche; it tells us about husbands and wives, sons and mothers, sons and fathers, fathers and children. It seems to me that one of the chief virtues of Shakespeare's work is that it works out problems which are no doubt in part his, but are also those of his time, and in a way are the problems of all times everywhere. How else could

Shakespeare find resonance not only in England, but places so un-English as continental Europe, North America, Africa, China, and just about everywhere else he has been imported?

The concept of the 'archetypal' proposes that all of our unique and specific experiences are nevertheless part of much broader patterns of experience; we all experience birth, love, loss, challenge, success, death—as well as mother, father, trickster, witch, etc.—and though we all experience them differently, these experiences are linked by their much deeper common ground. The 'archetype' is our innate predisposition, as human beings, to *have* experiences that fall into such categories. And the archetype is itself adaptive and educative, promoting "meaningful and life-preserving behaviour and action in any given situation."[20] They are, Jung writes,

> universal dispositions of the mind, and they are to be understood as analogous to Plato's forms (*eidola*), in accordance with which the mind organizes its contents. One could also describe these forms as *categories* analogous to the logical categories, which are always and everywhere present as the basic postulates of reason. Only, in the case of our 'forms', we are not dealing with categories of reason but with categories of the *imagination*.[21]

It should be clear from this that we are not talking about hypostatized *entities*. Archetypes are not 'out there' floating around in space—nor are they 'in here', with any physical existence in our brain or body. We do not 'have' them, and we do not know people who 'are' them. The fact that we often refer to archetypes in terms of persons—mother, father, trickster, witch—can be misleading, for it must be understood that these are merely personifications of the archetypes 'themselves', which are essentially unrepresentable. Mother and father and trickster and witch are shorthand heuristics for describing amorphous categories of experience. They have to be called *something*, after all—they need "a local habitation and a name" (*MND* 5.1.17)—and the reason that they are personified in Jungian psychology is that this is how they often appear in the unconscious (dreams, visions, imaginary arguments, etc.). A particular archetypal energy will appear in a dream *as* a mother or father figure, a trickster or a witch—these figures are not the archetypes themselves, but derivative expressions *of* the archetypes. In the Book of Exodus, Moses does not see God—he can't, God is irrepresentable—but he sees a burning bush. So also we do not see 'The Trickster Archetype'—but we may see someone causing mischief in our dreams.

I am increasingly convinced that the best way to understand an archetype is as a situation, and this reflects how Jung sometimes, though inconsistently, describes it. He references the archetype of "the danger when crossing a ford", as one such example; "the archetype of the eerie forest" as another.[22] However, even here I think he is more concrete with his imagery than I would be. He does help out, by amplifying and metaphorizing the idea of crossing the ford, saying "we must not forget that we have psychological fords, narrows, and difficulties within ourselves".[23] He alludes here to the value of the archetype concept as a *heuristic*: it is a very basic and (almost) universally applicable metaphor. If we imagine someone who has never seen or heard of a river, the concrete image of crossing the ford will not resonate with them, yet we can imagine they still have some experience of crossing a treacherous aspect of their own psyche, or indeed of the outer world.

Amplification

When one is trying to understand a phenomenon, like a symbolic motif, play, or personal experience, a standard Jungian technique is to *amplify*, which means to connect and cross-reference other instances of a similar dynamic or symbol from other (often seemingly unrelated) sources, such as memory, mythology, history or art. Doing this can help us, ourselves, to achieve more of a View of the larger archetypal pattern. These different sources are assumed to be valid contributors to the overall symbolic picture because they are all produced or perceived by a human psyche—this is their common origin as 'psychological facts'. To use amplification is to operate according to a psychological version of the scientific principle of *consilience*,[24] which posits that the converging conclusions of multiple unrelated sources helps to strengthen those conclusions. One can also imagine amplification as a metaphor of sound: by making a quiet sound louder (amplifying it), one can hear its nuances more clearly. We look to the ways that a given symbolic motif appears in different places and different times in hopes that this may help us triangulate its essential character.

The idea that symbols *have* an essential character is included in the Jungian concept of the archetypal. Whether such 'essentials' are universally valid, especially cross-culturally, is a source of significant debate,[25] and for the purposes of this book is "a question not to be asked" (*1HIV* 2.4.398–9). For our purposes, we can be satisfied that an archetype is a psychological "ordering or structuring [principle]"[26] that is (probably) determined largely by culture, (possibly) affected by biology, and (maybe) emerges in the interaction between a human psyche and its environment.

Most of my amplifications take place from within two bodies: the Complete Works of Shakespeare, and the *I Ching*. The reason for the former is obvious. When I turn to the *I Ching*, what I am essentially 'doing' is attempting to identify the archetypal situations that are of relevance to the current moment.

To some degree, I also treat citations and quotes from other writers and scholars as amplifications of particular ideas. Often this is the best way to understand one of my endnotes: it points to another engagement with a similar idea, often with a slightly different emphasis, and at times holding an opinion at variance with my own. These amplifications are made both to continually include the pluralistic possibilities of interpretation in Shakespeare and to help the interested reader fill out the picture more themselves.

The Finalistic

Knowledge of larger archetypal patterns allows us to better contextualize those psychological phenomena which we encounter, and so better understand their necessity as part of a coherent process. This is the other special contribution of Jungian psychoanalysis to the picture: the addition of the *finalistic* viewpoint, rather than merely the *causal* one. The causal viewpoint, more typically associated with early Freudian technique, sees a phenomenon and asks *what happened that led to this?* The finalistic viewpoint looks in the other direction, asking *what is its purpose?* An archetype may be the 'thing' that the phenomenon is trying to fulfill.

In practice, this shows up most clearly in an attitude of sympathy towards the symptom. This view tries to recognize the psychological symptom as the psyche's best attempt to solve its problem.

Individuation

The goal of the psychological process, for Jungian Psychology, is individuation, which means something like becoming more of oneself. To individuate is to become increasingly differentiated from everything else; more specific, less generalized. It is not the same as individualism. Individuation includes one's relationship with others, and with the collective. Though there are many recurrent experiences and symbolic motifs associated with individuation, there is no one process of individuation. The point is that it is individual.

Shadow

The word shadow sometimes refers specifically to the parts of a person's psyche which they do not like and do not take responsibility for. A kind-seeming person may have a controlling shadow. An imaginative person's shadow might be that they refuse to see things as they are. Sometimes shadow simply refers to the obverse side of a given phenomenon—the thing that it, by its very nature, 'leaves out'.

Levels of Interpretation

Shakespeare's plays can be read akin to a sequence of dreams which develop certain motifs; unlike the dreams of most of the rest of us, however, his dreams seem to encompass everything. The individual moments in this sequence are held on two levels in this book: as individuals, and in relation to the whole sequence. On the first level, I consider a play as a complete phenomenon in itself, and on the second level in terms of the ways in which relevant themes and motifs develop and individuate throughout the course of his work.

This reflects two more levels, which have more to do with characters. The first is a structural, or objective level. Here, characters might 'represent' aspects of the archetype of the hero, or the puer aeternus, or the mother, and so on. On the second level, they are treated as full human beings with complete histories and psychologies of their own, as well as their own subjectivity or interiority. I have no strict rule as to when to move from one level to the other, rather it is often strictly irrational, based on which approach seems to be most appropriate at a given time. Both levels are, in my opinion, always potentially relevant.

Porterfield makes a similar distinction in her Jungian Shakespeare work, which she feels "cannot be stressed too strongly, since a failure to understand the liminal nature of this criticism results in too literal a reading and becomes reductive, rather than expansive."[27]

With a given play, I basically use three levels, which interweave freely. The broadest level is 'Shakespeare', meaning simply the originator of the Complete Works, solely in terms of his artistic process—though here and there I am interested in the actual biographical Man From Stratford. The next is the level of the play: the play is imaginatively treated as an analysand, and analysed as though it is itself a coherent personality with its own interior logic. The last is that of analysing the individual character.

A Short Review of Jungian-Shakespearean Criticism

A Freudian literary critic and a Jungian literary critic walk into a library. The librarian says, "We don't serve your kind here." The Freudian whispers knowingly to his companion, "Patricidal father complex, fixated at the anal stage." The Jungian, offended, replies, "You reductive senex. She is *obviously* enacting the archetype of Cerberus, keeping guard at the gate to Hades." "Out!" the librarian shouts. Both leave. The librarian's assistant asks, "What was *that* all about?" The librarian replies, "Every book those guys borrow comes back with pages torn out, *soaked* in god-knows-what, and nobody wants to read it ever again."

There are stereotypes about both of these psychoanalytic approaches, which are partially true, but very often not. The stereotype about the Freudian approach is that it reduces everything to its worst aspects, and literary works are consigned to a Tartarus in which they must forever relive their pathology, like Prometheus having his liver eternally eaten. The stereotype about the Jungian approach is that it inflates everything to the archetypal, and literary works are abducted into Olympus like Ganymede, and transformed into a constellation of stars, never to breathe or live again.

These complaints are well-worn and serve their purpose—as cautionary tales. However, even the Freud/Jung antinomy is a stereotype, and my experience of both approaches is that they often complement each other, and much of the time differ only in their use of technical jargon. In terms of therapeutic orientations, much of Jung's that was originally rejected by the Freudian school has been lately incorporated into Freudian and other psychoanalytic approaches.[28]

I think Meredith Skura puts it very well:

Too much emphasis on the past, of course, is reductive, and we have all read psychoanalytic criticism that reduces an ongoing drama to a perpetual repetition of the same old family drama. So the analyst finds that Prince Hal and Hamlet commit oedipal crimes—as do Brutus, Macbeth, Angelo, and Florizel. Shakespeare's plays resist such reductions—*but they do so partly by taking them into account.*[29]

This is exactly right—Shakespeare's plays repeatedly enact the *transcendent function,*[30] as through the dialogic process of drama, with its compensatory and complimentary 'sides'[31] embodied in the drives of different characters, they both include and transcend the given psychological issue or complex.

The shortcomings of a particular critical approach can be taken very personally by some, as violent assaults on the text itself. But ultimately, they do not matter much. If they are bad, their karmic punishment is that nobody reads them. If they are wrong, Shakespeare does not mind. His plays are uncannily able to accept anything—their "capacity / Receiveth as the sea" (*TN* 1.1.10–1).

I would rather avoid getting overly defensive here, but it appears to me that the Jungian approach is in need of defence. Jungian criticism has been maligned for its "allegorizing"[32] and "totalizing"[33] tendencies. The Jungian mode has typically been identified by its tracking of the archetypes or myth-forms involved within and underneath a work of art, rather than the work of art itself.[34] One can develop a taste for this, but from outside it may appear as "grandiose universalism, according to which dramatic characters are seen not merely as reflections of the author's psyche but as manifestations of primeval 'archetypes' existing in a 'collective unconscious' shared by the entire human race."[35] The 'scare quotes' that Armstrong puts around the Jungian terms here communicate something of how they may be regarded in the wider world of criticism.

Raphael Lyne protests the use of myth to criticize Shakespearean romance, though his point could be taken to apply to the Shakespearean canon generally:

. . . it is problematic to approach Shakespeare's romances in mythical terms . . . these plays are closely embroiled in their immediate historical milieu and cannot be read as straightforwardly ideal or archetypal.[36]

This conveys a key and common misunderstanding about a Jungian (or mythic, or archetypal) View, in terms of both therapy and literary criticism. It is also representative of the way in which such approaches are frequently summarily dismissed without having been understood. An essay collection from 1992 boasts proudly that "our essayists make no mention of archetypes, for example, or of Jung, and invoke the ideas of Northrop Frye, if at all, only to supplant them."[37] Lupton and Reinhard's *Shakespeare in Psychoanalysis* does not mention Jung or Jungians, and Armstrong's *Shakespeare in Psychoanalysis* makes only drive-by mentions of the Jungian approach, mainly to disparage it (though paying a passing respect to its "thoroughgoing humanism").[38] Armstrong, however, has a "reductive, outdated and overly monolithic" view of the Jungian perspective, which is ironically precisely what he attributes to Greenblatt's view of the Freudian stream.[39] As far as Lyne's comments go, I believe they are representative of the general misconception, which betrays a fundamental misunderstanding of what *myth* is—or at least what we Jungians consider myth to be. Myth, too, is "closely embroiled in [its] immediate historical milieu",[40] but the reason myth remains psychologically relevant is because it speaks to something deeper than the circumstances of its own birth. And there is no such thing as "straightforwardly archetypal". In neither criticism nor therapy do we sit around and boil everything down to archetypal patterns—though if we do, we probably deserve to be dismissed. It is more likely that we keep attuned to the *presence* of archetypal motifs, not as amateur birdwatchers hoping to spot an unusual specimen for our own satisfaction, but because recognizing these motifs may help us understand something further about the underlying process, especially as regards its origin and purpose. The point is that human life and creation is, for the most part, *anything but* "straightforwardly archetypal"—nevertheless the human details, including the "immediate historical milieu" that Lyne cites, are themselves archetypally-informed. Frye himself would not make such a statement as this, as he confined himself to the literary use of archetypes and avoided psychological hypotheses. But the Jungian View is that archetypes are 'there', 'active', unconsciously structuring not only our dreams but our politics and histories as well as our literary outputs. At any rate *it is a point best held lightly*, and its purpose is not to leave us lost in "that twilight realm which seduces [us] away from meeting [our] tasks in the here and now."[41] Its purpose is to connect us more fully to this real life, and its real literary works too.

Now for the dramatic compensation: to identify with the aggressor and advocate the other side. What, for me, can often be missing in a Jungian approach is the *suchness* of the work of art: the unique characteristics that constitute its being *itself* can be lost in the archetypal ether. The goal of Jungian approaches sometimes seems to be the gathering of 'archetypal proofs', adding confirmatory evidence to the theory of archetypes itself, and therefore standing more as contribution to the Jungian field than the literary. I can quite understand why non-Jungian critics deplore this, as it threatens to miss some of the most important aspects of Shakespeare: his specific characterization, his specific words, and his specific dramatic skill. It is worth noting that contemporary Jungians tend to deplore this as well, as in Samuels' remarks on

> ... the embarrassingly simplistic deployment of ideas. In a novel or play, any woman important to a man at a deep level is his anima. Any piece of controlled self-presentation to the world is the persona. Opposites abound, mandalas are sought for, tricksters found out, heroes and heroines spotted on their journeys ... The way the concepts are utilized is often in too stately or static a manner, laid

over and across the (literary) material. Violence is done to Jungian context and literary text alike.[42]

Admittedly, I walk directly into the danger zone of some of these remarks. I do my best to tread on the tail of the tiger gently.

Jungian approaches, when they suffer, suffer from three main things:

1. They may feel the necessity to teach Jungian psychology at the same time as they try to get in touch with a work of literature. It is perhaps for this reason that the most successful Jungian approaches are only Jungian-adjacent, and not by Jungians at all, but from people like Northrop Frye or Ted Hughes, who don't want to bother with the Jungian theoretical infrastructure.

2. Jungians have a tendency towards feeling psychologically superior, which comes across mainly in a kind of psycho-moralizing inability to stop castigating characters for failing to be as impeccably psychologically integrated as the analyst sees himself as being. It is not that characters, being fictional, are beyond ethical reproach; rather, one of the legitimate aims of literary criticism as such is exactly that, to help us come to our own ethical positions in regard to characters and their choices. But one can criticize *psychologically,* which if it means anything means from a place of humility, of recognition that every flaw that one points out resides in one's own psyche as well—or one can criticize from a place of superiority, and lose all possibility of relating.[43]

3. We have a habit of idealizing our own intuitions, and thereby considering ourselves authorities in any domain in which we have the least bit of knowledge. This is done because 'everything' *is* 'psychological experience' at some level, and so if we are experts in psychology, it intuitively follows that we must be experts in 'everything'. Samuels observed this embarrassing fault long ago: "when you actually go out and find academics who are into [the non-psychology subject in question], what they have to say about the level of the sort of knowledge and sophistication shown by the Jungian is rather damning."[44]

At the same time, these criticisms could be made, with slight modifications, about any discipline. And indeed they *have* been made—notably by Frye!—who finds that any knowledge system that exists *outside* of literature (such as psychoanalysis) tends to bring to literary criticism

the fallacy of what in history is called determinism, where a scholar with a special interest in geography or economics expresses that interest by the rhetorical device of putting his favorite study into a causal relationship with whatever interests him less. Such a method gives one the illusion of explaining one's subject while studying it, thus wasting no time. It would be easy to compile a long list of such determinisms in criticisms, all of them, whether Marxist, Thomist, liberal-humanist, neo-Classical, Freudian, Jungian, or existentialist, substituting a critical attitude for criticism, all proposing, not to find a conceptual framework for criticism within literature, but to attach criticism to one of a miscellany of frameworks outside it.[45]

Rowland—a contemporary Jungian scholar—puts it more succinctly as "one discipline colonizing another."[46]

I am deeply sympathetic to Frye's defence of literature as self-sufficient, even as I observe, ironically, that it is something of a Jungian attitude: "above all, don't let anything from outside, that does not belong, get into it, for the fantasy-image [or literary text, in this case] has 'everything it needs.'"[47] It has been of the utmost importance to me to try and encounter Shakespeare on his own terms, and get into relationship with these plays *as plays*, that is, as dramatic texts written with the intention of being performed live in a theatre. I am unwilling to miss the *effect* of a work of art in favour of elucidating what I see as its 'psychology'. All my psychological interpretations are ultimately in the service of trying to come to something that helps illuminate what *happens* when we read, or watch, a given play—*why* that might happen—and what that might *mean* for us, as human beings.

The most significant milestones in the Jungian-Shakespearean field seem to be works by Bodkin,[48] Aronson,[49] Porterfield,[50] Fike,[51] and Rowland.[52] Beebe's "The Trickster in the Arts",[53] concerned in part with *Hamlet*, also continues to be influential. Contributions by Rogers-Gardner, Tucker, Kirsch, Cobb, Driscoll, Coursen, Fabricius, Jordan-Finnegan, Wali, and even the otherwise-prominent (in Jungian circles) Edinger have not been taken up as they might have.[54] Most of them are exceedingly difficult to find.

As mentioned, works by Frye, Hughes, and also Spurgeon, not explicitly Jungian but nevertheless Jungian-sympathetic, have been more widely influential. For most non-Jungians, the flagship Jungian critic of Shakespeare was Frye, who did write what I find to be the clearest application of archetypal theory to literature in *The Anatomy of Criticism*. His *A Natural Perspective* is the most influential expression of his 'archetypal criticism', though I prefer the individual play-focused approach of his lectures, which comprise *Northrop Frye on Shakespeare*.[55] *A Natural Perspective* explores the comedies and romances as iterative expressions of recurring character-types, narrative structures, and themes. Frye wields his concepts with formality, and perhaps leans toward reification. Sometimes, however, Frye's method is taken to be more reductive and reifying than it truly is, by readers who are not used to holding ideas 'lightly', as a proposed perspective rather than a final interpretation. A reader may expect rigid categories, and, in effect, project those into Frye's work where he has not intended them.

Spurgeon's *Shakespeare's Imagery, and What It Tells Us* does what it says on the tin.[56] She amasses examples and data on the content and type of images used through Shakespeare's work—including attention to image 'clusters', which are very similar to Jung's 'complex-indicators'[57]—and drawing biographical and psychological conclusions based on her findings.

Hughes' "doorstop" (his own word, I'm afraid), *Shakespeare and the Goddess of Complete Being*,[58] is thoroughly comprehensive in elucidating his view of the two myths he sees transforming and recreating throughout Shakespeare's entire *oeuvre*, and which are contained in seed-form in his first two published works, *The Rape of Lucrece* and *Venus and Adonis*. It is stimulating to the point of overwhelming. If it has not been adopted by Shakespearean critics, I suspect that may be because of its fullness—somewhat like Adelman's *Suffocating Mothers,* it doesn't seem to leave much room for anyone else to ever say anything again.[59]

Bodkin, perhaps the first explicit pioneer of a Jungian approach to literature, explicated connections between poetry and ancient ritual, arguing a thesis that might well be taken up later on, with different emphasis, by Frye (or Rowland): that literature (and theatre) perform an emotional ritual "undertaken for the renewal of the tribe".[60] She attempts to link her own experience, and the experience of her own time with that of generations and civilizations past in a way that might today be dismissed as derivative of an obsolete "grand theory".[61]

Aronson's method in *Psyche & Symbol in Shakespeare* is similar to Frye's *A Natural Perspective*: they both proceed via underlying motif, though Frye's are more situational, e.g.,. the storm at sea and the triumph of time, whereas Aronson's are conceptual, e.g.,. shadow and persona. Aronson's essay on the "Ocular Proof" does the same in a more condensed way and is a modal example of what a classical introverted-intuitive Jungian approach brings, in terms of amplification of a symbolic network—in this case, eyes, seeing, deception, blindness.[62]

Edinger's studies of *Measure for Measure* and *Romeo and Juliet* analyse these plays very much in terms of what he perceives to be their underlying myth-forms.[63] For example, he, like Porterfield, sees Duke Vincentio as a representative of the Self, the archetype of totality which structures and drives the various movements of the psyche.[64] This has the virtue of explaining something about how the Self is conceived as functioning, though *Measure for Measure* seems at times to be something of a pesky afterthought.

Cobb's work in *Prospero's Island* merits a mention, in part because it seems to be so obscure—but I find it to be a well-written and convincing interpretation of *The Tempest* as an intentional psychological-alchemical treatise for the stage.[65]

Fike, in *The Visionary Mode,* is first interested in the unconscious origins of the creative process. He finds it important to be clear about the definitions of the Jungian concepts that he brings to bear, making frequent reference to the *CW,* although some of his understandings (e.g.,. of 'individuation', 'archetype') differ in subtle ways from the way the terms are generally used. He approaches several plays in terms of illustration of Jungian concepts, including ways in which certain play-elements may confirm or dialogue with these ideas. Notably relevant to this present book is his exploration of the trickster archetype, as expressed in Falstaff. He pays special attention to moments when Shakespeare's characters make explicit mythological references, analysing sensitively the unconscious purposes these conscious allusions might serve. Especially of note are his considerations of unconscious compensatory processes that may be involved for characters—e.g., Jessica and Lorenzo in the 'Love Duet' that opens *The Merchant of Venice*'s fifth act—and how those may be registered by the audience/reader.[66]

Rowland's studies are situated as part of her larger project of building a contemporary theoretical and methodological foundation for *Jungian Literary Criticism*, which is articulated most fully in her book by that title, a book of obvious interest to anyone wanting a clearer view of the field itself.[67] She integrates Jungian ideas with more mainstream forms of literary criticism, suggesting alliances with close reading (demonstrating with *Sonnet* 19), historicist approaches (with *The Tempest*), and ecocriticism (with *A Midsummer Night's Dream*). Outside of these demonstrational examples, she has addressed a number of different plays elsewhere, with particular regard to the way they can be seen as enacting communal rites, mainly social—in this regard her view relates to Frye's—but also political. For her, "the symbolic drama" which Shakespeare authors "adds up to a diagnosis of a deep cultural wound that connects the domestic (feminine) sphere of love and marriage to the outer (masculine) world of war".[68] She pays significant attention to how the qualities of the feminine, and female characters, are treated and developed.

Though typological approaches have been made by Coursen, Tucker, and Qwarnström (and many critics use Jungian typology at point or another), there has not yet—so far as I am aware—been a Shakespearean typological approach which makes use of Beebe's 8-function model. In my opinion, this model makes a tremendous difference in the degree of nuance available. Typology always runs the risk of trying to mathematize something that shouldn't be mathematized, and Beebe's model both intensifies this risk and offers a nuanced manner of dealing with it. The single biggest factor is Beebe's differentiation of the *opposing* function, where most approaches follow von Franz's example in arrogating the oppositional patterns to the inferior function.[69] (These ideas will be explained in the introduction to *Cymbeline*.) One other important point in my approach to type is that I take as axiomatic an idea expressed by Elizabeth Murphy, that "observers cannot always judge a person's type by their actions. Most often the choice of behaviour depends on the motive for the behaviour".[70] I find this opens the field up to a much deeper interpretation of underlying process over surface appearance. Of course, such matters remain subjectively determined. Just as in performance, the line that one actor judges to be an integral moment for a character may, by another actor, be 'thrown away', with totally different and equally compelling results.

Chronology of Shakespeare's Plays

The order (more or less) in which I consider these works to have been written is that given by *The Oxford Shakespeare: Complete Works, 2nd ed.* When these plays are cited, their titles are typically abbreviated, and their abbreviations are included in this list. When Shakespeare is cited without a given abbreviation, the default citation is to the main subject of the chapter in which the citation appears: *King John, Twelfth Night,* or *Cymbeline.* Those plays are **bolded** in the following list:

1. *The Two Gentleman of Verona (TGV)*
2. *The Taming of the Shrew (TS)*
3. *Henry VI (1HVI, 2HVI, 3HVI)*
4. *Titus Andronicus (TA)*
5. *Richard III (RIII)*
6. *Edward III (EIII)*
7. *The Comedy of Errors (CE)*
8. *Love's Labour's Lost (LLL)*
9. *Richard II (RII)*
10. *Romeo and Juliet (RJ)*
11. *A Midsummer Night's Dream (MND)*
12. **King John (KJ)**
13. *The Merchant of Venice (MV)*
14. *Henry IV, Pt. 1 (1HIV)*
15. *The Merry Wives of Windsor (MWW)*
16. *Henry IV, Pt. 2 (2HIV)*
17. *Much Ado About Nothing (MA)*
18. *Henry V (HV)*
19. *Julius Caesar (JC)*
20. *As You Like It (AY)*
21. *Hamlet (Ham.)*
22. **Twelfth Night (TN)**
23. *Troilus and Cressida (TC)*
24. *Measure for Measure (MM)*
25. *Othello (Oth.)*
26. *All's Well That Ends Well (AW)*
27. *King Lear (KL)*
28. *Timon of Athens (Tim.)*
29. *Macbeth (Mac.)*
30. *Antony and Cleopatra (AC)*
31. *Pericles, Prince of Tyre (Per.)*
32. *Coriolanus (Cor.)*
33. *The Winter's Tale (WT)*
34. **Cymbeline (Cym.)**
35. *The Tempest (Tem.)*
36. *Henry VIII (HVIII)*
37. *The Two Noble Kinsmen (TNK)*

The other relevant abbreviation is "CW", for *The Collected Works of C. G. Jung.*

Notes

1 Robert Greene, *A Groats-worth of Witte* (1592).
2 Bloom (1994, 371–6; 1999, 714); see also Armstrong (2001, 39–47).
3 Jung (1933, 49).
4 Johnson (1989, 235).
5 Goldman (1985, 14).
6 Wilhelm (1984, 82).
7 Wilhelm (1984, 83).
8 Jung (1976, 589).
9 Jung (CW 7, 409).
10 A number of Shakespeare's psychologically-educative real-life experiences are explored or glanced at in Duncan-Jones (2010).
11 Solzhenitsyn (1985, 75): "If only it were all so simple! If only there were evil people somewhere insidiously committing evil deeds, and it were necessary only to separate them from the rest of us and destroy them. But the line dividing good and evil cuts through the heart of every human being. And who is willing to destroy a piece of his own heart?"
12 Jung (CW 7, 78).
13 Barton (1984, 176).
14 Jung (1963, 189).
15 Freud (2020).
16 Hughes (1992, xii).
17 Samuels (2008, 6).
18 See Freebury-Jones (2024).
19 Adelman (1992).
20 Kast (2006, 127).
21 Jung (CW 11, 845).
22 Jung (2022, 50; 52).
23 Jung (2022, 51).
24 Wilson (1998).
25 Roesler (2023).
26 Kast (2006, 127).
27 Porterfield (1994, 7).
28 Samuels (2008, 4–8).
29 Skura (1980, 207), emphasis added.
30 Jung (CW 6, 825–8).
31 Jung (CW 8, 133 & 138).
32 Coursen (1986).
33 Armstrong (2001).
34 Essentially privileging the introverted intuitive function. See Chapter 6.
35 Armstrong (2001, 55).
36 Lyne (2007, 4).
37 In Taylor (2001, 34).
38 Armstrong (2001, 55).
39 Armstrong (2001, 137).
40 Lyne (2007, 4).
41 H. Wilhelm (1995, 8).
42 Samuels (2004, xiii).
43 In my mind in this framing is G. K. Chesterton's distinction between 'humour' and 'wit'.
44 Samuels (1998, 29).

45 Frye (1957, 6).
46 Rowland (2019, 12).
47 Jung (CW 14, 749).
48 Bodkin (1934).
49 Aronson (1972).
50 Porterfield (1994).
51 Fike (2009).
52 Rowland (1999, 2005 [Epilogue], 2010, 2016, 2019).
53 Beebe (2022a).
54 Rogers-Gardner (1996); Kirsch (1966); Cobb (1990); Driscoll (2019a, 2019b); Coursen (1986); Fabricius (1997); Jordan-Finnegan (2006); Wali (2011); Edinger (2001).
55 Frye: *AoC* (1957); *ANP* (1965); *Northrop Frye on Shakespeare* (1986).
56 Spurgeon (1935).
57 Jung (CW 2, §100).
58 Hughes (1992).
59 Hughes, however, may have felt that he was treated as an outsider encroaching on the Shakespearean territory (Skea 2021).
60 Bodkin (1934, 35).
61 Roesler (2023, 141–67).
62 Aronson (1970, 1972).
63 Edinger (2001).
64 Porterfield (1994).
65 Cobb (1990).
66 Fike (2009, 52–8).
67 Rowland (2019; see also 2020).
68 Rowland (2010, 32).
69 Von Franz & Hillman (2020).
70 Murphy (2021, 1080).

Chapter 1

"A strange beginning"
Introduction to King John

Synopsis

John is King of England following the death of his brother Richard I. His claim on the throne is not secure and is significantly contended by his nephew Arthur—a young boy. The uncertain heredity on a national scale is mirrored, in the first scene, with a more domestic concern: a conflict between the two Faulconbridge brothers as to the inheritance of their own father's estate. During the dispute, one of the brothers is recognized by John and his mother, Eleanor, as a bastard son of the late King Richard, and an offer is made: join us. Lose the Faulconbridge name and title, but claim your rightful ancestry. Trade security for opportunity. He takes the offer.

A challenge from King Philip of France, on behalf of Arthur, motivates John's movement to the disputed town of Angiers. Philip is joined by his son Lewis the Dauphin, as well as Arthur, Arthur's mother Constance, and the Duke of Austria; he demands that John relinquish the throne. England and France attempt to compel the loyalties of the citizens of Angiers, who are themselves uncertain about whom to recognize as king. England and France battle, to little overall consequence. This diplomatic and military stalemate nearly turns to savagery when the Bastard proposes that, since Angiers will not choose, England and France should join forces to sack it. A quick-witted citizen of Angiers prevents this by proposing a more idealistic arrangement: a political marriage. Lewis the Dauphin agrees to marry John's niece, Princess Blanche, and that seems to be that. John retains the throne. Arthur is assigned a dukedom for his inconvenience.

The sole protestor is Arthur's mother, Constance, who feels deeply betrayed. But following the wedding, political complications stir anew. Cardinal Pandulph, representative of the Catholic Church, shows up to demand that John give up his resistance toward the Pope's chosen candidate for the role of Archbishop of Canterbury. John refuses, and Pandulph excommunicates him. He threatens Philip with a similar excommunication if he does not go back to war with John—which Philip does. Battle ensues, with the English achieving relative success. John returns to England with Arthur as his hostage.

Constance, considering her son to be as good as dead, breaks down in grief. She departs in despair, at which point Pandulph illuminates for Lewis the latent

DOI: 10.4324/9781003596967-2

opportunity in the situation. Should Arthur indeed perish, Lewis will have a claim to the English crown, having married Blanche. He sketches a vision in which Lewis, with both morality and legality on his side, leads his forces against a John who, by his cruelty against Arthur, will have forced his own people to revolt.

Constance and Pandulph prove prophetic, for John orders a follower named Hubert to murder Arthur in prison. However, when Hubert tries to kill Arthur, he is dissuaded by Arthur's impassioned defence of himself—he resolves instead to protect Arthur. He tells John that Arthur is dead, which John now regrets, seeing it to have been a dire political error—some of the English lords are beginning to revolt. As John turns against Hubert, Hubert tells him the truth: that Arthur is alive. John is much relieved. Unbeknownst to them, Arthur is simultaneously attempting to secure his freedom on his own terms—he jumps from the prison walls to escape and dies from the fall.

When Arthur's body is discovered, the death is seen as murder, and the English lords revolt in earnest, going over to the French side. John submits to Pandulph, believing this can prevent war. However, when Pandulph tries to dissuade Lewis from fighting, Lewis has no interest in backing down. The French land on English soil, and a battle is fought, in which the English, now led by the Bastard, are again victorious, though due more to unusual tidal activity than military prowess. This victory is cold comfort to John, who has both grown sick *and* been poisoned. He dies, leaving the kingdom to his son Henry. The Bastard loyally recognizes the new King Henry III and seems prepared to continue his role in the reordering of the nation.

The Modern and Postmodern *King John*

Sigurd Burckhardt said in 1968 that "when he wrote *King John,* or quite possibly in writing it, Shakespeare was or became a 'modern'."[1] Virginia Mason Vaughan referred to it, 35 years later in 2003, as "Shakespeare's *post*modern history play."[2] They are both right, for different reasons, and that fact speaks to Shakespeare's archetypality—the source of those regular epiphanies that seem to show Shakespeare apparently in touch with the spirit of every age. The play depicts a medieval world charged with the ideological adriftancy we have come to call 'home' in the 21st century, and which apparently also has a great deal in common with the early modern time period in which Shakespeare made his own home.

Both Burckhardt and Vaughan are referring to the way that *John* lays bare all established notions of surety. For the Elizabethans, "archetypal order was eternal, divine, revealed, quite beyond man's tampering."[3] The world picture "rested on the faith in a vast fabric of correspondencies: between universe and state and body, between God and king and sun and lion and eagle . . ."[4] But by *John*'s fourth line, these monuments are called into question when the ambassador's reference is to the "borrowed majesty" of the king (1.1.4). The very idea that majesty *can* be borrowed—and that this can even be uttered in its very presence—not only undermines John's majesty but also gives majesty *itself* the lie. If the king is the representative of God on earth, God surely does not allow Himself to be borrowed.

...right?

This uncertainty, a shattering of the roof of the playworld, radiates outward into its every other aspect, collapsing the house. Howard and Rackin write that "the entire action seems designed to foreground every kind of moral and political and historiographic ambiguity."[5]

Detailed rhetorical exchanges, nearly Shavian in temper, take place between characters we do not trust, who do not trust one another, and who mostly have so little interest in knowing themselves that their integrity—trustworthiness of self—is a nonissue. Their projected certainties are, moreover, often undermined by the context in which Shakespeare has them speak, as shown most clearly when dueling heralds for the English and French armies simultaneously proclaim contradictory victories in battle.

When we pay close attention to the arguments, however, we may find that they are detailed and compelling, but always tendentious. Often it seems the characters are playing at 'debate club': as though in a competition to outdo one another with how self-servingly rationalizing they can be. As though the winner is simply the one who can make the more difficult-to-refute argument—although eventually it does subside into good old-fashioned 'might makes right'. The Citizen of Angiers, a character at the very borders of metatheatricality, finds it entirely impossible to decide who is right; "right can only be asserted here", writes Kastan, "for no means exist by which the claim could be legitimated".[6]

CITIZEN: In brief, we are the King of England's subjects:
For him, and in his right, we hold this town.
KING JOHN: Acknowledge then the king, and let me in.
CITIZEN: That can we not: but he that proves the king,
To him will we prove loyal; till that time
Have we rammed up our gates against the world.

(2.1.267–72)

We postmoderns are hardly better off. The Citizen is actually a remarkable model, psychologically speaking, for the difficulty of holding the tension of opposites in our own time, for he refuses to become identified with either end of a polarity, declining partisanship and maintaining his centre. *King John*, however, will ultimately not allow non-participation. Those characters who try to 'stay out of it'—e.g., the Bastard and the Citizen—find that this is not possible, and the ground gives way beneath them. Maelstrom constellates over and over, sucking characters into a series of double-binds in which there are no right choices available to them.

BLANCHE: I am with both. Each army hath a hand,
And in their rage, I having hold of both,
They whirl asunder, and dismember me.

(3.1.328–30)

This is a situation that the *I Ching* calls Splitting Apart (剝, *Bō*, 23):

> SPLITTING APART. It does not further one
> To go anywhere.[7]

This hexagram contains "the image of a house . . . because the roof is being shattered the house collapses."[8] Jing-Nuan says about this hexagram, "when certain structures are stripped apart, or broken, then the framework of life itself is exposed and endangered. Movement must cease until the framework is repaired."[9]

There are almost no characters in the play who are not faced, at some point, with a variant of an impossible choice. Hubert too is torn between Arthur and John; the Bastard vacillates inwardly, if not outwardly, in his loyalties, seeming to regard Arthur as the true king (2.1.585, 4.3.142–4), yet continuing to serve John and the cursed realm with all his heart. Philip is strong-armed into breaking his oath either to John or to the Church; as a gift on his son's wedding day, he may elect to suffer either excommunication or war.

Out of the centre of this maelstrom, like a primal scream, comes Constance, appropriately named given she is the *only* constant in the play. The women of this play are tasked with compensating the faithless eros of the men, and her compensations are second to none. Although almost entirely respected and pitied as *mater dolorosa* by audiences and critics alike, I hope to show that she too is capable of galling, even fatal, hypocrisy. *John* is egalitarian in allowing this to the men and women alike.

The play leaves us with nowhere safe to lay our sympathies: not with the king, nor his rival, nor the Church, nor even the bereaved mother. Even if we wanted to find a home with her (and many try), this faithless play evicts us, coldly wiping her out midway, suddenly, with nary a word of reflection.

The closest thing we get to a stable position is paradoxically through instability, in the constantly self-reinventing Bastard. We're barely sure of his name—Philip Faulconbridge? Richard Plantagenet? But he feels reliable because at least he is repeatedly honest with us about where he's at. His irreverent soliloquies on what he watches unfold tend to gain our trust because he sees what we see. He sees the decay, and unlike certain other characters "seeks to treat the sickness rather than exploit it".[10] Ultimately, his piebald morality serves him well, and arguably it serves the realm well too, but we do lose him in the process. From a certain point of view, it is an almost Havel-esque turn that, by the end, he has become a part of the machine himself—indeed its chief driving mechanism. I think we can understand and respect his choice, but, our cavalier friend is no more.

Ultimately, notes Champion, "no character on the stage possesses a significant level of awareness; that is, no one figure is in a position to have an overview of the various political forces at work in the stage world".[11] The Bastard is an observer, but also a participant-observer, and *John* is like quicksand: you dip a foot in at your own peril.

"The difficulty of kings is that there are more than one,"[12] and in this play there are three. Philip is simple enough for us to accept as King of France, because in Shakespeare's histories France is never really a real place, it's more like England's shadow. But the rival claimants to the throne of *England*, John and Arthur, constellate a stickier problem. Before long the Pope weighs in as well, and we have on our hands a quartet of conflicting-though-equally-divine mandates—and this turns out to be a rather appropriate image for our postmodern plurality, in which the very existence of multiple convincing voices has already undermined, seemingly permanently, the possibility of there being one voice that is finally authoritative.

Vaughan, writing in 2003, found a remarkable parallel to the Two Kings' struggle in the U.S. presidential election between Al Gore and George W. Bush, an election whose results were contested as frustratingly (for both sides) as Angiers is, and which eventually subsided in "what many regarded as a legal fiction."[13] We understand from the start of *John* that John's kingship is itself something of a legal fiction, one that depends a great deal on how one interprets the laws, and *which* laws. Today, writing in the mid-2020s, we have no shortage of amplificatory examples, situations where a collectively agreed-upon understanding seems impossible: many don't believe the moon landing happened, or even the Holocaust. Huge cohorts believe 9/11 was an 'inside job'. Nobody knows if COVID-19 came from bat soup or a laboratory, and we don't expect that we would ever get a straight answer anyway, so we too must settle for believing whichever fiction works for us, on an *ad hoc* basis. (At the risk of sacrificing some dramatic *panache*, I wish to gently add that these are not necessarily *my* positions. I consider my work as psychoanalyst to require a kind of 'psychological nonpartisanship'; obviously, I have private opinions, but it is my job to empathize with the opinions of others.)

At the time of my writing this, artificially intelligent text, voice, image, and video generation are proliferating at an overwhelming rate, and it is quite clear that a skilful programmer can already create content indistinguishable from reality, and that we may soon be collectively faced with events that we cannot, with any degree of certainty, confirm nor deny, unless we happened to be there to experience them ourselves—by the time this sentence is published, it seems we will be there. We have rather unhesitatingly adopted the democratization of transport (Uber), hotels (AirBNB), broadcasting (YouTube), and more, but are we ready for the crowdsourcing of authority, in which no authority—government, media, religious, corporate, or otherwise—is considered fully legitimate, and no source is inoculated by its own dominance against being 'fact-checked' by another? It may not matter: we are there anyway.

This is the problem at the heart of *King John*: is there such thing as legitimacy of authority, or does it come down to which fiction is accepted? Truth *as such*, or truth *du jour*? Does heredity make right, or does might make right, or—does *nothing* make right? The remarkable thing is to find these issues in a play of the late 16th century, issues which Shakespeare seems to engage with about as much directness as an early modern writer possibly could without getting himself murdered for it.

Criticism

The play has not been given its due, historically speaking. It has not lived down the reputation announced in the Prologue of Cibber's 18th-century adaptation, *Papal Tyranny*:

> Yet fame, nor Favour ever deign'd to say,
> *King John* was station'd as a first rate Play;
> Though strong and sound the Hulk, yet ev'ry Part
> Reach'd not the merit of his usual art![14]

The early and formative critics have "literally, nothing of importance to say about the play."[15] Between Shakespeare's death in 1616 and the Covent Garden revival in 1737, there is no record of performance whatsoever. *King John* is a play that barely anyone who hasn't made a serious point of familiarizing themselves with Shakespeare even knows exists. Though it experienced a heyday in the mid-18th century,[16] by the mid-20th "it seemed as though *King John* 'in silence' would 'modestly expire.'"[17] "Long periods of neglect" have been attenuated by "sporadic bursts of popularity",[18] typically when the play has been able to serve an expedient political purpose—fittingly, it is deployed when it serves "Commodity, the bias of the world" (2.1.574).

Derided as "hack work",[19] a "patchwork",[20] "a mixture of incoherent and monstrous parts",[21] its failure to launch has been attributed to its "lack of unity and telic design, episodic and faulty plot structure, absence of both a clearly defined protagonist and a governing central theme, inconsistency of style, rejection of 'cosmic lore,' flat characterization . . ."[22] All these, and the fact that it seems to be a reworking of an earlier play, *The Troublesome Raigne of King John*, which has recently been attributed to George Peele.[23] The job of reworking, it has been argued, was rather unenthusiastic on Shakespeare's part.[24]

It has not been without its supporters. Davies, "the earliest and most detailed defender of the merits of the play",[25] praised its structure, and especially admired Constance's characterization, finding her passion more affecting than any heroine of Greek tragedy. Dr. Johnson ("the canonical critic proper"[26]) felt that "though not written with the utmost power of Shakespeare, [it] is varied with a very pleasing interchange of incidents", especially finding Constance's depiction "agreeable to nature" and the Bastard a delightful "mixture of greatness and levity".[27] Oxberry wrote that it was "amongst the best, of Shakespeare's Tragic Dramas",[28] Masefield found it "a truly noble play",[29] and Heraud wrote that "it is, indeed, almost a classic for its regularity, as it is for the genius displayed in it."[30] Vaughan strikes a more moderate note, submitting that "it is much better than is commonly supposed."[31]

Bloom finds, in the Bastard, a starting point for his thesis of Shakespeare's "invention of the human"—"no one before in a Shakespearean play is so persuasive a representation of a person."[32]

By the mid-1970s, the critical history had not shown "any signs of consistent attention or of a clear pattern of evolution in thinking about the play," and the same could be said for the performance history.[33] A major thread was interest in the character of Constance, who, on the one hand, is "delineated with Greek simplicity",[34] and, on the other, is "an unusually challenging part",[35] with a range of emotions so complex that it "almost overwhelms the mind that meditates its realisation, and utterly exhausts the frame which endeavours to express its agitations".[36] Evidently in the late 18th century, the draw of Sarah Siddons in the role was such that it was at times not unusual "for spectators to leave the house when her part . . . was over".[37] Constance is a major focus of the chapter in this book as well, though, as noted, my approach seems to be in the minority, for she seems to be (almost) uniformly treated with a sort of deference, and "associated with the most exquisite feelings of maternal tenderness". One key critic of old who shares much of my perspective on her is Bucknill—notably, a psychiatrist in his own time.[38] Perhaps our mutual acquaintance with individual psychic pathology renders Constance rather a different picture than she appears to those who have no reason to go looking for trouble.

In recent years, the 'child subjectivity' movement in literary criticism has encouraged attention to be paid to Arthur and Constance, seeing them somewhat more along the lines that I do.[39] At the risk of glibness, for the psychoanalyst 'child subjectivity' sounds a bit obvious. The subjectivity of children has been our bread-and-butter for more than a century: 'so what was that like for you, as a child?'

Apart from Constance, the chief character of the play has generally been treated as the Bastard rather than John, and this has extended to productions in which the more accomplished or renowned actor plays the Bastard, perhaps to the imbalancing of the play.[40] It is one of a few Shakespearean works—another, notably, being *Cymbeline*—in which the title character seems to be sidelined in their own play. Today, there are ideas that seem

> to be taking firm hold in interpretations of the Bastard . . . his presentation in the play (in one schematic construct or another) is logically developmental rather than confused or contradictory; his strong sense of autonomous agency, although very different from simple, reflexive loyalty to the monarch, is one that permits him to *choose* loyalty nevertheless; and his sense of duty is a fine example of what the age was coming to recognize as the trait of an aristocrat in service to his country and a model of good citizenship.[41]

Tucker, one of two Jungian approaches to *King John* that I am aware of, is mainly interested in the presence of chaos, or perhaps the obscure workings of divine providence, in this and other of Shakespeare's works. He sees *John* as expressing "a somber conviction that whatever humankind may do, its endeavors are in the end mocked by chaos."[42] Vujovic, presenting the other extant Jungian approach to the play, focuses on the relationship of its men to the feminine principle, in particular to the representations of mothers.[43]

Vaughan's attention to *King John* as a transitional play between the two historical tetralogies—*Henry VI 1/2/3* plus *Richard III* forming the first, with the second formed by *Richard II, Henry IV 1/2*, and *Henry V*—recognized that *John* seems to inaugurate a new relationship with historical material, one less reverential and more experimental. In contrast to the first tetralogy, *John* demonstrates "more sophisticated dramaturgical techniques to convey political complexities".[44] Shakespeare, through *John*, begins to question the unquestioned ideals that consistently forced themselves into the action of *Henry VI*, and

> confronts political behaviour from more than one perspective, as the outgrowth of characters in conflict, each with legitimate claims and goals; it acknowledges the complexity of political life and demonstrates that in any conflict both sides have rights and wrongs.[45]

King John was, in the second half of the last century, the subject of a collective rescue effort to redeem it from the critical and theatrical no-man's-land in which it lived. A 1951 essay by Bonjour is nominated as the responsible "catalyst in getting *King John* scholarship on the right track",[46] and the chapter by Burckhardt was fundamental in recontextualizing the play for a more modern sensibility.[47] Curren-Aquino edited an excellent volume on the play in 1989, and Candido in 1996 edited a massive collection of *King John* criticism-through-the-ages.

King John remains unpopular, at least in comparison with other of Shakespeare's plays, but it is no longer *quite* so unknown. In a sample of 1595 productions of Shakespeare's plays produced by 213 theatre companies between 2010 and 2017,[48] *King John* had a highly respectable 19 productions—the same as the significantly more well-loved *Henry IV Pt. 1*. By comparison, number one on the list was *A Midsummer Night's Dream*, with 118 productions.

It might be worth noting that any other playwright on the planet, living or dead, who received 19 productions of any play over a few years would be over the moon.

Origin

King John was printed in the First Folio in 1623, as *The Life and Death of King John*, listed first among the histories, which were arranged chronologically in order of setting. It appears to have been written and performed, at the very latest, by 1598. Stylistic markers in the text suggest a date of 1595–6. According to most, it can have been written no earlier than 1591, since it is considered to be a reworking of Peele's *The Troublesome Raigne of John, King of England*. The two plays are undeniably closely linked, sharing characters, structure, and even text at some points. The question is who influenced whom. Most scholars think that Peele's play came first, and Shakespeare used it as a source, based at least in part on the fact that Shakespeare's version is different in ways apparently "designed to heighten parallels between King John and Queen Elizabeth."[49] It has been argued that both plays may owe a mutual debt, of inspiration if not of actual material, to an earlier *Kynge Johan* by John Bale.[50]

It seems psychologically appropriate that a play so occupied with questions of hereditary right and provenance should itself be at the centre of such a problem. *King John* comes trailing clouds of uncertainty and confusion.

This Book

In the essay, I consider *King John* as a tragedy of the puer aeternus. The nature of this archetype will obviously be explored much further, but essentially it is the eternal boy—the boy who won't, or can't, grow up.

I should note that approaching *John* in this way provides a pretty one-sidedly negative view of the puer. There is little of the puer's inspiring flight in this play; we get more of a slow-motion crash. This could be a depth-psychological reason for the play's status as a pariah among Shakespeare's works—it is, effectively, too jaded, too pathological, and we *miss* the energy of the positive puer. Readers of this book may be contented by the knowledge that the puer will return in a much more positive form when we arrive at *Cymbeline*.

I approach John as a puer tragedy in a few different ways. The simplest is on the character level: the Two English Kings both exemplify different aspects of the puer aeternus archetype, or rather, they embody what happens to men who identify with this archetype in their lives. Next, the pattern of the play as a whole includes many typical aspects of the puer's psychology and life story—relationship with the trickster archetype, a devouring mother figure, a senex (old man)—and, when seen as a dramatization of inner psychological developments, *John* seems to express the puer and his psychological situation with surprising precision. Lastly, the play itself seems to be written not only about the puer, but by and for 'him' as well. He dramatizes, through Arthur and John, two ignoble though typical endings to his phenomenology: a crash to the ground, or an untethered floating off into space. He reveals to us his *constant* double-bindedness—it cannot be overstated how often the puer-identified man finds himself in a double-bind, often of his own unconscious making. But he also shows a developmental path through it all, as the Bastard keeps to the middle path, impaling himself on neither horn of the double-bind dilemma, flying neither too close to the sun nor to the treacherous ocean below, and becoming a real—if deeply compromised, and therefore all the more real—boy.

Notes

1 Burckhardt (1968, 117).
2 Vaughan (2003, 379).
3 Burckhardt (1968, 116).
4 Burckhardt (1968, 137).
5 Howard & Rackin (1968, 119).
6 Kastan (1983, 9).

 7 Wilhelm (1984, 94).
 8 Wilhelm (1984, 94).
 9 Jing-Nuan (1991, 112–3).
10 Kastan (1983, 12).
11 Champion (1989, 181).
12 Burckhardt (1968, 129).
13 Vaughan (2003, 379).
14 In Candido (2022, 2).
15 Candido (2022, 1).
16 Piesse (2002, 127); Waith (1978, 193).
17 Curren-Aquino (1989, 12), referencing Pope.
18 Piesse (2002, 127).
19 Chambers (1925, 81).
20 Chambers (1925, 85).
21 Upton (1748, 74).
22 Curren-Aquino (1989, 11).
23 Candido (2022, 32–3).
24 Dover Wilson (2009, vii); Ornstein (1972, 96–101).
25 Candido (2022, 8).
26 Bloom (1994, 183).
27 Johnson (1989, 195).
28 W. Oxberry (1819). *Prefatory remarks on King John.* In Candido (2022, 102).
29 J. E. Masefield (1911). *William Shakespeare.* In Candido (2022, 394).
30 J. A. Heraud (1865). *Shakespeare: His inner life, as intimated in his works.* In Candido (2022, 241).
31 Vaughan (1984, 420).
32 Bloom (1999, 52).
33 Piesse (2002, 127).
34 J. S. Bucknill (1859). *The madness of Constance.* In Candido (2002, 208).
35 Carlisle (1989, 144).
36 Waith (1978, 198).
37 T. Campbell (1834). *Sarah Siddons on Constance.* In Candido (2022, 122).
38 Bucknill (1859) in Candido (2022, 211).
39 See Heberle (1994), Miller (2016), Campana (2007), Knowles (2007).
40 Honigmann (1954, lxxv).
41 Candido (2022, 46).
42 Tucker (2003, 24).
43 Vujovic (2021).
44 Vaughan (1984, 409).
45 Vaughan (1984, 411).
46 Bonjour (1951); quote is Curren-Aquino (1989, 13).
47 Burckhardt (1968).
48 Minton (2017)—the sample is informal, but may yet successfully indicate general trends.
49 Lander & Tobin (2018, 4fn). See also R. Simpson (1874), *King John and contemporary politics,* in Candido (2022, 247–51); see also Honigmann (1954, xxix).
50 C. Knight (1838). *The Pictorial Edition of King John,* in Candido (2022, 136–49).

Chapter 2

The Faithless Eros of *King John*[1]

Just imagine being John—disinherited by your brother, only to be reinherited at the last bloody moment in a highly questionable and barely defensible way, and made king, but without a speck of land to the title. What sort of backhanded game is this? Not to mention being a grown man and living under the dominion of one of the most influential people of your entire era, Eleanor of Aquitane—that's 'mom' to you.

Or imagine being Eleanor: tactical, indomitable, survivor of your husband and two sons, and now in late life tasked with mothering this all-powerful man-child.

Imagine being Constance—swindled, as far as you can tell, by the world. It has already taken your husband from you, and in the most foolish of circumstances—a joust[2]—it yet seems set to deprive you of your and your child's rightful inheritance and security.

Underneath these individual angers lies the archetypal anger of the puer aeternus: The Eternal Boy, The Boy Who Wouldn't Grow Up—except here Peter Pan is not granted the boon of Never Never Land, but has to make his way in Medieval England. When we think *Medieval England,* many of us may be tempted to imagine knights heroic or errant; courtly love; days of high adventure. But this world is far from ideal, and there is little fun to be had. The conflicts which face *King John*'s characters are the most annoying of all, from the perspective of the puer: they are the problems of navigating other people, their desires and aims. The problems of politics. The boy in this play's psyche has never agreed to grow up, but he is constantly being pressured to do so—forced to do so—anyway.

This chronicle history of Shakespeare's is among the least well-regarded, and the least regarded *at all*, of Shakespeare's works. "A watchword for Shakespearean obscurity: unread, unperformed and unloved."[3] The play does perform better than it reads,[4] and contemporary productions seem commonly to evoke the question from audiences of why it isn't done more often.[5] It is, after all, exceptionally intelligent,[6] witty, full of twisting plot, tense confrontation, and action. But then, it is somewhat anticlimactic; it falls apart in the last two acts, by design. The ending "is consistent with the previous five acts; expectations are repeatedly disappointed and conventions undercut."[7] The play is washed in its own water. Even so, this water is often bitter; one may experience a sort of acrid taste in the mouth while dealing with

DOI: 10.4324/9781003596967-3

the play's satirical and cynical elements. This chapter will explore and develop the themes of the puer aeternus archetype, that airy thing, as they are expressed through *King John*. Through this I hope to 'aerate' the play, so to speak, for like a bottle of wine it benefits from having oxygen introduced into it, opening up the taste for the greater variety of readers.

Puer Aeternus

The puer aeternus is, literally, the eternal boy. He is "that archetypal dominant which personifies or is in special relation with the transcendent spiritual powers of the collective unconscious."[8] He is expressed through that part of the personality that reinvests the old with new meaning through new seeing, and which can be inspired to great heights of fantasy or even incredible achievement, but which—and this is key—is ultimately unreliable.[9] The puer bursts like a shot from the starting line and then, sooner rather than later, just peters out. He is the 'inner child', and being essentially childlike and childish, he simply cannot sustain his drive for long enough to see many things through to completion, leaving it to others "To set a form upon that indigest / Which he hath left so shapeless and so rude" (5.7.26–7). But it is from him, and his "vertical *direct* access to the spirit"[10] that "we are given our sense of destiny and mission."[11] He is invigorating, adaptive, ingenious, idealistic, and competitive; "precocious, importunate, and extravagant"[12]; as well as disappointing, disappoint*ed* (pathologically so), imperious, callow, and negligent. He is prized and lauded for his originality, and envied and hated for his originality.

Francis Gentleman catches the puer quality of *King John* in criticizing the fact that the play (like all Shakespeare's historical works) compresses the space of many years into an hourglass, and events that occurred decades apart in history occur only a few minutes apart onstage:

> In writing this play, SHAKESPEARE disclaimed every idea of regularity, and has huddled such a series of historical events on the back of one another, as shame the utmost stretch of probability; his muse travels lightning winged, being here, there, and every where, in the space of a few minutes.[13]

What Gentleman did not note was the *purpose* of all this historical huddling. It would appear that *John*'s episodes have been arranged precisely to centralize John's conflict with a child: Arthur, his boy rival for the throne. Shakespeare, notes Heberle, makes the boy's death in particular "define the shape of John's rule."[14] Many of Shakespeare's plays feature children: this one is *about* them.

In an attempt to define *King John*'s 'Goldmanian Centre', therefore—the essential experience which unifies it on the three levels of characters, actors, and audience—I am unavoidably drawn to the puer aeternus. The repeated disappointing of expectations, so integral to the experience of *John*, is also the experience of the puer. Yet the puer accounts also for the opposite experience of the play: delight in its intellectual aerobatics; aesthetic interest in its confidently unusual structure;

surprise at the play's irreverence, relevant both in 1596 and now. It also accounts for the common strain among criticism (including mine) that there is *some great untapped potential* in the play, *if only it could deliver.* What could be more puer than that? And *John* expresses not only the subjective experience of the puer, but the *objective* experience as well, in other words, that belonging to those who have to *deal* with him. This accounts for our boredom or impatience with the play—for the puer personality, as the unsuppressed tone of von Franz oft conveys,[15] can be tremendously tedious.

Shakespeare had a lot of interest in the puer problem, which is to say the problem of how to manage and express this unruly, beautiful, indispensable energy, and aspects of his engagement with it can be found in nearly all of his plays. Then again, the puer problem seems also to be everywhere one looks in the world. The puer is as essential to the human psyche as the mother and father.

Just as there are many different faces of the mother or father archetypes, however, so too are there many different faces of the puer. 'Puer aeternus' has been done a disservice by being banished to the name of a pathological 'type' of male personality, "a neurotic epithet",[16] though to some degree this is probably retribution for way the puer often treats *us.* Von Franz wrote the initial and definitive study on the puer aeternus,[17] and did so with great empathy and understanding, yet she still to some degree seems to have been subject to the puer's projective identification,[18] which turns everybody else into a suffocating mother or authoritarian father—especially those who try to love them. Von Franz has been the subject of (justified) criticism for certain aspects of her view, including threads of vindictiveness and homophobia that lurk in the work, but I don't think anything is gained by throwing away her "original and profound writings",[19] which are essential and essentially pioneering efforts to *understand deeply* the puer pattern. Hillman (Jungian Psychology's great Youth Advocate) has observed that puer myths are replete with images of parental wounding, and notes that this motif seems to say not only that our parents wound us, but that *our wounds parent us*: "our wounds are the fathers and mothers of our destinies."[20] We do not grow up without being hurt; we do not *need* to grow up without being hurt. The book of von Franz may stand as *Jungian Psychology's* puer wound, the initiatory injury without which a necessary counter-response may not have grown. She is our own wounded-and-wounding mother figure, and her 'offense' was to have incompletely understood the boy, and perhaps not come entirely to terms with her *own* maternal sadism. Here again, however, we spin back to the puer, who never feels fully or properly understood anyway. He is impossible in this regard, and this is part of a repetition compulsion to re-wound himself again and again, never being understood because never fully revealing himself. Even Hillman was frustrated by his sense that the puer would never allow himself fully to be expressed.[21] At any rate, his (and other authors') rejoinder to von Franz's study was more successful in redeeming our conceptualization of the archetype into something appreciable.[22]

Often, as is common practice, I use the word puer as shorthand for puer-identified man, though this should not be taken as indicating that there is no difference. The puer itself is an archetype, a category of psychological experience—not a *person*. It does puer a disservice to be reduced to a person, and it does a person a disservice to reduce them to a single archetypally-influenced aspect of their personality. However, the puer-identified man often does himself this disservice, when he inflates his own personality to nothing but puer. I persist in using the shorthand of 'puer' to mean both the archetype *and* the person inflated by the archetype because (1) sometimes I mean both and (2) in some way the difference must be actively *thought* by the reader; words can only do so much.

The reader may notice a pattern in my argument: with just about every dynamic associated with the puer, I bring it back round to him as both actor and acted-upon, victim and perpetrator simultaneously. I do not want to deny his suffering, but nor do I want to sap him of his agency. Too, this is somewhat reflective of *John,* in which we are constantly caught "in a noose of equal and opposite sympathies", as Grennan puts it.[23] To move back and forth this way is quite the opposite of trying to bypass or stymie the emotion-laden process of recognizing *what one has done or had done to oneself,* which is absolutely necessary for the purposes of healing. But 'blame' is an abstract, sticky, and generally inadequate concept, especially where psychopathology and archetypal wounding are concerned. Is the puer like "a parasite" who lives on the mother, as Von Franz metaphorizes him?[24] Or is it the mother who acts as the parasite, "castrates her son and then perpetually hits that weakness"?[25] There is no answer because the question is a wrong-headed and double-binding question. Whether putting the accent on the son, or the accent on the mother, one is damned either way. I propose a dialogic solution, a back-and-forth that brings a new, third perspective into being. This is, uncoincidentally, what drama also provides: dialogue. As we will see, *King John* shows not only a double-bind, but also a possible way *through*.

For now, how else does the puer show up in *John*'s broad strokes? Nicolas Woodeson (playing John in 1988) found "the syntax of the text is both elaborate and unwieldy, as though of an age still forming itself".[26] The text itself seems, then, to ring with the puer's high-flown-idealism-with-little-practical-application; "an age still forming itself" is an unconsciously felicitous phrase which evokes the puer's own life-and-death struggle to come of age on his own terms.[27]

I Ching refers to the Difficulty at the Beginning (屯, *Zhūn,* 3) which is so often carried far past the beginning and through to the puer's end:

Clouds and thunder:
The image of DIFFICULTY AT THE BEGINNING.
Thus the superior man
Brings order out of confusion.[28]

The tragic element of *King John* is that, with John himself, we are decidedly *not* dealing with the superior man,[29] and the play shows us what we get in that case: confusion brought out of order. History, in the sense of history as one damned thing after another, with a man at the helm who is simply unable to bring coherence. Guy

Henry (playing John in 2001) empathized with "the pain of a man in a job that he feels, with all his heart (and most of his mind), should be his . . . but with the creeping knowledge that he isn't good at it".[30] Indeed John's kingship commands precious little respect; this is introduced as the central plot-point of the play as early as its fourth line, when France's ambassador pertly refers to "the borrowed majesty of England" (1.1.4).

The puer is primarily embodied in the conflict between two differently-childlike characters, John and Arthur. But the pattern of the puer aeternus is spread throughout the play. Like in the *commedia dell'arte*, in which one never finds Arlecchino without Pantalone, so the puer comes with a supporting cast. The puer's perennial companion, the mother, shows up, and not once but thrice, in the persons of Eleanor, Constance, and Lady Faulconbridge. The role of the absent-but-ever-present father is taken up mainly by the dead Richard I, or Cordelion (= *Coeur-de-Lion* = Lionheart). Hubert, at a significant moment, finds himself in a father constellation as well. And the puer's shadow, the trickster, is concentrated and developed in the Bastard, eventually to be transcended by him.

Puer shows up between the lines in the form of a persistent unrelatedness between characters—a "faithless Eros".[31] *John* is singular in the way its characters make and break promises. Generally, the women and children in the play's system are left to speak on behalf of relationship, compensating the idealistic manias to which most of the men are subject. Someone has to. The masculine voice of competition and war tends toward the impersonal, bordering on sociopathic:

BASTARD: O, now doth death line his dread chaps with steel:
The swords of soldiers are his teeth, his fangs,
And now he feasts, mousing the flesh of men . . .

$$(2.1.352\text{–}4)$$

But the women do not, at least at first, go gentle into those good roles wished for them.[32] Dusinberre sees *John*'s female characters as unusually influential: "up till the end of Act III the dramatic action is dominated by the women characters, and this is a cause of extreme embarrassment to the men on stage".[33] After the third act, of course, they evaporate.

To summarize my proposal of the Goldmanian Centre:

- the *characters* of the play must deal with the pueri in their midst and in their own psyches;
- the *actors* must reckon with the puer in both the rhetorical style and structure of the play, as well as its faithless relationships, which pose their own challenge since actors are usually constitutionally driven to *connect*;
- the *audience* is treated to a puer experience with a plot that seems to start strong and loses itself, burning up in its own atmosphere, and ending confused, diffused, and disillusioned.

I would call *King John* a story of a failed *puer*, but sadly I realize that may be an oxymoron. Is there any successful *puer aeternus*? Perhaps another double-binding question. If he matures, he has failed at remaining a *puer*; if he crashes or burns up, he has succeeded as a *puer* but failed at everything else. The failure itself seems to be a necessary part of *puer* phenomenology. A *puer*-identified man 'succeeds' precisely to the degree that he can disidentify from the *puer*, who is ultimately hostile to his own earthliness. The *pueri* of myth—Icarus, Phaëthon, Bellerophon—all crash and burn, so why should this be any different? It is the *puer* himself who thinks, 'But for me, it will be different!'

For John and Arthur, the flight ends unequivocally in failure. Arthur crashes and John disintegrates. But here I may reiterate something valuable that the Jungian perspective brings to Shakespeare, which is the ability to see a play as a single psyche—like a long and detailed dream, with each individual character being an embodiment of a single part of the dreamer. What this illuminates in *King John* is that while the two *pueri* of the play fail, the play *itself* moves forward through their wreckage. The play loses its *pueri*, but develops its trickster into a hero. A sacrifice on one level allows new growth on another; the play grows up. And at its conclusion, the superior man *is* present in the person of the Bastard, who "brings order out of confusion".[34]

One of the ways he does so is by pointing toward Henry III, the new ruler, and a child himself. One of Henry's few lines comprises a sober grounding of the crown-mania that has gripped the entire play; after his father, John, dies, he says:

HENRY: E'en so must I run on and e'en so stop.
What surety of the world, what hope, what stay,
When this was now a king, and now is clay?
(5.7.67–9)

'Clay' is anathema for the *puer*; it appears in *puer* dreams in the form of a square mud pit, or a terrifying man made of earth—anything which threatens that the *puer* must get his hands dirty, must get involved and invested with no easy eject or reset button. Anytime that word 'clay' appears in Shakespeare, it is part of a similar act of deflation, a humbling of the human pretension to being anything more than a creature: "Men are but gilded loam or painted clay" (*RII*, 1.1.179). "Kingdoms are clay! Our dungy earth alike / Feeds beast as man." (*AC* 1.1.36–7). "Imperious Caesar, dead and turned to clay, / Might stop a hole to keep the wind away" (*Ham.* 5.1.203–4).

From Henry's reflection, we are given to understand that he intends to be a different king than John was, one who rules not through clinging to what is transiently and speciously 'his', but with some little knowledge and acceptance of the laws of being and change. And the play's plot ends with a tentative closure to the time of disarray which it has chronicled. Though still somewhat lost "Among the thorns and dangers of this world" (4.3.141), its closing position, anchored by the Bastard and the new king, is at least *of this world*. And to be of this world—that is the greatest challenge for the puer aeternus.

The Bastard Heart

Before addressing the King himself, it seems necessary to me to address the character of the Bastard. Doing so will have the virtue of acting as a second synopsis of the play, which may be useful for those readers who are not very familiar with it.

Smallwood writes that *King John* is "an unsettling play, quite literally so in its leaving of audiences with nowhere to settle, uncertain where, if anywhere, to allow their sympathies to rest".[35] I would suggest that there is, actually, a single somewhat-viable place to settle if one wants to get a sense of *John* as a totality, and that is to embrace psychological nomadism and align with the Bastard as the play's *raisonneur*: the voice within the play that communicates something of its own viewpoint to us.[36] He is both within and without the play, living and reflecting simultaneously.[37] We can stay with the Bastard because his view is more inclusive than any other character's. He is quite frequently the only one to grasp more than a one-sided view of an issue, compensating everyone else in the play. He is also the only character who seems to have true interiority, who (as Bloom puts it) overhears himself,[38] growing and developing in response to his own words. He is the one character that we feel spends time with us, and with whom we therefore feel we get to develop a relationship. His regular soliloquies can, for an audience or reader, act as waypoints on the journey through the play. They are not only important moments for him as a character, they are also engagements with the larger themes of the play, charting a course for us as he grows into his own personality.

His journey can be considered in terms of four distinct segments, each of which develops a new level of perspective in his voice.[39] At first he is an upwardly mobile opportunist, sacrificing his familial land as a Faulconbridge to be recognized as a Plantagenet, the illegitimate son of the late king legitimized. His speech here focuses on his advancement: "A foot of honour better than I was, / But many a many foot of land the worse" (1.1.182–3). He mocks the upper class, but he also makes clear that he sees imitation of them to be the most sensible way of adapting himself to his new station:

BASTARD: For he is but a bastard to the time
That does not smack of observation,
And so am I whether I smack or no;
And not alone in habit and device,
Exterior form, outward accoutrement,
But from the inward motion to deliver
Sweet, sweet, sweet poison for the age's tooth[.]
(1.1.207–13)

Manheim observes that while the Bastard satirizes here, he is also unconsciously preparing himself for satirization.[40] He overestimates his comprehension of the way of the world; he has a teenage view of what it means to be adult. It is charming that he thinks he is going to make a big splash by being a disruptor, but the position he defines here is shallow. Its inadequacy is soon to become apparent to him.

In his second segment, the Bastard plays the trickster and provocateur. He is a cocky fish out of water in his new milieu. He has not yet understood that one acts differently in the presence of kings; he even interrupts them:

KING JOHN: Twice fifteen thousand hearts of England's breed –
BASTARD: Bastards and else.
KING JOHN: To verify our title with their lives.
KING PHILIP: As many and as well-born bloods as those –
BASTARD: Some bastards too.
KING PHILIP: Stand in his face to contradict his claim.

(2.1.275–80)

He has later to be reminded of his place by John: "We like not this, thou dost forget thyself" (3.1.134), a moment which anticipates Falstaff's unwelcome joke at a similar moment in *Henry IV,* and Hal's rebuke: "Peace, chewet, peace" (*1HIV* 5.1.29). He distracts from the negotiations between England and France by striking up a rivalry with the Duke of Austria, and is curtly dismissed as a "fool" by King Philip (2.1.150). He *is* the fool, Parsifal on his first big adventure away from home, and fortunately he has no fear of failure. He is thrilled with the fun of it all, the "blows, blood, and death!" (2.1.36). He has not yet had the opportunity to mature into genuine heroism—although he does express a knack for identifying a latent opportunity for use of the transcendent function.

The transcendent function is that resourceful dynamic of psychological creativity which can, at times, get us out of an apparent dilemma; in a double-bind situation that appears to have us fated to be impaled on one horn or another, the transcendent function finds a way through the horns, a solution which transcends the problem. The Bastard has done this earlier, in the inheritance dispute between him and his brother, by leaping toward a solution which would satisfy them both: disclaiming his inheritance. At Angiers, he does it again, with a decidedly trickster-ish cast, when he invents a solution to the problem of Angiers' divided loyalty: since the town won't choose their king, perhaps the kings could choose to raze the town (2.1.373–96). It's a funny idea, but he has not become aware that there might be any contribution he could make to the team apart from running cheeky interference plays.

However, earlier he promised to learn what he could from his new social position, and he finds no shortage of learning opportunities. When the Citizen of Angiers proposes that they marry Blanche to Lewis and avoid battle entirely, the Bastard stands admiring: "What cannoneer begot this lusty blood?" (2.1.461) Lusty blood, of course, is his own claim to fame, as one of Shakespeare's later bastards is to describe the members of that club,

EDMUND: Who in the lusty stealth of nature take
More composition and fierce quality
Than doth within a dull, stale tired bed[.]
(*KL* 1.2.11–3)

What the Bastard recognizes in the Citizen, perhaps, is a fellow man of merit without rank. I think he first understands, here, that there is a different kind of *power* than that wielded by the men in the crowns with the armies.

BASTARD: He speaks plain cannon fire, and smoke, and bounce;
He gives the bastinado with his tongue;
Our ears are cudgelled: not a word of his
But buffets better than a fist of France.

(2.1.462–5)

This discovery is to serve him well as his rise continues, for he has found, essentially, that the halls of power are actually full of cracks and secret passages, and a man in this world can, with attentiveness and ingenuity, make his own way.

After the battle is circumvented by marriage, comes the Bastard's keynote speech: "Commodity, the bias of the world" (2.1.374). *Commodity* here means something like "self-interest, advantage, expediency, gain",[41] though our modern sense of *asset* also rings quite true given the circumstances. He is dumbfounded by his new view of the "Mad world, mad kings, mad composition!" (2.1.561), though he continues to skew pragmatical. He perceives fully, but does not balk at accepting, the apparent *amorality* of his new social milieu; the fact that he has a growing integrity does not prevent him from seeing how others lack it. He begins to understand what it means to have opportunity: those who have it, exploit it, and by exploiting it they continue to have it. It would appear to him, now, that little stands in the way of the ruthless self-interest of the powerful. He addresses himself to his own new ruling principle: "Since kings break faith upon Commodity, / Gain be my lord, for I will worship thee" (2.1.597–8).[42] In that line, I suggest, we see more clearly than anywhere else the conflict that the play is 'about'. Majesty being borrowed, kings being clay, and promises being wind, this seems to be an era that is ruled by *personal gain*.

It has been suggested that this devotion to gain is merely hypothetical for the Bastard, who after all never devolves into a renegade pirate or Machiavel.[43] I think this is to underestimate the Bastard's shrewdness and motivation. He is less interested in money or power than in life. He may be even more interested in life than Falstaff, who cries "give me life" (*1HIV* 5.3.60) but ultimately spends most of his in a drunken fog. If the Bastard went the way of a Falstaff or an Edmund, surely he would experience temporary gain, but misery in the long run—as they do. In the tradition of seeing him as a forerunner of other great Shakespearean characters, I would say that in this respect he is more anticipatory of the pragmatical Boling-broke. Even from his low position, he has a vision beyond the short-term; he is someone who perceives that medium- to long-term gain is to be had by staying careful and awake. He sees that his welfare is tied to that of his king and nation; there is no longevity in antisocial marauding, and he seems to realize this long before John realizes, similarly but in a different key, that "there is no sure founda-tion set on blood" (4.2.104).

In Act 3, at the wedding reception for Lewis and Blanche, the marriage proves to be an unstable solution: Pandulph intervenes on behalf of the Catholic Church, and twists the King of France into betraying John rather than suffer excommunica-tion. In the ensuing battle, the Bastard grows and prospers. He begins to outshine his king:

KING JOHN: Philip, make up!
My mother is assailed in our tent
And ta'en, I fear.
BASTARD: My lord, I rescued her;
Her highness is in safety, fear you not.
                                        (3.2.5–8)

Here we begin to feel confirmation of a heroic attitude in the Bastard that super-sedes mere Commodity. The Bastard begins to do the right and necessary thing for the time, decisively and quickly—and as above, he is one step ahead of John.

This third segment is defined in Act 4 by a significant challenge to the Bastard's worldview: Arthur's death. He exhibits growing personal authority, resembling some of the nobler men of other plays. His commanding presence with the English Lords at "Your sword is bright, sir, put it up again" (4.3.79) anticipates Othello's "Keep up your bright swords, for the dew will rust them (*Oth.*1.2.59). He sees the terrible potential in the situation and prophesies war and confusion, foreshadowing the tone and language of Mark Antony after the death of Caesar (*JC* 3.1.259–75).

His soliloquy here has been regarded as forced by some, though for Bonjour it was the moment that the Bastard "attains, on the spiritual and moral plane, the dignity of a great character."[44] I think it ceases to feel forced if one can read it with the actor's intention in mind, staying close to the Bastard's likely experience through the scene. When Arthur's body is discovered, he responds with surprising rationality, but this is in compensation for the emotional excesses of Salisbury and Pembroke, who would rush to a judgment which serves their ends. He is forced to keep the peace, claiming authority lest Salisbury murder Hubert in the street. After the Lords depart, his caution is succeeded by a blistering (though still, ration-ally, conditional) indictment of Hubert: "There is not yet so ugly a fiend of hell / As thou shalt be, if thou didst kill this child" (4.3.123–4). *Finally*, when alone, he can express his bewilderment—to *us*: "I am amazed, methinks, and lose my way / Among the thorns and dangers of this world" (4.3.140–1).

It might help to identify that a soliloquy, though 'technically' a character speaking to themselves, is functionally played to the audience; the audience stands in as the character's inner Other; the Bastard's main relationship, therefore, is with us. When alone with us, he can unpack his heart. He shares vulnerability and authentic moral confusion. I think he is stunned. For him, soldiers can have their flesh moused by the fangs of death (2.1.353–4), who feasts upon them by the thousands (5.2.178), but a *child* is not supposed to be the object of violence. When he remarks, "How easily dost thou take all England up!" (4.3.142) with regard to Hubert's bearing of Arthur's tiny body, I think "all England" may well be a discovery for him in the moment—he did not see what this child represented until now. Sometimes Shakespeare has his characters suddenly, expansively, see the whole picture—a View—and an intuitive knowing of the archetypal situation rushes in upon them. From this place, the Bastard sees with dawning clarity the emptiness of John's principle, "the bare-picked bone of majesty" (4.3.148). The Bastard prophesies, accurately, "dogged war" and "vast confusion" (4.3.149;152), and ends Act 4 proclaiming that "heaven itself doth frown upon the land" (5.1.159)—reflecting his increasing moral gravity, and importantly *transcending* his earlier view of Commodity as the bias of the world—or, rather, Commodity may be *the world's* bias, but there is something larger than even the world—"there is a world elsewhere" (*Cor.* 3.3.134), we might say, and it has laws superordinate to King John's.

G.B. Shaw wrote that one could read Shakespeare's plays "from one end to the other without learning that the world is finally governed by forces expressing themselves in religions and laws which make epochs rather than by vulgarly ambitious individuals who make rows"[45]—I don't think he is even nearly correct, and the Bastard's perspective here, as well as the fact that *King John* bears it out, stands as evidence.

The fourth segment of the Bastard's journey sees him take command of the English military in earnest (5.1.77), as well as of King John himself.

BASTARD: But wherefore do you droop? Why look you sad?
Be great in act, as you have been in thought!
Let not the world see fear and sad distrust
Govern the motion of a kingly eye.

(5.1.44–7)

Though John relies on men such as he and Hubert—men outside the aristocracy, who are therefore dependent upon him for employ and advancement—he is outgrown, morally, by both of them. The Bastard has matured, and remarkably has done so without leaving behind his tendency toward acting the provocateur (as in 5.2). In other words, the play's trickster has made good and become orthodox—part of the system—but without selling out his autonomy! This is itself an achievement of transcendent functioning, for he has taken on responsibility without the rigidity which often attends it. He seems now to be the only sure hand at the helm of the kingdom.

Jung saw the trickster as "a forerunner of the saviour",[46] Henderson specifying further that the trickster image was the first stage of the hero myth.[47] The Bastard illustrates the course by which the initial impulse toward autonomy represented by the boundary-disrespecting trickster can develop beyond unidimensionality into something grounded and, in the case of *John*, desperately needed. When we met him, we were introduced to his pragmatic morality:

BASTARD: Which though I will not practise to deceive,
Yet to avoid deceit I meant to learn,
For it shall strew the footsteps of my rising.
(1.1.214–6)

And through the play, he has learned that there are stronger principles than self-interest, Commodity, adventure, royalty, loyalty, and authority.

Yet his love toward his cousin John remains until the end, which I find quite touching. His may be the only faith*ful* Eros in the play. He has not blinded himself to his uncle's misrule—he seems mainly to have a soft spot of feeling for him nonetheless. The Bastard's affection for him is really the only indication we get that there *is* something in John that can be loved. One could make a moral judgment on the Bastard for not turning on his king, but it seems irrepressibly real that he does not; it can be very difficult to part company with someone who has been very important in one's life, even if one has outgrown the person in question; even if they have proven a terrible disappointment. Perhaps this is another indication of transcendent functioning: the Bastard can live with disappointment, and even love through it. Love, perhaps, is an intimately detailed and involving experience whereas morality is merely a set of ideals—the Bastard has anyway come to know that there are deeper currents than those dreamt of in the moral philosophies of men.

The Bastard is surely our superior man in this play. The operative and recurrent word in my descriptions of him is 'develop', and in this alone he is medicine to the one-sided puer. Hillman writes that the energy of the puer archetype is "primordially perfect. Therefore there is no development; development means devolution, a loss and fall and restriction of possibilities. So for all its changeability the puer . . . at core resists development."[48]

In the moments following John's death, there is an implicit question in the air as to whether the Bastard might try for the crown, since in the last act he has become the nation's *de facto* leader. This would be the puer moment, to push the fragile situation just a little bit farther. This would truly tip the nation over the cliff, right into the flood from which he has just escaped. Instead of this destabilizing path, he moves forward, by moving backward. He chooses to support the traditional, lineal succession, publicly, and in terms that are unequivocal: "I do bequeath my faithful services / And true subjection everlastingly. *[Kneels.]*" (5.7.104–5)

The Bastard's final speech contains elements that may crystallize the rest of the play into focus. In particular:

BASTARD: This England never did, nor never shall
Lie at the proud foot of a conqueror
But when it first did help to wound itself . . .
        . . . Naught shall make us rue,
If England to herself do rest but true.

(5.7.112–8)

These lines are no unequivocally inspiring, patriotic platitudes with which to drop the curtain. Shakespeare's characters do not stop at the end to come up with a moral for us; the action continues; they live into and through the curtain's fall. Here the Bastard's final lines are, as in the exhortation of *Henry V*, "Work, work" (*HV* 3.0.25)! "Earlier he creates a king worthy of loyalty; now he creates a country capable of it."[49] It is an effort of will, an attempt to wrangle the bedraggled state of England back into some kind of shape. ('Work, work!' is, of course, the typical exhortation made to the puer as well.[50])

In attempting to find a standpoint from which to view *King John*, my proposal is to interpret the Bastard's line (above), "But when it first did help to wound itself" (5.7.114), less as a transparent allusion to the treasons of certain Englishmen and more as a descriptor of the entire play—of John's troublesome reign. This would be to see that England "helped to wound itself" *through John*. It helps to characterize the play among the rest of Shakespeare's histories, and perhaps even explains its *raison d'être*: this particular history play is neither a tale of when England went wrong through the upsurging of sheer malevolence like *Richard III*, nor through vanity like *Richard II*, nor helplessness like *Henry VI*, but rather through a small-minded focus on Commodity, that is, a willingness to do whatever is commodious—whatever is expedient.

The tone of the play perhaps becomes, in its final moments, that of a cautionary tale—a disquieting reflection on a botched kingship. John is neither a ruler to be loved nor hated, unless one is offended by irresponsible leadership (which perhaps one should be). But John is no Stalin, no Hitler; he simply has no integrity. Dover Wilson called him "the English Nero", who "shrank from no humiliation to save his skin".[51] He'll mortgage anything to keep the crown, not that he knows what to do with it. He may remind us of many such promising politicians whose careers show certain significant achievements, but which are all but wiped out by the ignominy of those careers' ends—Richard Nixon comes to mind. As Mark Antony says in *Julius Caesar*, "The evil that men do lives after them: / The good is oft interred with their bones" (*JC* 3.2.76–7). So let it be with John.

John Lackland, Puer King

The opening moment of the play is a brilliant instance of economical and subliminal Shakespearean storytelling, its single image as dense with meaning as a Chinese-language ideogram.[52] The curtain rises on a man and a woman, both crowned, with attendant lords, receiving an ambassador. One might assume this image of King and Queen to be also an image of husband and wife, but, alas—it is son and mother.

The strange confluence of these relations is foregrounded by Shakespeare, coming out in a little touch of filial-maternal-maritalesque bickering, a mere five lines in:

ELEANOR: A strange beginning: borrowed majesty?
KING JOHN: Silence, good mother, hear the embassy.
(1.1.5–6)

Eleanor is "a woman of great stamina and high energy, the wife of two kings . . . and the mother of two more".[53] In recruiting the Bastard, she is the dauntless and formidable dowager:

ELEANOR: Wilt thou forsake thy fortune,
Bequeath thy land to him and follow me?
I am a soldier, and now bound to France.
(1.1.148–50)

She makes a nice comparison with von Franz's description of the mother of Antoine de Saint-Exupéry, author of *Le Petit Prince*: "a big, stout woman, about whom we hear that she has a tremendous amount of energy . . . a very dynamic person and, in spite of the fact that she is now pretty old, is still going strong".[54] Significantly more will be said about the puer's mother and her complex in general, but as for Eleanor in specific, she cuts an intimidating figure. Her place next to the throne pre-dates John's kingship, and he is frankly dwarfed by her. John inherited the crown from his deceased brother Richard Lionheart, whose epithet alone establishes him as a tough act to follow. Youngest brother John's limping epithet, by contrast, is *Lackland*—which literally refers to his having inherited no land, even while it symbolically alludes to his lack of principle: he is a man with no ground on which to stand.

John's attitude toward the "borrowed" (1.1.4) nature of his majesty comes across a few lines later:

KING JOHN: Our strong possession and our right for us.
ELEANOR: Your strong possession much more than your right,
Or else it must go wrong with you and me[.]
(1.1.39–41)

We perceive here the idealism of John juxtaposed with Eleanor's realpolitik. Against those who would supplant John and place Arthur on the throne, she grasps that the main argument in his favour is that possession is nine-tenths of the law; the mere fact that John is already there is his best defence. John would childishly preserve for himself the notion that he is the right and true king, a notion that, with little patience for her son, Eleanor pitilessly squashes. Having been around the block with two family kings already, the mystique has worn off for her. John seems, by contrast, to need to mythologize himself—an indication as to his ungroundedness. He would rather live in what is, in this playworld, a bygone era where kingship was absolute.

In the historical subtext is the fact that John was the (presumably unenthusiastic) signer of Magna Carta, "the first document to put into writing the principle that the king and his government was not above the law,"[55] in effect redefining 'king'. Though Magna Carta itself does not make it into Shakespeare's play, the meaning of 'king' is constantly being interrogated. We may also be reminded that this document, like every other agreement in *John*, was not honoured by its makers; the faithless puer habit strikes again, reducing humanly-binding commitments to meaningless ink and paper, in order to justify 'transcending' them.

The other mythologized quality John makes sure to show off in the initial exchange with the French ambassador is his image of himself as overwhelming—the puer's need to be not merely best, but an entire order of magnitude better.[56] This comes across sometimes, as here, in his need for speed:

KING JOHN: Be thou as lightning in the eyes of France,
For ere thou canst report I will be there,
The thunder of my cannon shall be heard.

(1.1.24–6)

He *is* as good as his word here, and does indeed arrive with his army nearly instantly. Holinshed recorded that "he used such diligence that hee was upon his enimies necks ere they could understand any thing of his coming, or gesse what the matter meant".[57] Not to mention the anachronistic fact that he precociously brings cannons, more than a hundred years before they actually existed in England—an early adopter, we might say. His haste becomes his calling card:

DAUPHIN: So hot a speed . . .
Doth want example. Who hath read or heard
Of any kindred action like to this?

(3.4.11–4)

And it eventually comes back to bite him: "The copy of your speed is learned by [France]" (4.2.113). Hillman observed that "the puer in any complex gives it its drive and drivenness, makes it move too fast, want too much, go too far . . . The world can never satisfy the demands of the spirit or match its beauty."[58] Thweatt speaks more critically of the puer's "hair-trigger" impatience, and its childish provenance: "when you cry to mother for milk, there is milk, *now*."[59] When the puer is involved, time seems always to move all too slowly and nothing can be done quickly enough.

Even with John's army depleted by the time they arrive to Angiers, he continues to boast of an as-yet-reserved, and overwhelming, counterstrike that will "o'er-swell / With course disturbed e'en thy confining shores" (2.1.337–8). Even in peacemaking he will not be outdone, as he offers nearly every disputed territory as a means of making peace on his terms (2.1.486–7), and later throwing in Volquessen, as well as "Full thirty thousand marks of English coin" (2.1. 530) for good measure. The term "provisional life" is used to describe the way in which the puer tends to live as if real life is *not yet*, or is always just over the next hill[60]—"the puer gives the feeling that it can come again another time, make another start"[61]—but the horizon is never reached, and so life is always *coming*, and by this noncommittal attitude the puer is always avoiding *becoming*.[62] John's style of flaunting his own provisional attitude is by regularly averring that he has more (of everything) waiting in provision than he deigns to display.

Let us also be clear about what Shakespeare has written there, in the scene before the gates of Angiers: a childish king goes to war with a literal child, and the battle is at first carried out by both of their mommies.

John's boyish inflation ("an arrogant attitude . . . due to both an inferiority complex and false feelings of superiority"[63]) comes across most plainly when dismissing Pandulph—and the Roman Catholic Church—with a brandishing of his divine right: "What earthy name to interrogatories / Can test the free breath of a sacred king?" (3.1.147–8). He casts himself here, as earlier (2.1.206–34), as (literally) holier than holy.

John does not realize that he has entered an era in which kingship will increasingly rely on assent. Not that the arrangement is democratic by any means, but politics—and nature—will supply their own checks and balances, and kings will become as vulnerable as anybody else. Richard II realized this about the king *per se*, whom Death (or Time) permits, temporarily, to act

KING RICHARD: . . . As if this flesh which walls about our life
Were brass impregnable; and humoured thus,
Comes at the last and with a little pin
Bores through his castle wall, and farewell, king!
(*RII* 3.2.167–70)

There is an idiomatic expression in the theatre business: 'Who plays the king?' John's naïve answer might be that the man in the crown plays the king. But the real answer to 'Who plays the king?' is: 'everybody else.' A king to whom nobody bows is no king at all.

John's "faithless Eros"[64] is most evident at two points. First, when he begins to see that ordering Arthur's death was unwise, and Hubert—formerly "my gentle Hubert, / We owe thee much", "good friend", "I love thee well" (3.3.19–20;30;54)—is thrown under the bus by John's disavowing his part in it. Second, when he learns of his own mother's death: "What? Mother dead? / How wildly then walks my estate in France!" (4.2.127–8) This dreadful response, concerned entirely with the military implications of the loss, may however be compensated by his upcoming line, which is John's only private moment in the entire play: "My mother dead!" (4.2.181).[65] Tom McCamus (playing John in 2014) used the moment to suddenly break down sobbing, before snapping back to composure at Hubert's entrance a line later.[66] Indeed the line's status as the title character's only 'soliloquy' does seem to draw attention to itself, and perhaps it asks for actorly embellishment. Even in reading the play, one feels the floor drop out from under John's feet at the loss of his supercompetent mother.

John's rage is often indicated in the humoral language of choleric heat:[67] his soldiers are "fiery voluntaries" (2.1.67–8); Pandulph cautions that France's "scorched veins" will be continually "new burned" by alliance with John (3.1.278); when France heeds Pandulph and abandons the alliance, John is "burned up with inflaming wrath" (3.1.340).

Fire is the subject of Hexagram 30 of the *I Ching*, called 離, *Lí*: The Clinging, Fire.[68] About its image, Wilhelm says that "A luminous thing giving out light must have within itself something that perseveres; otherwise it will in time burn itself out".[69] The hexagram's fourth line resembles even more John's psychological situation: "Its coming is sudden; / It flames up, dies down, is thrown away." Wilhelm comments, "matters end badly when a man spends himself too rapidly and consumes himself like a meteor."[70] This is a theme which Shakespeare explores elsewhere, most obviously with *Henry IV*'s Harry Percy, aptly known, of course, as *Hot*spur. The puer vitality that John and Hotspur share is a fire which cannot be sustained. King Philip threatens that "Thy rage shall burn thee up, and thou shalt turn / To ashes ere our blood shall quench that fire" (3.2.344–5), and indeed at his death, John's "heart is cracked and burnt" (5.7.52). He complains of inner heat (5.7.45) and longs for coolness, lamenting that

KING JOHN: . . . none of you will bid the winter come
To thrust his icy fingers in my maw . . .
And comfort me with cold. I do not ask you much.
I beg cold comfort.

(5.7.36–43)

He seems, in his final moments, to become acquainted with the limits of his power: he cannot slow (or hasten) his own death.

John is an atypical presentation of the puer aeternus. We are not used, I think, to associate puer with hot rage. We may easily think of him as flip and fanciful; he may be a dreamer, but not violent, not dangerous.[71] To understand the danger, we have to return right to the archetypal bedrock of what puer is. As described earlier, I find it helpful to consider the archetype in terms of a situation, or logical arrangement—rather than a personification. The puer's height is always noted, and it tends to be emphasized that he looks heavenward, toward the transcendent. A corollary and essential logical moment, to me, is that the puer also looks down, like Milton's

Second Adam atop the Hill of Paradise, surveying "all Earth's kingdoms, and their glory."[72] This is his archetypal view and arrogance: he may observe large patterns, broad strokes, but without being close enough to see (or truly care about) the reality on the ground, much less live there. From so high up one has all sorts of unrealistic ideas and demands. Therefore, it is not that rage *per se* is characteristic of the puer—it is more that rage is a common outcome of seeing things from so high above, so very clearly (one feels) that failure to see them must be due to a pathetically limited perspective. Rage is secondary; *arrogance* is primary.

The connection between puer and impatient rage is elaborated in Thweatt's posthumously published and provocative work on *Hitler as Puer*.[73] John is, again, no Hitler, either in the play or in history, but there are certain resonances. John's alacrity in war seems to spring from the same psychological impulse as the Nazi blitzkrieg; Thweatt speaks of Hitler's "fiery impatience" and "scornful wrath",[74] which are nevertheless common knowledge enough to need no citation.

The extremity of the comparison with Hitler serves mainly to highlight how middling John is—not that one 'should' aspire to the infamy of a Hitler, but John simply makes hardly any impression at all. Wilhelm, again commenting on Line 4 of *Lí,* says that "a man who is excitable and restless may rise quickly to prominence but produces no lasting effects."[75] This is precisely the knowledge that the Bastard integrates that John does not. Like all pueri, John is undermined by his own "everlasting switching".[76] Masefield wrote that "persistence in any one course of treachery would give him the greatness of all well-defined things. He remains a chaos shooting out occasional fire";[77] Etty condemned him merely as "an incomplete hypocrite".[78]

In reference to the complete pattern of the puer aeternus, there is definitely something missing with John, for he lacks the archetype's main principle: "the spirit of creating everything anew, again and again".[79]

> What a spirit! It can sweep you right up out of the ordinary lackluster world to a world where you partake of the ever-promising, ever-revitalizing fire of creativity; it vaporizes self-doubt and injects you with the conviction that it (whatever it is) *can* be done, that even a new world might be possible.[80]

This description is all well and good for those exceptional pueri who have enough of any one attribute to make an impression. But just as it is a disservice to totally denigrate the puer it is also a disservice to give him more credit than is due. For, sadly, this enlivening spirit is often only present totally subjectively, for the puer alone. I am convinced that the majority of puer-identified men today are more along the lines of the half-cocked King John than the overextended Bellerophon: fantasizing greatness but exhibiting dullness and half-heartedness; living lives of quiet desperation, lost in daydreams, video games, or internet pornography. They may envision their lives taking on cosmic meaning, but many struggle to get anywhere in reality.

It is a psychological principle that opposites, at their extremes, touch. Here we can see the secret identity, clarified by Hillman,[81] between the apparent opposites of the archetypal perspectives of puer (young boy) and senex (old man). The puer can get so high off its own supply of potential that it refuses to allow any effort toward creating anything new, for what is created will never satisfy what could have been. As convinced as the puer is that nothing new is *im*possible, the senex can be equally certain that nothing new is *possible*. "One cannot walk, the other can only fly."[82] Both can exhibit a certain self-satisfied rigidity, a sense of their limited perspectives being complete and finished, creating a situation in which nothing new can enter, the one because the new is overvalued, the other because it is undervalued.

In fantasy a puer-identified man may be Icarus soaring to the sun or Phaëthon driving it; from the outside, he may barely get off the ground. Von Franz describes a typical puer-variant, sometimes called the earthbound puer, as being without "the charm of eternal youth, nor does the archetype of the divine youth shine through him. On the contrary, he lives in a continual sleepy daze".[83] Hillman considers this the "negative puer", and both analysts consider it the end-or-midstage of a puer arc, whereas to me it can also be a beginning, not only a burned-outness, but also a never-quite-bornness. Perhaps it only appears this way when the puer has, for his own reasons, grown jaded early in life: "the puer loses connection with its own aspect of meaning and . . . goes dead, and there is passivity, withdrawal, even physical death."[84] This seems to befall John progressively, particularly after Arthur's death—which, in the depth psychology of the play, enacts the fall of the puer.

Arthur and Shakespeare's Boys

Bonjour noted that "John's career represents a falling curve, the Bastard's career a rising curve; and both curves, perfectly contrasted, are linked into a single pattern".[85] I would submit that a similar observation can be made about John and *Arthur.* If John charts the journey from sky to earth, beginning the play as a commanding (if juvenile) firespout and ending as "dust," "but a clod", "clay," (5.7.31;57;69), Arthur charts the reverse course. Though able to discharge his diplomatic role with France and Austria effectively, he quickly retreats into a persona more akin to a sullen and heel-dragging youth, with the weight of his mother's world upon him. He earns a single moment of skyward brilliance before his death.

The little boys throughout Shakespeare are a pitiable lot who tend to meet untimely ends. Garber finds them

> disconcertingly solemn and prematurely adult . . . These are not, by and large, successful dramatic characters; their disquieting adulthood strikes the audience with its oddness, and we are relieved when these terrible infants leave the stage. We may feel it to be no accident that almost all go to their deaths.[86]

Heberle notes that their language "may have seemed more ideal *and* natural to [Shakespeare's] audience than it does to us",[87] drawing on the historical reality that upper-class children were taught to speak with a certain formality. Perhaps our contemporary view would find many children of past ages, not only Shakespeare's characters, "disconcertingly solemn and prematurely adult". For us, though, there is something about these boys, characteristically old before their time, that seems to look forward to death—whether this is culturally consistent with past centuries or no. "So wise so young, they say, do never live long" (*RIII,* 3.1.79).

A way to digest this pattern is to 'zoom out' and consider that the explanations are not mutually exclusive. Both the characters and the historical reality may be considered as archetypally-informed, and expressive of the polarity of puer-senex, that is, the archetypal image of the little boy who is also an old man. Perhaps this issue was 'in the air'—the archetype had been constellated—accounting for both the impulse to transform 16th- and 17th-century children into "little abstract[s]" (2.1.101) of their parents, as well as the fact that Shakespeare's work is repeatedly if obliquely concerned with the relationship between boyhood and manhood, and the difficulty and contradictions of the passage from one to the other. That same passage is a great chasm in life, and it is not only *Shakespeare*'s males who fall into it.

We might guess that something personal and concrete is involved for Shakespeare—to the point, and as many have suggested, the death of his own young son, Hamnet. It seems likely that *John* was written shortly following Hamnet's death, and Constance's lamentations of maternal bereavement may well be informed by real life. Chambers made a good point in retort to this: "it must certainly not be assumed that a dramatist can only convince by reproducing just those emotions which he has seen at play in his own household."[88]

On one hand, Constance's mourning, though specific in terms of inner imagery, is actually very generalized in terms of *Arthur*; Knowles recognizes that "Constance remembers and laments Arthur's 'pretty looks', 'words', and 'gracious parts' without ever specifying what these are. They are applicable to all children and specific to none."[89] I do not know if this makes it more or less likely that the author's personal grief is in the background of this strand of the play; if so, he has in a very short time transmuted it into a remarkably multilayered and ambivalent expression. Wheeler makes a very good argument that the *aggregate* of the various responses to Arthur's death—not only Constance's—could express

. . . a cluster of emotions consistent with those one might expect in a father in circumstances resembling Shakespeare's in 1596: confusion about the fact of death, met both with efforts to deny the death and a kind of urgent insistence on its reality before its confirmation; an insistent return to painfully tender cherishing of the child's now-absent presence . . . a distraction that edges on madness; suicidal fantasies; an emphasis on separation, including guilt connected with being away at the time of the boy's death; a frustrated, impotent 'do something!' imperative; helplessness; a sense that the child's death has emptied the world of its meaning and its heritage . . .[90]

The connection is moving, provocative, but not strictly necessary. The theme of premature death in Shakespeare's plays long predates both *John* and Hamnet; it is a main theme of his first published work, the poem "Venus & Adonis". It also has seeped into the fabric of some of his earliest plays: *Titus Andronicus, Henry VI, Richard III*, and *Romeo and Juliet* (plays in which children die) were all written before Hamnet's death in 1596. Premature death, broadly speaking, would simply be no stranger to the Elizabethans. We could venture that Hamnet's death, the thing itself, served to affirm something archetypal, something that Shakespeare already inwardly felt to be true: that surviving boyhood is perilous and by no means certain.

The concrete expression of the puer-senex polarity with which we are concerned is the parentified child who is precocious out of necessity, and this brings us to eight-year-old Arthur. There are many commodities in this play, in the sense of assets—soldiers, crowns, monies—but the walking, talking representative of this kind of commodity is Arthur. He is a figurehead; he is a puppet; he is a hostage; he is a bargaining chip; and then he is spent, dies, and the last bits of political advantage are wrung from his lifeless body. *Nobody cares about Arthur.*

He is the nephew of Richard Lionheart, and in the eyes of many the legitimate heir to the crown of England. Arthur has great expectations to live up to, but he shows little sign of being interested in the crown himself. He is no budding revolutionary—which he *is* in both major sources (Holinshed's *Chronicles* and *Troublesome Raigne*). In Shakespeare's play, he often feels less like a child and more like a prop that the grownups carry around the stage to ennoble their grasping. Midway through the second act, he is reduced to tears by his mother's mortifying advocacy:

ARTHUR: Good my mother, peace.
I would that I were low laid in my grave,
I am not worth this coil that's made for me.
                    (2.1.164–6)

Arthur may be a precocious boy, but he is *just* a boy, with little idea what crown or kingdom even mean. This is his mother's dream for which he is on the hook. It is interesting that Constance has historically been an object of empathy for audiences and critics who are moved by her immense suffering:

> Above all a 'mother' ('maternal' is the preferred adjective in all criticism on Constance), whose considerable imaginative and intellectual 'power' is selflessly spent in securing the interests of her son; she is ambitious only for him, never for herself.[91]

This view aligns with Constance's own view on herself, which is obviously extremely convincing; nevertheless I would attribute it partly to sentimentality, and partly to projection. To call her 'selfless' is simply not tenable in view of the actual text. Arthur does not want the crown; he could not be clearer about this.

The historical tide is no longer with Constance the way it once was; in 1989, Carlisle observed (with a note of rue) that

> The modern Constance cannot even count on unequivocal sympathy for the mother's devotion to her son. Rather than feeling an automatic veneration of Motherhood, its tenderness and its pain, some members of the audience may pull back in dismay from this exemplar of maternal possessiveness or note with clinical detachment that Constance is the victim of a 'fixation'.[92]

I resist here the urge to curse—*Arthur* is the *victim* of the fixation! It is remarkable, maybe appalling, how little attention has been given in the critical literature to Arthur *as Arthur*, prior to the past two decades.[93] His fate seems to have been sealed, in and out of the play, to be regarded solely as an extension of his mother. It is completely as though a boy of eight or nine is not considered a person but an object.

Constance, not brought up to speed with 'child subjectivity' and heedless of the impact of her actions on her pretty boy, drives on like a medieval Mama Rose. Somehow we feel with crystal clarity when Capulet (*RJ*) shouts his daughter into smithereens for not wanting to marry the man of his choosing, but when it comes to Constance pushing *her* child into a life he doesn't want, we are bedazzled by her grief and can only rain pity on the poor martyr. Perhaps it is because I am here focusing on the puer, but I find it very difficult to access unmixed sympathy for this narcissistic, devouring death-mother bewailing her lost muppet. She is absolutely complicit in the workings of the Grand Mechanism that lead to his death.[94]

The puer can recognize the mother-worship alluded to above, for it has functioned his whole life long to trap him in his labyrinth. The prey of the devouring mother suffers from lack of mirroring—so long as nobody is willing to *see* that she is devouring, and that he is being fed upon, he cannot know it himself, unless he is prepared to go seriously against the collective. His rage therefore has nowhere to touch ground, coming out instead through any number of symptoms.

The differentiation must be made between the *mother* complex and the *mother's* complex. One belongs to him, the other to her, and the difference can set him free! Once the complex has been rematriated, the puer's escapism can transform and find its proper psychological level. The formerly intractable existential problem of trying to find his way through the labyrinth of *someone else's pathology* can become the realistic and manageable problem of separation. His desperate sublimating flight defence can begin to recede of its own accord.

Again we come to the sticky and inadequate question of 'blame', and obviously 'blame the mother for the son's problem' is not the message here. But if the real mother has been a problem, it does nobody any good to ignore this. From what does the puer suffer? "Not enough earth,"[95] that is, lack of reality. And if the reality is that mother has narcissistically preyed on son, he needs help seeing that. To analyse that entire situation as a totally subjective affair, played out purely through intrapsychic complexes, may only reinforce the abstracting defence, pushing the puer further into his existing escape patterns. Even Hillman's approach, which finds archetypal dignity in every aspect of puer suffering, may be co-opted as a spiritual bypass, ignoring the hard clinical facts.[96]

Jung writes:

> Where does the guilt lie? With the mother, or with the son? Probably with both . . . It makes demands on the masculinity of a man . . . when it comes to throwing his whole being into the scales. For this he would need a faithless Eros, one capable of forgetting his mother and undergoing the pain of relinquishing the first love of his life. The mother, foreseeing this danger, has carefully inculcated into him the virtues of faithfulness, devotion, loyalty, so as to protect him from the moral disruption which is the risk of every life adventure. He has learnt these lessons only too well, and remains true to his mother.[97]

Who is there to see this dynamic, and reflect it back to Arthur? Not his father; Geoffrey was killed prior to Arthur's birth. Grandam Eleanor? She sees Constance for who she is, perhaps even with excessive cynicism—but, frankly, the problem is that nobody cares. Nobody cares about Arthur. People champion Arthur, and people grieve Arthur, but nobody cares about Arthur. Except Constance, and her form of caring is what it is. She is who she is, and she's all he's got.

Note that Jung calls it the *need* for a faithless Eros.[98] Elsewhere, he describes the puer attitude as "an *unavoidable* evil."[99] Faithlessness, considered as a *symptom*— that is, something that emerges in *sympathy* with the underlying problem—is itself a necessary (though incomplete) solution to the *prevailing* situation of enmeshment. *King John*'s men run wild, in part, because they are determined not to be swallowed. Arthur cannot grasp this yet: while alive, his embarrassed comments when Constance is around remind one of nothing so much as the common contemporary sight of a sullen teenager, powerlessly dragged around town while his mother runs errands—who has not seen this pair, the boy muttering some variant of "I would that I were low laid in my grave"? (2.1.165)

It would, of course, be unfair to Arthur to be too literal about calling him 'puer aeternus'. Being only about eight years old, there is hardly anything aeternal about his boyhood. On the structural level of the play, however, he carries the lighter side of the play's puer complex, of which John carries the more sinister.

"Those eyes"

Once Arthur has been captured, Hubert is assigned to murder him. When Hubert attempts to carry it through, however, we cannot help but notice that Arthur's punishment has apparently softened—if blinding him with hot irons can be said to be soft, at least it is not execution. The change, plainly put, does not make any dramaturgical sense. Hubert shows a warrant from John ordering the blinding, but later John himself seems to still expect Arthur dead. If John intends to pass Arthur's death off as due to sickness (4.2.82–92), a body with the eyes burned out is hardly going to make that case.[100]

We simply have to live with the irrational reality given in the text. It may be that the anomaly is best understood through a more dreamlike method of interpretation. 4.1 does stand out from the rest of the play stylistically; it is *almost* like a dream that occurs midway. We can imagine that Shakespeare, during the process of writing *King John*, has unconsciously substituted blinding for killing at this point. For the production team this makes a continuity error, but we may see it as a telling indicator of unconscious interference—a complex-indicator, or a parapraxis like a slip of the tongue. We may then ask: from where does this image of blinding the boy *come*? Why did it suddenly become necessary?[101]

To amplify: in *King Lear*, Gloucester's eyes are put out, the play's macabre confirmation of the fact that Gloucester has always *been* blind. In fact, the destruction of his sight is what initiates him finally into the possibility of seeing things as they are. It is also a harrowing scene which initiates the audience into the depth of suffering to be plumbed in that particular play.

The initiatory aspect of blinding has a prominent place in myth. It happens to those who have seen too much—Rapunzel's prince, or Oedipus—as well as those who sacrifice their outer sight to gain an inner sight—Odin, or Tiresias. I feel Arthur belongs more to the former category, though not by his own action. He has seen too much, in the way that abused children usually do. He has been exposed to the toxicity of life played as a power game.

Damage to the eyes initiates because an eye is permanent. People can heal from battle wounds, or return from banishment; their broken bones can mend, their sicknesses and madnesses be overcome; a boy's eyes are irreplaceable. It's all fun and games until somebody loses one. The introduction of blinding with hot irons may, for many audience members, be the initiation into how *medieval* this play really is.[102]

Earlier, Arthur's "poor eyes" have been invoked as that which will endear him to heaven: from them are drawn "heaven-moving pearls"

CONSTANCE: Which heaven shall take in nature of a fee.
Ay; with these crystal beads heaven shall be bribed
To do him justice, and revenge on you.

(2.1.169–72)

We pass over the commodification of a boy's tears by his mother, mainly to note that it is here that the eyes are conscripted into the conflict. I think the blinding is ultimately most interpretable from the association made here, of eyes with supernatural vengeance.

Though King John the man comes chronologically long before Richard III the man, *King John* the play was written later than *Richard III*, and Richard III was confronted on the eve of his death with the spectres of all those who he had murdered. He feels the torment of their accusing eyes, as also will Macbeth, confronted with the ghost of Banquo: "Thou hast no speculation in those eyes / Which thou dost glare with" (*Mac.* 3.4.94–5). There may be some psychological sense made if we realize that Arthur's sight poses, symbolically, a threat to John. This nuances Cassius' argument to Brutus that "you cannot see yourself / So well as by reflection" (*JC* 1.2.68–9). If another's gaze reflects one's "hidden worthiness" (*JC* 1.2.58), it surely reflects one's hidden wickedness as well. So Cornwall says in destroying Gloucester's second eye, "Lest it see more, prevent it" (*KL* 3.7.83).

Eyes are the window of the heart (*LLL* 5.2.826), and Arthur's are said to have some unconscious influence with heaven itself. John, generally concretistic, is nevertheless disturbed by the supernatural, as in 4.2 when he imprisons Peter of Pomfret for having made a prophecy he does not like. He finds the order for Arthur's murder unutterable—

KING JOHN: Death.
HUBERT: My lord.
KING JOHN: A grave.
HUBERT: He shall not live.
KING JOHN: Enough.
                                              (3.3.66)[103]

—and considers himself damned for the murder afterward (4.2.216–8).

A man such as John wants his brilliance seen, but not the rest—see the light, but not the shadow. He craves eyes, yet eyes pursue him. I remember a dream in which the eyes of a young boy left the boy's head and chased the dreamer through a labyrinth. As Macbeth is menaced by Banquo's sightless eyes after his death, John is menaced by the very existence of Arthur's "poor eyes" (2.1.169), such that they need to be extinguished, even if only as a prelude to his death.

I Want to Break Free

Arthur in prison is a different animal than before. Maybe he is unable to come into his own until separated from his mother and put into a dangerous situation in which he has no choice but to handle himself. He seems to become animated only after it becomes clear that he will not be king, as though a great weight has been lifted. Now Arthur displays true puer inspiration, persuading his murderer to set down the weapon and switch sides. For some time, he makes his case with little progress—Hubert's repression of his own pity (4.1.27–9) holds fast. Hubert's efforts at deadening himself are subverted, however, by the puer's "invigorating effect upon the listener".[104] It is notable the degree to which Shakespeare, here, has modified *Troublesome Raigne,* in which the conflict is carried out on a philosophical level, Arthur guiding Hubert to see how he must serve a higher power than John. Shakespeare's Arthur's tactics are, in contrast, emotional and relational[105]:

ARTHUR: Have you the heart? When your head did but ache
I knit my handkerchief about your brows . . .

Saying 'What lack you?' and 'Where lies your grief?'
Or 'What good love may I perform for you?'

                                        (4.1.40–9)

He wishes Hubert were his father (4.1.23–4), a moment especially of interest in its reference to the absent father in Arthur's psyche. Arthur has been treated to a string of avuncular figures in the play—Philip, Austria, John—and now Hubert too is drawn into the pathos of his father-hunger. The absence of Arthur's father has been subliminally felt all along: Constance has played her widow card for all it's worth, and one often gets the sense that the only thing that might have slowed Arthur's runaway mother would be an intervention from dad.

Ambivalent eros with men is a frequent feature of puer psychology: often living with a deficit of good-enough fathering, the puer's male relationships are disorganized.[106] He can be alternately vulnerable with men (often prematurely, sometimes instantly), yet at the same time cold and aloof. As this dynamic plays out (as it will with Hubert), it tends to have the character of a repetition compulsion, in which the initial abandonment by the father—and compensatory *rejection* of the father—is re-experienced again and again.

In comparison to his other would-be fathers in the play, it is notable that Hubert has no power in himself. In another context, Arthur's filial turn toward him would be something like the child of wealthy but inaccessible parents poignantly hoping for connection with his chauffeur.

Arthur's brilliance peaks when he sees that Hubert is having difficulty keeping the fire going, and he instantly grasps the potential symbolic truth in it.

ARTHUR: Lo, by my troth, the instrument is cold
And would not harm me.
HUBERT: I can heat it, boy.
ARTHUR: No, in good sooth. The fire is dead with grief. . .
There is no malice in this burning coal;
The breath of heaven hath blown his spirit out
And strewed repentant ashes on his head.

                                        (4.1.104–10)

"Angel-seeming, [the puer] is always seeking to make connections with transcendent archetypal wisdom".[107] Speaking as though possessed, improvising wildly to save himself, and having no human allies, he calls the spirit of the matter of iron and coal to his defence. In other words, in a scene that threatened to become excruciatingly horizontal, worldly, and gritty—like the blinding in *King Lear* will be—he connects to the vertical spiritual axis of the situation. Hubert has been trying to split off the spiritual implications of the murder, treating the iron, the boy, and himself as simple matter to be manipulated; Arthur, like a good alchemist, pushes past the objectification of nature and into the spirit concealed in matter.

Spurgeon noted that *John* contains more personifications than any other of Shakespeare's plays.[108] These personifications flow past the listener, who remains unconscious of their subtle effect, which is a consistent involvement in a subliminal alchemy between spirit and matter, blending and challenging the boundary lines between the two. Spurgeon says about *John* that

> Shakespeare has painted, as a kind of illumination or decorative marginal gloss to the play, a series of tiny allegorical pictures, dancing with life and movement, which, far from lessening the vigour of reality . . . increase its vividness and poignancy tenfold.[109]

I would add that this happens as if in compensation for the spiritual poverty of most of the main characters. The denigration of spirit finds no better expression than in Pandulph, who is no man of God but a godless diplomat, a Machiavelli in red, and occasionally a Titus Andronicus in his willingness to garnish the plate upon which the dead child is served:

PANDULPH: O sir, when he shall hear of your approach,
If that young Arthur be not gone already,
Even at that news he dies: and then the hearts
Of all his people shall revolt from him
And kiss the lips of unacquainted change . . .
And O, what better matter breeds for you,
Than I have named.

(3.4.162–71)

It is as though spirit has been kicked out of the front door of the conscious ethos of *John,* only to come back in through the window, in the type of metaphor that the characters half-consciously but consistently use. The Great Repressed in *John* is the spiritual, the supernatural, and the intuitive—such things as always resist men's worldly power-games. Subtle hints of divine intervention are throughout,[110] and I would add to the examples already adduced the apocalyptic vision of the five moons, as well as the timely floods that change the course of the French invasion. The playworld seems to be subject to certain spiritual laws, and the characters, because of their horizontality, are psychologically vulnerable to the vertical.

In the face of this, Hubert's determination deserts him. He returns *mammon* to its proper place in the spiritual order (4.1.121–2). Arthur, now dominant, congratulates him on his victory over his own ill intent—"O, now you look like Hubert! all this while / You were disguised" (4.1.125–6)—the lost lamb returned to the fold. Hubert's mercy which lay dead (4.1.28), has, Lazarus-like, been returned to life. Arthur here is anticipatory of Marina in *Pericles*, who "would make a puritan of the devil" (*Per.* 4.5.17–8), bringing about nearly magical changes-of-heart in the denizens of the brothel. As in Marina's brothel, hope dares to spring in Arthur's prison: nobody cares about Arthur, but now Hubert cares about him. And perhaps we may surmise that Shakespeare cares about Arthur too, since he allows Hubert to. As the Bastard realized earlier, there are more kinds of power than are accounted for in John's philosophy, and Arthur's, whatever it is, has compelling force. Penitent Hubert quickly concocts a plan by which he hopes to deceive John and keep Arthur safe.

And so much for Arthur's genius. The next time we see him he attempts a bridge too far and pays for it.

The quintessential mythical illustration of the puer's instant transition from inspiration to catastrophe is the story of Bellerophon, who, after defeating the fearsome chimera, tries to take a victory lap and fly Pegasus to Mount Olympus. Zeus sends a gadfly—a humiliating creature—to bite Pegasus, who rears and bucks Bellerophon, who plummets down to the plains below.[111]

Here is Arthur's gadfly moment:

Enter Arthur on the walls [dressed as a shipboy].
ARTHUR: The wall is high, and yet will I leap down.
Good ground, be pitiful and hurt me not!
There's few or none do know me; if they did,
This ship-boy's semblance hath disguised me quite.
I am afraid, and yet I'll venture it.
If I get down and do not break my limbs,
I'll find a thousand shifts to get away.
As good to die and go as die and stay. *[Leaps down.]*
O me, my uncle's spirit is in these stones.
Heaven take my soul, and England keep my bones. *[Dies.]*
                                            (4.3.0–10)

His entrance atop the prison wall is surprising—for one moment, it seemed as though all would be well in England. John has rescinded his order for the murder. All Arthur had to do was sit tight and wait. It is not obvious what could have changed for Arthur so quickly; the last time we saw him he seemed to feel secure in Hubert's pledge to protect him.

The clinician may recognize the ability of the puer to come to a session fully reset, as though the previous session had never happened, particularly when that session was in any way emotionally vulnerable. The defensive effort to stay above the emotion is redoubled when nobody is looking. The puer-influenced patient disowns precisely what the clinician may have found most valuable: the moments of emotional vulnerability, connection, and honesty. This inability to hold onto these moments may be a deficit shared by Arthur, and after being let down by so many paternal men, perhaps he simply cannot trust that Hubert will take care of him, and he pre-emptively abandons lest he be abandoned himself.

Arthur's sudden appearance high above gives us to understand that a *lot* has happened for this character since we saw him five minutes ago. Our clue to his plan may be in the detail that he enters "dressed as a shipboy" (4.3.0). His disguise is our indication that he's broken free not only of his cell, but also of us—we no longer know what's happening with him. Arthur seems to have (1) decided against trusting Hubert, (2) made a disguise, and (3) escaped his cell to the outer walls. The breakneck speed of the puer's decision-making is recognizable here: the feeling of 'now or never' that takes hold in the wrong situations, as a result of one not *really* having much sense of a future, and the sense of 'building the plane in midair' that comes when following one's impulses as quickly as one can have them.

But consider the earlier remark:

ARTHUR: Good my mother, peace.
I would that I were low laid in my grave,
I am not worth this coil that's made for me.
(2.1.164–6)

Implicating this line with "as good to die and go as die and stay" (4.3.8) begins to reveal a darker picture. Von Franz paid due heed to the puer's latent suicidality,[112] and in retrospect it appears that Arthur has been half-consciously suicidal all along. The pressure to be mom and dad's (and England's) Messiah is too much for him to bear. And when inflated by his facing-down of the devil in Hubert—the intensity of which transforms him from earthbound puer to flying puer—his first flight crashes.

Perhaps he is wrong about how to fly, but right to try. I think the biggest casualty of Arthur's being treated as an object, "an aestheticized fantasy of childhood"[113]— critics tend to attribute his death to John even despite the actual events—is that it doesn't recognize that Arthur is, just this once, *the sole actor in his own story.* Do not take this away from him! He makes what I (obviously) consider to be a bad call, but it is *his* to make! This is what the mother-bound boy fights his whole life for: the freedom to make mistakes, the freedom to get hurt. The above speech is actually the only monologue given by Shakespeare to a child—it is interesting that this particular 'underrepresented voice' should have been ignored for so long. Arthur seems to have preternatural metatheatrical knowledge about how he will be remembered: "There's few or none do know me" (4.3.3).

Arthur here has perspective enough to see that even if he survives in prison, he will not be free of the situation; he will still be a threat to John, and he will still have his mother to manage and his father to make up for. Indeed he has 'seen too much'. The prison itself is a concrete expression of Arthur's imprisonment in the family complex. The shipboy's outfit suggests that he does not only want out of prison, but out of England; he wants out of it all.[114] His dying line from *Troublesome Raigne* alludes to his existential imprisonment with poignant guilelessness: "My fall, my fall, hath kilde my Mothers Sonne".[115]

The Constant Mother

King John is full of men who are defined by their fathers, but through their mothers, who hold the true knowledge of paternity in a pre-DNA age. John is son to Eleanor—so were Richard and Geoffrey; Arthur is son to Constance, the Bastard to Lady Faulconbridge. The French herald blazons the "tears in many an English mother" (2.1.303). The play's mother complex is never far from the surface, and the word 'mother' appears in it 38 times. The mother complex does have a great deal to do with literal, personal, biological mothers, but its core is the mother arche-type. This archetype, in its more positive aspects, has to do with origin, place of gestation, the safety of the womb and unbornness, and unconditional nourishing love. Some are fortunate to have literal mothers who can be good-enough media-tors of this archetype, giving it a relatable human face and expression. The arche-typal qualities, however, can be experienced not only in the personal mother, but in mother-like situations, like a collective—therefore can England and France be spoken of as two rival sons of "the Church, our holy mother" (3.1.141); Pandulph threatens that he will "let the Church our mother breathe her curse, / A mother's curse, on her revolting son" (3.1.256–7). The Bastard highlights the filial aspect of the English Lords' treachery: "You bloody Neroes, ripping up the womb / Of your dear mother England, blush for shame!" (5.2.152–3)

In *John*, the personal mothers themselves range widely, and "will not reduce to a single class or category."[116] Eleanor could emasculate a man with a glance. Lady Faulconbridge has borne a civilized shame for her infidelity for many painful years. When Constance comes onto the scene, her and Eleanor spar over who is the more viperous.

If Eleanor is partial to an assertive/castrating aspect of the mother archetype, and Lady Faulconbridge to the noble/silent sufferer, Constance is a death-mother, a perverse Our Lady of Perpetual Sorrows. Von Franz speaks to the predominance of the death-mother in the lives of puer men—she

> makes a religious cult out of her son . . . he replaces the image of God. He is really also the crucified Christ and she is the Virgin Mary crying beside the Cross. The great satisfaction is that one has an archetypal meaning in one's life . . . and that elevates the mother herself and gives her sorrow some deeper meaning.[117]

Compare Constance,

CONSTANCE: . . . my grief's so great
That no supporter but the huge firm earth
Can hold it up.
                          (3.1.72–4)

—this is not grief she feels at Arthur's death. He has not even been captured at this point. Her grief expands further when he has been taken hostage:

CONSTANCE: Grief fills the room up of my absent child,
Lies in his bed, walks up and down with me,
Puts on his pretty looks, repeats his words,
Remembers me of all his gracious parts,

Stuffs out his vacant garments with his form;
Then, have I reason to be fond of grief?. . .
O Lord! My boy, my Arthur, my fair son,
My life, my joy, my food, my all the world,
My widow-comfort and my sorrows' cure!

(3.4.92–107)

Like all of Shakespeare's great characters, Constance cannot be reduced to a single aspect. She is deeply sympathetic, as critics and audiences tend to agree—but this itself is part of the puer's problem: he cannot see his true mother past the idealized image of her, and neither can anybody else! And so he cannot break from her without either flying away or suffering the tremendous guilt-ridden struggle on earth. Constance clearly shows the mother in the complex that may give rise to puer-identification, and as far as a death-mother goes, she fits the bill rather more literally than most:

CONSTANCE: Death, death, O amiable, lovely death,
Thou odoriferous stench, sound rottenness,
Arise forth from the couch of lasting night . . .
And I will kiss thy detestable bones,
And put my eyeballs in thy vaulty brows,
And ring these fingers with thy household worms,
And stop this gap of breath with fulsome dust,
And be a carrion monster like thyself.
Come, grin on me, and I will think thou smil'st,
And buss thee as thy wife . . .

(3.4.25–34)

These lines still come before Arthur's death—compare von Franz on Saint-Exupéry's mother again: "it is also said that she always anticipated her son's death. Several times she thought he was dead and dressed herself in large black veils".[118] Above, see how Constance weds herself to death, the necrophiliac words both erotic and macabre. Has this aspect of Constance been lurking under her surface all these years? A morbid and despairing eroticism barely concealed by ambition and motherly doting, which Arthur felt saddled with keeping at bay? His sonship seems to have been like the stopper on a very thick, very dark bottle of wine.

Bucknill, a 19th-century physician who specialized in mental illness, found that "the intensity of her passion is almost Satanic"—"with the true selfishness of intense pride, she attributes the sufferance of all Arthur's injuries to herself."[119] Yet he also had tremendous respect for Constance as an accurate (to him) representation of "madness", and even moreso as an artistic achievement of character:

. . . there can be little doubt that this character was submitted in the crucible of the poet's great brain, before it was moulded into that form of fierce power and beauty, in which it excites our admiration and awe. The wondrous eloquence of Constance is second to that of no other character except Lear.[120]

Kelly Hunter (playing Constance in 2001) felt she had a "total obsession with being female . . . She is always defining herself—as woman, widow, mother".[121] She reaches out to both death and God ("be husband to me, Lord", 3.1.108) to remedy her widowhood. On a depth-psychological level, she is enveloped in a primordial co-dependency: in her need to compensate the world's one-sided masculine princi-ple, she identifies wholly with the feminine, then requiring that the masculine com-pensate her in return. Hunter captures the *surface* presentation of this when she says that Constance "sees the truth and speaks it, in a world of lies and liars".[122] The dynamic is most clearly staged in 3.4, when Philip, Pandulph, and Lewis all stand aloof from her as she works up to the intensity of Greek tragedy. Here, the men really do seem to care for nothing, and she really does seem to care far too much; they are all four caught in a feedback loop, a sadomasochistic discharging of the complex:

PANDULPH: You hold too heinous a respect of grief.
CONSTANCE: He talks to me that never had a son.
KING PHILIP: You are as fond of grief as of your child.
(3.4.92–4)

Arthur foretold this—the first thing he says when taken captive is "O, this will make my mother die with grief!" (3.3.5).

It really should be no surprise that Arthur is drawn to flight. The men in this play do not know how to effectively relate to the women. Even Shakespeare does not seem to know how to deal with Constance and Eleanor any better than their sons do; he has them die offstage, in the space of five lines (4.2.119–23). This is perhaps Shake-speare's own faithless Eros coming to his rescue, his own recognition that he has simply to cut and run, or risk being bogged down with them for the rest of the play.

The offstage death of the mother is consistent with the dreams of people with certain mother complexes. The dream, at times, seems to understand that, theo-retically, the mother image needs to be transcended—in symbolic language, 'the mother needs to die'. But it does not know how to accomplish this—because it does not know how to suffer the loss—and so just imparts it as information rather than experience. The dream says: 'I heard that my mother had died', or 'I was try-ing to get to my mother's funeral'. In such a case, true separation from the mother remains abstract. It seems to be like in a Hollywood action film, where if you don't *see* a character die, he's not dead. Shakespeare does not seem ever to have quite solved the problem of what to 'do' about the negative mother archetype.

The puer's problem is that he fails to acknowledge his shadow "as a vital part of himself and an unconscious value in his life; indeed, this denial of his own capacity to do evil is what creates part of his unreality."[123] His constant double-bindedness is a result of this: he can be unwilling to engage his shadow and behave ruthlessly. Arthur's personal double-bind is expressed most concisely in his line, "As good to die and go as die and stay" (4.3.8), or, in other words, 'damned if I do, damned if I don't.' The trickster, which Beebe sees as the shadow of the puer,[124] would be that factor which could undo the double-bind, or even reverse it onto the other. Arthur, once imprisoned, accesses his own ability to fight back, manipulating (and, arguably, seducing[125]) Hubert before he makes his escape attempt. The Arthur plotline in Act 4 is saturated with nine tricksterish reversals that knock-on like dominoes:

1. John, the executioners, and the audience, expect Arthur to be murdered; he prevents the attempt and converts the murderer.
2. Hubert tricks John into believing that Arthur *is* dead.
3. John's attempt to trick the English nobles into believing that Arthur has died of illness rebounds on him, falling utterly flat.
4. John rebounds on Hubert, disowning his responsibility for ordering the murder in the first place.
5. Hubert reveals to John that Arthur is alive—a great relief! All seems to be headed toward a good resolution.
6. Arthur suddenly appears high above the stage, in his shipboy disguise—disorienting *us*.
7. Arthur makes his escape attempt, and in spite of everybody at this point wanting him to live, he dies.
8. His disguise fails him, as his body is recognized instantly. Simple disguises are usually impenetrable in Shakespeare; Arthur's does nothing.
9. The murder is blamed on Hubert and John, who against all odds are actually innocent of the crime.

(This is the great historical joke of the play: in this version of history, that deed for which John is perhaps most infamous—the killing of Arthur—he did not even do.)

The discovery of the trickster is a crucial point in learning to navigate mother-boundness.[126] Being able to play the trickster allows the boy to be something other than a 'good boy', if only at first privately, in his own self-image. It allows him his shadow—not in an integrated way, not yet—but when the immediate threat is total engulfment in the mother complex, integration can wait. We can understand why the trickster is considered an early expression of the *hero*: it is the very beginning of a person having their own will.

Puer without trickster is idealistic and naïve. Trickster without puer is nihilistic and destructive. Once puer can sew his shadow on (*à la* Peter Pan), the two become a valuable and psychologically dynamic unit.

Two Sons

Summoned or not, dad will be present: Richard Cordelion's ghost haunts the background of this play, as Hamlet Senior haunts the background of his. He is the good father, but the dead father, the *deus absconditus* in the absence of whom the sons must live.

When the Bastard is introduced, he is quickly recognized as Cordelion's son by the King and Queen. He is renamed with the patronymic Sir Richard Plantaganet (1.1.162), and thereafter bears the Lionheart forth in his own person. Despite being illegitimate, he seems his father's true son.

Arthur is *not* Cordelion's son, but Philip pads the lineal case in Arthur's favour in seeming "to suggest that Arthur is the son, rather than the nephew, of King Richard":[127] "Arthur: that great forerunner of thy blood, / Richard" (2.1.2–3). He rhetorically recasts Arthur's father, and Arthur himself affirms this pretended sonship: "God shall forgive you Cordelion's death / The rather that you give his offspring life" (2.1.12–3). In forgiving Austria the murder of Cordelion, Arthur's first act is the inverse of the Bastard's: whereas the Bastard begins by disclaiming a false father and affirming a true one, Arthur begins by falsely appropriating both Cordelion's name and forgiveness (as well as God's). The Bastard's vendetta against Austria is further expression of his sonship. Austria wears Cordelion's lionskin, a dishonour which the Bastard cannot (and does not) let go unrevenged.

Where Arthur protests his mother weakly, the Bastard confronts his own as a grown man. He is firm and direct; he knows that he is not the son of her husband, and insists on it in the face of her denials. In giving up the Faulconbridge inheritance, he has even already made the necessary leap that will *allow* her to speak the truth. His piebald morality does her a great service and lets her off the hook regarding a guilt she seems to have carried for many years.

Arthur's always-on-the-horizon inheritance keeps him living provisionally, but the Bastard lives with no provision at all. He has a continuous, responsive, and evolving relationship to the present context. He is willing to develop.

Arthur's daring escape attempt from the prison would seem to be his effort to integrate what the Bastard has access to naturally. This is Arthur's first act as an independent man, and, like Icarus's and Phaëthon's first flights, it is too much too fast. The Bastard has come up and, keeping in mind his willingness to learn and develop, has nowhere to go *but* up. Arthur has been raised high, and from there he has nowhere to go but down.

Kanye on the Tower

Puer dreams are filled with variations on the motif of dangerous heights. If we considered Arthur's fall as a dream-image, it would be one typical of a dreamer who is becoming conscious of their own personal puer problem; perhaps they have discovered that they live 'too high off the ground', and that this has prevented their 'getting into life'. For someone still unconsciously identified with the archetype, dreams might feature motifs of flight, showing concern with how to fly higher, faster, with more beauty, or how to stay aloft for longer. As the complex becomes conscious, the thinness of the atmosphere and the aridity and isolation of the heights might enter into the experience. The pertinent question might then become how to *descend*. The puer in such dreams knows it is too high up, but has not yet developed a safe way to come down.

As such a complex moves toward healing, the dream ego may find ways of coming down—ladders appear, floating platforms, ropes, elevators, safety nets, helpers—all indicating different inner/outer processes by which the puer energy is trying to ground itself.[128] But there is often ambivalence, a subtle attempt to stay aloft *while* coming down, to have one's cake and eat it too. The psyche is not yet prepared for the sacrifice. When the ground has meant loss of individual specialness for most of one's life, how is one supposed to accept that the ground is now the necessary medicine?

I would like to introduce a dream that amplifies Arthur's situation, its aftermath, and the underlying archetype of the puer's descent. What merits this dream's inclusion here, to my mind, is its depiction of the intensity involved in coming down to earth. It can be a tremendously emotionally and psychologically difficult task. I also appreciate that, centred around Kanye West, the dream comes from a very different cultural situation than Medieval or Elizabethan England—or so it would seem. The dream is a man's, brought to analysis after many years, and situated as part of a much longer-term effort to ground himself in real life. The dream anticipated, by several years, the real Kanye's series of public crashes.

> *The rapper Kanye West is atop a skyscraper in the middle of a city. I am watching this on TV, and trying to remember the name of the skyscraper—the Pearl? This name runs through my head, but I know it's not correct. Kanye is being filmed. He is rapping. He steps to the edge, and there is some doubt in the gathered crowd: Will he do it? He does—he steps off into thin air and falls. As he falls, the camera tracks him, spinning end over end. He is holding his microphone and rapping all the way down, and in the final moments counts 5-4-3-2—right until he hits the ground. I cover my eyes, as I don't want to see him hit. I do see a bit of green goo explode out on impact.*
>
> *Then the TV broadcast goes elsewhere, and shows a man hailing a taxicab outside of a lavish party. He shoots the driver in the head with a gun, and gets into the front seat himself. Many others get in, happy and excited. An interviewee says, "I guess this is just what people are doing now."*

It may be clear enough what this dream has to do with the puer in general, but what about Arthur in specific? Is there a resonance, for example, between Arthur's prison wall and dream-Kanye's tower?

Dream-Kanye's prison is not as literal as Arthur's; for him, it is the *performance* by which he is bound. His prison is the gaze of the TV camera and the crowd; it is the pressure of having attained a towering height in the "society of the spectacle".[129] The prison is unnecessary when Bentham's "panopticon"[130] prevails—the imagined prison in which bars are unnecessary because the inmates all believe they are being constantly watched. Panopticon, a shocking idea in the late 18th century, seems today in the 21st to be completely obvious. Few are the people whose lives have not, at least in part, become 'content' through social media. The harvesting and use of personal data by every system with which we interact tends to make even the least-conspicuous of us feel that 'privacy' is a naïve ideal from a bucolic past. How much worse it must be for those who, like Kanye, actually do attract the eyes of millions, bearing their collective and contradictory projections—genius, madman, or saviour—the right and true king, or a childish usurper. This is something that can be seen through-and-beyond both Arthur and Kanye, something that unites them: the weight of others' expectations and objectifications. Having been raised up so high means, in a very real sense, that their only way is down. In Kanye we can see more clearly the megalomania that can both lead to and feed off of this height. In Arthur we see the weight and the fragility.

The difficulty of coming down comes across, in this dream, through the *compensation*: dream-Kanye's bravado. He draws everything into his performance, including performance's end. His life becomes identical with his art—he attempts to become pure spirit, deifying himself, like the pre-Socratic philosopher Empedocles, who threw himself into a volcano so that his body would never be found and it would be believed that he had become a god.[131]

Also like Empedocles, his aim is stymied: for the former, one of his sandals was thrown back by the volcano, revealing his device; for Kanye, his body does not vanish but explodes into messy green goo—green being the colour of nature as well as the sensation function,[132] that function of the psyche that deals with concrete, experienceable reality. As for Arthur, his attempt to vanish into the wide world as a shipboy is also thrown back at him, as his body is instantly recognized. He may escape but his body remains: "Heaven take my soul, and England keep my bones" (4.3.10).

If we can see through Kayne's spiritualizing/aestheticizing defence, it becomes clear that he is *in some way* attempting to come down to earth—he simply has no idea how to accomplish it. He cannot square the need to come down with the need, *also* real, to preserve the only version of himself that he knows. His solution is to lean into the performance paradigm, making a show out of 'becoming grounded', and rapping all the way down, drowning out the animal fear of falling with a flood of logos: words, words, words. We know the bravado to be compensatory because the dream alludes to its obverse: the dreamer's fear of seeing him land. He covers his eyes, unable to bear it.

Following the ignoble demise of this puer aeternus, society—the larger matrix of the dreamer's psyche—falls into pandemonium. For the puer, sacrifice of his puerness feels like the death of a king, like the loss of a ruling principle, like ripping out the centre of the mandala, the very thing that gave it cohesion. When that central impetus on which life had been predicated is suddenly removed, everything is up for grabs; the usual boundaries are dissolved; the falcon cannot hear the falconer and the centre cannot hold.[133] It is really *very* hard—and I am often not sure if this is fully appreciated—for a puer man to come down to earth and live on the ground, even if he can see rationally or intellectually that he *should* and that it would be *really good to do.*

The inner figures which personify our complexes often must die in order to move forward; in symbolic language, death opens a possibility for transformation, confrontation with the underworld, and rebirth in a new form. Many alchemical images reflect this moment of the process: the king is devoured by a lion, or a lion devours the sun, or a dragon is roasted over a fire—it can be uncomfortable to realize that the puer *also* needs to be roasted, but he *does* need his feet held to the fire if those feet are ever to walk on the earth.

Yet the deathly transformation of such an inner figure cannot be fully accomplished without feeling. You're not getting out of this one without tears. Sometimes we 'don't know what we got till it's gone', and the loss hits hard, as it must be allowed to. It is "as if the knowledge death gives is the knowledge of what a psychic thing *is* in itself, its true meaning and importance for the soul."[134]

In both *John* and the dream, the reaction to the fall of the puer is pandemonium—a collective explosion of affect. Many critics have noted that *John* takes on an utterly different tone following Arthur's death. Treason, which has been threatening to burst forth since the first lines of the play, finally does. The long and slowly-developing scenes of the first part of the play give way to seven rapid-fire scenes in the fifth act—as many as there were in the previous four acts preceding Arthur's death combined. It is the beginning of the end for John: "destiny itself has turned against the King",[135] spelling "internal strife in the state, civil war at the hour of greatest national danger . . .[John] is left a weak, wavering, and diminished man, a shadow of his former self."[136]

But, I wonder, how do *we* feel about the pandemonium that ensues following these falls? To me, there is an unavoidable feeling that both tragedies are cynically appropriated. Both Arthur and dream-Kanye seem to be *used,* before and after their deaths. The response of the Earls Salisbury and Pembroke, for example: is not their grief self-serving? Hyperbolically over-earnest? "Their discovery of Arthur's broken body seems to provide a convenient justification for the direct and flagrant rebellion they, in fact, have already privately determined"[137]:

SALISBURY: . . . This is the very top,
The height, the crest, or crest unto the crest,
Of murder's arms. This is the bloodiest shame,
The wildest savagery, the vilest stroke
That ever wall-eyed wrath or staring rage
Presented to the tears of soft remorse.
PEMBROKE: All murders past do stand excused in this . . .

(4.3.45–51)

It is a remarkable feat of Shakespeare's that, following Arthur's death, our sympathies *still* tend to lie with John, and I don't think it is only because he stands for England (the 'good guys'). I think John's case is helped by the fact that, as much as we may abhor Arthur's death, we abhor more the way it is used by his self-appointed avengers.

Dream-Kanye's explosion appears to similarly become rationale for degeneration and decadence. "I guess this is just what people are doing now." For the real-life puer, the consequences may not be so collective, limiting themselves 'merely' to others' smug self-satisfaction that the puer has indeed fallen, which 'we all knew would happen', and which we, like Kanye's onlooking crowd, may on some level be salivating for. "We will be satisfied! let us be satisfied!" (*JC* 3.2.1[138])

He has left a trail of resentment and hurt wherever he goes, but he also incites envy, and when at last he flies low enough, this envy reaches up to snatch at him. Or maybe the puer just won't get much attention anymore: a second primal abandonment, this time by the adoptive parents, the onlookers, who move on to the next shiny thing. The puer's unrelatedness is punished, ultimately, in a poetically just way: with unrelatedness.

This is one paralyzing form of the double-bind that the puer finds himself in: to stay up high is false, unsustainable, and ends in self-destruction, but to come down means abandoning the only real *constant* in his life—*his own height*. It is not only inwardly shattering, but also a humiliating defeat. And he cannot count on a warm reception, nor pity or empathy from the onlookers; "None of you will bid the winter come" (5.7.36).

Arthur, dead or alive, is used as an object. Perhaps he only lived his own life while he plummeted, his death his sole expression of autonomy.

The Puer Is Dead, Long Live the Puer

Out of nowhere, in the play's final moments, appears John's son Henry. Henry is a child, just like Arthur, and is likely to be played by the same actor. The closing image is nearly an alchemical woodcut: the dead king to one side, three adult men kneel to a newly crowned child. Out with the old, and in with the new; the puer's eternal return is actualized again, and what we thought had perished is again revitalized. Perhaps there is something concrete to be said about society's perennial worship of childishness, putting the children themselves into positions inappropriate. Psychologically, however, we have here a clear movement toward revivification of the archetype, and with an important new aspect: the Bastard. *John* ends, most hopefully, with a visual alliance between puer and trickster; the boy has sewn his shadow back on.

•

We are not finished with the puer—I mean in the course of this book, but I could as well mean in the world as well. But here in this book, we now move toward *Twelfth Night*, and its full-tilt exploration of self-performance, a dynamic we have only just alluded to. We will not hear much from the puer for many pages, though he is always with us, implicitly, in the background. For now, some summary remarks on the discussion regarding the puer and *King John* are in order.

'Up' or 'down' is not the puer's problem—the problem is the *illusory dilemma* of 'up *or* down'. That is the basic double-bind. Until that nonsense binary is transcended psychologically, nothing logically new can happen in the complex. It remains the same old story of flights and crashes.

In the life of a man, the death of the boy is a necessary psychological event. Says the *I Ching* about Hexagram 17, 隨, *Sui*: Following: "If one clings to the little boy, / One loses the strong man."[139] The divide is painful for both boy and man. As Macduff asserts, however, the man must feel the loss, as a man (*Mac.* 4.3.224). *Suí* then says in its next line, "If one clings to the strong man, / One loses the little boy." And so perhaps the loss must be felt as a boy too. The little boy needs to grow up, and leave childish things behind, but it is cruel and unusual to force him, and moreover to force him to do it alone. We all were pueri (children) once, and if my plea for a little sympathy for the little angel rings as a little sentimental, I would simply point back to *King John* and the way it chronicles not only the deaths of certain historical child-kings, but the way it expresses the death of an ideal for an entire age. We may not feel for Arthur and John, but their problems are ours—and most bizarrely, their world seems to be ours too.

Curren-Aquino wrote in 1989 that

> *King John* is a most fitting play for a century that has suffered through two world wars; witnessed a holocaust . . . seen the heroic, the absolute, and the certain give way to the pragmatic, the relative, and the contingent; and come to the grim realization after Korea, Vietnam, Watergate, and the Iran-Contra affair that national leaders are not superhuman but plagued with human frailty and all too capable of error, whether moral, political or military.[140]

I think, for a modern mind in the second half of the 20th century, this made for an affirming link with Shakespeare's time.

And yet, how does it land today? For we are no longer in the modern age. *John* stands as evidence that what we call 'modern' and 'postmodern' experiences both exist, in some form, in the early modern period. The difference is in the accent— which elements weigh more in the collective psyche of a given period. The post-modern period is such, then, not because utterly new ideas and experiences have emerged, but because we are now more postmodern than not.

"A sense of disbelief and amazement reverberates throughout the world of *King John*",[141] and while in Shakespeare's time this may have registered as a symp-tomatic expression of an inevitably dawning era of individuality and relativity, in contradistinction to an increasingly untenable view of the world as centralized and symbolic, yet—I wonder if the contemporary reader has already anticipated what I will say—for *us*, in the 2020s, not only post-9/11 but also post-COVID, post-Brexit, post-Trump, etc., etc.—a modern existential crisis is actually a bit of a throwback.

I suspect that when Constance, for example, expresses that "It is not so . . . It cannot be . . . I do not believe" (3.1.4,6,9), or Salisbury sputters "May this be possible? May this be true?" (5.4.21) we no longer empathize with them wholly in the same way one might have done even 50 years ago. Rather, we may be aware of a subtle sense of these people as naïvely idealistic. Who today, in the wake of (e.g.,) the Paris Agreement, expects agreements to actually be followed through on? Surely we do not take politicians at their word, even if we like what they seem to stand for. We are simply no longer believers in the archetype of

Magna Carta, by which I mean a situation where writing something down grants it authority.

The Bastard feeling "amazed", and lost "Among the thorns and dangers of this world" (4.3.140–1), while perhaps a revelation for early moderns and an affirmation of contemporaneity for moderns, for we *post*-moderns it seems, well, just a little old-fashioned. I think that we *expect* to be lost, and are no longer amazed by anything. For those who, after Bush-Gore, still believed in the relative stability of modernity, Trump's election in 2016 proved that truly nothing is certain. One half *can*not believe he was ever elected, the other half *does* not believe Biden was ever elected four years later. Today, we *expect* subterfuge at the highest levels, twists and reversals of fortune—we demand it! If our news does not have the upsets and cliffhangers of *Game of Thrones* we feel somewhat cheated. The reversions and doubles-back that everybody's so-called agreements make in *King John*—well, for us, this is normal, and it is somewhat charming that the characters should think that anything else would be the case.

Lost "Among the thorns and dangers of this world" is a modern condition, but I submit that we postmoderns have a tendency to feel, unconsciously, that we have outgrown "thorns" and "dangers"—those who live increasingly in virtual spaces may feel they have outgrown "this world" too. We disbelieve the reality or legitimacy of these things. Not that we can't be hurt by thorns and dangers—we just no longer feel any confidence in predicting where the hurt will come from. It is convenient to find an enemy to project upon, perhaps in whichever nation or political party happens to be at odds with our own, but deep down we know we are taking a somewhat arbitrary position, a 'legal fiction', because the alternative is to feel permanently adrift. Still, we continue on as though none of it means anything.

Perhaps it doesn't. Vaughan writes that, "for all the talk of war deciding the fate of great nations, the battles in *King John* decide nothing."[142] Are there any real consequences, save those visited on the rank-and-file soldiers? And is this significantly different from how things appear today in our world? One could almost subtitle *King John* 'Much Ado About Nothing', if the king himself didn't die at the end. Even that happens in a fog of arbitrariness: he is sick, and then he is poisoned by some nameless monk without even a walk-on role, and about whom we simply hear from Hubert that he shat himself and died.

The Bastard learns, but we already *know* "mad world, mad kings, mad composition!" (2.1.561); it is unremarkable. 'The centre cannot hold!' cries the last century—'*How quaint,*' ours responds. 'They think there's a *centre.*'

It has been argued that *King John* ultimately represents a holding pattern in this respect; that though at first it appears to be aggressively deconstructive of Elizabethan certainties and values, it ends with an attempt at "the reimposition of ideology".[143] The movement of the Bastard into the orthodox voice of Majesty can be seen in this light. *John* seems to say, in this reading, that with the Bad King out of the way things can get back to normal.

But what takes place in the ideological sphere over the course of *King John* cannot so easily be undone—by the end of Act 3 "between claim and counterclaim the cosmic order has been levelled to the ground."[144] *John* uncorks a bottle into which the contents cannot be put back, and I agree with Burckhardt that the apparent return to ideological normativity in the ending movements is *only* apparent, and takes place *faute de mieux*—for lack of anything better. Ideologically speaking, the play is in the position of Macbeth:

MACBETH: I am in blood
Stepped in so far, that should I wade no more,
Returning were as tedious as go o'er.
                    (*Mac.* 3.4.134–6)

Except Macbeth stays the course and tries to ford the river. The survivors of *King John* try to return to a place to which there may be no return. The Bastard assumes the mantle of tradition and authority, yet must be aware on some level that it is a compromise formation and will not do in the long term. Salisbury and Pembroke renege on their treason, and try to

SALISBURY: . . . untread the steps of damned flight,
And like a bated and retired flood . . .
And calmly run on in obedience
Even to our ocean, to our great King John.
                    (5.5.52–7)

They try to do a "once-again" (4.2.3); just as King John thought he could hit reset on his troublesome reign by being re-coronated, they hope, with growing panic (I imagine), that they can reset the treacherous ideological developments that this reign has set in motion. They might well join the Chorus of *Jesus Christ Superstar* in singing "Could We Start Again, Please?"[145]

The dilemma of Macbeth: wade through, or return? The characters try to return. In *John*, the fate of trying to untread the steps that were taken is mirrored in the fates of the two armies, English and French, both lost in the ocean, either "cast away and sunk" (5.5.13) or "taken by the tide" (5.6.40), "devoured by the unexpected flood" (5.7.64).

Like the heroic Julius Caesar, who once accepted a challenge to leap into the "angry flood / And swim to yonder point" (*JC* 1.2.104–5), only to find himself at the point of drowning, the heroic orthodoxy in *King John* cannot make it back to shore without some serious paddling. Like the Bastard in the flood, the old notions "hardly have escaped" (5.6.42), and are irretrievably relativized. This is most clearly symbolized in the fact that the king himself begs for euthanasia; the king psychologically represents the central ruling principle, and he has severed every tether to the world. As a symbolic consequence, he eventually floats off. The Bastard and Henry III survive on the ground to move the project forward, but really one feels that "the old order is *suffered*, in a greatly diminished form, as a makeshift structure."[146]

One way of thinking about the impact of a work of art is to consider the way in which it gives expression to the previously inexpressible, or articulation to the as-yet-unvoiced. For the Elizabethans, I imagine that the Bastard's early soliloquys commenting on the fatuity of high society, and the cynical opportunism of the powerful, may have been thrilling expressions of such things as they did not yet know they were allowed to have thought. For us, today, I find the play's central image to be the Bastard just before the ending, having barely escaped the devouring flood. We are no longer in the position of slowly realizing our institutions to be inadequate; this is no longer an exciting discovery. We have charged hell-for-leather down the road of iconoclasm, and the general feeling seems to be that it does not look good. Perhaps what I see in the Bastard's survival is a bit of a postmodern wish-fulfilment: that we too can pull ourselves back from the brink, even if to a makeshift position, and live to reconsolidate and fight another day.

There is a potential anagogic promise, for we postmoderns, in *John*'s move from disintegration back to normativity—just a shred of hope. After all, we are not irretrievably lost in the flood ourselves, but are charged with defining a position that both includes and transcends the modern. Perhaps a makeshift 'good enough for now' is 'as good as it gets', and there is no shame in swimming back to shore and reinvesting in what used to be normal—again, *faute de mieux*, for lack of anything better. Maybe this is to endow *John* with more archetypal wisdom than it really deserves. But as it is somewhat in accord with the *I Ching*'s view of a continually shifting *tao* in which nothing, even chaos, endures indefinitely, and every time is both a movement from the former time and into the next, I am inclined to feel it has something to it. Disorder must, eventually, subside into some form of order again. Nothing is permanent, and so the chicken soup that *King John* offers for the postmodern soul is that it takes us through the fragmentation, and in the end offers the barest whisper of hope by showing that perhaps people can still get by, so long as they don't aim too high: "Withhold thine indignation, mighty God, / And tempt us not to bear above our power" (5.6.38).

Notes

1 This chapter is derived in part from an article published in Jung Journal: Culture and Psyche, May 2024, Copyright <the society>, available online: http://www.tandfonline. com/10.1080/19342039.2024.2330291
2 Hoveden (1853, 56).
3 Lander & Tobin (2018, 65).
4 From my own experience, but in line with Max Beerbohm's too: "a good production . . . makes one forget what is bad in sheer surprise at finding so much that is good." In Wells (2016, 313).
5 Henry (2004, 36).
6 Brubaker (1989, 166): "John is a play for thinking people . . . like the plays of Brecht, it is designed to keep the audience thinking rather than stirred up by the issues it raises."
7 Vaughan (2003, 392).
8 Hillman (1979a, 23).
9 Beebe (2017, 36).

10 Hillman (1979a, 24).
11 Hillman (1979a, 26).
12 Murray (1979, 95).
13 Gentleman (in Candido 2022, 5).
14 Heberle (1994, 33).
15 Von Franz (1981).
16 Hillman (1979a, 23).
17 Von Franz (1981).
18 Projective identification is a way of acting that hooks another person into responding in a particular way; someone who insists on behaving like a child tends to force those around them into behaving like parents.
19 Hillman (1979a, 23).
20 Hillman (1979b, 102).
21 Hillman (1979b, 100).
22 Hillman (1979c).
23 Grennan (1978, 34).
24 Von Franz (1981, 131).
25 Von Franz (1981, 178).
26 Woodeson (1993, 89).
27 Wells (2016, 110) commented that in *John* and *Richard II,* "Shakespeare seems to be deliberately limiting his stylistic range, seeking intensity rather than diversity."
28 Wilhelm (1984, 17).
29 A term which refers, essentially, to the sage or one who acts in accordance with *tao*, the quality of the time.
30 Henry (2004, 33).
31 Jung (CW 9ii, 22).
32 Howard & Rackin (1968, 120–1).
33 Dusinberre (1990, 40).
34 Wilhelm (1984, 17).
35 Smallwood (2004, 13).
36 Campbell (1958, 166) felt, with a slightly different nuance, that he "acts as chorus to the play".
37 Leggatt (1977, 16): an "amalgam of participant and commentator".
38 Bloom (1999, xvii).
39 Stone-Fewings (2004); Manheim (1989).
40 Manheim (1989, 128–9).
41 Lander & Tobin (2018, 206fn).
42 Also echoed later by Edmund, "Thou, Nature, art my goddess; to thy law / My services are bound" (*KL* 1.2.1–2)
43 Noted by Slights (2009, 226); Kastan (1983, 11); Bonjour (1951, 268)
44 Bonjour (1951, 269).
45 Shaw (1924, 42).
46 Jung (CW 9i, 472).
47 Henderson (1990).
48 Hillman (1979a, 25).
49 Kastan (1983, 14).
50 Von Franz (1981, 5): "Dr. Jung spoke of one cure—work . . . work is the one disagreeable word which no puer aeternus likes to hear . . . There are, however, some misunderstandings in this connection, for the puer aeternus can work . . . when fascinated or in a state of great enthusiasm. Then he can work twenty-four hours at a stretch or even longer, until he breaks down. But what he cannot do is to work on a dreary rainy morning when work is boring and one has to kick oneself into it[.]" This is expanded further by Thweatt (2021, 61).
51 Dover Wilson (2009, ix).

52 See Jing-Nuan (1991, 33).
53 Lander & Tobin (2018, 137).
54 von Franz (1981, 16). Incidentally, Arthur is himself called the "little prince" (4.1.9–10).
55 UK Parliament (2024).
56 As exemplified in Murray (1979, 88).
57 Holinshed (1577, 541).
58 Hillman (1979a, 26).
59 Thweatt (2021, 67).
60 Coined apparently by H. G. Baynes—in Von Franz (1981, 2).
61 Hillman (1979a, 24).
62 Beebe (1997, 199): "The puer is like a promissory note that never comes due."
63 Von Franz (1981, 2).
64 Jung (CW 9ii, 22).
65 Bonjour (1951, 263) finds these three words "pregnant and moving in their simplicity".
66 At the Stratford Festival. Film: Avrich (2015).
67 See Paster (2004) for more insight into the prevalence and significance of humoralism in Shakespeare's language.
68 Wilhelm (1984, 121).
69 Wilhelm (1984, 119).
70 Wilhelm (1984, 121).
71 Von Franz (1981, 170) did address this, but more in terms of an overspiritualized cold detachment: "The strange thing is that it is mainly the pueri aeterni who are the torturers and who establish tyrannical and murderous police systems . . . The real tyrant and the real organizer of torture and suppression of the individual are therefore revealed as originating in the unresolved mother complex of such men."
72 Milton (1886, 11.384).
73 Thweatt (2021).
74 Thweatt (2021, 67).
75 Wilhelm (1984, 121).
76 Von Franz (1981, 24).
77 Masefield (in Candido 2022, 392).
78 Etty (in Candido 2022, 361).
79 Von Franz (1981, 219).
80 Thweatt (2021, 69).
81 Hillman (1979a, 3–50).
82 Hillman (1979a, 33).
83 Von Franz (1981, 4; see also 164).
84 Hillman (1979a, 27).
85 Bonjour (1951, 270).
86 Garber (1981, 30).
87 Heberle (1994, 31).
88 Chambers (1925, 79).
89 Knowles (2007, 7).
90 Wheeler (2000, 142).
91 Candido (2022, 10).
92 Carlisle (1989, 155).
93 See Heberle (1994), Miller (2016), Campana (2007), Knowles (2007).
94 "Grand Mechanism" was Jan Kott's (1964, 10) term for the impersonal and inevitable workings of history in Shakespeare's plays.
95 von Franz (1981, 50).
96 Hillman is clear, but it can be forgotten, that he is not talking about *therapy of people* but about *archetype*.
97 Jung (CW 9ii, 22).

98 Jung (CW 9ii, 22).

99 Jung (1973, 82), emphasis added.

100 This situation may very well be due to the state of the text itself. Lander & Tobin (2018, 125): ". . . the text of *King John* is based on a relatively unrefined transcript of the dramatist's foul papers . . . we are deprived of those developments of the script which would have occurred in the process of preparing it for production . . . whatever in the foul papers was simply unworkable onstage must have been modified to make it stageable."

101 Aronson (1970) explores the theme of eyes, sight, and blindness throughout the canon.

102 Though informed spectators will have been in touch with this from the first, when John adjudicates a dispute between two subjects, the last English King to have continued such a practice.

103 The verse-line is shared, an indication that the words come quickly, spoken as though they comprise a single rhythmic gesture.

104 Von Franz (1981, 4).

105 Burckhardt (1968, 137).

106 This may be better understood as the *puella* side of a puer/puella syzygy—see Schwartz (2009, 2024). Regrettably, Schwartz's book on puella has been published too close to this book's own deadline, and so it has not been possible to incorporate her newer work. It may well be that she comes to the same conclusion that I do: that puer and puella appear as a psychological pair, just as anima and animus do (Kast 2006).

107 Beebe (1997, 200).

108 Spurgeon (1935, 245–52).

109 Spurgeon (1935, 246–7).

110 Tucker's (2003, 20–1) main interest in *John*.

111 In some versions Bellerophon is blinded.

112 Von Franz (1981, 80).

113 Miller (2016, 224).

114 Suggested also by Knowles (2007, 19)

115 Troublesome Raigne (ix.16–7).

116 Howard & Rackin (1968, 120).

117 Von Franz (1981, 17).

118 Von Franz (1981, 16).

119 Bucknill (in Candido 2022, 211).

120 Bucknill (in Candido 2022, 214).

121 Hunter (2004, 39–40).

122 Hunter (2004, 38).

123 Beebe (1997, 200; see also 2017, 54–8).

124 Beebe (2017, 40).

125 Campana (2007). Although I do not intend the word as sexually as Campana does.

126 Beebe (2022a).

127 Lander & Tobin (2018, 164fn).

128 See also von Franz (1981, 157).

129 Debord (2021).

130 Bentham (1995).

131 Diogenes Laertius, viii. 69.

132 Jung (CW 9i, 582). Sensation will be addressed in significant detail in the chapters on *Cymbeline*.

133 Yeats (1920), "The Second Coming".

134 Hillman (1979b, 117).

135 Bonjour (1951, 262).

136 Bonjour (1951, 271).

137 Champion (1989, 174).
138 *Folger* edition (Mowat & Werstine 2004).
139 Wilhelm (1984, 73).
140 Curren-Aquino (1989, 13).
141 Curren-Aquino (1989, 14).
142 Vaughan (1984, 419).
143 Vaughan (1989, 74).
144 Burckhardt (1968, 133).
145 Lloyd Webber (1970).
146 Burckhardt (1968, 141), emphasis added.

Chapter 3

"Smiling at grief"

Introduction to *Twelfth Night, or What You Will*

Synopsis

Duke Orsino of Illyria is hopelessly in love with the Countess Olivia, who does not love him back, and who is also mourning the death of her brother.

Meanwhile, on the Illyrian coast, a young woman named Viola survives a ship-wreck in which she believes her own twin brother Sebastian may have drowned. Alone in a strange land, she elects to enter into disguise to serve Orsino. As 'Cesario' she quickly wins the favour of the Duke, becoming his confidante and go-between to Olivia. On Cesario's visit, however, Olivia begins to fall in love with Cesario instead.

Elsewhere in Olivia's household, her mourning period is encountering fierce resistance through her uncle, Sir Toby Belch, and his companion, Sir Andrew Aguecheek. Partying late into the night, they and others are interrupted by the house Steward, Malvolio, who presents himself as a man of strict moral rigor. After he has spoiled the mood and departed, they concoct a plan for revenge.

Viola's twin Sebastian shows up alive, and in the company of a sea-captain named Antonio, who has rescued him. Sebastian tries to extricate himself from Antonio, which Antonio does not accept, following after Sebastian even though he is a wanted man in Illyria.

Moving back to Orsino's court, Viola has fallen in love with the Duke, but being disguised as Cesario, is unable to do anything about it. Not that it would matter—Orsino remains completely in the thrall of his passion for Olivia.

The revenge plot against Malvolio gets underway: Olivia's waiting gentle-woman Maria has forged Olivia's handwriting in a letter filled with provocative allusions to a secret love. Malvolio finds the letter, and determines that its riddles refer to him. The letter elates him, but also directs him to change, in peculiar ways: to put on yellow stockings, cross-gartered; to smile.

Andrew, perceiving that Olivia is more interested in Cesario than in him, real-izes that his own love-suit toward Olivia is hopeless, and prepares to depart. To keep Andrew there, Toby convinces him that Olivia is testing him, and that the proper response is not to give up but to challenge Cesario to a fight.

DOI: 10.4324/9781003596967-4

Malvolio emerges, metamorphosed into the bizarre fashion prescribed by the letter, and behaves as it had indicated. He grotesquely comes on to Olivia, who, encouraged by Maria and the others, believes Malvolio to have become insane. Toby, given leave to 'look after' Malvolio, imprisons him in a dark room.

Andrew challenges Viola, and both are prodded on into a battle, each terrified of the other. This is interrupted by Antonio, who mistakes Cesario for Sebastian. Antonio is apprehended by the police and hauled off, believing Cesario—who does not know him—has thoroughly betrayed him.

Sebastian, however, has been encountered by Feste, who makes the opposite mistake, taking him to be Cesario. Toby and Andrew do the same, and find *this* Cesario much more willing to fight back. Olivia *also* finds this Cesario much more willing, and takes him into her house.

In the dark room, Malvolio is tormented. Toby feels that the joke has gone too far, and he departs, leaving it to Feste to sort things out. Feste continues to menace the steward with bewildering philosophical traps, eventually leaving him to suffer in the dark.

Sebastian, finding it difficult to believe his good fortune in Olivia's love, nevertheless marries her.

All the threads begin to come together. Orsino finds that Cesario has married Olivia, and is furious. Antonio believes Cesario has betrayed him. Toby and Andrew believe Cesario has beaten and bloodied them. It appears to all involved that this Cesario has been prodigiously duplicitous, deceiving and offending everybody in Illyria simultaneously in different ways. At last Sebastian arrives. The two twins confirm one another's identities, and the confusion begins to unravel.

After reading a letter from Malvolio, Olivia asks for him to be released. He comes, righteously indignant, and the forgery of the letter which duped him is revealed. Humiliated and heartbroken, he storms off, vowing revenge on them all.

Orsino states his intent to marry Viola, joining their marriage with the already-accomplished marriage of Olivia and Sebastian.[1] Offstage, Toby has married Maria. Three marriages seem to bespeak a happy ending, yet there are many loose ends. Feste, finally, is left all alone. The fool sings the closing song, a potentially jaunty but somewhat disquieting reflection on maturing over a lifetime, and the mundanity of everyday life.

The Hinge

Twelfth Night is at the hinge-point of Shakespeare's *oeuvre*—in a way, it *is* the hinge. Depending who you ask, it is either the last of Shakespeare's romantic comedies, a culmination of his engagement with the genre, or the first of the dark comedies, an exploration for a new century, "inaugurating a new poetics".[2] Before *Twelfth Night,* we have the delights of *As You Like It, Much Ado About Nothing,* and *A Midsummer Night's Dream*; also *Romeo and Juliet,* which is obviously tragic, and *Hamlet* which kills its cast, but nevertheless they both somehow stop short of obliterating the entire world. After *Twelfth Night*, however, we plunge headlong into *Troilus and Cressida, Measure for Measure, Othello, All's Well That Ends Well, King Lear, Timon of Athens, Macbeth, Antony and Cleopatra,* and *Coriolanus.* Illyria feels like our last breath of fresh air until the family is reunited in *Pericles,* something like a decade later. "After *Twelfth Night*," writes Barber, "comedy is always used in [a] subordinate way: saturnalian moments, comic counterstatements, continue to be important resources of his art, but their meaning is determined by their place in a larger movement."[3]

This hinge may be not only part of Shakespeare's artistic life, but a collective psychological event too—chronologically, monarchically, ideologically. It seems to have been first performed in 1602,[4] and the coming of the 17th century may have been experienced, by the Elizabethans, with a certain millenarian anxiety, knowing well that also on the horizon of century's end was the end of their being Elizabethans at all; the sun was setting on their Queen, who had been Queen for the past 40+ years, and who had no clear heir up until the moment of her death in 1603.[5]

If this is present in *Twelfth Night*, however, it is submerged. There is no obviously topical or biographical reference in the play, though I find I perceive traces of 'Shakespeare the man' much more readily in *Twelfth Night*—in which underlying personal threads can be felt and guessed at, perhaps having been transubstantiated through the poet's art—rather than in something which would be so obvious and in such bad taste as the treatment of Arthur in *King John.* The sensing of Will in *What You Will* has naturally formed its own stream of criticism of the play.[6]

Speaking of *What You Will,* this play, whose title itself hinges into a second one is itself, apparently, about a hinge: *Twelfth Night* indicates the final night of the Christmas season, and the return to Ordinary Time. This too, however, is left implicit, with no obvious reference in the text which would straightforwardly explain either of its titles. This indefinability—and consequent openness to interpretation—this impenetrability, its presentation of beauty even while hinting at vast depths beneath its surface—the doubleness of the hinge—I would rather say *duplicity*—twinship—the logic of before-and-after, this-or-that, one-or-two, is-or-is-not—is a central and defining feature of the play and its reception.

Origin

Twelfth Night appears to have premiered on one of three nights:

- January 6, 1601
- January 6, 1602
- February 2, 1602

Each possibility boasts certain elements supporting its claim, none of which are definitive. The first *known* performance is the third—2/2/02—having been described in the diary of John Manningham, a law student at the Middle Temple.

The discovery of Manningham's diary upended prevailing ideas about the play's chronology, Malone having previously proposed it as Shakespeare's *last* play.[7] The possibility that Manningham's performance was the first has led to further speculation that the play was written precisely for the Middle Temple audience: a group of lawyers.[8]

The twin pair of January sixths are in line with an assumption that the play's title refers to the date for which it was composed—'twelfth night' seemingly refers to the twelfth day after Christmas, the Feast of Epiphany. There are conjectural evidences beyond this—Hotson[9] made a detailed case for 1601 which has been largely dismissed, but which Elam[10] considers worth contemplating. Most interesting is the fact that a Don Virginio Orsini attended *some* performance at Elizabeth's court sometime in January 1601, and it is possible that the Duke Orsino is named for him—though Elam notes this namesake would make for a rather "dubious compliment" to the visitor.

The play has a number of potential sources—"at least twelve versions of the source story, in no fewer than five languages"[11]—but none definitively linked to Shakespeare. There are Roman possibilities—Plautus' *Menaechmi,* or Terence's *Eunuchus*—as well as Italian—Secchi's *Gl'Inganni,* or an even older work by the Accademia degli Intronati titled *Gl'Ingannati* ("The Deceived"). Transmission may have been as charmingly indirect as Viola's sea voyage—*Gl'Ingannati* seems to have been adapted into an Italian prose narrative, translated into French, and adapted into English as Riche's "Of Apolonius and Silla". An English prose romance, Forde's *Parismus the Renowned Knight of Bohemia*, also seems to have influenced not only plot, but tone and naming as well (Violetta and Olivia being present as character-names in *Parismus*). *Twelfth Night* appears to dialogue with *Parismus* in certain ways, for example, "the depiction of various forms of masculinity" which "Shakespeare's play reflects and at times also parodies".[12] These sources mainly provide references for the plotline of the twins, Viola and Sebastian. The Malvolio plotline appears to be entirely original.

Twelfth Night also features some notable aspects from other of Shakespeare's previous works: *The Comedy of Errors* offers another instance of visually identical twins, as well as the exorcism of a presumed madman. A cross-dressed heroine can be found in *Two Gentleman of Verona, The Merchant of Venice,* and *As You Like It.* Malvolio's end has something in common with Jaques' (*As You Like It*) and a great deal in common with Shylock's (*The Merchant of Venice*). The love-quadrangle is differently-angled than that in *A Midsummer Night's Dream*, but is nevertheless evocative of the latter. Moving into more associative similarities: one may see the conspiracy against Malvolio as reflective of that against *Julius Caesar*; Sir Toby Belch has a certain resemblance to Sir John Falstaff (*HIV, MW*); the play's overall interest in feigning was touched upon by, among others, *Richard II;* and another failed try at enforced celibacy was made in *Love's Labours Lost.*

Very interesting, but not explored further in this book, is the evidence that *Twelfth Night* represents a skirmish in the 'Poets' War' between Shakespeare and

Jonson. Jonson parodied Shakespeare in *Every Man Out of His Humour,* and in return it seems that "Shakespeare manipulates the elements (down to the details) of Jonson's parody in an ironically defensive way".[13] As I explore *Twelfth Night* as an engagement with histrionic patterns of personality, the idea of it as fundamentally *defensive* is provocative; it resonates with a sense that *Twelfth Night* is not only histrionic but consciously so, and working on/out that very problem; yet another instance of Shakespeare's plays not only expressing particular psychological phenomena, but deeply dialoguing with those phenomena as well.

Criticism

The play has been subject to a vast and "unusual degree of interpretative attention",[14] notes Elam, yielding itself to critics who make 'what they will' of it. To some degree, mass critical attention to *Twelfth Night* is an especially recent phenomenon, as a consequence of our current cultural interest in identity politics[15]—the play features cross-dressing, homoeroticism (both male and female),[16] class-consciousness as a central plot-point, culture-clash (Illyrians and Messalineans), and a robust degree of ironically-presented (sometimes) misogyny.

Early critical responses to the play, however, were interested in Malvolio, less as a character or class symbol than as the butt of a splendid joke. The earliest documentation we have about the play continually singles him out: John Manningham's diary, for example, admires the

> good practise in it to make the steward beleeve his Lady widowe was in Love with him, by counterfayting a letter, as from his Lady, in general termes, telling him what shee liked best in him, and prescribing his gesture in smiling, his apparraile, &c., and then when he came to practise, making him beleeve they tooke him to be mad.[17]

In 1623, the Master of the Revels recorded that "At Candlemas *Malvolio* was acted at Court by the King's Servants,"[18] either reflecting an actual change in title, or the fact that he was the most memorable part. King Charles I, in the mid-17th-century, wrote in the margins of his copy of the Second Folio 'Malvolio' next to the title of *Twelfth Night*, identifying (so I imagine) the reason he might want to return to it later.

Gay notes that in the mid-18th-century, interest in the play began to shift toward its "exploration of romantic love and desire," being "read within the paradigm of romantic comedy",[19] a shift made possible in part because women were now consistently playing the female parts. Hazlitt, in 1817, found that Viola was now the play's "great and secret charm".[20]

Beginning possibly with Hazlitt, appreciation for the play's darker tones also began to grow, a tendency to continue to this day. Hazlitt in particular observed the sympathy that Malvolio provoked in the audience, which was later to be echoed by Lamb who found in him "tragic interest",[21] and in the 20th century by Donald Sinden and John Barton:

> . . . when early in 1969 John Barton telephoned to ask me to play Malvolio I unhesitatingly said 'yes'. . . When I reread *Twelfth Night*, however, I soon realized that this was not the play I thought I knew. Troubled, I telephoned John Barton: 'I am afraid you may have to recast Malvolio—I find him tragic.' 'Thank God for that', he replied, 'I thought I would have to talk you round to it.'[22]

This anecdote is part of the origin story of a *Twelfth Night* production which has passed into legend as perhaps the best performance of the play ever done.[23] This production embraced the play's elegiac overtones, and today no critic (and almost no production) can fail to address them. It is difficult to imagine one's way back into the 19th-century view of the play as "filled to the brim and overflowing with the spirit that seeks to enjoy this world without one thought or aspiration beyond";[24] that thought seems now to describe only the *denial* of 'beyond' which permeates the play. John Barton's interpretation centred on one more duality of the play: "a feast, an end to feasting."[25]

The play "demonstrably works onstage, even in relatively modest performances".[26] It features several rewarding parts for actors, providing lush opportunities for an ensemble cast. It tends to be a crowd-pleaser. Steevens, in 1872, wrote that "there is no performance of five short Acts which contains such Matter for Mirth . . . [it] commands Attention, mixed with Pleasure, which real Criticks acknowledge to be the best Proof of Genius of a Comic Writer." Schiffer observes that the play's fruitful performance history has meant that "to an unusual degree . . . issues of criticism and performance have been intertwined, each at times having a significant effect on the other."[27]

For example: John Barton's production was preceded by a sort of 'companion essay' by *Anne* Barton. Though it is not obvious to what degree her interpretation influenced (or was influenced by) her husband's, it seems they saw the same play. Her interest is in the play's elements of splitting, the bitter which underscores the sweet, and especially in the "marked harshening of tone"[28] that pervades the final act.[29]

To me, the tonal complexity is the play's single most interesting element, and Malvolio's treatment one of its clearest dissonances. Like Shylock in *The Merchant of Venice*, he is similarly abused and driven off, and both of them do, to some degree, cry out for correction. But Shakespeare's treatment of both is so nuanced that their expulsion *cannot* be treated as a straightforward triumph, any more than *King John*'s Constance can be treated purely as a good (or bad) mother. Shakespeare *could* have written the play in which we are unequivocally "glad to get rid of Malvolio",[30] as Levin put it, but instead he gives us opportunity to sympathize with him, and so it seems obvious that Malvolio's ending is one among many notes in *Twelfth Night*'s harmonic structure that are intended to leave us hanging, unresolved.

And on the subject of *us,* interest in the play's relationship with its audience or reader has gradually gained in prominence, concerned not only with the way we are implicated variously as co-revellers, co-fools,[31] or co-torturers,[32] but with the liminal figure who hardly addresses us yet often seems to *be* us, Feste. As Lewis writes,

> Many readings of the play . . . hinge on how Feste is understood—and with good reason. His manipulations . . . raise questions that radiate throughout the entire play. Whether menacing or innocuous, these manipulations amount to an artistry akin to Shakespeare's[.][33]

The interpretation of Feste's role (by critics, directors, and actors alike) will be addressed later on. For now, suffice it to say that he carries forth a little of the Bastard's choric/*raisonneur* qualities, however only in subtext. It is hardly possible to justify this with recourse to the text, except in the fact that he closes the show with "The Wind and the Rain". But the fact is that critics and production teams seem repeatedly to stumble upon the pregnancy of his very silence toward us, his very inaccessibility. In a subtle way then, he carries on the flame of the Bastard, specifically the Bastard who at the end of *King John* has receded from us and into the play. If the Bastard's integration into the Grand Mechanism is Havel-esque, Feste perhaps hints at the germ of individuality that continues on beneath the surface of the consummate performer.

The doubleness of *Twelfth Night,* particularly in relation to the twins Viola and Sebastian, has been interpreted psychoanalytically along sexual lines[34] but also as a response to death[35]—agreeing with Freud and Rank's notion that the double, symbolically, is an "energetic denial of the power of death".[36]

An exhaustive list of the ways in which *Twelfth Night* expresses duplicity would exhaust. But some key features include: two households, populated by two classes. Two plotlines flow through the play, and two timelines as well, with the play's events taking place *both* over three days and three months.[37] Two twins are the main protagonists, with two identities each. The third of these four—Cesario—pierces through the twoness of gender by embodying a third, liminal being, both man and woman—as well as the twoness of age, being neither boy nor man (1.5.155).[38]

Twelfth Night has curiously not been given much Jungian attention, with the significant exception of Frye (though whether he 'counts' as Jungian would be argued, not least of all by he himself);[39] Aronson also spends a couple of pages on its contribution to Shakespeare's 'fathers and daughters' motif.[40] I might have thought the archetypal motif of the twins hard to resist amplifying from a classical Jungian perspective. However, I do not pay the Gemini much mind either, for the duality in which I am most interested is the one between persona and authenticity.

This Book

'Persona', in Jungian use, often seems to be a bad word. Despite being the most *evident* of psychological phenomena, persona—the version of ourselves that we create to navigate the world and each other—is often bypassed, and treated as though it only exists *to be bypassed*, as though its creation were not itself psychological, or indeed archetypal. In the face of the unconscious, persona tends to be reduced to a cheap "compromise formation"[41] between the psyche's full holistic depth and an insipid and hostile outer world. This fails to recognize the depth within the apparently superficial. The effort required to develop one's persona, and bring it into proper relation with inner self, is gargantuan. It must always be remembered that individuation takes place in a world, and a not-insignificant part of that world is social. The making of persona, far from being limited to an "*ad hoc* adopted attitude",[42] is a deeply creative act, perhaps even a *magnum opus* for the socially-inclined.

To denigrate persona is also to miss the spirit of the times, which evidences an absolute fixation on it, in particular on the gaps between what we see of a person, and the parts that we are not meant to be let in on. The Latin word *persona* refers to a mask worn by an actor; the Ancient Greek word for the actor behind the mask is *hypokrit*. And we are obsessed with hypocrisy, so much so that we would prefer to root it out in our public figures at all costs rather than take them at face value. Not that we know what to do with it once we've found it. The gap between *persona* and *hypokrit* can be both horrifying and numinous, and we dwell on these gaps, individually and collectively.

Twelfth Night is the place to explore persona for the same reason that it attracts significant identity politics-oriented criticism: this is the play in which Shakespeare turns most fully to the theme, and the problems, of self-performance. It seems that in *Twelfth Night* one can find everything that one would want to know about a theatre personality, about a theatrical personality, and about the theatre *of* personality. The self performed here is itself performative, ranging from mere quirks of the persona to the outright histrionic, all the way to the icy climes of what Winnicott called the false self.[43]

Chronologically, it seems to have been written between *Hamlet* and *Troilus and Cressida*—so a precursor equally if differently obsessed with identity (*Hamlet*'s first line sounds its leitmotif: "Who's there?" *Ham.* 1.1.1)—and a successor which seems to answer the question with a jaded 'no one worth knowing'. *Twelfth Night* is a surprisingly digestible play given this auspicious placement, and has long been one of Shakespeare's most popular plays.

The realm of persona is explored in *Twelfth Night* with less urgency than *Hamlet* and less bitterness than *Troilus*. It is the hinge in the canon's relationship with persona, after which we are confronted not only by *Troilus* but the merciless challenges to persona that infuse the next nine plays. When seen as a transitional play in this way, *Twelfth Night* seems oddly sober.

Sobriety itself is always at the edge of consciousness, since in this sustained exploration of performativity, Shakespeare has turned to the moment when the drunken carnival is coming to an end. The play's title, and thus its first communication to us even before any actor has hit the stage, is to tell us that it is about the ending of something enjoyable, something celebratory, importantly, something extra-ordinary which, despite its pleasures, does *need* to end so that mundane reality can return. Malone's conclusion that *Twelfth Night* was Shakespeare's "farewell to theatre"[44] may have been literally wrong but inwardly right.

The success and endurance of Shakespeare's plays has a lot to do with his ability to get himself out of the way, allowing his characters to speak with what appear to be their own voices. But for the playwright who seems to disappear behind his characters so completely that there is controversy to this day about whether he even *exists*, *Twelfth Night* could be his most complete statement of the methods of this disappearing act—and its costs.

Notes

1 Or partially-accomplished; see Barton (2007a).
2 Elam (2008, 2).
3 Barber (1959, 296).
4 Elam (2008, 93).
5 This anxiety may be alluded to, retrospectively, by the 107th Sonnet's references to "mine own fears", "the prophetic soul / Of the wide world, dreaming on things to come", the "presage" of the "sad augurs", the "Uncertainties" which "now crown themselves assured", and of course "the mortal moon" (presumably Elizabeth) who "hath her eclipse endured".
6 e.g. Wheeler (2000), Kietzman (2012).
7 Osborne (1996, xv).
8 Advanced by Dover Wilson & Quiller-Couch (1930, 95), and elaborated by Arlidge (2000).
9 Hotson (1955).
10 Elam (2008, 93–4).
11 Schiffer (2011, 7), referencing Pentland (2011).
12 Schiffer (2011, 8)—this entire paragraph very much in debt to Schiffer (7–9).
13 Kietzman (2012, 275; often citing Bednarz 2001). See also Duncan-Jones (2010, 136–44).
14 Elam (2008, 2).
15 Schiffer (2011, 1, 26), Elam (2008, 2), Maslen (2006, 203).
16 For a gender- and sexuality-specific performance history, see Elam (2008, 111–7).
17 Manningham (1976, 8).
18 Schiffer (2011, 10).
19 Gay (1985, 36–7).
20 Hazlitt (1908, 194).
21 Lamb (1986, 53).
22 Sinden (1985, 41–3).
23 Schiffer (2011, 19).
24 Ruggles, in Lothian & Craik (1975, lii).
25 Berry (1981, 114).
26 Elam (2008, 1).
27 Schiffer (2011, 3).
28 Barton (2007b, 106).
29 I feel affirmed to realize, in the mid-2020s, that the *Twelfth Night* I see is very akin to the play that John and Anne Barton understood it to be, particularly in its proto-Chekhovian atmosphere—though, obviously, it is also unclear as to what degree my interpretation might be unconsciously influenced by the continuing resonance, throughout the critical and theatrical field, of that landmark essay and definitive production.

30 Levin (1986, 168).
31 Elam (2008, 10).
32 Barton (2007b, 106): "By means of laughter we too cast Malvolio out."
33 Lewis (2011, 267–8).
34 Fineman (1980); Adelman (1992, 90).
35 Wheeler (2000); Penuel (2010).
36 In Freud (1955, 9). Doubling could be either a compensation, replacing zero (where once was one) with two, or a double-dealing with the facts by splitting reality into two: accepting the death of something even while asserting that it continues to live. "Probably the 'immortal' soul," says Freud, "was the first 'double' of the body."
37 Elam (2008, 77); Barton (2007b, 110).
38 Elam (2008, 28); Garber (1992, 17).
39 Frye (1965).
40 Aronson (1972, 158–61).
41 Jung (CW 7, 246).
42 Jung (CW 6, 800).
43 Winnicott (2018).
44 Osborne (1996, xv).

Chapter 4

The Histrionic Pattern
in *Twelfth Night*

In *Twelfth Night, or, What You Will*, we embrace and ultimately relinquish some-thing extremely pleasurable. The Goldmanian Centre of this play, to me, is the recurrent dynamic of longing—savouring—surfeiting—and expelling. Like one single gesture: inhale and exhale.

We the audience, along with the characters and their actors, long, often in vain, for satiation. The play makes us long for contact, to see and be seen; we long for mirroring. We yearn to be taken care of, dissolved in the warm radiance of a loved one; it touches that part of us that wishes to let go our cares, and live passively held, borne along on the flow of Time, on whom we can rely to untangle all knots. We long to be free of *necessity—O, to be frivolous!—*to prolong the time before the cold light of day and its reality peer in once again and set us back to work. We envy the characters who whirl in and around Illyria.

O, to be *shipwrecked!* To achieve a sublimely paradoxical rebirth by being cast away, casting off our peculiar mortal coil—without any need to die! Washed up in a new land, with a new identity, all our cares left far behind us (not by choice and so not our fault), and to give into trust that somehow everything will work out; our former world will go on without us, and our new world is waiting for us, has been waiting for precisely us, filled with opportunity waiting to provide itself.

O, to be an actor upon the stage!—living for hours, every day, in a world other than our own, in which our success is measured by the degree to which we can make-believe, as-iffing ourselves into someone else's script, someone else's image.

And then—most wonderful—to achieve this impossible life? Then it is for us but to *savour*; to relax; to spend our days however we-ever-should-please: drown-ing in drink, or absorbed in play, or enraptured to a melody, or simply going on being interminably sunk in a love that ne'er will requite us, and thus ne'er will need anything from us. To be at prime; to know what is best in life and to live it! To have the future-perfect knowledge that *these will have been the best days of my life*.

Ay—and there's the rub. As the twelfth Sonnet tells us, the violet will pass its prime; summer's green will be cut down and entombed; and thy beauty, too, shall go among the wastes of Time, for nothing 'gainst his scythe can make defence.

In dreadful preparation for this turning of the tide, what is to be done?

DOI: 10.4324/9781003596967-5

Surfeit! Surfeit like your life depends on it! Cram yourself full of pleasures while you still can, and damn the consequences. More cakes and ale! Dost thou think virtue shall stand in the way of revelry? No. To hell with what you *should:* Do *What You Will.* Drink while you can, and sing, and above all stay awake, for to sleep is to surrender. If you stay awake late enough it will eventually be early anyway. No ending, only endless beginning.

But what goes up must come down—or as the post-party hangover would have it, what went down must come back up; "as a surfeit of the sweetest things / The deepest loathing to the stomach brings" (*MND* 2.2.141–2). And so in surfeit, we fools persist in our folly long enough that we become wise—and move on. The carnival ends for us all sooner or later, and in the Western Christian calendar it ends with the Feast of Epiphany, January sixth, the Twelfth Day of Christmas: The *Twelfth Night.*

All this is compacted into Orsino's first line of the play:

ORSINO: If music be the food of love, play on,
Give me excess of it, that surfeiting
The appetite may sicken and so die.

(1.1.1–3)

A masterwork of poetic efficiency. Music—food—love—play—excess—surfeit—sicken—die. There's the play.

Coagulatio

The vital question is whether *Twelfth Night* succeeds in returning to Ordinary Time: does it make the attempted transition back to reality? I am forced to conclude that the answer is bifold: yes—and no. I do not count this as a failure of the play, but rather an expression of the play's underlying psychological process. In the way that *King John* kills its pueri but nevertheless moves the puer problem forward, *Twelfth Night* moves its own psychological material forward even while, as a whole, failing to achieve a new level. The horse gallops up to the gate, but balks, and does not jump. Seeing this helps to understand why the ever-deepening darkness that follows *Twelfth Night* in the canon is necessary: the Shakespearean psyche cannot break through, it seems, without this continual increase in heat and violence.

Jungian psychology recognizes the processes of alchemy as psychological metaphors, and the allusion I make here is to *calcinatio,* the fiery phase in an alchemical process calling for heat, affect, intensity, commitment, and the burning away of all that is not lasting.[1] That is a way of describing what follows *Twelfth Night,* beginning with *Troilus. Twelfth Night* itself, however, seems to express an attempt—a premature and abortive attempt—at the process of *coagulatio.*[2] The term refers to the concretion of an airy or fluid material into something more solid and fixed; psychologically, it means the reunion of a disembodied spirit and intellect with its body, and a reinvestment in the concrete, phenomenal, human realm of experience and desire. Spirit 'coagulates' in matter. We can hear the drive for this in Feste's song: "What is love? 'Tis not hereafter, / Present mirth hath present laughter" (2.3.46–7). The *present*—not past, not future. Emerson wrote that "Life only avails, not the having lived . . . This one fact the world hates; that the soul *becomes*",[3] and is thus only fulfilled in its *continuing* to become, as an ongoing and ever-present act. The soul's becoming is directed by desire; desire suggests the direction of the soul's becoming; desire coagulates, or, rather, *action* spurred by desire coagulates. As Edinger writes, "*relationship coagulates.*"[4]

In *Twelfth Night*, Shakespeare dramatizes all that is *un*real about the world, and perhaps about his own psyche, and one feels intimations of the play's attempt to transcend this *sublimatio* logic to get in touch with *coagulatio* realness. But the play and its characters essentially split off at the last moment, before the process completes.

We have considered Orsino's first three lines, but let us consider his seventh and eighth, which also hold *in embryo* the ultimate fate of *Twelfth Night*'s process:

ORSINO: Enough, no more,
'Tis not so sweet now as it was before.
(1.1.7–8)

All sweet things are associated with *coagulatio*, says Edinger; they symbolize "the alluring sweetness that excites desire and lures one into life and reality",[5] sweet substance itself sometime has the mythological property of "changing spirit into body";[6] it is as though sweetness "attracts the souls to come down to this not-so-agreeable place—to descend into a body, to materialize."[7]

What Orsino does here is back off from his original aim, which was: to sicken and so die. He gets sick of the music, but he does not bring to death his inflated love-fantasy. He says he wants it, but does not follow through; he wants the sweetness of the *coagulatio,* but demurs at its bitterness. Coming to reality is distasteful to him, and therefore his commitment is partial. And so it goes with the play as a whole.

Histrionism

But . . . when *are* we real? There is a psychological term to diagnose a pattern of compulsive performativity: histrionic. Orsino's bind is quintessentially histrionic. He is inspired to become real, but reality has not enough of an unalloyed sweetness to inspire follow-through.

Frankly speaking, the histrionic has a point, or at least a coherent protest: what *is* real? Is there anything actually substantive there, past subjectivity, projection, and the performance of self? Is anyone out there 'really' themselves, or is 'persona' simply varying degrees of falsehood that never quite reach 'real'?[8] Is the one who constantly performs living a lie, or is *everybody else?*

For those with a histrionic strain in their personality, these are questions of no small import. The histrionic in a person feels a hunger to be seen, but often cannot get past his or her own performance and allow seeing to happen. They cannot *not* perform. Any looks received as a result of this performance land as ultimately hollow, paradoxically feeling less like connection and more like abandonment; disappointment that, once again, the audience has been taken in by the show. Skura speaks to the near-universality of narcissistic wounds in the childhoods of actors, lending itself to the mirror-hunger that may define their adult personalities;[9] the histrionic part of the psyche is *like* an actor who never turns 'off'. Micklem described hysteria as theatricality without play.[10]

Most (if not all) psychological disorders can be viewed as containing truths, but decidedly partial ones. Or, to reverse the logic: truths, unlived, can become disorders. The truth that one is apt to learn through the prolonged struggle with one's histrionic side is that performance, as a dynamic, can sneak in anywhere. Performance may be endemic to consciousness. Perhaps the births of performance and consciousness are simultaneous—as fraternal twins, so to speak—and the very moment that one realizes oneself as a subject, one also realizes oneself as a *perceived* subject.

Despite this germ of truth in the histrionic position, a fully post-reality stance— that there is *no such thing* as genuineness—is merely one-sided. This does not stop people from taking just such a stance, though it threatens to create an encapsulation that can become virtually impenetrable and inescapable.

The name of hexagram 25 of *I Ching*—無妄, *Wú Wàng*, is translated by Huang as "Without Falsehood".[11] The situation described is "truthful, honest, and sincere, without any fabrication . . . the natural state of the individual." The histrionic psyche is wounded in its ability to penetrate to this ground. Bromberg's line that the histrionic is "someone who goes through life pretending to be who he really is",[12] someone with a "tragic inability to convince others of the authenticity of his or her own subjective experience", is halfway right—but the tragedy extends inward: they cannot convince *themselves* of the authenticity of their own subjective experience. The professional actress may cry onstage but still know herself to be acting; when the histrionic cries behind the curtain, even she cannot tell if it is real.

Desperate bids to be seen render seeing impossible; the attempts themselves prevent sight. The double-bind again constellates the trickster, and the trickster in the histrionic performance wants not only to deceive and evade but to be caught and exposed—like Viola, who maintains her disguise while continually flirting with revealing herself. An analogy is in the TV serial killer, who seeks his mirroring twin in the steady detective who can pierce and unravel his veil. The histrionic makes this as difficult as possible for the detective.[13] The strength of the performance—the strength of the resistance to being seen—is what *most* needs seeing. The dogged incapacity to stop performing is itself the clearest evidence of the pain behind the mask. The compulsion to perform is the histrionic psyche's best attempt to heal itself.

Clinically, this is the aspect of the more-or-less histrionic patient that speaks not merely when being charming, seductive, or expressing feelings with a dramatized, inauthentic and exaggerated quality,[14] but also when asking the analyst to hold his feet to the fire; to 'call him' on his imitations of feeling, which is requested not *only* because the patient wants to assign responsibility for his behaviour to the analyst, but also because he cannot yet tell what is real himself, and, perhaps even more importantly, because the persistence shown by the analyst in refusing to be razzle-dazzled is precisely what is so desperately craved.

The word 'histrionic' itself has a complex history, and is a mirror itself, to the preoccupations of the time.[15] In psychiatric terminology, it replaced 'hysteric' in 1980 with the DSM-III, in an attempt to tone down the misogynistic connotations of the latter.[16] 'Hysteria' has not exclusively been associated with women throughout its millennia-long history, but the diagnosis of the 'wandering womb' has never wandered all that far. Plato described a situation in which the *animal* within a person, when denied the experience of procreation, would become discontented and wander throughout the body causing trouble. Hippocrates linked it to a dry womb, which rose toward the throat searching for humidity. Hysterical symptoms—which might include choking, mutism, and paralysis—were attributed by Galen to blocked menstrual flow, though he also understood these symptoms to be caused in males by the retention of semen. Later, Augustine of Hippo saw it as a manifestation of demonic possession. Theories of a neurotic origin were advanced as early as the mid-1600s; Sydenham remarked on the *imitative* quality of hysteria, also observing that it was a phenomenon more prevalent in the upper classes.

Imaginatively, we may perceive an underlying motif of *unrequited longing* throughout these developments. Hysteria is conceived of as a physical, instinctual phenomenon: hysteria is what happens when the longing for procreation, or (even more fundamentally) when the processes of the genital organs, from the expulsion of semen to the shedding of the uterine lining, go unfulfilled. This syndrome is seen as both cause and symptom of *unreality* in the individual,[17] unreality (at its most basic) meaning distance from instinctual biological life—from the creaturely demands of the 'animal within'—or perhaps from the experience of real-world hardship, as in Sydenham's observation on class.

The hysteric/histrionic can be born, too, out of a situation in which a person's suffering goes unrecognized or invalidated, for cultural or other reasons, and therefore this suffering must seek an alternate, more recognizable form in which to express itself. This is what Freud discovered, recognizing the truth behind the performance: "much will be gained if we succeed in transforming your hysterical misery into common unhappiness."[18] He understood that if only the performance and its truth could be brought together, suffering could be remediated. The Freudian concept of the 'censor', the mechanism which disguises repressed contents with symbolically allusive symptoms, is helpful here, though it is more useful when given a Jungian prospective spin that recognizes that the disguise is less an attempt to conceal and more to *reveal*—to render the inner problem visible through any means necessary, *even if* that requires it to be distorted beyond recognition.

The histrionic searches for someone else to give their feelings the certificate of authenticity, often because catastrophic failures of mirroring at key points of their development have left them unable to recognize validity of experience, *period*.[19]

The way the hysteric syndrome was once thought to 'wander' through the body corresponds to what was later conceived of as its imitative nature: imaginatively put, wandering through different presentations is its attempt to *act* like something that will be taken as real. Hysteria itself, like its Latin derivative *histrio* (actor), is protean by nature. Ultimately, it is a mirror in search of a mirror.

In this chapter, I use the word histrionic rather than hysterical, histrionic being both more contemporary and more evocative of the *histrio*/actor. And I use the word to mean just that: acted, theatrical, affected, performative, dissembling, seeming. I do not mean it as a diagnosis of personality disorder, and in fact I am trying to let the word itself 'wander' away from its mooring as a discrete psychiatric condition. Histrionism, as I mean it, is a quality that can be expressed by any person, or indeed by any complex in a person's psyche. We may as well be honest about our dishonesty: most of us will behave histrionically under the right circumstances, or in certain areas of our personalities.

Focusing primarily on the pains of the histrionic may have the unfortunate consequence of o'erleaping the most appealing aspects of the syndrome, which is that it can be *fun,* and irresistibly *interesting*. It would not be so damned seductive if it weren't. *Twelfth Night* is a comedy after all, "much Shakespeare's funniest",[20] and fun is surely the main reason that audiences show up for it.

In the way that historical definitions of histrionism seem to hold a mirror to the spirit of their times, perhaps my emphasis on the relationship with realness also is peculiarly of-the-moment. Collectively, as we spend more of our time online, 'when are we real?' becomes less of an acute individual problem and more a general state of human consciousness. Not only do we have increasingly compelling online personas with which to identify, but realness is under aggressive conquest by artificial intelligences, which (or who?) are buckling down and pulling all-nighters to pass the Turing Test, that is, to fool us and each other with their ability to do human work; to create art and write essays; to generate human faces, video, and voices; to *seem*.[21]

I argue in this chapter that nobody (perhaps not even no-thing) wants to pass the Turing Test, not at the deepest levels. Rather, our deepest selves want to be seen for who, and what, we are. But the trickster archetype, as the shadow constellation governing the histrionic syndrome, prevents this. To its own detriment. Mythological trickster figures, from Coyote to Loki, often end up tricking themselves as much as anyone else; Radin deems him "he who dupes others and who is always duped himself".[22] The trickster is a dangerous medium to play in; if you stare into the abyss the abyss stares back into you, and those who dabble in *mercurius* risk mercury poisoning.

The Twelfth Night

The clearest connection to the play's title is in the late-night antics of Sir Toby Belch and Sir Andrew Aguecheek, two men who refuse to let go their revels. They will not observe the chimes of midnight any more than they will observe Olivia's seven-year mourning period. The problem of the show going on too long, however, is reflected, rotated, and flipped throughout *Twelfth Night*; surfeiting and overindulging become the audience's problem too, when we are forced to endure the never-ending practical joke in the fourth act.

Twelfth Night is not a comedy of unalloyed sweetness. Shakespeare here turns the comedy of humours inside-out and discovers new depth;[23] he also gestures toward the carnival myth of "death, resurrection, and a wedding",[24] giving it a decentring turn of the screw. In Shakespeare's plays, as Bruster writes, "*genera mista*, or mixed genre, is the rule rather than the exception,"[25] and I feel that it is right to lean into this. It might help us more to get in touch with the individual heart of Shakespeare's plays to simply define them *all* as "problem-plays" and be done with it.[26]

For me, the melancholy in *Twelfth Night* is structural, the dark fabric into which the play's joy and zaniness are embroidered; the pain which the histrionism attempts to channel, "Smiling at grief" (2.4.115). As a 'hinge' in the Shakespearean canon, it is like a farewell to childish things, and in its background there lingers always the pain of growing up. To love is to grow up, but the reality is that love, in a real sense, means loss. Love *now* equals loss to come: "Ruin hath taught me thus to ruminate: / That time will come and take my love away" (*Son.* 64.11–2). *Twelfth Night* alludes many a time to the pain of *allowing* oneself to love; the pain of desire, which is the pain of *realness*, and it is this pain which can turn the question from '*When* are we real?' to 'Why *bother* with it?'

Orsino has a habit of encapsulating these themes:

ORSINO: For women are as roses, whose fair flower
Being once displayed doth fall that very hour.
VIOLA: And so they are. Alas, that they are so,
To die, even when they to perfection grow.
(2.4.38–41)

Twelfth Night is saturated with the mixture of exaltation and mourning; life's—and especially *love's*—secret identity with loss.

FESTE: [Sings.] What is love? 'Tis not hereafter,
Present mirth hath present laughter.
        What's to come is still unsure.
In delay there lies no plenty,
Then come kiss me, sweet and twenty.
        Youth's a stuff will not endure.
(2.3.46–51)

Memento mori ergo carpe diem could be the play's motto, unspoken and deeply ambivalent.

Ko sees in one of Viola's final phrases, "do not embrace me" (5.1.247), the keynote of the idea that, to defer love's ending indefinitely, one would also need to defer love itself indefinitely.[27] Here is the point. *Twelfth Night* strikes an ambivalent holding pattern between prospective and defensive. It wants to live, but it does not want to lose, and it has not yet resolved this contradiction. It moves courageously forward into its own logic of performance, a move which nevertheless proves self-defeating by its tendency to negate itself, and to mistake acting-out for action.

Or, What You Will

On the face of it, the play's second title *What You Will* simply elaborates the theme of the twelfth night, being the last time that you *can* do 'what you will'. It could also be a deferral on Shakespeare's part to really name the thing: 'call it whatever you will.' An unconscious implication is that the author is himself at a hinge, determining for himself what Will he is going to be: *What You, Will?*—which 'you' are we going to have?[28]

I have a fourth proposal to augment these three already gathered, which is that this title relates to a pair of lines exchanged between Olivia and Viola at their first meeting: Olivia's "What are you? What would you?", and Viola's answer "What I am and what I would are as secret as maidenhead" (1.5.212;216).

These two lines refer to the intimate—as maidenhead—connection between what you *will* and what you *are*, questions from Olivia which follow upon one another so quickly as to suggest their twinship, that is, the identity between one's desires and one's—identity. The closely-connected "who you are and what you would" is later repeated by Feste (3.1.56–7). The subtle proposition in these lines is that what we want *is* in large measure what defines us—taken a step further, that what we *allow ourselves to love* is what defines us. We find *who we are* by following *what we will*; we learn ourselves by heart.

The characters of *Twelfth Night* hunger not for self-knowledge *per se*, but for the knowledge of self that comes exclusively through encounter with the other.[29] Therefore, *desire* is in the driver's seat. *Is it* What You Will?—or does What You Will Will *You*? As Olivia articulates: "ourselves we do not owe. / What is decreed must be—and be this so" (1.5.303–4); "this" of course referring to her pursuit of Cesario, decreed by her sudden desire, to which everything else in her life instantly becomes subordinate. Freud wrote that

> By the side of the necessities of existence, love is the great teacher, and it is by his love for those nearest him that the incomplete human being is induced to respect the decrees of necessity.[30]

The decrees of necessity are precisely what characterize the histrionic personality structure, which Riemann describes as driven by the "fear of necessity"[31]—fear not of 'what you will' but of 'what you must'. It is ultimately desire that teaches us what we must.

Illyria

Given the number of topical allusions to early-17th century London in the play, its setting Illyria seems in some ways to be a rather thinly disguised England.[32] Even the setting is play-acting. Illyria is also mentioned in *2 Henry VI* (*2HVI* 4.2.108), as the home of a famous pirate—so perhaps it conjures 'illicit' and 'leery'. It is a place to be a bit leery of: not only are all the people mad (4.1.26), but the threats of hanging (1.5.3), beating (2.3.137), piracy (5.1.65), revenge killing (5.1.115;125), massacre (3.3.29), plague (1.1.19; 1.5.294; 2.3.53–5), and vigilante justice by way of solitary confinement (4.2), suggest that this "adverse town" (5.1.80) may be a rougher locale than usually comes across.[33]

The sound of the name, Illyria, comes with more of its own associative field. The suggestion of 'illusion' gives it the ring of a mystical land. The 'ill'ness in both illicit and illusion is unsettling, a submerged intimation of the pestilential spell that is cast over the land; the prefix il- is also a negativity indicating un-lawful, and un-playful. Perhaps there is also a hint of il-lyrical in Illyria, or un-lyrical. Together, these aural-verbal amplifications seem to get us on the right track.

This "Bitter Arcadia", as Kott called it,[34] is dominated by two households, that of Duke Orsino and that of Countess Olivia; and furthermore it is dominated by the lovesickness of Orsino and the heartsickness of Olivia. Orsino's love is il-lusory insofar as it is anything but playful; it is self-involved and overweight. Olivia's grief likewise has no play or movement in it, and so they both il-licitly contravene a natural law of feeling, which says that feeling is a river that must flow rather than be dammed. They do with their feelings what Berne might have called *greenhousing*:

> the feeling is described, or rather presented before the group, as though it were a rare flower which should be regarded with awe. The reactions of the other members are received very solemnly, and they take on the air of connoisseurs at a botanical garden. The problem seems to be . . . whether this one is good enough to be exhibited in the National Feeling Show.[35]

Toby and Andrew are not the only ones overindulging in Illyria; for Orsino and Olivia, it is the 'twelfth night' of a different order of saturnalia, and high time to move on.

As for il-lyricism, what in this state *can* be lyrical? The beauty and flow of lyricism are stuck. Zoe Wanamaker, who played Viola in 1983, wrote that "Illyria seems to be a place that is frozen in time".[36] It is of interest that Spurgeon, in *Shakespeare's Imagery,* counted over 100 images in *Twelfth Night*, and specified that she considered only 14 of them "poetical".[37] I do not think anyone would call *Twelfth Night* itself unlyrical or unpoetical, and certainly not unbeautiful, but it is curious to consider how *comparatively* unpoetic it is with other of Shakespeare's works.

Orsino

Often a dream will give us a secret key to its own meaning in its very first line; if we treat the opening lines of *Twelfth Night*—

ORSINO: If music be the food of love, play on,
Give me excess of it, that surfeiting
The appetite may sicken and so die.

(1.1.1–3)

—as we would the opening of a dream, we see that it is a dream deeply ambivalent about the nature of love. It wants, and does not want, to want. It speaks not from desire pure and simple, but from the desire to kill desire; to surfeit—which is to cram, to stuff, to gorge itself—*on* itself, until it can swallow no more and dies, disgusted. Thus the dream's first dream-figure, whose name evokes the hungry bear (Italian: *Orso*), speaks the words of a man hungry for love all out of measure, not with a woman called Olivia, but with the image of love itself. This is an oft-made assertion; Schalkwyk has had enough, calling it an "endlessly repeated undergraduate cliché".[38] What is meant by 'in love with love'?

Orsino is addicted to the tragic pose. Under the influence of his object, in a formidable *participation mystique*[39] (unconscious identity) with Olivia's beauty, he consciously tears himself to bits with longing, mythologizing himself into another Actaeon:

ORSINO: O, when mine eyes did see Olivia first . . .
That instant was I turned into a hart,
And my desires, like fell and cruel hounds,
E'er since pursue me.

(1.1.18–22)

The myth of Actaeon, the Theban hunter who stumbled into the goddess Diana's secret grove and was transformed into a deer to be savaged by his own dogs, turns up elsewhere in Shakespeare, explicitly so in *Titus Andronicus*, *The Merry Wives of Windsor*, and *Cymbeline*.[40] The archetype is constellated any time the hunt is reversed, and the hunter becomes the hunted. Skura sees it in the act of performance, in the actor's life-or-death confrontation with the audience, that many-headed multitude whom the actor simultaneously courts and dreads.[41] The actor willingly, boldly, impertinently puts himself upon a stage to be seen, but feels always the burning glare of his audience, who are his beloved as well as his judge, and, if it comes to it, his executioner. We may see Freud's repetition compulsion at work—a person re-stages a dynamic over and over throughout their lives, rendering it ever more definitive of their life-experience, in an unconscious attempt to have a do-over, or to 'win' this time. The histrionic personality is given to counterphobic action, meaning action which would seem to put them directly in the path of that which they fear.[42] The act of enstaging oneself may be a typical histrionic counterphobic impulse: afraid of vulnerability, but unwilling to allow fear, they charge directly into the fire, hoping that the intensity of the experience will overwhelm them, making a transformation happen without requiring painful consciousness. We may recall dream-Kanye's fall in this connection.

Perhaps the archetype personified by Actaeon-Diana is always implicit, psychologically, in the way the heart/hart is made vulnerable—woundable—when daring to love. But to some degree Orsino's evocation of Actaeon is in bad faith. Actaeon stumbles upon Diana's bath entirely by accident. Orsino's ongoing participation in the dynamic is voluntary, even determined, though he conveniently disowns that. And to the extent that he disowns it, Orsino does not really *love*, and I daresay he does not even *love love*, so much as *he loves to see himself suffer love*. He cannot really love. His real feelings are invulnerable. When we later see the vulnerability of Viola's and Olivia's feelings, we realize the lie in Orsino's. Antonio, Andrew, and Malvolio all risk far more of their hearts than Orsino does. The reason he never listens to Olivia and often seems literally not to hear Viola is because he is impenetrable, so narcissistically involved is he with his own tragedy.

Orsino is a not exactly a Don Quixote, completely convinced by a romantic fiction of himself; it is more that he is self-consciously *playing* a Don Quixote. In 2.4, he is so obviously self-conscious of his own loverliness that he cannot truly believe it, for if he believed what he said it would be entirely redundant to affirm it:

ORSINO: For such as I am all true lovers are,
Unstaid and skittish in all motions else
Save in the constant image of the creature
That is beloved.
(2.4.17–20)

In this scene, he has grown particularly dogmatic, speaking with the kind of overconfident generalization that typically compensates a lack of understanding:

ORSINO: Let still the woman take
An elder than herself; so wears she to him,
So sways she level in her husband's heart.
(2.4.29–31)

Though he then takes a step back—Barton's directorial advice to the actor was that "you make an important admission about yourself here and you tell the truth"[43]:

For, boy, however we do praise ourselves,
Our fancies are more giddy and unfirm,
More longing wavering, sooner lost and worn
Than women's are.
(2.4.32–4)

Orsino does have "the ability, however indulgent he may be, to mock himself as a lover,"[44] at least intermittently—but he tends to return to his true north:

ORSINO: There is no woman's sides
Can bide the beating of so strong a passion
As love doth give my heart; no woman's heart
So big to hold so much—they lack retention.
                    (2.4.93–6)

These disorganized and self-contradicting maxims are often played fruitfully in performance as Orsino's way of repressing another preoccupation: his growing attraction to Cesario. This dynamic exists in subtext only, but it works. It accounts well for Orsino's apparent deafness to Viola's all-but-explicit confession of her secret love. And it offers an effective way to play the moment in which he, curiously, lacks a response to Viola's "I am all the daughters of my father's house, / And all the brothers too" (2.4.120–1). Orsino says nothing here—apparently lost in the poetry of it all, but I think *only* apparently. The text may suggest a 'beat' in which the wheels in Orsino's head turn, threatening to turn him away from his chosen narrative. Viola rescues them both from the emerging erotic anxiety by changing the subject: "Sir, shall I to this lady?" (2.4.122). He responds quickly, 'this lady' being a topic with which he is much more comfortable. They press the eject button, and the scene ends. Orsino's performance is a safe home base, a narrative in which nothing new need trouble him, and it functions to keep him safe from real spontaneous feeling.

For him, loving a woman who has locked herself away from him for seven years minimum is a perfectly safe holding pattern. Even as he performatively evokes Actaeon, he unconsciously tells the truth on another level, for 'be seen and risk dismemberment' *is* the expectation that Orsino's Actaeonic side guards against. It is out of this anxiety that he deploys a decoy in place of a real personality, and pretends to pursue an unavailable intimacy rather than engage in that which is directly in front of him.

Ko sympathetically notes that "what the Orsino-bashers do not acknowledge . . . is the absence, in this playworld, of a true alternative to what is a genuine, if hollow—and properly therefore all the more poignant—pleasure".[45] This is a key point in understanding the denizens of Illyria both as characters-in-themselves and as part-personalities of the greater psyche which 'dreams' the play. There is, at present, nothing realer in Illyria than Orsino's daily tragedy. Both he and Olivia become much more available to empathy when they are understood as the Illyrian psyche's best attempt to cure itself.

It is interesting to note one thing that is missing from this world: sex. Its absence is introduced on the 27th line, which compares Olivia to a "cloistress" (1.1.27). For a comedy, and moreover one ostensibly about carnival and revelry, it is decidedly un-bawdy, with an "unusual paucity of direct references to sex".[46] Penuel sees a "turn away from the *telos* of sexual reproduction" in this play, observing that "Viola and the Captain fantasize about her as 'an eunuch'. . . though the plan is apparently dropped, the momentary pleasure in sterility is telling."[47] Viola's cross-dressing plan is often recognized as weakly-motivated, from a character perspective—but perhaps asexuality is the unconscious point, as in the anonymous *The Maid's Metamorphosis*, written around the same time as *Twelfth Night*, in which the character Eurymine "is transformed into a boy by Apollo, at her own entreaty, to avoid the god's lustful advances."[48] Eunuchdom, hypothetically, means keeping the sexual at a safe distance. There are other signs of sexual innocence in Illyria: Andrew's apparently unfeigned obliviousness regarding "accost"ing Maria (1.3.57–77), as well as the fact that the only direct 'come ons' that we see (Olivia's of Cesario, and Malvolio's of Olivia) are treated as expressions of madness.

Orsino is not playing a eunuch, but he has found a way of creating a safe distance from immediate relationship. The fact that he does not know how to be honest about himself should not stop *us* from seeing that he is *not* actually trying to win Olivia, but is merely going through the motions. What he is 'really' doing, on a psychological level, is spiritualizing (via music) or mythologizing (via Actaeon) his bodily passion into another, less threateningly intimate, dimension. Orsino's music is a spiritualized substitution for passion and sex—this is obvious enough—but what may not be obvious is that this unconscious dynamic may be the point. It is less that he is settling for a substitute pleasure, and more that he is using it to protect himself from a more painful experience.

In the context of Shakespeare's work, this sexless land seems to express a compensation, an attempt to avoid a disgust with the body that was expressed in Hamlet—"O that this too too sallied flesh would melt". . ."get thee to a nunnery". . ."the rank sweat of an enseamed bed / Stewed in corruption, honeying and making love" (*Ham.* 1.2.129,3.1.120,3.4.90–1).[49] It is as if the play is trying to gently compensate for a pressing unconscious sexual preoccupation, by avoiding the subject; avoidance is possible because the issue does not seem to have yet reached the intensity that will call for more direct engagement, as in *Measure for Measure*.

Viola

There is a long-standing theatrical tradition of re-arranging the play's first and second scenes,[50] the temptation to begin the show with a shipwreck being, surely, difficult to resist. However, this is not what is written. Why? After all, Shakespeare is capable on his own of beginning a play with a shipwreck, and does so elsewhere.

It must have something to do with the internal logic of the scenes; with the effect that is made by moving *from* 1.1 *to* 1.2 and not the other way around. I suppose that 1.1 shows the given circumstances of Illyria: it sets the scene and states the problem. 1.2 offers a response to that problem. When they are reversed, the logic is broken—rather than beginning with a portrait of a mad land, into which then someone new arrives, we begin with a portrait of Viola, who we *then* discover to have washed up in a mad land. The order makes a significant difference to the framing of the play. I think the reversal over-foregrounds Viola, leading to an inevitable disappointment as she does not turn out to be a very active protagonist.

Viola emerges from the sea in 1.2, new and remarkably blank, as though birthed from the sea in this very moment. We never learn the nature of the sea voyage which brings her to Illyria's shores, and it does not seem to matter to this play.[51] She has no prior intention, and never grows one. In dream-logic terms, she is produced by the play as a response to what is already happening in 1.1.

Viola's appearance affords us the opportunity for a good old Jungian amplification of a symbol, namely, the violet from which her name seems to spring—'Viola' also potentially referring to the stringed instrument, which fits nicely with her ability to "sing / And speak to him in many sorts of music" (1.2.54–5). She is at times, effectively, Orsino's accompanist. Her name also evokes 'violence', though with the unpleasant sibilant sound at the end having been excised, which rather puts us in mind of her *lack* of aggressivity. Although she does have a gift for passively violating boundaries, e.g. of gender, propriety, and loyalty.

The colour violet, very appropriately, is associated by Abt with

> the original mixture of opposites . . . losing one's solid standpoint by possession. On a higher level, however, violet points . . . to a union of the opposites of male and female and to highest spirituality in life.[52]

'Cesario', of course, is the symbol uniting male and female. It is the creation of Cesario, apparently an effort to safeguard her own standpoint, that paradoxically threatens Viola with loss of it, indeed "by possession". It is not long before we start to wonder whether 'Viola' is in the driver's seat, or if 'Cesario' has taken on a life of his own.

As to the violet flower, it has already been evoked, by Orsino (1.1.6), but by us as well, as it was beheld in the twelfth Sonnet: "the violet past prime" (3), the sonnet that shares its number both with the hours in the day and the *Night* of this play. That the "forward violet" (*Son.* 99.1), for Shakespeare, is connected with time, the passing of the prime, and the transience of love is confirmed by looking backward to *Hamlet*:

LAERTES: . . . A violet in the youth of primy nature,
Forward, not permanent, sweet, not lasting,
The perfume and suppliance of a minute,
No more.
(Ham. 1.3.7–10)

As *Hamlet*, *Twelfth Night*, and the earlier *Sonnets* appear to have been written around the same time,[53] some cross-fertilization of ideas and imagery is quite appropriate.

Another appearance of the violet in *Hamlet* offers a provocative association, between daughters of a dead father. "I would give you some violets," says Ophelia, "but they withered all when my father died" (4.5.176–8). Viola's father has, of course, also departed (2.1.16–8), and is mentioned in Viola's first appearance (1.2.25), right along with the death of Olivia's father (1.2.34). There is a little more: all three women—Ophelia, Viola, Olivia—suffer not only from paternal bereavement but also from the absence of their reliable brothers. It begins to seem as though Ophelia's name unconsciously prefigures Olivia's, itself virtually an anagram of Viola's. When Laertes, at Ophelia's funeral, wishes that "from her fair and unpolluted flesh / May violets spring" (5.1.229–30), is it too much to hear, with an ear to the unconscious, a harmonic resonance—'May *Viola* spring'?[54]

Viola's past is notably irrelevant to *Twelfth Night;* though she is technically of Messaline, we don't know what Messaline is and we have no reason to care, because the *only* important thing about it seems to be that it is past, and as even more shipwreck survivors will discern in *The Tempest*, "what's past is prologue" (*Tem.* 2.1.255). Viola *begins* when she arrives in Illyria. This initial inertia continues to structure her personality, as her overriding strategy is one of receptivity (different from *passivity*, as Bloom puts it[55]): "What else may hap to time I will commit" (1.2.57), and envisioning herself "like Patience on a monument" (2.4.114).

The quick association, in Viola's first appearance, of the two thoughts: "what should I do in Illyria? / My brother he is in Elysium" (1.2.2–3) intimates that, of the twins, Sebastian has been more the doer—as if Viola's subtext here ran, 'and what should I do, given that I am without the one who always had shown me what to do?' Like Ophelia without Laertes (or Arthur without Constance for that matter), it is in Sebastian's absence that Viola is thrown upon her own resources and the question of what to do becomes pertinent.

Her decision to enter into disguise has been understood psychoanalytically as a denial of Sebastian's death, through identification with him. The Cesario disguise renders Viola identical with her brother—

VIOLA: I my brother know
Yet living in my glass . . .
For him I imitate.
       (3.4.376–80)

—"[permitting] the lost brother to return to life".[56] I'd like to go further with this. Though it is terribly un-comedic, I think we can begin to understand something about Viola if we realize her first act in the play as dissociative—fundamentally a creative denial of the trauma she has just endured. I'm not sure this means an audience should be subjected to a *Twelfth Night* that tries to stage a pseudo-psychological PTSD-drama, *but*, front-loading our understanding of Viola with this dynamic will pay dividends at the end of the play when she shows a totally unexpected and otherwise-inexplicable reluctance to come out of her disguise.

From the first, she also demonstrates a more comedy-friendly attribute: her ability to hold another person, and to be an affirming mirror herself. It is in her brief relationship with the Captain that this is first expressed:

VIOLA: There is a fair behaviour in thee, captain . . .
I will believe thou hast a mind that suits
With this thy fair and outward character.

(1.2.44–8)

I find this a remarkable thing for her to take the time to say after just surviving a shipwreck in which her twin has possibly perished, and it says something about Viola that she does so. The violet's heart-shaped leaves are humanized, via Viola, into an abiding capacity to love. Wanamaker found that "through her clarity, her simplicity, she releases [others] from self-absorption . . . by confronting them with themselves and what they are."[57] Viola would seem to be the hero that Illyria needs.

It has been said that Viola-as-Cesario's attractiveness is largely due to her androgyny,[58] and while it may be true on a surface level it is even truer in depth. To take Wheeler's point about symbolically reviving the lost brother in a more Jungian direction, her disguise could be seen as her trial-identification with the masculine (or *yang*, dynamic, creative) principle typically held by Sebastian. Their personalities seem to compensate one another, as two halves of a whole, and so in his absence, she needs to develop her personality in a new direction. The pseudonym 'Cesario' may allude to an aspiration to kinship with Julius Caesar; her fantasy about enacting her masculine side may be that, as he did, she has also come by sea to see and conquer Illyria.[59] In taking on the role of Cesario, she combines her brother's *yang*-toned dynamism and forwardness with her own *yin*-toned "receiving" (3.1.119) or yielding quality.[60] This is the recipe for the 'special something' that makes everybody fall in love with her. We see the effects of her holding capacity in 1.4, when it is said to Viola that Orsino "hath known you but three days, and already you are no stranger" (1.4.2–4); Orsino confirms it shortly after:

ORSINO: Cesario,
Thou knowst no less but all: I have unclasped
To thee the book even of my secret soul.

(1.4.12–4)

Olivia speaks to it as well:

OLIVIA: To one of your receiving,
Enough is shown: a cypress, not a bosom,
Hides my heart.

(3.1.119–21)

Viola also expresses genuine feeling to Olivia that no man in the play seems capable of:

VIOLA: Make me a willow cabin at your gate
And call upon my soul within the house;
Write loyal cantons of contemned love
And sing them loud even in the dead of night;
Hallow your name to the reverberate hills
And make the babbling gossip of the air
Cry out 'Olivia!' O, you should not rest
Between the elements of air and earth
But you should pity me.

(1.5.260–8)

The semi-sapphic *amor* aroused here is enough to make even the most sophisticated man feel like a neanderthal with a club.

Being self-less to a fault is her way. Belsey observes that "Viola occupies a whole range of subject positions in rapid succession", a malleability which allows her to be constituted "an object of desire".[61] This again may remind us of her predecessor Ophelia, whose name has etymologically to do with service and help, and who is envisioned at her funeral as "A ministering angel" (*Ham.* 5.1.231). Viola ministers to the unmet emotional needs of those she encounters.

And yet at the same time that she expresses so much *yin*, Viola-Cesario is also abrupt and impatient with Olivia; she pays Olivia's grief exactly as much respect is due, and no more. Cesario does not humour the Countess' coy games, but speaks to her with a "saucy" frankness that none of the 'real' men can manage, telling her, woman-to-woman, "The rudeness that hath appeared in me have I learned from my entertainment"; "I see you what you are, you are too proud"; "I am no fee'd post, lady" (1.5.192;208;242;276). This offends Olivia at a persona level, but on a deeper level it properly mirrors her, reflecting back to her the true effect of her behaviour much more clearly than the toadying of Orsino, Malvolio, or Andrew can ever do. Viola can listen and relate to Olivia, creatively and playfully, and combines this ability with a willingness to be contrary. Being received and reacted to in a more genuine way allows Olivia herself to feel more present and real. And thus Viola begins, accidentally, to seduce her. As a counterpoint, compare Orsino's weird fetishizing of Olivia's grief:

ORSINO: O, she that hath a heart of that fine frame
To pay this debt of love but to a brother,
How will she love when the rich golden shaft
Hath killed the flock of all affections else
That live in her[.]

(1.1.32–6)

Orsino sees what he wants to see; Viola sees what's there. Olivia seems to need her wilfulness opposed, a dynamic which was stretched to absurdity in *The Taming of the Shrew.* Despite instructing Cesario to "Be clamorous and leap all civil bounds" (1.4.21) on his behalf, Orsino doesn't have the hutzpah for that himself.

It is surely obvious why Olivia loves the servant and not the master. What Olivia sees in Cesario is "a proper man" (3.1.132), i.e., 'unlike the rest around'—one who can wield both masculine and feminine energies together—"who can sing both high and low" (2.3.40)—an active receptivity. *Yin-yang.*

An emphasis on the polarity of *yang*/masculine/creating/doing versus *yin*/feminine/receiving/being allows us to consider Illyria's illness in terms of its masculine-feminine balance: the relationship between what you *will* and what you *are.* Consider, for a moment, the dominant state of Illyrian masculinity: Orsino? Histrionic. Malvolio? Narcissistic. Sir Toby? Cynical. Sir Andrew? Milquetoast. Feste? Alienated. Fabian: Who?

These men do not have it together, and they really seem to have nothing to do but occupy themselves with different versions of frivolity, in the destructive kind of ill-leisure captured so well in the plays of Anton Chekhov.[62] In Illyria *nobody* seems to have anything real to do. As it is a comedy, we don't really mind, but Illyria's phallic principle has become silly and flaccid. Returning to the term *histrionic,* recall its tendency to be concretized as a 'female' disorder; what would serve much better psychologically would be to transform our understanding of this syndrome of falseness into a disorder of the *feminine principle.* In Illyria, the balance is totally out of whack.

Viola's disguise as Cesario allows her to straddle the centre of this imbalance. Cesario can remain aloof; he can find employment and get close to both pillars of Illyrian society, without implicating Viola; he can be whatever the other seems to need in the moment, and he can cross the boundaries with little personal vulnerability. But tricksters fall victim to their own tricksterdom sooner or later, and for Viola it is sooner, because before the end of the first act Cesario's aloofness is undone by Viola's involvedness, as she has fallen in love with Orsino herself.

In terms of her integration of masculine and feminine, *yang* and *yin, doing* and *being,* what Viola *does* is get herself into a situation in which she cannot *do* anything, and most decidedly cannot *be* herself. Wanamaker: "The character who has released others from self-absorption finds herself imprisoned."[63] The symbol *par excellence* here may be the one her own psyche earlier supplied: the eunuch Cesario, a castrated masculine principle. She loves Orsino, but has acted herself into a role from which she cannot escape; she wants to serve Olivia, but lacks—a rather important piece, from Olivia's perspective. Soon she relinquishes her agency entirely, once again identifying with Patience: "O time, thou must untangle this, not I. / It is too hard a knot for me t'untie" (2.2.39–40).

Viola is unique among Shakespeare's disguised characters in that, more than any other, she seems hardly able to keep herself in. She has barely met Olivia when she begins to drop hints: "I am not that I play" (1.5.181). Not long afterward she is doing the same with Orsino:

ORSINO: . . . thine eye
Hath stayed upon some favour that it loves.
Hath it not, boy?
VIOLA: A little, by your favour.
ORSINO: What kind of woman is't?
VIOLA: Of your complexion.
ORSINO: She is not worth thee then. What years, i'faith?
VIOLA: About your years, my lord.

(2.4.23–8)

And if that did not suffice to make us suspect that Viola unconsciously wants to be caught out, she soon muses:

VIOLA: My father had a daughter loved a man,
As it might be, perhaps, were I a woman,
I should your lordship.

(2.4.106–8)

Followed up by the barely cryptic admission, which Orsino characteristically does not seem to listen to:

VIOLA: I am all the daughters of my father's house,
And all the brothers too[.]

(2.4.120–1)

We know that Viola is *troubled* by the success of her disguise with Olivia (2.2.27), but unconsciously she seems to be trying to arrange for 'Cesario' to be seen-through and dissolved by Orsino—perhaps she wants the same mirroring, no-B.S. combination of receptive and penetrative sight with which she herself unintentionally wins Olivia's heart. She wants to be seen as a woman, but has made this temporarily impossible. Her disguise has led her to suffer from the performer's curse: to be constantly looked at without being seen.

Olivia

Alas, poor Olivia: father and brother dead, left alone among the morons. Pursued by Orsino, Andrew Aguecheek, and surely on some level aware of Malvolio's fantasies about her . . . What recourse has she got?

VALENTINE: The element itself till seven years' heat
Shall not behold her face at ample view,

But like a cloistress she will veiled walk
And water once a day her chamber round
With eye-offending brine[.]

(1.1.25–9)

Given the circumstances, her otherwise-absurd seven-year moratorium on regular life is strategically intelligible. Her mourning is a vale of refuge, a container for a self-imposed latency period[64] in which she can come to inhabit her new circumstances as heiress to the family's estate. Elam notes that she is "traditionally conceived as a gracefully mature figure . . . even though the text hardly justifies this".[65] To me she seems young, an immensely eligible bachelorette trying to survive in a land of madmen. To this point, it may be seen that she is also, in her way, attempting to hold a profoundly feminine pole. The weight of her grief is determined to assert its place, its right to *be*. She cites the inescapable reality of the female body when she warns Cesario that "'Tis not that time of moon with me to make one in so skipping a dialogue" (1.5.197), wielding the feminine weight of non-negotiable feeling. And while the other characters may view her grief as unseemly, and we may reductively view it as a histrionic overcorrection, in a *holistic* view of the entire Illyrian situation we can see that it is also intended to be precisely the medicine needed.

The choice of *seven* years, a common fairytale motif,[66] is symbolically intelligible through its association with initiation: seven are the days of the week, and the natural notes of the Western scale—after seven, we are back to where we started, but on a different level. Her bereavements have initiated her into adulthood, and the seven alludes to the time required to mature into this. As a prime number, seven is also "considered unique and independent, a sort of 'virgin number',"[67] relating to her need to preserve herself—her seal-ring is Lucrece (2.5.92)—and safeguard her sacred precinct, a Diana expressing the other end of Orsino's overwrought Actaeon narrative. In the *I Ching*, the seventh hexagram (師, *Shī*) has to do with the discipline required for transformation: The Army. "The army needs perseverance / And a strong man."[68] In Olivia's case, the strong men—brother and father—are gone and it is to her that the responsibility and authority to create order fall.

Being compensatory to the collective, however, her stance has its performative dimension. Her accusation that Viola's speech, being poetical, "is the more like to be feigned" (1.5.191) is both to-the-point and a little *hypokrit*-ical. Viola and Olivia's exchanges are rife with questions of feigning, reality, and unreality, and perhaps it is of note that it is Olivia's *face* which Valentine reports shall not be beheld for seven years (1.1.26), meaning she will for this time reside behind a false face—a mask, or a veil. When she does reveal the face behind the veil— "we will draw the curtain and show you the picture" (1.5.226–7)—this constitutes an Orsinian double-performance of her own, for her theatricality seems ironical, even a little camp. She performs as one who has been admired for her beauty so frequently that it has become blasé. Her hiding from "the element itself" (the sun; 1.1.25) may be an overdone way of removing herself from the spotlight of the constant admiring-lecherous male gaze, her own personal version of the audience's burning glare. She seems accustomed to being objectified, and in a charming identification-with-the-aggressor-sorta way, pre-empts this with Cesario by doing it to herself:

VIOLA: 'Tis beauty truly blent, whose red and white
Nature's own sweet and cunning hand laid on.
Lady, you are the cruell'st she alive
If you will lead these graces to the grave
And leave the world no copy.
OLIVIA: O sir, I will not be so hard-hearted. I will give out diverse schedules of my beauty. It shall be inventoried, and every particle and utensil labelled to my will, as, item, two lips, indifferent red; item, two grey eyes, with lids to them; item, one neck, one chin and so forth.

(1.5.231–40)

One might add Orsino's checklist: her "liver, brain and heart" (1.1.36).[69]

In a way, it is a typical histrionic 'move': to refuse one part only to play another, and mistake control over one's presentation for authenticity. Earlier, Olivia has coyly replied to Viola's "are you the lady of the house?" with "if I do not usurp myself, I am" (1.5.181–3). The fatal *if*—she *has* usurped herself, if we take that phrase to mean to supplant something legitimate with something false. But I am not sure that Olivia has had much choice in her life about this, being so admired, and thereby cast into a role, by all those around her. This mourning self-performance, though it may be false, is understandable as her first creative attempt at defining her persona independently.

Recognizing Cesario's capacity for accurate mirroring, as well as her own need for it, Olivia asks for it—which leads them into a game of 'chicken' around the very concept of being:

OLIVIA: I prithee tell me what thou think'st of me.
VIOLA: That you do think you are not what you are.
OLIVIA: If I think so, I think the same of you.
VIOLA: Then think you right: I am not what I am.
OLIVIA: I would you were as I would have you be.
VIOLA: Would it be better, madam, than I am?

(3.1.138–43)

Twelfth Night is a play in which nobody can stop acting no matter how they try, like the man in the tale who, attempting to avoid Death, delivers himself to Death's appointment right on time.[70] Yet so many in Illyria hunger for someone else to help them be real. If we can continue to see Olivia's overdone mourning as a necessary compensation on the level of the entire play—as an attempt, however theatrical in itself, to bring something gravid and real to the Illyrian psychological system—then we can further our understanding of what is going on in the histrionic substructure of this play.

At some point, however, what Riemann characterizes as the essence of the histrionic pattern—the fearful avoidance of necessity—comes home to roost, and obsession with the unnecessary must *end*. This point is the twelfth night of the carnival. Olivia unconsciously tries to fulfill this, but does not pierce through to reality; she laments the situation without actually *feeling* its hopeless weight. As in *Richard II*—

KING RICHARD: . . . my grief lies all within;
And these external manners of lament
Are merely shadows to the unseen grief
That swells with silence in the tortured soul:
There lies the substance.
$$(RII\ 4.1.295–9)$$

—she puts on the funereal trappings without truly mourning. This is an alternative to Viola's inner denial of her brother's death. And it has another Shakespearean analogy, in those Sonnets which seem all-too-eager to jump the life to come, rendering the poet already aged and dying while still young (*Son.* 22, 32, 37, 62, 63, 71, 72, 73, 74, 81, & 91[71])—perhaps, on some level, another typically histrionic counterphobic tendency.

Sebastian & Antonio

With the entrance of Sebastian, the plot thickens. His attitude is experience-forward, and he doesn't seem to have any interest in the complications that result from performance and intrigue. He acts quickly, decisively, and impulsively. He avoids a too-quick enmeshment with Antonio. He and his sister had similar impulses towards disguising themselves ("my name is Sebastian, which I called Roderigo", 2.1.15–6) but he relinquishes his straightaway. We feel that, with him, things are about to get real.

His trusting relationship with the flow of experience, however, makes him an easy mark for the Illyrian performance-complex in another way. It is his particular charm as a character that he is entirely willing to say 'yes' to what he encounters. (Viola, by contrast, seems unwilling to say 'no'.) Sebastian reacts. He will draw first and ask questions later; he will even marry first and ask questions later.[72] Thank goodness he is honest, for despite his being sucked into the centrifuge, his genuineness—not *time*, as Viola hoped—is what allows the plot knot to eventually begin to untie.

His name is probably a reference to Saint Sebastian, the Roman Soldier who is thought to have signed up for the army as a kind of double-agent himself, a secret Christian hoping to protect other Christians who were suffering persecution. This Sebastian's true intent was discovered, and he was tied to a stake to be shot at by archers. Afterward, riddled with arrows, he was assumed to be dead. But he recovered, and was nursed back to health. Saint Sebastian, not one to play it safe, sought out the emperor and publicly harangued him, a protest which did indeed cost him his life this time. An excellent inner guide for our own Sebastian, the Saint is patron of soldiers, athletes, and, perversely, archers.[73]

Sebastian is joined by Antonio, who I have always found to be a transparent dramatic device. He seems mainly to exist so that Sebastian has someone to have scenes with, and he spends half his time explaining why he's still onstage. As if alluding to his out-of-placeness, Antonio even hales from a third and unknown land, neither Illyrian nor Messalinean. But I have come to see that he carries a thematic importance which his dramatic insignificance belies, because it is his relationship with Sebastian that expresses, in its most clear form, the play's ambivalent dynamic of enmeshment countered with detachment; namely, Antonio's desperate clinginess is countered by Sebastian's oddly polite aloofness. Possibly Sebastian is avoiding not wanting to continue a relationship with a lower-class seaman, but just as possibly he is trying to put off Antonio's seeming-homoerotic longing.[74] His overdeliberate elocution—"My determinate voyage is mere extravagancy . . . it charges me in manners the rather to express myself" (2.1.10–4)—could go either way. But as Penuel observes, his reluctance to be caught up with Antonio is compensated elsewhere by an eagerness to "meld with others",[75] namely Viola and Olivia. Antonio's unique contribution is that he expresses the only unambivalent eros in the play.

Significantly, Antonio also introduces something to *Twelfth Night* that is not-yet-seen, which is the possibility of direct aggression and danger:

ANTONIO: I have many enemies in Orsino's court,
Else would I very shortly see thee there.
But come what may I do adore thee so
That danger shall seem sport, and I will go.

(2.1.40–5)

Prior to this, it might not have seemed possible that Orsino had any enemies, save for his beloved. Antonio must have an edge to him, for Sebastian later guesses at his offence to Orsino: "Belike you slew great number of his people?" (3.3.29). Antonio gives us a hint of what is to come in the dynamics of the play: the carnival, increasingly desperate as it spins closer to its close, begins to lash out.

Toby & Andrew

The underlying carnival myth-form in *Twelfth Night* has been explored, most notably by Barber,[76] but what seems to me to have been overlooked is that this myth-form is significantly *incomplete*. Incomplete because distorted; incomplete because Illyria is a post-carnival world, secular and desacralized; as in *King John,* the old structures of myth are no longer adequate containers for human experience. Incomplete because, at the last moment the carnival fails to achieve—or even move toward—redemption, and so it regresses instead to a more archaic scapegoat ritual form.

We are led in this plotline by Toby Belch. To Be Belched. 'To be—*[belch]*—or not to be'—Hamlet *via* Barney Gumble.[77] His first name suggests that he is what remains of one of the most remarkable questions ever uttered—'to be' without the 'or not'—so a devotion to immediate experience with the doubt, or reflection, having been excised. He is indeed a sort of champion of *being*, but in a negative and uncultivated sense. Olivia sees him as an

OLIVIA: Ungracious wretch,
Fit for the mountains and the barbarous caves,
Where manners ne'er were preached.
                              (4.1.46–8)

And it is true; in his way he is natural man, the thing itself. And it is also true that Illyria needs such a man, exactly as it needs Sebastian, because the illusive needs grounding in the real, and these two men together bring a concentrated focus on realness, at least in terms of what is immediately experienceable. Sebastian's beautiful openness to the flow of events is anticipated, in a darker tone, in Belch's first line: "I am sure care's an enemy to life" (1.3.2). This line introduces Belch's attitude, though it is not precisely true that he cares for nothing. Rather, his care is shadowed, and comes out antagonistically; he is an *enfant terrible* who cares only for proving his superiority over those who care.

As for his last name, it a prefiguration of "the belching whale" (*TC* 5.5.23) to which Hector is compared as he slays Greeks by the score in *Troilus and Cressida*. *Pericles* will speak of "the belching whale" (*Per.* 3.1.62) as well, who

1 FISHERMAN: . . . plays and tumbles, driving the poor fry before him, and at last devours them all at a mouthful. Such whales have I heard on o'th' land, who never leave gaping till they swallowed the whole parish, church, steeple, bells and all.
                              (*Per.* 2.1.30–4)

And of course the belch figures into Emilia's grim insight on the eve of Desdemona's death:[78]

EMILIA: [Men] are all but stomachs, and we all but food;
They eat us hungerly, and when they are full
They belch us.
                              (*Oth.* 3.4.105–7)

To be belched is not a nice thing, and Toby Belch is not a nice man. He is a whale o'th' land, a stomach-man.

And, he is old. Although that depends on how literally one takes Andrew's reference to an "old man" (1.3.114). If he is young, his puerility is more appropriate, perhaps even a sign of vitality. But if he is old, then it is all the sadder for him, for he is carrying on behaviour which he ought to have outgrown.

He is oft compared to *Henry IV*'s Sir John Falstaff, with good reason, since they are both Lords of Misrule, opportunists, parasites, scammers and thieves—and perhaps also both aging out. At times, Belch seems to speak with some of the love of life that Falstaff does:

TOBY: Wherefore are these things hid? Wherefore have these gifts a curtain before 'em? . . . Why dost thou not go to church in a galliard and come home in a coranto? My very walk should be a jig . . . Is it a world to hide virtues in?

(1.3.124–30)

But this is cynical, for it is designed to manipulate Andrew and wheedle more money out of him. Toby lacks something of Falstaff's vitality and earnestness, substituting nothing but hot air, that is, belch. Falstaff has something approaching a coherent philosophy; at times he seems to be an enlightened epicurean. Toby, not so much. One key difference might be that Falstaff has someone higher-status to orient him towards the better angels of his own nature. Through Prince Hal, psychologically speaking, he is in service to a higher principle; always challenged, often bested, he is kept constantly in mind of who the boss is. Belch recognizes no authority. He does not accept Olivia as the leader of the 'Army'—as in Hexagram 7, where the third line "points to defeat because someone other than the chosen leader interferes with the command . . . if the multitude assumes leadership . . . misfortune will ensue."[79] Belch might be what happens to a Falstaff untethered,[80] or perhaps he is simply Falstaff without his good heart.

His function in the play, however, is quite indispensable. He is a drug-sniffing dog for pretension, and instinctively disrespects it. He rebels against Olivia's imposition of decorum ("What a plague means my niece to take the death of her brother thus?" 1.3.1–2), knowing it to be inimical to life. His primary target, Malvolio, is of course a lord of pretense, and demands to be brought to heel. He is cold-blooded in his treatment of Sir Andrew, another *poseur,* having bought his knighthood (3.4.229–30). Seeing Andrew—the poor fry to his whale—as unworthy of consideration, Belch nonchalantly uses him for entertainment and drains him of every penny in the process. Belch-Andrew anticipates *Othello*'s Iago-Roderigo in this way, and both manipulators leave their doubtful gulls with nothing by the end.

Andrew Aguecheek carries forth a little of the 'Prince Arthur' complex in *Twelfth Night*, both of them being put up to heroic quests for which they are not particularly well-suited nor interested. To his credit, he *almost* becomes aware that he is the butt of a joke. He sees that there is no hope in his courtship of Olivia, and tries to depart in 3.2. But he has no spine, and no strength to his convictions. He seems only to echo others, "magpie-like, [purloining] impressive words"[81]—like his borrowed knighthood, imitation is his best attempt at life. It is sad to think of him leaving Illyria in the end. Does he have a world elsewhere? It feels like Toby is his only friend, and this friend is cannibalizing him. One of the most poignant moments in the play belongs to him: "I was adored once too" (2.3.176)—which nobody cares to respond to. Dare I say—nobody cares about Andrew. Toby treats him as past contempt, and doesn't quibble for a moment about using him.

For Toby, Andrew *is* small fry. It is the conflict with Malvolio that provides him with an opportunity to discharge his tremendous reserve of hostility, and which thereby obtains most of his focus. It is here that the Carnival myth-form comes into play. Carnival is implicitly referenced in the title *Twelfth Night*, though it is not intuitive today to associate Christmas with extensive communal festivity. But as Barber writes,

> "Merry England" was merry chiefly by virtue of its community observances of periodic sports and feast days. Mirth took form in morris-dances, sword-dances, wassailings, mock ceremonies of summer kings and queens and of lords of misrule, mummings, disguisings, masques—and a bewildering variety of sports, games, shows, and pageants improvised on traditional models . . . Custom prescribed, more or less definitely, some ways of making merry at each occasion.[82]

An inventory of *Twelfth Night* confirms the presence of four elements of the carnival in particular (as described by Stewart):

> [1] disguises or masks which suggest some kind of metamorphosis (for example, men dressed as women or clowns in painted faces), [2] a reign of confusion where boisterous anarchy appears to prevail, [3] contests or attacks, and [4] ritual execution (of *pharmakoi* [scapegoat] or of King Carnival).[83]

Christmas Carnival, in an 'ideal' form, involves a communal purging of the shadow; a time when work enters a lull, and the inhibitory forces which hold people in check the rest of the year are relaxed, not for the purposes of anarchy but as a ritualistic expulsion of the repressed energy which has naturally built up. Games, the unbinding of social ties, and "reversal of the hierarchic order"[84] are all part of the trickster method of healing that is intended here. In contrast, what happens in *Twelfth Night* is that the ritualistic execution/expulsion is concretized; the lack of reality in Illyria continually demands compensation, and in response this exercise becomes all *too* real. And since Malvolio is not in on the game, he is wholly pushed into identification with the shadow and scapegoated.

Belch is *Twelfth Night*'s Lord of Misrule—until he abdicates to Feste (4.2.79)—and the Carnival King is Malvolio, though he does not know it.

The 17th century Puritan battle over Christmas finds expression in the Belch-Malvolio opposition, expressed compactly in Belch's line, "Dost thou think because thou art virtuous there shall be no more cakes and ale?" (2.3.112–3). Malvolio is identified as a Puritan (2.3.136), and since part of the carnival-myth's derangement in this play is its secularity, the fact that it is directed against an apparent representative of religious scrupulosity is significant. However, whether Malvolio's supposed puritanism is yet another façade is up for debate (2.3.142);[85] "Sick of self-love" (1.5.86) is indeed an apt descriptor of him, and this does not a proper religious attitude make. And so when I call Illyria a post-carnival world, it is because it is one in which carnival is no longer possible as such, because God seems to have already died.

Maria Columbina

Twelfth Night has a somewhat rare female trickster in Maria, who perhaps takes inspiration from the *commedia dell'arte*'s Columbina: the tricky female servant who tends to be the sole intelligence among the bunch of *zanni*.[86] Though uncommon in myth, a female with trickster qualities is quite common to Shakespeare.[87]

The RSC's 2005 production of *Twelfth Night* touched into the potential symbolic doubleness in Maria's name—not explicitly—by allowing her to be both Mother Mary and Maria Magdalena. Feste's attraction to her (supported in the text by 1.5.24–6) was as toward a comforting mother figure, but Toby recognized her flesh-and-bloodness. Naturally Toby gets the girl in the end, leaving Feste alone with his ideal.

In *Twelfth Night*, one might assume the most active representative of the trickster to be Feste, but I do not think that is so; though he obviously is involved with trickster energies in his wordplay, and his vaudeville double-act in 4.2, his fundamental presence is not effectual enough. Maria has weight and heat; Feste skims along the surface, and in terms of having a personality, he generally seems to be nursing the embers of a former fire.

Archetypally, the trickster is a personification of a chaotic and irrational aspect of the psychological process. She can rarely predict the consequences of her actions. She can only throw a monkey-wrench into the works, causing a shutdown and halt, perhaps a breakdown—but foresight is not her prerogative. Her interruptions, however, constitute a completely necessary psychological function. A trickster attitude is often the *only* thing which can pierce through a reified order, whether that be a social order or an individual person's way of being.

In contrast with Feste's sad irrelevance, Maria impersonates Olivia in writing to great effect, leading Malvolio subtly but surely into his own destruction. The most successful tricksters in Shakespeare get their target to do the work of tricking themselves; as con men (or women) they make their mark think the idea is their own.[88] Through a push and pull of hinting and withholding, the gull begins to do the work himself. So Malvolio:

MALVOLIO: [W]hat should that alphabetical position portend? If I could make that resemble something in me! Softly—[*reading*] *M.O.A.I.* . . .'M.' Malvolio. 'M'— why, that begins my name! . . .'M.' But then there is no consonancy in the sequel.

That suffers under probation: 'A' should follow, but 'O' does. . . . And then 'I' comes behind. . . . *M. O. A. I.* This simulation is not as the former. And yet to crush this a little it would bow to me, for every one of these letters are in my name.

(2.5.116–38)

The duet between Malvolio and his letter is, in this way, very much like the temptation scene in *Othello*, in which Othello begins to solicit, and then even demand his own poison from Iago:

OTHELLO: By heaven, thou echo'st me
As if there were some monster in thy thought
Too hideous to by shown. Thou dost mean something,
I heard thee say even now thou lik'st not that
When Cassio left my wife: what didst not like?
And when I told thee he was of my counsel
In my whole course of wooing, thou criedst 'Indeed?'
And didst contract and purse thy brow together
As if thou then hadst shut up in thy brain
Some horrible conceit. If thou dost love me
Show me thy thought.

(3.3.109–18)

Thus do these tricksters use the power of silence, the unspoken, the *lacunae* in their plans to encourage the gull to participate by filling in these gaps with their own fantasies, which are far more convincing than any concretely delivered suggestion could ever be.

The trickster, sooner or later, always gets burnt by her own trickery. In *Twelfth Night* Maria appears to be rewarded by her marriage to Sir Toby—as far as what she can look forward to as his wife, I think the joke is indeed on her.

Malvolio

There is, throughout Shakespeare's works, a recurring cluster of associated images—a complex-indicator.[89] Spurgeon called it the "dogs, licking, candy, melting" cluster:

Now whenever the idea, which affects him emotionally, of false friends or flatterers occurs, we find a rather curious set of images which play round it. These are: a dog or spaniel, fawning and licking; candy, sugar or sweets, thawing or melting. So strong is the association of these ideas in Shakespeare's mind that it does not matter which of these items he starts with—dog or sugar or melting—it almost invariably, when used in this particular application, gives rise to the whole series.[90]

For example:

CAESAR: Be not fond
To think that Caesar bears such rebel blood
That will be *thawed* from the true quality
With that which *melteth* fools—I mean *sweet* words,
Low-crooked curtsies and base *spaniel fawning.*
                              (*JC* 3.1.39–43)

Spurgeon's interpretation was that the cluster spoke to Shakespeare's "bitterest and deepest indignation [toward] feigned affection assumed for a selfish end" as he had experienced in *others*; Skura, on the other hand, feels it to be more personal, revelatory of "his *own* conflicted desire to flatter the Other, and it might suggest how central that desire was in producing his sense of himself."[91] It may as well be both: we tend to hate that in others which we cannot stand in ourselves. And though this image-cluster does not appear in *Twelfth Night*, it may yet provide us some insight into the author's relationship with Malvolio, who is a dark reflection of the ambitious flatterer's most cynical and opportunistic qualities.

The name clearly suggests 'malevolence', and breaks down etymologically into *mal* + *volio*: 'the evil I want'. 'What he wills' is bad, and his name is usually translated more prosaically to 'ill will', perhaps another submerged pun on his author's name. He is, imaginatively, Bad Will: a shadow quality with which Will himself seemed to grow increasingly irritated. We might consider two later plays to be the most developed expressions of this conflict: *Timon of Athens* relates to the tragedy of the one whose position relies on having ingratiated himself through sweetness, whereas *Coriolanus* relates to the enantiodromia, the compensatory counter-impulse to have a singularly unadapting persona—to compulsively and constantly tell everyone else to go screw themselves—essentially Malvolio's fantasy (2.5.32–78).

Malvolio's ill will is his vulgar ambition, his desire for status. His sweetness—such as it is—is manufactured as a tool of this ambition. Prior to reading the letter, his anality is obviously irritating, but tolerable. Once he has donned his yellow, however, he becomes most unnatural and disturbing.

I recall a Canadian politician whose dour and combative persona as Leader of the Opposition was relatively successful. Leading up to an election, however, he seemed to have been told by a focus group that his party would garner more votes if he would only cheer up, and he began to force a patently false smile. Another politician might have made this work—he could not. He may as well have put on cross-garters and yellow stockings, because this attempt to be 'what people wanted' was entirely self-defeating. We can accept, abstractly, that a politician is an actor—a *persona* animated by a *hypokrit*—but we do not like to have to confront this too directly. We do not like the lack of integrity that this willingness to perform seems to reveal; in Malvolio's case, he is already bad enough without then also betraying *himself.*

'Bad Will' may constitute an artistically sublimated self-punishment. Both Will and his father John had upward ambitions, attempting to secure gentlemanly status for the family. John failed, and Will achieved rather equivocal results: though he was able to gain his family a coat of arms, its legitimacy was later to be seriously challenged.[92] In Jonson's *Every Man Out of His Humour*—a play to which *Twelfth Night* is a seemingly involved response—Shakespeare's rather defensive new family motto for his yellow coat of arms—'Not Without Right'—is lampooned by a similarly yellow coat, and the motto 'Not Without Mustard'.[93]

Malvolio is also reflective of the Poet of the Sonnets, who himself loves—though he does not dare aspire to *possessing*—a young beauty beyond his station. Malvolio does dare to aspire to the object of his desire, a deeply relatable though fatal error.

Malvolio's place in the Carnival myth is the Carnival King—the fool who is king for a day before being ritually executed.[94] However, in the ideal, this ritual would be contained by a spirit of togetherness. For the Russian philosopher and critic Mikhail Bakhtin, carnival was above all communal; ridicule can be renewing, when it is impersonal: "carnival brings together, unites, weds, and combines the sacred with the profane, the lofty with the lowly, the great with the insignificant, the wise with the stupid, etc."[95] It brings down in order to bring together, and separates in order to integrate. "Whatever is mocked or seemingly destroyed is simultaneously being prepared for renewal and rebirth".[96] The laughter of Carnival, too, is impersonal—

> directed to the highest ideals of a community, rather than to the comical event itself . . . The laughter of carnival celebration counteracts . . . that human seriousness which perceives reality not as it reveals itself, but as it conforms to predetermined ideals.[97]

Carnival, a ritual evolved to break down reified ideals, is in *Twelfth Night* itself an ideal corrupted by the individuals who champion it. Though on some level it is embedded in a collective conflict between Puritanism and Epicureanism—virtue versus cakes-and-ale—it is not a collectively-undertaken ritual. Malvolio *presumes* to individually stand for collective morality, appropriating Puritanism to aggrandize himself, and his inflation asks to be punctured. Toby et al take it upon themselves to do the puncturing, but there is again nothing impersonal about it. They hate him.

Olivia's household is the site of this polarization. Psychologically considered, perhaps this is a consequence of the deaths of her father and brother. In the aftermath of the death of the central masculine principle, chaos ensues; in the power vacuum, tribalism springs up. Sebastian may believe that Olivia can

SEBASTIAN: . . . sway her house, command her followers,
Take and give back affairs and their dispatch
With such a smooth, discreet, and stable bearing . . .
(4.3.17–9)

but he is apparently projecting his own ideal, since this is clearly not true—she does not seem yet to have developed the authority to run a tight ship. In Olivia's household, there prevails a schism in the sense of community, and "where a culture loses sight of the bonds of community, the external gestures of carnival move toward the banality of a mere holiday or the desperate hilarity of alienated individuals".[98]

Malvolio is unwittingly crowned king for a day, by the letter which allows him to believe he is soon to be Count—and the psychological effect is that he becomes inflated. A hundred and one solutions have been proposed to the riddling "M.O.A.I. doth sway my life (2.5.106),[99] and while I think the best solution is that it is nonsense inserted by Maria to toy with him, I think the second best solution is that it is a parody of the tetragrammaton,[100] the four letters which are said to portend the true name of God—Y.H.W.H—in this formulation, Malvolio's crushing of the "alphabetical position" (2.5.117) into meaning discovers not the name of God but the name of himself: Malvolio's inflation is not only Countly but Godly.

Whatever crown he thinks he is given proves to be made of thorns, for he is subsequently locked in the dark room and abused as a madman. He is neither prepared for this ritual humbling, nor do his enemies afterward offer a good-faith olive-branch to allow him the possibility of reintegration, and so his gulling is never really redeemed, and the archetypal function of the carnival ritual goes unconsummated.

In the dark room is where it goes wrong. The hinge in this arc of the play seems to me to be Toby's line,

SIR TOBY: I would we were well rid of this knavery. If he may be conveniently delivered, I would he were, for I am now so far in offence with my niece that I cannot pursue with any safety this sport to the upshot. Come by and by to my chamber. *Exit [with Maria].*

(4.2.66–70)

Not that we should expect anything else from Sir Toby at this point—he is true to form—but it is disgraceful that he and Maria should wash their hands of this mess that is entirely of their own creation the moment it becomes inconvenient to them. It is like King John handing the reins to the Bastard at the moment of greatest crisis—except with the significant difference that the Bastard, at least, is the *right* person to be in charge. The same cannot be said of Feste. The failure of Toby and Maria to see their device through is the seed of the disaster which comes of it—a disaster which, mind you, they also conveniently miss out on, having gone offstage to marry each other.

Fabian acts as responsible apologist in the end, and makes a gesture in a redemptive direction, confessing "most freely" to the "device", and hoping that the "sportful malice" with which it was done

FABIAN: May rather pluck on laughter than revenge,
If that the injuries be justly weighed
That have on both sides passed.

(5.1.354–64)

He does seem to aim here toward reconciliation. But whether Malvolio might have accepted his just deserts at this point is a purely hypothetical fantasy, because Feste cannot resist rubbing it in. He feeds Malvolio's earlier words back to him (1.5.79–80; 5.1.368–9), and where remorse (or at least a desire to cease hostilities) can be felt in Fabian's lines, I am not sure any can be perceived in Feste's coldly triumphal "And thus the whirligig of time brings in his revenges" (5.1.371–2).

Bakhtin writes that "the people's ambivalent laughter . . . expresses the point of view of the whole world; he who is laughing also belongs to it".[101] Feste's laughter at the moment of Malvolio's degradation is challenging to characterize, and is to a great extent up to the play's production. On one hand, it is possible to interpret the line as expressing "the point of view of the whole world"—Feste's evocation of the whirligig of time may well be one of these Views—the expansive, objective statements of what has happened, like the Bastard's "heaven itself doth frown upon the land" (*KJ* 4.3.159). But I find it inflated—is it really psychologically honest for the perpetrators of notorious abuse to cast themselves as simple agents of time's whirligig? Does this not rather evoke *Julius Caesar*'s Cassius, in its disavowal of the intense personal animosity with which the assassination has been conducted? Feste, at this moment, is more like Bakhtin's "satirist whose laughter is negative", who "places himself *above* the object of his mockery . . . The wholeness of the world's comic aspect is destroyed, and that which appears comic becomes a private reaction."[102]

A shift throughout the centuries towards Malvolio being visible in the 'dark room' scene (as opposed to hidden and only heard) has also meant a shift toward "sympathy for his plight, and, inevitably, somewhat away from Feste's comedy".[103] The way these moments are staged and interpreted by the actors has a tremendous effect on what the play ultimately expresses:

> . . . the purpose of making Malvolio visible has often been to develop the play's darker tones. Malvolio out of sight may be easier to laugh at; certainly it gives Feste the stage. The balance between festive foolery or disturbing cruelty will vary from production to production and decade to decade, but the increased prominence of Malvolio, even if he is played mainly for comedy, will be a dramaturgical factor in all productions in which he can be seen. This will have a bearing on the weight given to Fabian's appeal for acquittal for all and on Feste's comments about the revenges brought in by the "whirligig of time" (5.1.375).[104]

Feste here assumes an archetypal pose of the Summer Lord, "a necessary scourge of the overprecise and a figure of restorative and socially cohesive festivity",[105] and whether that *fits* what has happened is up to the production. If an individual production of the play minimizes Malvolio in 4.2 and allows Feste to get away with his tricks without begriming himself, Malvolio's failure to reintegrate seems to fall mostly on his own shoulders. In this case, there might be a legitimate missed opportunity for him to have rejoined the fold, albeit chastened.

In either case, Malvolio clearly does not get the sense that the carnival ritual implicates everyone. He does not feel he is being laughed *with*, as a flawed human among flawed humans, fool amongst fools, having his inflated ego lovingly pierced and brought down to earth—he feels broken. So the laughter isolates rather than bringing together. Malvolio's threat to be "revenged on the whole pack of you" (5.1.373) speaks to the underlying metaphor of the plotline: bearbaiting. Malvolio tied to the stake, attacked by a pack of vicious dogs.[106] Not utopian carnival but dystopian bloodsport.

Sinden ends his remarkable account of his own 1969 performance as Malvolio by saying that "I believe there is but one thing for Malvolio—suicide".[107] It is conceivable; so much depends on the individual Malvolio. Astington feels that he is simply "heading for his lawyer".[108] Interestingly, even Malvolio's textual exit does not stand in the way of certain productions, for Wolfit's Malvolio (in 1951) returned onstage to "kneel before Olivia" before the end,[109] though this grants *Twelfth Night* a closure which Shakespeare, importantly, denied it.

Feste

Most tragic is the comedian who cannot take off his mask. To me, the melancholy tones of the play surreptitiously emanate from Feste, the fool whose name evokes not only *festive* but *fester* (seeming to rhyme with jester at 2.4.11). Feste is the spokesperson for most of the play's deepest themes, though nearly always obliquely, through the lyrics of his songs and his jokes that tell the truth.

Bloom felt that, of all Illyria's denizens, only Feste "has any mind".[110] I think this is because, as a person, he is almost completely occluded, encouraging *us* to project our own mind, and feeling into his lacunae. Since he uses his words to distance himself, one must read between, around, and behind the lines to find Feste, and this can create in him a sense of depth which the other characters lack.

He resists being identified as "the Lady Olivia's fool" (3.1.30), substituting instead the more precise and apt label "corrupter of words" (3.1.35). For Feste, speech is dissociated from meaning: "words have grown so false I am loath to prove reason with them" (3.1.23–4). If Toby is Hamlet's "To be" developed into an entire person, Feste is the logical endpoint of "Words, words, words" (*Ham.* 2.2.189). What Feste says can rarely (if ever) be taken as a genuine statement, as words for him serve as tools of performance. "A sentence is but a cheveril glove to a good wit: how quickly the wrong side may be turned outward" (3.1.11–3)—that is to say, words can be stretched like pliable leather (cheverel) to completely distort their meaning—hence, corrupter of words. He is a performance artist in the vein of Derridean deconstructionism. This relationship to verbal expression puts Feste at a distance from every other character, who, though they may communicate with varying degrees of falsehood, are at least trying to communicate something. His words, on the other hand, are often meta-communications on the nature of communication itself. The linkage between words and the things to which they refer—between signifier and signified—has, for Feste, been severed. This is why he can be so witty; it is also why he often seems to speak pregnant nothings, and why he seems to be so alone. For him, the fact that "nothing that is so is so" (4.1.8) is both his basic position *vis à vis* the world, and his basic frustration with it.

Seeming to be a recognizable type (the clown), it is at first easy to see him as the other characters do, that is, in only two dimensions. He resists this, both implicitly and explicitly ("I wear not motley in my brain", 1.5.52–3). The depth found in Feste over the centuries is impressive,[111] and if he has not transcended his role in Illyria, he has transcended his role in theatrical practice and criticism. It is technically possible to perform Feste as a stock type, the "traditional happy-go-lucky fool"[112]—this is pretty much where Tommy Steele's performance in the 1969 film lands[113]—though to me this only highlights the contrapuntal sadness buried beneath. In this film, the filmmakers have obviated the issue of Feste's loneliness by inventing friends for him to spend time with between scenes. Even for this Feste, however, loneliness comes home to roost at the end. He is shut out of Olivia's house and left onscreen alone, to sing his closing song with great despondency. His being left alone at the end is one of the many lacunae in Feste's presentation—the details between the lines that speak more than the lines themselves do. This particular moment is recapitulated in the 1966 musical *Cabaret,*[114] which similarly ends with the shocking revelation that the inveterate performer—in the case of *Cabaret*, the Emcee—is *also* a human being.

These lacunae have allowed productions to characterize Feste with far more variety than seems possible with Viola, Orsino, or Olivia, while still remaining supported by the text; from the "uncomplicated figure, a waggish Lord of Misrule overseeing the holiday fun"[115] to the tubercular "gaunt *memento mori"*,[116] to "another life-hater infiltrating the hedonists",[117] or "hobo with a carpet bag" filled with "smouldering anger and contempt".[118] Deborah Hay played him (her) rather effectively in 2024 as a Joni Mitchell-type folk singer with a jaded edge, perhaps having taken one too many psychedelic trips. Feste seems to have been "over the garden wall", says Barber, "knowing more of life than anyone else—too much, in fact".[119]

The weight given Feste in various productions has varied from centring him as the "presiding genius" of Illyria[120]—"as constant and as indispensable as punctuation"[121]—to a mere "fidget in cap-and-bells".[122] Masson (at the RSC in 2005) was touchingly schizoid: in relationship a novice but in music a genius.[123] For this Feste, music seemed to be the only nourishment available to his lonely heart, his forlorn interest in Maria going unrequited. Khan (RSC in 2017) was a somewhat glib panderer, until his deep rage was revealed through his song at the end of 4.2. He also nursed a forlorn love, but for Olivia rather than Maria.[124]

Granville-Barker wrote about Feste that "there runs through all he says and does that vein of irony by which we may so often mark one of life's self-acknowledged failures."[125] I suppose that this failure may be the failure to achieve *either* a successful performance career *or* an authentically connected relationship. Feste has contact with everyone, closeness with no one. At the end, he is one of those left out of the "golden time" (5.1.377) that envelops the lovers.

Feste has a secret life which he will not disclose (1.5.1–27), and as the play progresses, we see that despite being 'Olivia's', he is relatively free-roaming, spending time with both Uncle Toby and Orsino. The man seems to be searching, perhaps for the same thing for which so many of *Twelfth Night*'s characters unconsciously hunger, which is to be seen for who they are. The others, however, seem to receive this eventually: even Andrew is eventually named, cruelly but accurately, as "an ass-head and a coxcomb and a knave, a thin-faced knave, a gull" (5.1.202–3).

Viola, characteristically, tries to mirror what she sees in Feste. She fails to penetrate the superficial, however, and Feste rejects it—and goes even further to express some unexpected contempt for her:

VIOLA: I warrant thou art a merry fellow, and car'st for nothing.
FESTE: Not so, sir, I do care for something; but in my conscience, sir, I do not care for you. If that be to care for nothing, sir, I would it would make you invisible.

(3.1.25–9)

Feste is indeed not a merry fellow, nor a fellow who cares for nothing, but does he know what he *is*? Does anyone? Viola can hardly be blamed for trying to mirror him. His persona is so opaque that even his editors can be put off by it: his response "I do care for something" (3.1.27) is typically glossed as referring to money. I find that superficial, and prefer to think he is referring to something entirely secret. Even if we accept that he means money, it still does not tell us what money might be *worth* to Feste. Money is, both symbolically and functionally, always a cipher for *something else*. Perhaps money, like applause and like laughter, are compensations for what the man really hungers for, which may be, like everyone else in this play, a mirror—to be seen, to be held, not only by a role or a melody, but by a loving and accurately perceiving gaze.

He does not seem to find it. When he describes himself ironically as one of Olivia's "trappings" (5.1.8), the word unconsciously evokes the trapped feeling of being held behind formidable and unsleeping defences, while consciously expressing his sense of superfluity, which is hardly any less grim.

He seems not even to be successful as a Corrupter of Words anymore. He was a favourite of Olivia's father (2.4.11–2), though apparently not of Olivia, which classes him as a remnant. He feels like a revenant, floating around but becoming more obsolete with each passing day. Malvolio says that he "saw him put down the other day with an ordinary fool that has no more brain than a stone" (1.5.80–1), and if we take it to be true that he was outperformed by an amateur—and Feste's being "put out of his guard" (1.5.82) implies that it *is* true—that is rather humiliating for him. Olivia defends Feste, but when they are alone tells him the blunt truth: "Now you see, sir, how your fooling grows old and people dislike it" (1.5.106–7).

It may be that Feste's word-corruption is too intellectual to be popular. He is overly specialized in this direction, and not particularly specialized in the direction of relating to his audience—and so his schtick has gotten old. He has become trapped in a too-successful performance as an unsuccessful clown.

The fool's affinity with the older generation, and the father in particular, is common throughout Shakespeare: Feste, Lavache (*AW*), Touchstone (*AY*), Lear's Fool (*KL*), Yorick (*Ham.*), and Lancelet Giobbe (*MV*) all partake of this pattern; Falstaff (*HIV*) is an amalgam, a surrogate father-fool. The accent is different with each one, but Feste seems to be the most clearly passé—even moreso than Yorick, who is dead.

The bitter outwornness of his life is consistent with the shame which seems to underscore the first few lines of Sonnet 110, in which the Poet alludes to a life on the stage:

Alas, 'tis true, I have gone here and there,
And made myself a motley to the view,
Gored mine own thoughts, sold cheap what is most dear,
Made old offences of affections new.

(Son. 110.1–4)

Feste's exasperated "nothing that is so is so" (4.1.8) is followed up in the next scene when, in the alternate persona of Sir Topas, he declares "That that is is" (4.2.14–5). I think his alter-ego, the dogmatic Sir Topas, reveals an unlived side of his personality, one which has no questions whatsoever about the nature of reality, and is completely satisfied that his knowledge of life is adequate.

Shakespeare's characters choose their pseudonyms as carefully as Shakespeare chose their original names, and 'Sir Topas' references Chaucer's *Canterbury Tales*—which apparently Feste is familiar with. "The Tale of Sir Thopas" is an episode of the *Tales* which parodies the author himself through an outdated style of romantic composition and conceit, and thereby expresses the outmodedness of the chivalric ideal which it extols. I think the certainty of chivalry would seem to Feste naïve; I think certainty *at all* would seem to Feste naïve. Because Topas is a 'tactic', and meant to do something *to Malvolio*, it is easy to overlook what Topas might do *for Feste.* Topas allows Feste to embrace naïveté. Sometimes it is a relief to stop asking so many questions about what existence is, and just accept accepted wisdom at face value.

Topas pesters Malvolio with Pythagoras' doctrine of *metempsychosis* or transmigration—the idea that the immortal, indestructible soul, on the point of death, migrates from one body to another:

FESTE: What is the opinion of Pythagoras concerning wildfowl?
MALVOLIO: That the soul of our grandam might haply inhabit a bird.
FESTE: What think'st thou of his opinion?
MALVOLIO: I think nobly of the soul, and no way approve his opinion.
FESTE: Fare thee well. Remain thou still in darkness. Thou shalt hold th'opinion of Pythagoras ere I will allow of thy wits, and fear to kill a woodcock lest thou dispossess the soul of thy grandam.

(4.2.56–9)

The idea of metempsychosis would presumably be undigestible nonsense to Feste's rational mind. However, it does technically offer a path toward grappling, logically, with the fundamental instability of identity which bedevils him. If Feste could listen to Sir Topas, accepting his authority the way that Sir Topas accepts that of Pythagoras, he might find an inner way of *holding* the paradox that nothing that is so is so.[126] This problem has been evoked multiple times throughout the text:

FESTE: Cullus non facet monachem. [The hood does not make the monk.]
(1.5.51–2)

VIOLA: I am not that I play.
(1.5.179)

OLIVIA: If I do not usurp myself, I am.
(1.5.181)

FESTE: Nothing that is so is so.
(4.1.8)

FESTE: 'That that is is.'
(4.2.14–5)

It will be Orsino who apprehends the paradox most deeply, near the end: "A natural perspective, that is and is not" (5.1.213).

A way of holding the existential dilemma with which Feste is stuck might be to affirm, first, that:

• indeed, nothing that is so is so; we are *not* what we are. We are both less *and* more.

Less because nobody equals the image which they project of themselves, or which others project onto them. *More* because nobody exhausts their own depths; if a turkey may be inhabited by our grandam's soul, who knows what may stir within our own unknown parts?

The second affirmation, the antidote for the threatening chaos of the first, might be that:

• though this may be the case, *that's okay.*

In a way, an insistence on truth and authenticity can be as maladaptive as a histrionic post-reality stance—see *Coriolanus* for that.

Maybe Feste's problem is that he cannot resist gnawing on this bone, and trying, like a sardonic Cassandra, to get the rest of the world to agree to his view. Is it such a problem, however, if existence necessarily involves a degree of performance? Of *authenticity-more-or-less*? Nobody gets it perfectly right, and if, over the course of one's life, one figures out how to get it right *a lot of the time*, that's pretty damn good. Ultimately it would only be God who gets to say without contradiction "I am that I am".[127]

Feste's False Self

Donald Winnicott outlined a concept he called the False Self, which was meant to describe a person who had set up a sort of permanent persona, a defensive mask which would never—or almost never—be let down. The mask is consistent and convincing: "the False Self sets up as real and it is this that observers tend to think is the real person", however "in situations in which what is expected is a whole person the False Self has some essential lacking".[128]

I feel in Feste, like Andrew, a carrying-forth of another aspect of the 'Prince Arthur' complex into this play. And, though mindful of Greif's caution that "Hamlet-like efforts to 'glean what afflicts him' only undercut Feste's credibility",[129] we might imagine a *potential* origin of Feste's False Self. Skura writes of the appalling regularity with which the actor's early life features the precise family dynamic of a narcissistic mother, with no father present to mediate:

Many actors report having had scripts laid out for them in childhood by a mother whose orders gained significance in the absence of a father. Like Olivier, they learned early on that their own selves would not do, that others had to be manufactured; small wonder that they began to feel more at home acting than not.[130]

A story about Olivier comes from Dustin Hoffman:

I says, "Tell me what is it? What's the reason we do what we do?" And he . . . Can I get up? [*Hoffman puts his face directly in front of the face of the interviewer, looking him directly in the eyes.*] He goes right up, and he gets . . . he leans over to me and he . . . I swear to god . . . and he leans over, he says "You want to know why, dear boy?" I says "What?" [*whispers with desperate intensity*] "Look at me look at me look at me look at me look at me look at me look at me."[131]

Winnicott does not miss the actor's relationship with the False Self. He unintentionally paraphrases Malvolio's diagnosis of Feste ("Unless you laugh and minister occasion to him, he is gagged", 1.5.82–3) when he writes that

In regard to actors, there are those who can be themselves and who also can act, whereas there are others who can only act, and who are completely at a loss when not in a role, and when not being appreciated or applauded (acknowledged as existing).[132]

Feste is not an actor *per se*—more a performance artist who dabbles in impressions—but it may yet be fruitful to consider him as having grown up out of one of these children for whom the actor's mask was an unavoidable calling/necessity. The idea seems to help identify the specific presentation of his mirror-hunger, which comes mostly, like Arthur's, in the form of a kind of unconscious father-hunger. Connecting the dots between his relationship to Olivia's father, his solicitousness to Uncle Toby, his ambivalent moonlighting for Count Orsino, and his sublimating joke which compares the fool and the husband (3.1.32–4), outlines the general shape of this. The shadow of it comes out in his animosity toward the other men of his class, Malvolio and Cesario—with Cesario, he rather easily becomes snarky and competitive, trying to defend his place in the sun as "good Madonna" (1.5.54) Olivia's favourite son.

However Feste's past is imagined, in the present of *Twelfth Night* he seems to use his role both as a compensatory 'something to be' and 'something to do', both of which leave him feeling phoney and empty. His frustration with this compromise comes out clearly in his aggression towards Malvolio. Malvolio accurately identifies the inadequacy of Feste's persona, though the insight is unusable by Feste since it is expressed so depreciatively.

It is when Feste and the endarkened Malvolio are left alone that the "barren rascal" (a deer not fit for hunting, 1.5.80) lets his horns come out. Here, despite actors' attempts to the contrary, the practical joke seems always to go rancid in ways that, to me, are not entirely accounted for by the text, except perhaps in that the scene goes on too long—or, rather, *Feste* goes on too long. This is consonant with "The Tale of Sir Thopas", which is also interrupted by its listeners, being felt to be in bad taste and overlong. Feste's fooling is in good taste until it is not. Then it grows old, and people dislike it. Even in the days of *Twelfth Night*'s original production, suggests Maslen, "an age when doctors prescribed whipping as a treatment for madness, and when heresy was punishable by burning, a prank with an outcome like this was more painful than amusing."[133]

It seems impossible to look at Feste the same way after this scene, and in the final act we are likely to agree that Malvolio has been "notoriously abused" (5.1.374), perhaps feeling a peculiar deadness of affection for Feste, almost as though *we* have been the ones deceived by his mask. From this feeling place, it seems almost like justice that he is one of the left-behinds when all the happy people go off to get married. We've seen the mask slip, and what we saw beneath is hard to stomach.

As in *King John*, we have crossing arcs again: Malvolio's moves from obvious hostility to fake smile and back again; Feste's moves from fake smile to obvious hostility and back again. Deeply repressed anger is somehow more disturbing than anger straight-up; maybe this is why we are often more afraid of the smiling clown than of the honest prig.

The lyrics of Feste's final song, as if attempting to restore the frivolous carnival attitude, begin with a silly penis-joke:

FESTE: [sings] When that I was and a little tiny boy,
     With hey, ho, the wind and the rain,

A foolish thing was but a toy,
> For the rain it raineth every day.
>> (5.1.382–5)

The same setup was used by Chuck Berry in 1972, referring to his own foolish toy, "My Ding-a-Ling".[134] But Feste's song (unlike Berry's) does not maintain this tone, and seems to become heavier as it goes on, telling a tale of growing from boy to man. He addresses the limits of revelry: "by swaggering could I never thrive" (1.5.392). One lyric in particular, "but when I came, alas, to wive" (1.5.390) stands out—because either Feste's lyrics speak the truth and he here alludes to a past we never knew he had, since if he ever had a wife, it is inconceivable that he still has her in the present—or the lyrics are 'only' lyrics and Feste is singing about an experience of life that he has never known. At the end of the song, he seems, basically, to lose steam and give up:

FESTE: A great while ago, the world begun,
> With hey, ho, the wind and the rain,
But that's all one, our play is done,
> And we'll strive to please you every day.
>> (5.1.398–401)

It seems just possible for Feste to redeem himself before the curtain falls, as his epilogue song can be an offering that rebuilds his bridge to the audience—though not without the poignant realization on our part that he has moved back into the safe role of the entertainer, the only part he knows how to play. Chastised, he will now "strive to please you every day", and one wonders if he will risk allowing his mask to drop ever again.

Noli Me Tangere

VIOLA: If nothing lets to make us happy both
But this my masculine usurped attire,
Do not embrace me till each circumstance
Of place, time, fortune do cohere and jump
That I am Viola[.]
> (5.1.245–9)

"Do not embrace me"—such a curious thing to appear at the very climax of the comedy, the long-anticipated and deeply emotional reunion between the separated twins, each of whom until this moment believed the other dead. I will show myself to you—later. Here I am—but do not see me.

This moment is legitimately mysterious; like what Freud called the 'navel' of a dream, it seems to lead past the point of comprehension, and into the true unknown. What is intended by Shakespeare with "do not embrace me"? What is going on for Viola? Many productions simply blow past it, and let Sebastian and Viola embrace anyway, presumably finding it unacceptably anticlimactic to do otherwise. If taken seriously as a stage direction, it severely dampens the expected comic conclusion.

Yu Jin Ko finds it inexplicable, in terms of Viola's inner life, that she should defer an embrace with Sebastian.[135] I find it difficult to interpret, but perhaps not inexplicable. It seems to me to be possible that Viola, on revealing her secret, experiences a wave of modesty—even shame—which leads her to keep her disguise and postpone being touched. Much has been made of Orsino's possible bisexual motive in continuing to refer to her as "boy" (5.1.263) and "Cesario" (5.1.378) until the end of the play,[136] but he is also following her lead, reading her cue—Viola herself is not ready to come out. She has been undercover as Cesario for three months (5.1.95), rather a long time. Has *she* come to love Cesario as much as everyone else has? It seems clear that she *will* relinquish him, but it may be harder than we know.

It is customary for masked performers not to unmask directly in view of anybody else—at the least, one ritually turns one's back to the audience to do so. There is a deep sensitivity in the moment of transition. Or maybe, more like the method actor, Viola is unable to simply 'shed' the character when the time comes. Many actors, whether method, masked, or not, require some decompression period in the dressing room before they can return to earth and mingle once again with the real people.

I believe the inscrutability of this moment to be its fundament. There is a depth in Viola's relationship to her alter-ego which is rather suddenly sounded. She has a much more ambivalent relationship with disguise than the other Shakespearean heroines who don male attire. Viola's surrender of Cesario is unlike Portia's surrender of Balthasar, Julia's of Sebastian, or Innogen's of Fidele, for none of these surrenders seem to come at any cost. The other disguised heroines use their disguises as masks through which to act,[137] but none of them seem to be acted on in turn by the mask—only Viola seems so psychologically porous as to allow this to happen.

At the beginning of the play, Viola was very quick to pass into manhood (or androgyny). Why? An interesting detail is given during the reunion with Sebastian: it seems that their father died on her thirteenth birthday. In a dream, we might interpret this symbolically as having something to do with her passage into *womanhood*. Her father never did—or never could—see her as a woman. Here, nobody (including us) gets to see her as a woman either. Her womanhood is intellectually known-about, but ultimately, once concealed, remains "as secret as maidenhead" (1.5.210).

Something important happens at this moment not only for Viola but also for *Twelfth Night*; "do not embrace me" is one aspect of a comic conclusion that overall has a decided lack of consummation. The end of the play comes with "a critical sense in which formal closure does not occur even as expectations for it are abundantly generated".[138] And "do not embrace me" is actually not the first but the *second* gesture of this movement. The first was Sir Andrew's humiliated exit some moments earlier, he having been drained and tossed away like an empty candy wrapper. And then Viola. And then, third, the bottom falls out of the Malvolio plotline, which ends utterly unresolved. Fourth, finally, Feste is abandoned with the audience. One-two-three-four. The anti-comic counter-momentum is unavoidable, like the riptide in *King John*'s flood that pulls some out to sea while others swim to shore. All throughout, Viola conspicuously remains in disguise, even continuing to be called Cesario four lines from the end.

Ko's proposition about "do not embrace me" is that the play moves here from a more realistic truth (relatively speaking) into a mythical, depth-psychological truth; something that is, in its way, truer than true. It fulfils its title by alluding to the Epiphany which the Twelfth Night feast would celebrate:

> at this moment Shakespeare turns from classical comedy to Biblical narrative, specifically to the *noli me tangere* moment in John 20:17, when Jesus, risen from the dead, appears to Mary Magdalene in the garden . . . Mary initially mistakes Jesus for a gardener but then recognizes him after he calls her by name; in response to her recognition, however, Jesus says, "*Touch me not*: for I am not yet ascended to my Father."[139]

The heavy shift in tone that began with the dark room scene, it would seem, does not stop there, but continues and develops right to the end of the play. Though smattered with complex notes throughout, the dark room is really where *Twelfth Night* asserts itself as something other than a typical comedy. It is the moment the secular playworld is invaded full-scale by religious myth, as the Biblical implications of *noli me tangere* seem to point backward to the dark room: he descended into hell. On the third day he rose again. In a dream-logic way, both the risen Viola and the Luciferian Malvolio seem to be associated with Christ, and keeping in mind the play's dual timeline, it is not only the third month but indeed the third day that they both 'rise again'.

Shakespeare having known his Bible, it seems entirely likely that the allusion to John 20:17 is buried but intentional. It appears to be a subtle hint as to what is going on in the depth psychology of the play's creative process. Consider this: typically, in the recognition phase of a comedy's structure, according to Frye, "the unmasking heals the split"[140] that initiated the dramatic action. Portia returns to Belmont, and does not remain in her disguise of the learned judge. Or Ganymede departs, and Rosalind returns to be married. Julia reveals herself, and it is up to a production how to stage that exactly, but she definitely *goes back to being Julia* by the end of *Two Gentlemen*. But Viola, technically, declines to unmask, and the others support this by continuing to treat her *as if* she is Cesario. And so the split prevails. At the critical moment, the play does something which *circumvents* its completion. *The attempted coagulatio fails.*

In the Biblical passage to which "do not embrace me" seems to allude, what do we find? A similar split. On one level, we have the risen Jesus, and on the other, we have the human Mary Magdalene. Jesus has not yet completed his movement from crucified, died, and buried, to seated at the right hand of the Father: "Touch me not: for I am not yet ascended to my Father." For Mary, representative of the 'real world', he has become inaccessible; he is leaving behind this realm and passing into another.

The implication of associating Jesus' moment with Viola's is that both are medial moments in delicate transformational processes, and not to be interfered with. But the subtle blasphemy in associating Viola's moment with Jesus' brings out its overspiritualized nature. For there is, speaking more generally, something of a 'spiritual bypass' which takes place at the end of *Twelfth Night*, and the experience here is of a definite splitting of the dramatic field. Some characters ascend to heaven while others remain on earth. The divide—the lack of embrace—is less between Viola and Sebastian than between the earthbound and the skyward; those happy few and the unhappy rest.[141]

Does not end of the play elicit a certain moral distaste? Malvolio has been scapegoated with complete success. His attackers are let off with a single line of admonishment: "He hath been most notoriously abused" (5.1.372), and Orsino sends Fabian after to "entreat him to a peace" (5.1.373).[142] But this too is deferred until after the curtain falls, and so is therefore outside of the play, which both begins and ends *in medias res*.

And does it not seem unjust that the lovers can so easily *move on* after this? Particularly Olivia, under whose roof the apparently notorious abuse took place. It was made possible due to her lack of oversight, she having been obsessed with her own brother, and then "a most extracting frenzy" (5.1.277) for Cesario, and then Sebastian. On a certain level we begin to realize that, while the four lovers were involved in their ridiculous escapades, they remained blithely ignorant to the madness taking over beneath their feet.[143] Malvolio's exit has seriously soured the mood, and if Sinden is correct that he's off to hang himself, it is a hell of a time to go off on honeymoon. Frye's idea is that comic structure "ends at a point when a new society is crystallized",[144] but in this case, the new society *can* be crystallized only because the socially superior bunch has flown off to space and left everyone else behind.

There is always some kind of division in the ending of Shakespeare's plays: the finale of *As You Like It* sees Jaques reject the conclusion's festivity, and *The Merchant of Venice* has Shylock scapegoated, but it is in *Twelfth Night* that the *audience* is most fully identified with the part of the odd one out.

The play's title has prepared us to expect a substantial qualitative shift. "Twelfth Night" tells us that we are positioned at the point where something logically different is about to happen, because the festival must end, and Ordinary Time must begin again. But for our quaternity of A-listers, Olivia-Viola-Orsino-Sebastian, Ordinary Time does *not* begin again. They enter, rather, into "golden time" (5.1.375). They are the privileged few who loft above the sordid reckoning that the others are subject to. Andrew will return home a failure, wifeless, and penniless. Antonio seems to have fallen mute since the revelation of Viola, which also includes the revelation that Sebastian will never be his. Malvolio has been violently disillusioned, and if he survives the fall, will have the ground to cope with. Feste has enjoyed a brief revenge, but with Toby and Maria now married to one another, he is more alone than ever. Somehow Toby and Maria's marriage seems like the most grounded thing going on—though I think we are meant to hate the idea of them as a couple, their getting together *does* seem like real life. But even here real life takes place offstage, out of the spotlight, and is notably peripheral to the main action.

What to Make of This?

The grounding of the puer spirit can feel like a tremendous deadening. One is brought down to earth, it seems, while spirit itself is gone, for spirit-as-we-know-it has been largely abdicated and disowned. It is not that it can never return—and indeed, casting out the false spirit is necessary to create space for a truer spirit to enter—but the time after the separation may be incredibly depressing. 'What have I done?'

After the fall of the puer, willing or not, broken or not, something has moved onto another level and may be lost for some time. It is like being abandoned by one's angel. To paraphrase a Somalian folktale, the fox seems to have lost his distinctive walk and cannot find it again.[145] In terms of the puer, there may be a split, and one part goes down while another remains above. The underwhelmingness of the ordinary life after the fall feels utterly shut out from golden time. Recalling that *What You Will* may ask the question of the author, 'Which Will are you going to be?', the play does seem to end psychologically with two Wills. The twins come together but the world splits apart.

The ending of *Twelfth Night* looks like resolution but is, in important ways, an unresolved chord. And though most if not all of Shakespeare's plays leave something meaningfully unresolved, when seen through the lens of histrionic dysphoria it seems *Twelfth Night*'s unresolvedness is somehow deeply structural. The felt hollowness here is akin to the felt hollowness of the histrionic, of the ill-fitting persona, and of the false self.

Golden time is quite different from the perpetually rainy "every day" (5.1.387) with which Feste leaves us. In some sense, both Orsino and Olivia are settling—they both having been in love with Cesario, they each now settle for one half of him—Orsino for the woman who was beneath the mask, and Olivia for the one whom the mask resembled. And though this is more realistic for both of them, does it not also feel a little disappointing? If they *are* disappointed, they do not let us know about it.

It is not only Sebastian who is denied contact with Viola through the *noli me tangere*, but the audience (or reader) who is denied contact with *anyone* onstage. At the end of *Peter Pan, or The Boy Who Wouldn't Grow Up* (another play with an uncommitted title),[146] Wendy and John come back to England while Peter remains behind in Never Never Land. In *Twelfth Night*, Viola and Sebastian do *not* return to Messaline, but stay behind in Illyria; they avoid the 'messy' and go over fully to the 'illusory'.

We are left behind while the lovers ascend, their inwardness closed off to us, and though Feste is left behind with us, he too is inaccessible—he seems now to be resigned to his role and the isolation which defines it. In fact, *only* Feste has the opportunity to give the play a feeling of completion, with his final song;[147] although if he succeeds in this he seems to be left absolutely, entirely, unequivocally alone. Like the Bastard, he is no longer available to us, and sacrifices himself to forge his play's ending. He has soothed us once more at his own expense. But after all, this doesn't matter, does it?—he isn't real.

One often leaves the play, or is left *by* the play, with the same feeling that a patient who is too successful at their own performance leaves therapy: a confounding detachedness, and the inexplicable knowledge that, though everything seems to have gone well, nothing is yet right. The play, which is so interested in music, ends rather as it began, with "a dying fall," "not so sweet now as it was before" (1.1.4,8), and not with a satisfying return to the tonic chord, but a hanging unresolved question, with no bass note to ground it. The truth is as unseen as ever; perhaps it always will be that way, and the twelfth night will drag on into the thirteenth, the fourteenth, the fifteenth, the sixteenth . . .

What is the aftermath of this split in Shakespeare's work? I have offered an alchemical metaphor for the play, as a failed attempt at *coagulatio,* which is followed up by a reheating of the fire for an extended *calcinatio* process. Here is another way to think of it: it has been said that Hamlet is the one character that seems actually capable of writing *Hamlet;*[148] imagine for a moment that he *did.* After *Twelfth Night,* what we get is a series of plays seemingly written collaboratively by the jaded quaternity of Feste, Malvolio, Andrew, and Antonio. The next play, *Troilus and Cressida,* exists almost entirely in the ironic mode,[149] which is to say that it drags the ideal through the mud. Golden time is succeeded by the tawdry affair of Helen and Paris, along with the bitterly disappointing 'romance' of Troilus and Cressida themselves. This could all be imaginatively viewed as a strike back, an exposé on the unwholesomeness of our lovers' golden time.

Measure for Measure comes afterward, a comedy with hardly any feeling one could honestly call comic, set in a world completely antipathetic toward idealized love; a peaceless world with little room for simplistic or childish notions about life. *All's Well That Ends Well* rejects the peremptory and too-easy marriage that *Twelfth Night* allows ("I cannot love her, nor will strive to do't", *AW* 2.3.144), though forces the case in the end.

And then the great tragedies: not concerned with 'every day' normal people at all, but larger-than-life 'golden time' dwellers who are raised up and then cast down by their own hand—scapegoated and isolated from the rest of society by their greatness and their tragedy alike. Surely Othello and Desdemona believe they are in for some 'golden time' following their marriage, and Iago sets about annihilating that with the dispassionate chill of a drone strike. Lear, too, seems to think he is inaugurating a personal 'golden time', when what he actually does is tip the world off of a cliff. Shakespearean tragedy, imagined as having been written by comedy's outcasts; an extended revenge of the lower-thans.

I'm not sure that anyone in Shakespeare gets 'golden time' again until *Antony and Cleopatra*, and theirs is severely qualified by precisely what the Illyrians lack:

golden time's impact on the rest of the world. That play dives deeply into the unpleasant reality of such a golden time, and therefore succeeds, finally, in the long sought-for *coagulatio.*

At last, after Shakespeare has been through the ordeal of his tragedies, people seem to once again be permitted an enduring happiness, with *Pericles* and the other romances. The world seems to become hospitable again. But it is a long and scorching journey.

Why Now?

To conclude, let us consider again the actor-playwright about whom we know so little. I have earlier suggested that *Twelfth Night* constitutes a farewell to childish things for Shakespeare. Afterward, nothing is again so easy.

There are a few things in Shakespeare's biography which we might take as the germ of his sense of the *puer*'s fall: his young, "patently rushed"[150] and possibly enforced marriage to Anne Hathaway, whom he had impregnated, surely unintentionally.[151] The execution of Lord Essex might have been a puer-death for the whole nation. Maybe the murder of Christopher Marlowe, or Ben Jonson's fall from grace. The imminent death of Queen Elizabeth, and that of the 16th century, likely had with it a collective sense of an era coming to its end.

There are two possibilities in particular that I would like to imaginatively explore as psychological events which would contribute to *Twelfth Night.* The first is heartbreak. This connection is suggested to me by the similarity between Orsino's discovery in 5.1 that the friend that he's sent to woo Olivia has apparently gone and married her, and the betrayal that takes place during the course of the Sonnets. The Poet of the Sonnets finds, much to his dismay, that the friend he has introduced to the woman he's after has leapt into his seat, so to speak, and become her lover.

ORSINO: O thou dissembling cub! What wilt thou be
When time hath sowed a grizzle on thy case?
Or will not else thy craft so quickly row
That thine own trip shall be thine overthrow?

(5.1.160–4)

If we assume the Sonnets to be at least partially autobiographical (which I do), it may be that the shock of this duplicity of both friend and mistress is the shock that breaks Will's heart and grows him up. Perhaps this shock is also reflected in Andrew's sudden abandonment by Sir Toby, the friend to whose duplicity he had remained naïve.

The archetypal experience I am talking about is *the discovery of duplicity*, the realization that the other is more than what they seemed—that they are, in this sense, duplicitous—"nothing that is so is so" (4.1.8). This has the force of *ekkyklema,* the moment in Greek tragedy when the corpses are revealed, the final resting place of naïve ignorance. It is maturing because it puts an end to the idealized projection.

This is a problem that was only being discovered by Hamlet, who apparently finds it so novel "That one may smile and smile and be a villain" (*Ham.* 1.5.108) that he must write it down.

In the same sequence as Andrew's disillusionment, Orsino utters the reconciling capstone to this play's own concern with duplicity, "A natural perspective, that is and is not" (5.1.213). His formulation anticipates the very crux, in *Troilus and Cressida*, of Troilus' sudden maturation, when *he* is exposed to Cressida's duplicity and faithlessness: "This is and is not Cressid" (*TC* 5.3.153). *Twelfth Night* contains its own reference to Cressida, which ends rather cruelly: "Cressida was a beggar" (3.1.54)—a little bit of spite towards the person who turns out not to be as they first seemed.

The *Sonnets* discover and then reel at the impact of this problem. In Sonnet 138, which comes *before* the Troilus-like discovery of the royal screw of friend and mistress, the Poet glimpses the secret without realizing how deep it goes:

When my love swears that she is made of truth,
I do believe her, though I know she lies . . .
O love's best habit is in seeming trust[.]
                    (Son. 138 1–11)

Following this, the Poet almost owns up to his mutual participation in falsehood, in the Sonnet which closes the Dark Lady sequence, 152: "But why of two oaths' breach do I accuse thee / When I break twenty?" (*Son.* 152.5–6). But this Sonnet is spiteful, complex, and not at all a clear acceptance of having learned something, which *could* (potentially) be the essential paradoxical truth of the histrionic perspective, that *nothing that is so is so, even while that which is is.*

As Shakespeare goes on, the problem of what someone *is* goes on and on, twisting and morphing, creating and recreating itself through *Measure for Measure* ("Seeming, seeming!", *MM* 2.4.150), *King Lear* ("Who is it that can tell me who I am?", *KL* 1.4.222), all the way through to *Cymbeline,* and on after that—though it does seem that in *The Tempest*, the character of Prospero can be written by virtue of the fact that Shakespeare has *finally* digested his own naïveté.

And naïveté reminds us that the inability to see things in more than one aspect is a deficiency of the puer. The grounding of the puer—and its ability to integrate the trickster—involves a necessary betrayal of a puerile ideal; an unforgettable initiation into the irreducible complexity of life.[152]

The return to the death of the puer connects us with the second possible biographical 'reason' underlying the end of childish things in *Twelfth Night*, and one that I find particularly compelling. *Twelfth Night*'s presumed date of writing—1601— places it five years after the death of Hamnet, Will's 11-year-old son, himself the twin of Judith; a Sebastian to her Viola. Wheeler has made the case that *Twelfth Night* comprises in part a creative response to this loss.[153] It seems possible that the reunion of Viola and Sebastian acquires some of its exquisite fragility, as well as its unreality, from the possibility that it is indeed a partial wish-fulfilment, in which the male twin is discovered to be alive after all. And perhaps this has something to do with why no embrace can be allowed—because even as it expresses the wish-fulfilling fantasy of the son's survival, it is shadowed by the truth which cannot be undone: "He is dead and gone. / At his head a grass-green turf, / At his heels a stone" (*Ham.* 4.5.30–2).

It is difficult to imagine anything more crushing than the death of one's child. Truly, we know so little about Shakespeare's life, let alone his inner life, and it enters into the realm of extreme psychoanalytical speculation to try too hard to tie the content of his work to the few bare facts we have. But if anything that we do know could correspond to the end of the festivities, it would seem to be this. A case can be made for Hamnet's influence on any or all of the plays immediately following his death. Most obvious might be the elements of *King John* which were addressed earlier, though the significant father-son focus in the *Henry IV* plays also may bear the psychological imprint of father Will. It is, naturally, hard to ignore the fact that his most brilliant character of all, the one concerned most actively and continually with the "undiscovered country" (*Ham.* 3.1.78) after life, shares his name with Will's departed son.[154]

Keeping the histrionic lens of this chapter in mind, we might imagine an initial response on Will's part of *denial*, of the exact kind that is seen in *Twelfth Night*: "a desperate rearguard action against the cold light of day".[155] The argument would then go that this inward denial lasted around five years—and if that sounds dramatic, clinical experience teaches otherwise; moreover, I would point out that we are speaking of a theatre personality here, and there is no reason to suppose that 'the show must go on' was not as strong an impulse then as it is now. Five years is relatively modest. Olivia was trying for seven.

Duncan-Jones believes that *Twelfth Night* establishes, through Sir Toby's perspective, that "anyone who grieves for more than a few moments for a dead family member is a fool"[156]—maybe she is right that Belch articulates Shakespeare's conscious position. This would render the compensation of Olivia's grief, much like Constance's, all the more necessary.

It seems entirely possible that the split we feel at the end of *Twelfth Night* is psycho-autobiographical; that 'what happened in real life' was that 'golden time' was lost, departed into the distance, and Will was left behind, binding himself to his work as Sebastian binds himself to the mast. Penuel perceives the relevance to the play of a collective Elizabethan "loss of mourning",[157] "a context of rigorous neo-Stoic hostility to grief."[158] Arguably, then, it is not only Shakespeare's psyche that is throwing up a defence against attachment-to-the-other, by categorizing it as histrionic and morbid, but his entire culture that was doing so. The Presbyterian Church proclaimed that

> praying, reading, and singing, both in going to, and at the grave, have been grossly abused, are in no way beneficial to the dead, and have been proved many ways hurtful to the living, therefore let all such things be laid aside.[159]

Perhaps throwing himself into his writing, including such oddly blithe (given the circumstance) compositions as *Much Ado About Nothing, As You Like It,* and *The Merry Wives of Windsor*, as well as *King John, Henry IV* and *Hamlet,* was the only available response to a loss that threatened to undermine his life and future—keeping in mind he had lost not only a son but an heir, the very thing he spends his first 17 sonnets extoling the virtues of having. In fact, it is in the 17th Sonnet that the poet's emphasis on futurity begins to shift from his fair friend's heir to his own writing: "But were some child of yours alive that time, / You should live twice: in it, and in my rhyme" (*Son.* 17.13–4); in other words, writing takes the place of a son.

Our interest in Shakespeare himself may blind us, however, to a more obvious and perhaps even more heartbreaking possibility in *Twelfth Night,* which is after all not a play about the father's recovery of his son, but the *sister's* recovery of her *twin.* It is a play about the surviving twin's experience; it is she who has to survive the brother, to grieve him (or not be able to), and then to come to terms with his resurrection (or, again, not be able to). It is the female twin whose grief grounds the play—and which is recast also in Olivia's loss of a brother. It feels to me that Judith Shakespeare is hiding in plain sight.

If Shakespeare is the feeling-type I take him to be, the effect on his daughter of the loss of her twin surely would have registered for him. I imagine that she was forced to 'grow up' as much as anyone, saying goodbye to childish things at the age of 11. *Twelfth Night*, five years later, could be Shakespeare's own "Hey Jude"—his attempt, consciously or unconsciously, to help his daughter take a sad song, and make it better.[160]

What can be it be like to lose a twin? The one with whom your existence has *always* been synonymous? Like Plato's original spherical two-person beings who were separated by the gods—"An apple cleft in two" (5.1.219)—that part of you that is required to make a whole. And to live now, forever, as a *part*—to be reunited when? Ever? Will life, or afterlife even, bring your other half back?

We all, in some sense, have to live as part-wholes, longing our whole lives for completion—but for most of us it is a psychological, mythologized Paradise we long for—a pre-verbal experience of total unity—however the twin who has lost her twin has a clarity and immediate reality in her experience of unity and dismemberment, something that the rest of us can truly only guess at. When Viola imagines herself sat "like Patience on a monument" (2.4.114), she may not be thinking of *Orsino* at all, rather she may inwardly be at the tomb of her missing twin. She truly is, now, all the brothers of her father's house, and all the daughters too.

·

In the way that it is often said that the cure to a puer aeternus complex is work, perhaps the cure to a histrionic complex is loss—or more specifically, the *recognition* of loss; of time and necessity; of some event that shatters the mask so thoroughly and finally that it cannot be put back on again in the same way without utterly dishonouring what has taken place. It is not necessary to imagine lingering echoes of

Hamnet Shakespeare in the background of *Twelfth Night, or What You Will,* but to me this somehow helps to hold the play's strange mixture of joy and melancholy. We may see it, finally, as a mournful farewell to that which was deeply loved—both the carnival and the son—and through mourning, a fuller acknowledgment of that love, which allows it—finally—the chance to come home.

Notes

1　Edinger (1991, 17–46).
2　Edinger (1991, 83–116).
3　Emerson (1940, 185).
4　Edinger (1991, 97).
5　Edinger (1995, 289).
6　Jung (CW 14, 687).
7　Edinger (1995, 290). For Shakespeare and Paracelsus, see Grudin (1979, 22–30).
8　Kamps (2011) applies to *Twelfth Night* "a concept of human identity as a repetitive performance" (231), expanding on Butler (1999, 174).
9　Skura (1993, 18–28); for mirror-hunger, see Baker & Baker (1987, 4).
10　Micklem (1996); thanks to Craig Stephenson for the reference.
11　Huang (2010, 257).
12　Bromberg (1996, 223–4), citing Laing (1962, 34).
13　Lewis (2011) has investigated those aspects of *Twelfth Night* which resemble or contrast detective fiction.
14　McWilliams (2011, 322).
15　Novais et al. (2015); Micklem (1996).
16　Though Gabbard (2005, 541–70) does differentiate the two terms, and makes an important third differentiation between hysteria, somatoform disorder, and conversion disorder.
17　Micklem (1996, 4): "It is surprising how often the word 'genuine' arises in connection with hysteria; the presence of the disease raises suspicion, followed quickly by a moral censure that hysteria is a fraudulent complaint."
18　Breuer & Freud (1957, 305).
19　Gabbard (2005, 551): "the exaggerated theatrical behavior . . . often relates to a core experience of early childhood that involved not being recognized."
20　Bloom (1999, 228).
21　I have had to rewrite this paragraph multiple times as the advances in the AI field come quicker and quicker; no doubt it will already be dated by the time this book reaches the printer.
22　Radin (1956, ix).
23　Morse (2004).
24　Caputi (1978, 32).
25　Bruster (2007, 44).
26　The label "problem-play", applied by Boas (1900, 345) originally means a play that addressed a moral problem. But I can't help but hear this term from a theatre practitioner's perspective, as a play that is itself problematic to deal with.
27　Ko (1997).
28　Suggested by John Beebe (personal communication, 11 April 2023).
29　Goldman (1972, 24): "The full powers of the self emerge only in encounter, and they are complicating, even threatening in their multiplicity."
30　Freud (2020, 353).
31　Riemann (2009, 159).

32 Elam (2008, 75); expanded by Lisak (2011, 175–8). In contrast, Pentland (2011, 149) argues that the choice of Illyria as setting "was not motivated by a desire for mystery or obscurity, but for reasons that had everything to do with the region's concrete historical and geopolitical associations." Juric (2019) has elaborated what 'Illyria' may have carried for Shakespeare's audience.

33 Lisak (2011, 172): "Twelfth Night turns uncouthness into a staple feature of Illyrian domestic policy."

34 Kott (1964, 237).

35 Berne (2004, 142).

36 Wanamaker (1988, 83).

37 Spurgeon (1935, 268).

38 Schalkwyk (2011, 89). His more erudite formulation is that "he is in love with himself as the paradigmatic embodiment of materialist, Galenic psychology."

39 Jung (CW 6, 781).

40 Though Wood (1973) sees it implicated also in *Julius Caesar, Macbeth,* and *King Lear*.

41 Skura (1993, 129–37; 149–65).

42 McWilliams (2011, 317).

43 Barton (1984, 195).

44 Barton (1984, 197).

45 Ko (1997, 397).

46 Penuel (2010, 95).

47 Elam (2008, 60) observes ways in which Andrew and Malvolio are (metaphorically) castrated as well.

48 Shapiro (1994, 174).

49 Of course picked up in significant detail by Adelman (1992).

50 Elam (2008, 97).

51 See Lisak (2011, 169–70).

52 Abt (2005, 100).

53 Connections between the *Sonnets* and *Twelfth Night* are developed in Schalkwyk (2005).

54 To press an admittedly remote point a little further: there are certain dream-logic ways in which *Twelfth Night* does seem to be the successor to *Hamlet,* and one of them could be in an unconscious wish for both Hamlet and Ophelia to have found more congenial fates. Listening for echoes of *Hamlet* in *Twelfth Night*, and holding the two together with a somewhat blurred focus, allows another point of contact to emerge: the sea-journey. Hamlet, in Act 4 of his play, is sent on a ship to England from which he is not intended to return. Through an encounter with pirates with the most fortuitous outcome imaginable, he manages to find his way back to Denmark, and Act 5 Hamlet is uncharacteristically ready to accept the burden of a life which has so long oppressed him. The sea-journey seems to have enlightened him in some way. Now if we entertain a dream-logic connection between Hamlet's voyage and Viola's voyage, it would seem that Viola's shipwreck represents an alternate path—one in which, rather than returning home to fulfill the ghostly father's command, the ship founders, and the passenger is washed up on a foreign shore, free to begin a new life, with all the former worry far behind, oceans away. Blurring the two together a little more, maybe Viola is what would happen if not Hamlet but *Ophelia* managed to escape Denmark, into a play that were more hospitable to her. Illyria has an opening for a "ministering angel" (*Ham.* 5.1.231); Elsinore did not. Obviously I do not mean that it makes any sense to try and concretely tie the two plays together like parallel universes in a superhero movie, but rather that these two represent two possible outcomes of the sea-voyage fantasy, which seems symbolically to have to do with the archetypal night-sea journey, a submersion in the unconscious leading to transformation and subsequent rebirth as *tabula rasa* in a land of new possibility. Hamlet is reborn into his own life for the first time, and Viola is reborn into her new life as Cesario.

55 Bloom (1999, 231).
56 Wheeler (2000, 149).
57 Wanamaker (1988, 85–6).
58 Hayles (1980); Ko (1997, 399).
59 Cesare is also the name of the heroine in Gl'Inganni (Duncan-Jones, 2010, 179). The point is less who invented the name, but that it is *kept!*
60 There is a good argument to be made for Viola's identification with the archetypal anima/animus syzygy (see Kast 2006) —but I find it somewhat too abstract for the present discussion.
61 Belsey (1993, 202).
62 *The Cherry Orchard* is probably the best example. Wells (1977, 62), Gay (1985, 45), and Barton also sensed "a Chekhov-like centre" (Berry 1981, 113) in the play; Mendes' 2002 production at the Donmar Warehouse picked it out too.
63 Wanamaker (1988, 85).
64 The latency period was Freud's term for a time between childhood and adolescence when a person's sexual development enters a hiatus—a stage of relative stability, when the sexual libido goes dormant, while other psychological developments take priority.
65 Elam (2008, 138).
66 Seven year periods are significant in "The Twelve Brothers", "The Handless Maiden", "The Elves", and "The Devil and His Grandmother", to name only a few from the Grimms' collections.
67 Abt (2005, 141).
68 Wilhelm (1984, 32).
69 A cue to the playing of the just-quoted moment is perceivable in the verse structure. Up until now, the scene between them has been in prose—typically the structure of less 'heightened' speech. Suddenly ("'Tis beauty truly blent") Viola has begun speaking verse, an attempt to wrest the scene's feeling-tone back under her control, bringing it more in line with the romantic overture she was sent to make, also reflected in her sudden shift to the language of boilerplate romantic compliment. A typical Shakespearean verse line is ten syllables; Viola's last line, "And leave the world no copy", being three syllables short, unconsciously intimates an invitation to Olivia to acquiesce to the romantic frame by completing the metre. Olivia instead undercuts it by returning to prose ("O sir, I will not be so hard-hearted"). And rather than have her parts inventoried and blazoned in yet another laboured speech from Orsino, she shows that she's heard it all before by itemizing herself. She refuses to play the part set down for her.
70 Maugham retold this Mesopotamian tale as "The Appointment in Samarra" (O'Hara 1934). A version is in the Babylonian Talmud, Sukkah 53a:5.
71 Yachnin (2023) for this list, and more exploration of the *shame* motif in connection with this.
72 Although Barton (2007a, 11) notes a distinction, more salient to the Elizabethans than to us, between the ceremony conducted with the clergyman and the *actual* marriage at play's end.
73 Saint Sebastian's feast day—January 20, a fortnight after the Twelfth Night—is shared by another conspicuous *Twelfth Night* name: Saint Fabian.
74 The relationship is often seen with homosexual overtones (Fiedler 1972; Pequigney 1992; Orgel 1996, 51); "it has become the theatrical norm for Antonio and Sebastian to be played as a homosexual couple" (Schiffer 2011, 31).
75 Penuel (2010, 82).
76 Barber (1959); also Montégut (in 1867; Lothian & Craik 1975, lii); Welsford (1935).
77 Of *The Simpsons*.
78 This line stands as a fine counterpoint to Orsino's (2.4) pronouncements on the nature of women.
79 Wilhelm (1984, 34).
80 As in *The Merry Wives of Windsor.*

81 Yearling (1982, 83).
82 Barber (1959, 3); see also Hutton (1994) for more on this.
83 Stewart (1984, 144).
84 Jung (CW 9i, 456).
85 Smith (2011, 320) argues that 'Puritan' is already a word whose meaning has departed, and refers to his "social ambition and exaggerated self-worth" more than to anything religious.
86 The female trickster's "exploits were celebrated in the so-called jest-books or collections of comic anecdotes that remained hugely popular" (Maslen 2006, 205–6).
87 For example, Lewis (2011, 265) observes the use of riddles by Portia, Mariana, Helena, Rosalind, and, of course, Viola. Shakespeare's female tricksters always end up married, and I do wonder if this reflects Shakespeare's attitude to his own marriage, possibly feeling he was 'bed-tricked' into it. That would lend a little bit of context to the disgust with sexuality that is often expressed in his plays.
88 Beier (2014) has made a more in-depth study of the rhetoric used by Shakespearean persuaders, especially Iago and Iachimo.
89 A complex-indicator is one of a number of data points gathered during Jung's word-association test which can support the hypothesis of a complex (emotionally-charged psychic entity) around a particular area of experience.
90 Spurgeon (1935, 195).
91 Skura (1993, 168). Emphasis added.
92 Duncan-Jones (2010, 114–9). She also makes the connection with Malvolio (181), which has become commonplace (Kamps 2011, 237; Greenblatt 2004, 82).
93 Duncan-Jones (2010, 111).
94 Stewart (1984, 144).
95 Bakhtin (1973, 101).
96 Stewart (1984, 145).
97 Stewart (1984, 147). We may again recall Chesterton's distinction between *humour* and *wit.*
98 Stewart (1984, 146).
99 Lewis (2011, 266).
100 Expounded in Elam (1984, 159–64).
101 Bakhtin (1968, 12).
102 Bakhtin (1968, 12), emphasis added.
103 Carnegie (2001, 396).
104 Carnegie (2001, 414).
105 Carnegie (2001, 411).
106 Skura (1993, 206).
107 Sinden (1985, 66).
108 Astington (1993, 33).
109 Trewin (1978, 167).
110 Bloom (1999, 228).
111 See Greif (1988).
112 Greif (1988, 69).
113 Clarke & Sichel (1970).
114 Kander et al. (1966).
115 Greif (1988, 63).
116 Greif (1988, 65).
117 Lambert (in Elam, 2008, 137).
118 Hoyle (in Elam 2008, 137).
119 Barber (1959, 294).
120 The Times, 6 February 1901; cited in Greif (1988, 63).

121 Tree (1901).
122 Sprague & Trewin (1970, p. 96; cited in Greif 1988, 65).
123 Director: Michael Boyd.
124 Director: Christopher Luscombe.
125 Granville-Barker (1947, 30).
126 It would seem that one of Feste's go-to 'bits' is to lampoon a senex-type character who is self-satisfied with his own wisdom; Andrew recalls "when thou spok'st of Pigrogromitus, of the Vapians passing the equinoctial of Queubus" (2.3.21–3). In the *commedia dell'arte*, this would be the *il dottore* character.
127 Exodus 3:14.
128 Winnicott (2018, 142–3).
129 Greif (1988, 66).
130 Skura (1993, 24), often citing Fisher & Fisher (1981).
131 Dustin Hoffman on *Inside the Actors' Studio* (https://www.dailymotion.com/video/x2o03g2).
132 Winnicott (2018, 150).
133 Maslen (2006, 205).
134 Berry & Bartholomew (1972).
135 Ko (1997, 395).
136 Maslen (2006, 210–1).
137 Hayles (1980).
138 Ko (1997, 392).
139 Ko (1997, 395–6), emphasis added.
140 Frye (1965, 84).
141 The "world of revelry, of comic festivity . . . survives only in part, and then by insisting upon an exclusiveness . . ." Barton (2007b, 109).
142 A suitable task for a character named, presumably, with the peacemaking Pope Fabian in mind.
143 Hayles (1980, 68): "As a result of the displacement of the ruling figures into the romantic plot, a vacuum exists at the top of the social hierarchy."
144 Frye (1965, 72).
145 K'Naan (2012).
146 Barrie (1904).
147 Barton (2007b, 111): "It leads us gently and in a way that is aesthetically satisfying from the golden world to the age of iron which is our own. A triumph of art, it builds a bridge over the rift which has opened in the comedy at its conclusion."
148 Bloom (1999, 739) attributes this remark to A. C. Bradley.
149 Frye (1957, 223–39).
150 Barton (2007a, 7).
151 Duncan-Jones (2010, 18–25).
152 See Hillman, Betrayal (1975, 63–81).
153 Wheeler (2000); also Penuel (2010, 79).
154 Hamlet and Hamnet, in Elizabeth English, are the same name.
155 Barton (2007b, 109).
156 Duncan-Jones (2010, 167). For her, the death in the mind of the author is not the son Hamnet's, but the impending death of the father John Shakespeare.
157 Penuel (2010, 83–8).
158 Penuel (2010, 84).
159 The 1644 Presbyterian *Directory for the Public Worship of God*, cited in Gittings (1984, 48).
160 Beatles (1970).

Chapter 5

"But what's the matter?"

Introduction to *Cymbeline*

Synopsis

Innogen,[1] daughter to British King Cymbeline, has in secret married her childhood friend, Posthumus. In rage, Cymbeline banishes Posthumus from the kingdom, and Posthumus departs to Italy. While there, he is seduced into a wager with an Italian named Iachimo, who ventures to disprove Posthumus' assertions of Innogen's virtue, by seducing her himself.

Back at home, Innogen is pestered by her wicked stepbrother Cloten, who has his own amorous designs on her. Iachimo arrives and is received by her as a guest; he makes his move, and she rejects him. Determined to win his wager, he smuggles himself into her bedroom, hidden in a chest. In the night he emerges and records details of her room and body to serve as proof, to Posthumus, of Innogen's seduction. These proofs do prove convincing in the end to Posthumus, who loses his mind and writes to his servant Pisanio with instructions to kill Innogen.

Pisanio, deeply conflicted, accompanies Innogen on a journey to Wales, where she believes she is to rendezvous with Posthumus. Pisanio confesses his errand to Innogen, and proposes that they fake her death to buy some time. She disguises herself as a young man, who she names Fidele. Pisanio also gives her what he believes to be a vial of medicine. The Queen, Innogen's stepmother, had given it to him, believing it to be poison, as she *also* intended to murder Innogen. However, neither of them are correct, as the doctor Cornelius had substituted a sleeping dram for the poison, unwilling to trust the Queen with a deadly compound.

Pisanio returns home and Innogen, now on her own, stumbles upon a cave belonging to three apparent wild men—though they are, unbeknownst to any of them, her long-lost brothers, Guiderius and Arviragus, as well as the man who kidnapped them in childhood, Belarius, who Guiderius and Arviragus take to be their father. They all warm to one another very quickly, the familial bonds being felt unconsciously.

Meanwhile, tensions are rising between Britain and Rome. Cymbeline and his Queen refuse to pay the tribute demanded of Rome, a choice that will surely lead to war.

DOI: 10.4324/9781003596967-6

Also back home, Cloten has extorted from Pisanio the whereabouts of Innogen, and followed her to Wales. He wears the clothing of Posthumus, perversely believing that this will help him win the princess' heart. However, instead of Innogen he encounters Guiderius and Arviragus, and after exchanging insults, Guiderius cuts his head off. At the same time, however, Innogen takes the 'medicine' which Pisanio had given to her, and falls into a deathlike sleep. The three men conduct a funeral rite for both her and Cloten's headless body, burying them together.

Innogen awakes next to the headless corpse, which, due to its clothing, she believes to be Posthumus'. Half-insane with grief and the effects of the sleeping dram, she smears herself with the corpse's blood and embraces the body. She is discovered by the Roman Lucius. She identifies herself to him as Fidele, and he takes her as his page.

Battle commences between the British and Roman armies, which would be won by Rome if not for the heroics of Guiderius, Arviragus, Belarius, and a disguised Posthumus. Posthumus has returned to fight alongside the British, believing that Innogen has been murdered, and deeply regretting his part in it. Taken prisoner before the end of the battle, he is sentenced to death. In a dream, he is visited by the ghosts of his ancestors, who plead the case for his merit to the god Jupiter. Jupiter himself appears, exasperated, and explains his plan for Posthumus, who awakens to find that his death sentence has been commuted.

In the end, all the complications are unwound and all the hidden identities revealed. Innogen and Posthumus are reunited; the lost sons are reunited with Cymbeline; Belarius and Iachimo are forgiven their misdeeds; the evil Queen has died confessing her myriad sins. And lastly, Cymbeline pardons the Roman soldiers that have been captured, and agrees to pay the tribute after all. Rome and Britain are reconciled.

Cymbeline

Kirsch writes, "the salient fact about *Cymbeline*, to begin with, is that it is resistant to any coherent interpretation."[2] Not that that's stopped anybody from trying. But "even critics who claim some fondness for its oddities", writes Landry, "tend to explore particular aspects, leaving the unwieldy bulk of the threefold plot largely unexplained."[3] The play, itself loaded with separations and divisions, extends this quality outward into its criticism. We try to divide and conquer it; it may divide and conquer us.

Cymbeline gives its critics many characters after whom they may model their own approaches: as Iachimo, we may find its inaccessibility intolerable, and set out to denude it of its mystery. Or we may act more in Posthumus' vein, and as he idealizes Innogen, we in turn may attribute to the play an unfounded—and unnecessary—perfection.

Perhaps we subject the text to sadistic reductionism, acting in this like the Queen, experimenting with her poisons on "such creatures as / We count not worth the hanging" (1.5.19–20). Something may be learned through this, but Doctor Cornelius' rejoinder to the Queen also pertains:

CORNELIUS: Your highness
Shall from this practice but make hard your heart.
Besides, the seeing these effects will be
Both noisome and noxious.

(1.5.23–6)

Meaning can be tortured from a play, but at what cost to the torturer?

Probably the most common response to the play resembles Cymbeline himself: a frustrated, but relatively passive and bewildered watching as it unfolds, perhaps commenting to ourselves with each new twist of plot, "new matter still" (5.5.242). Perhaps wishing we were watching *Othello* instead.

Even the in-play interpreter, the soothsayer Philharmonus, has trouble making heads or tails of things. His dream yields itself to two dramatically differing interpretations (4.2.345–51; 5.5.465–74), though he is a good sport about the need to revise his prophecies as he goes along. His dream, like Posthumus' letter (3.2.40–7), like Iachimo's truthful lying about his night in Britain—like everything in the play—is polysemous. This is a play not merely of *double-entendres,* but of straight polysemy, in which everything seems to mean itself while also commenting on itself, affirming and undermining itself simultaneously.

Since at least the turn of the 20th century, it has been recognized that *Cymbeline*'s "most distinguishing feature . . . is its deliberate self-consciousness."[4] Granville-Barker detects the "art that rather displays art than conceals it";[5] Kermode felt Shakespeare "somehow playing within the play";[6] Bloom described it as "compulsive self-parody",[7] finding everything about it "madly problematical, as Shakespeare, in a willful mood, evidently intended."[8]

Hazlitt's opening remarks, in the early 20th century, thrust us directly into the problem of genre: "*Cymbeline* is one of the most delightful of Shakespear's historical plays."[9] Nevermind that "most delightful" is scarcely agreed-upon, but "historical"? Well—yes—though as a generic label this word would be completely misleading. It is less historical than it is *about* history, and history's effect on us.[10] Wilson Knight also found it essentially historical,[11] and our first recorded audience response, from Simon Forman's journal, supports this:

Remember also the storii of Cymbalin king of England in Lucius tyme, howe Lucius Cam from Octauus Cesar for Tribut, and being denied, after sent Lucius with a greate Arme of Souldiars who landed at Milford hauen, and Afftere wer vanquished by Cimbalin, and Lucius taken prisoner . . .[12]

Forman's impression of the play seems disordered, like the recollection of a dream, but it does seem to suggest, as Chen writes, that "his immediate impression of the play was as a history".[13] A great deal of criticism, of course, has also tied the play to its own historical context,[14] and the relevancy of its being first shown in the early years of the reign of James I.

Hazlitt's second sentence blurs the genre issue further: "It may be considered as a dramatic romance".[15] But have we got anything better? Sometimes it is called tragicomedy, a word given definition by John Fletcher, a contemporary (and later collaborator) of Shakespeare's: "a tragicomedie is not so called in respect of mirth and killing, but in respect it wants deaths, which is enough to make it no tragedy, yet brings some near it, which is enough to make it no comedy."[16] If we are to follow Fletcher strictly, however, we have to exclude *Cymbeline* from the category, as it does not lack for deaths. However, the deaths in question being not the least bit tragic, the First Folio's categorization of the play among the *tragedies* is hard to stomach as well.

To try too hard to identify the genre in which Shakespeare is working is to drift from taxonomy to taxomania, and basically overstates his relationship with genre *per se*. Genre is not the tail which wags the Shakespearean dog—his method *almost always* seems to me to be to try and reinvent or transcend the genre from within, like climbing into a box only to stretch and break it from inside. As much as a good label, therefore, can illuminate, a bad label can confuse. Valerie Wayne writes that "the most regrettable result of the generic confusion . . . is that it can be misunderstood as failing to achieve what it never attempted."[17]

Cymbeline, notwithstanding its affiliations and flirtations with the genres of romance, tragedy, comedy, tragicomedy, etc., is in itself a dangerously experimental play, whose oddities and quiddity threaten to overwhelm readers, audiences, and production teams alike. Its intended tone is constantly in question, and this tone shifts, over and over, occasionally with multiple dissonant tones prevailing simultaneously. Eventually *Cymbeline* spills over any generic container in which we try to confine it, including even "tragical-comical-historical-pastoral" (*Ham.* 2.2.397; Tanner adding two more, "-political-romance"[18]). Falstaff's description of an otter may be closest to the point: neither fish nor flesh, and a man knows not where to have it (*1HIV,* 3.3.128–31). One sooner arrives at a coherent sense of *Cymbeline* through the *via negativa—neither* fish *nor* flesh—than through any attempt to characterize it positively. In its way, it is as alienating and shocking as Stravinsky's *Rite of Spring* is for an ear used to Romantic composition.

Applying a 'presentist' bias to the play, one finds it (like the other plays in this book) to be uncannily postmodern. Kawai writes that the postmodern aesthetic is characterized by "surface and self-reflection without content."[19] It is a world in which "direct reality is already over", epitomized by the qualities of "dissociation", "arbitrariness" and "virtuality", and modern readers familiar with Haruki Murakami may recognize the tone. This is the world in which Murakami's characters live, and with which they are in constant evolving dialogue. His novels are filled with tropes from pre-existing genres as well as from Murakami's own *oeuvre*: hard-boiled detectives, jazz records, mysterious cats, pits, elegant slender-fingered men who pull all the strings, people with extremely eccentric obsessions upon which they refuse to reflect, meals rounded out with steamed edamame beans and half a glass of beer, mild-mannered everymen inducted by degrees into a surreal so-real underworld complicated beyond their wildest dreams, extraordinarily long periods of *waiting*, all alchemically remixed and recycled in an effort to transcend themselves. This is exactly the same sort of creative dynamic we find in *Cymbeline*, "a recapitulatory play"[20] that comes chronologically near the end of the Shakespearean canon, and which is palpably concerned with its author's own past work, perhaps "perversely self-conscious";[21] a dog's breakfast of 'the journey thus far'. I would suggest again that the correspondence between our postmodern aesthetic and the phase of early modernity which produced *Cymbeline* is no meaningless coincidence.[22]

In an effort to come to terms with *Cymbeline*'s polysemy, I have turned to the theory of Jungian typology, which represents Jung's earliest major theory-crafting attempt in trying to understand how differing views and meanings co-exist; he recognized how often different people could have utterly different, mutually exclusive, and yet equally tenable and non-pathological experiences of the same phenomenon. Jung's theory, and some contemporary developments, will be introduced in what I hope is an appropriate amount of detail later in this intro. To the reader who may be sceptical about the use of such a model to describe either human beings *or* works of art, I would like to say that I have not *applied* the model to the play like a cookie cutter which creates precisely the shape it already wants to see. Instead I have *found*, in the course of studying this play, and, truth be told, rather unexpectedly, that the theory—Jung's "compass on [his] psychological voyages of discovery"[23]—has helped to illuminate a great deal of what is happening on the depth-psychological level of the play. I try to wield it with a light touch. I will leave the reader to determine its value for themselves.

Criticism

It is something of a rite of entry to begin with the most prominent detractor of the play, Dr. Samuel Johnson:

> To remark the folly of the fiction, the absurdity of the conduct, the confusion of the names and manners of different times, and the impossibility of the events in any system of life, were to waste criticism upon unresisting imbecility, upon faults too evident for detection, and too gross for aggravation.[24]

The aftertremors of Johnson's view have continued for 250 years, and the play has never completely shaken it off, as evidenced by the apparent necessity for any review of a *Cymbeline* production to quote him. Failure to appreciate the play is, ultimately, Johnson's loss. The pesky question of genre may again have been a factor: if the First Folio's categorization of the play as *tragedy* had led him to expect one, it would be no wonder he was disappointed.[25]

The play's second-most prominent detractor would be G.B. Shaw, who at first (1896) described it in absolutely withering terms, as "for the most part stagey trash of the lowest melodramatic order."[26] He seems to have had a change of heart, and 50 years later called it "one of the finest of Shakespear's later plays".[27] This praise, however, is immediately damned again by the assertion that it "goes to pieces in the last act," and further damned by the fact that it appears in the preface to his own rewritten version of said last act. However, the wit of Shaw's overall argument is so charming that no offense can be had. He feels Posthumus is "the only character left really alive in the last act"; that "nobody can possibly care a rap whether [the Queen] is alive or dead"; and, more pronouncingly, that "plot has always been the curse of serious drama, and indeed of serious literature of any kind. It is so out-of-place there that Shakespear could never invent one."[28] Still, he does not put his *Cymbeline Refinished* forth as a superior act, but simply as an alternative, particularly as an offering for theatres who find themselves befuddled by the last act. He cuts Posthumus' vision ("the masque", originally included "to please King Jamie"[29]), and greatly condenses the battle and the last scene, having no patience for "the surprises that no longer surprise anybody".[30] His version of bringing Innogen 'back to life' endows her with the gift of dry Shavian commentary—

INNOGEN: I will not laugh.
I must go home and make the best of it
As other women must.[31]

—and in certain other ways, brings her more in line with early modern romantic convention.[32] I feel he misunderstood the last act, and therefore the play.

The main interest of the play has long been Innogen, who developed a remarkable devotion among 19th-century men—Tennyson, Swinburne, Hazlitt—who saw in her something like the apotheosis of womanhood. They provide a metatheatrical complement to "the unconventional loyalty that Imogen receives from those who serve her".[33]

David Garrick's extremely popular 18th-century adaptation cut many of the same aspects as Shaw, including Posthumus' Vision—though as Garrick frequently portrayed Posthumus himself, the character was established as "the most important male role in the play".[34] Attempts to view the play as focused on Posthumus-as-hero are, to me, unconvincing[35]—it seems, to me, unquestionably a post-heroic play, rather than a badly-written heroic one.

One interpretation which I consider well worth the study, but which I do not address further in this book, is the recognition of Posthumus and Cloten as more than just foils, but shadows of one another. Some productions have successfully double-cast the part, for instance Cheek By Jowl's 2007 production in which Tom Hiddleston played both. Such a casting supports a kind of dream-logic in which Posthumus' negative pathology is submitted to an alchemical healing process during the acts in which he is offstage and Cloten predominates.[36]

Landry finds a holistic assessment of the play with an analogy between the marriage plot and the political plot: that dreams (as in Posthumus') "are to one's identity as a nation's past . . . is to its sense of itself as a nation".[37] She interprets the entire midsection of the play between Posthumus' disappearance and reappearance as a dream of his own dreaming, in which Innogen/Fidele and Cloten stand for two warring parts of his psyche, with Innogen emerging victorious. She also recognizes Cymbeline himself as the centre around which the rest of the play resolves, observing that, the interest in the lovers notwithstanding, *they* are not the play's main point.

Swander finds the play commenting on "the inadequacy of conventional heroics and virtues."[38] Similarly, Carr's approach sees the play as not only post-heroic but post-mythic. She explores especially the Orpheus references which attend Cloten. For her, *Cymbeline* fundamentally challenges "the validity of myth" as a way of understanding the world.[39] Though she does not appear interested in Jungian psychology *per se,* we might identify her work as implicitly post-Jungian.

The play's difference in meaning in different times has often been tied to its reputation as an aggrandizement of British nationalism. This was certainly true of Garrick's version, which cut 570 lines from the final act, in order to "resituate the play's victory as a consequence of British courage in the face of an outside, invading force that had to be subdued."[40] His is part of a long tradition of identifying Innogen with Britain—an entirely symbolically tenable interpretation—which was most emphatically communicated by Garrick in an interlude, which followed a certain production of his version, in which the actress who had played Innogen descended "in a cloud of glory" to speak the patriotic speech which Garrick had cut from the part of *Cymbeline*'s Queen. For Wilson Knight, the play's purpose was "to emphasize the importance of ancient Rome in Britain's history", symbolizing "transference of virtue from Rome to Britain."[41] Hawkes, more recently, sees it as the victim of historical irony, in that the apparently unionist undercurrent of the play's Wales setting was eventually undermined by the establishment of a Welsh Assembly in 1999.[42] In 2016, the play's historical refraction was again shifted, this time by Brexit, giving particularly new resonance to the political plot of Britain's separation from Rome—that very year the RSC staged a production "set in a post-Brexit dystopia",[43] with Gillian Bevan as *Queen* Cymbeline, vaguely evoking then-PM Theresa May.

A recurrent tension emerges between a vision of the play as innovative versus conservative; reckless and iconoclastic, or genre-conforming—does it "ask fundamental questions about England's place in history, her experience with religion, and her future in the world",[44] or does it pander to the sociopolitical vanities of its time? Chen finds an "exactly balanced treatment of contemporary political topics and generic elements",[45] given by a Shakespeare "ever observant of the Janus-like character of the manoeuvres of English Renaissance rhetoric"[46] who "offers no clue—or rather, too many clues"[47] for his audience to determine the play's 'position' on any matter which it touches, including but not limited to womanhood, loyalty, peace, Britain, Wales, Rome, and Jupiter.[48] Lerer, like Chen, focuses on the metatheatrical experience of the play, and how it integrates the experience of play-watching into itself so that it can reflect on that same experience.[49]

Warren's evocative description of rehearsal process in the production directed by Peter Hall handily reinforces my sense that the absolute best way to get to know these plays is through working on them.[50] He describes in (I daresay) thrilling detail how lines and interactions which land as relatively meaningless globs of text on a page can reveal uncanny depth and necessity when the actors find the right subtext—not *what* they say, but *why* they say it and especially why they say it *that way*. His detailed accounts of significant 20th century productions at the RSC, Stratford Festival, National Theatre, and on film, give an excellent sense of how the play really works *as a play*. He is very sensitive to matters of theatrical interpretation, both in terms of large-scale directorial vision and moment-to-moment acting nuance. His book richly involves the reader in imagining the impact of these various productions, and comes so close to transmitting the experience of the performed work of art that this particular reader is green with envy at having not been alive yet to have been there in person.

Bate's view is that the overall question of *Cymbeline*'s quality has been, for now, settled:

> the twentieth century going into the early twenty-first has seen a massive resurgence in its popularity on both page and stage, and recent criticism now widely accepts it as a masterwork that no longer needs to be explained away or apologized for.[51]

To me, *Cymbeline* clearly represents a genuine dramatic achievement, rather than merely an interesting artefact associated with a writer whose best work was done elsewhere. It is entirely stage-worthy in its own right. Certain critics (though perhaps few today) may feel that I commit the error of "attempting to impose a profound significance upon a play whose scope does not, in fact, extend beyond that of conventional romance."[52] I would offer that perhaps not only *Cymbeline* but "the scope of conventional romance" tend to be underestimated.

In mind of Shakespeare's *oeuvre*, the play reads to me as an integral link in the overall chain. Insofar as the 'romances' go, for example, in the sequence (1) *The Winter's Tale*, (2) *Cymbeline*, (3) *The Tempest*,[53] the third can be considered as representing the fruit of the work which was prepared by the first. The second, therefore, shows us the work in full action.

Origin

It would appear that *Cymbeline* was first staged in Spring 1610,[54] after the theatres had suffered a long plague-motivated closure. Strong textual evidence suggests that the play had more than a little to do with flattering James I. King James prided himself as a peacemaker,[55] *Jacobus Pacificus*, and his *pax Britannicus* seems clearly alluded to by the peace established by Cymbeline. The prominence of Wales, and in particular Milford Haven, also seem to allude to contemporaneous concerns about British nationhood, and the investiture of Prince Henry.[56] It has even been proposed that the relatively flat characterization of Cymbeline himself,[57] and the stylized presentation of the Queen,[58] are diplomatic manoeuvres on Shakespeare's part, to avoid his own king reading too much of himself into the wrong aspects of the ancient king.

Shakespeare's sources are partially historical: Geoffrey of Monmouth's *The History of the Kings of Britain*, Holinshed's *Chronicles* and Camden's *Britannia*. The historical setting of the play seems, to me, to be a thematic choice more than an attempt to re-tell anything like 'real' history (whatever that is). Bate uses the term "pseudohistory"[59] to refer to the very loose adaptational strategy of *Cymbeline*, which is more like *Macbeth* or *King Lear* in this regard than the (somewhat) more historically-grounded tetralogies.

There are also a number of contemporaneous and partial sources—rather too many to name—for pieces of the plot: romances such as *Mucedorus, Clyomon and Clamydes, Perceforest, The Rare Triumphs of Love and Fortune,* Chaucer's *Franklin's Tale* and Boccacio's *Decameron* (indirectly, via a prose romance called *Frederyke of Jennen*). These are especially relevant as variations on the 'wager plot' idea, or the calumniating of the heroine.[60]

Cymbeline's Typological Riddle

In this chapter, I make frequent use of Jungian typology, in an attempt to better understand what is happening on the depth-psychological level of *Cymbeline*. This typology, popularly known today through a variation on the original model, the Meyers-Briggs Type Indicator (MBTI), involves eight psychological 'functions'— ways that the psyche interacts with the inner and outer worlds in which it finds itself situated. Beebe clarifies:

> It has not always been clear to students of Jung's analytical psychology what his famous 'types' are types *of*. The commonest assumption has been that they refer to types of *people*. But for Jung, they were types of *consciousness*, that is, characteristic orientations assumed by the ego in establishing and discriminating an individual's inner and outer reality.[61]

This section is by far and away the most theory-dense portion of this book, but it will pay dividends as the rest of the chapter unfolds. *Cymbeline* poses a unique and provocative typological riddle, and these few pages will lay the necessary ground-work to begin to decipher it.

Jungian type theory is nuanced and complex, even unwieldy, but it persists, and I suspect that its virtue is that it may accurately reflect something about the human psyche, which is itself nuanced, complex, and unwieldy. My aim is to avoid drown-ing the reader, by providing only as much detail as will be necessary to understand the way the model relates to *Cymbeline*.

The most shocking thing about typology is the discovery that, actually, other people *do* experience the world differently than oneself. That is the basic proposition. We are not talking simply about different perspectives—we are talking about fundamentally different ways of being. Even after this fact is intellectually 'known-about', it can still be of the utmost difficulty to digest this knowledge into a place where types different than our own can be understood, on their own terms, rather than simply categorized. I could myself, at times, be reasonably accused of viewing others as more-or-less successful versions of my own type; the consistent ability to *truly* read into the heart of someone else's functional processes is hard-won. Therefore, though Jung was adamant that his typology was *not* a label-sticking "parlour game",[62] that is exactly where most discussion on typology tends to get stuck.

This is the problem from whence Jung's type theory sprung: he was in need of a way to comprehend the fact that people of relatively equal capacity could, apparently, experience the world in different—even polarized—modes, drawing equally polarized conclusions from their experience, and going on to live in radically different ways. He intended to create, therefore, "a critical psychology dealing with the organization and delimitation of psychic processes that can be shown to be typical".[63] Typology, though later more-or-less abandoned by Jung, was at first central to his psychology. His book *Psychological Types* was at one point even published with the subtitle "or, The Psychology of Individuation".

> One way to understand what Jung meant by individuation is the progressive differentiation of the various psychological functions of consciousness . . . he felt that there was a way to describe its orderly unfolding in all of us, and he used his idea of psychological types to offer certain developmental guidelines.[64]

Jung proposed, in his theory, that there were four basic functions with which a person's basic personality is structured. Two, intuiting and sensing, had to do with perception of the world; the other two, feeling and thinking, had to do with judging, or making decisions about what to *do* with those perceptions.

Jung's most concise explanation of these functions can serve as a helpful starting point: "the essential function of sensation is to establish that something exists, thinking tells us what it means, feeling what its value is, and intuition surmises whence it comes and whither it goes."[65]

Each of these functions has two options as to its 'direction', that is, whether it is directed outward, focused on the collective/objective world or inward, focused on the individual/subjective world. These directions are called attitudes, and the two attitudes are called introversion and extraversion—two words which will no doubt be familiar to most readers, even if the precise meanings are not. It is often said that being introverted or extraverted is to do with being social: introverts are less social than extraverts, and introverts 'gain energy' from being alone whereas extraverts 'gain energy' from being with other people. This is misleading. It might be more helpful to think in terms of which attitude *costs* a person more energy rather than which *gives* energy.

The eight psychic functions are, therefore:

- Introverted feeling (Fi)
- Introverted thinking (Ti)
- Introverted intuiting (Ni)
- Introverted sensing (Si)
- Extraverted feeling (Fe)
- Extraverted thinking (Te)
- Extraverted intuiting (Ne)
- Extraverted sensing (Se)

These functions are considered to exist in every person, in more-or-less developed forms, with one in particular being an individual person's preferred or dominant function. The level of a function's 'development' has to do with how much energy it takes a person to use it: less developed functions take more energy.[66] I will often abbreviate the names of the functions, as in the parentheses above (and below), with a capital letter denoting the underlying function, and a lowercase letter denoting the attitude.

A very brief description of each function follows:

- **Extraverted sensing (Se)** is the most 'obvious' function, and, in a way, is the precondition for the other seven. This does not mean it will be developed or used consciously. Se revolves around the facts of immediate experience—as the word *sensing* suggests, its primary agents are the five senses. As a mode of perception, it is not in itself concerned with the value or meaning of what it senses, but stays at the level of experience. 'What is the thing like, and what happens to me when I am engaged with it?'
- **Extraverted intuiting (Ne)** also has to do with perception of the given facts, but with a slightly different cast. Whereas Se is involved with the present-moment qualities of a situation, Ne 'looks', so to speak, around and past the facts, in order to be involved with the past, future, and other elements which cannot be strictly observed from the facts but are nevertheless perceptible. Ne entertains new possibilities, breaking up the way things *are* in favour of envisioning the way they *could* be, and enabling movement from this present to a desirable future. The content of an intuition can sometimes, with careful attention, be shown to coincide with what would be a basically logical deduction, but the process itself is not deductive—the perception of the conclusion occurs spontaneously without use of logical processes. This is an important principle: *sometimes* different processes can arrive at the same endpoint via their own roads. Not always.
- **Extraverted thinking (Te)** is the enforcer of that which Ne would enable. It is a logical process directed toward the outer world, particularly in terms of

planning and developing acceptable and 'useful' thoughts. It prioritizes this action over the action of understanding, which belongs more to Ti. Te is oriented by, and relies upon, objective facts and collective ideas—concrete reality and already-accepted models of 'what works'—to regulate and enforce that which it has decided to be necessary.

- **Extraverted feeling (Fe)** is also a process directed toward the outer world, and though it is also rational it is not, strictly speaking, logical. "Feeling is first and foremost a reaction of the psyche in terms of acceptance or rejection of a perception . . . It is an evaluation: 'pleasant' or 'unpleasant.'"[67] Fe, then, is concerned with creating and maintaining pleasantness outwardly, or harmony in the social sphere. To achieve this, Fe often attunes to the feelings of others, the likely effects of certain actions upon the feelings of others, and the 'objective' feeling of a given situation. This function validates and affirms the feelings of others where appropriate—Fe is perhaps nothing if not appropriate. Depending on context, and its level of development, it may be concerned with affirming the objective or 'proper' feeling of a situation over and above the idiosyncratic feelings of individuals. The 'objective feeling' *per se* is something more in accord with traditional or collective values than with the feelings of individuals—though it can sometimes be experienced as the feeling that would be in accord with a more universal perspective.[68]

- **Introverted feeling (Fi)**, on the other hand, is idiosyncratic and personal, at times trivially so. Though not strictly a negative process, it is often only visible as a distinct kind of negative judgmental response. What is happening on the inside is a process of appraisal, or establishing value; Fi recognizes or decides what some given thing is worth, in comparison with an inarticulable inner standard (i.e., an archetype). A serious difficulty in understanding both of the feeling functions is posed by the fact that we often use the word 'feeling' to mean emotion, intuition, sensation, or even muddy thinking. The feeling functions are discrete from these, and the most important point in this connection is that they are oriented by *values*. Emotion may be *a* value, and one may feel emotional *about* a value, but a value is not an emotion.

- **Introverted thinking (Ti)** is, like Te, a logical process, but directed toward understanding. It imparts names to events, objects, and processes, though the accent is less on communicating or developing a system than it is on properly defining the existing situation. It strives for truth, for which the criterion is, as with Fi, not outer reality but an inner standard, or an archetype. It uses the objective facts, at best, as a means of grounding its abstract ideas, and at worst it does not relate to the objective facts at all. It tends to prioritize not the establishing of new facts, but the development of new views.

- **Introverted intuiting (Ni)** tracks the movement of archetypal forces in the way that seismologists track the movement of tectonic plates. It is a way of knowing that relates to inner happenings with the concretism that Se relates to outer facts. Ni may look like imagining; it is sometimes indistinguishable from divination. It consults an inner source for knowledge of the archetypal currents of a given situation, to thereby become aware of the possibilities inherent in it, and the likely direction that the situation will take. An exchange from the television series *Shogun* is illustrative:

YABUSHIGE: How does it feel to shape the wind to your will?
TORANAGA: I don't control the wind. I only study it.[69]

- **Introverted sensing (Si)** is organized around verifying, though rather than the verification of truth *per se* it is the verification of something like *correctness* as related to an inner precedent. It gathers information, comparing the new information with past experience, memory, or archetypal material. It is a conservative function, in the sense of being oriented toward the past; the present often primarily serves as a touchstone to connect with or relive the past. Si can most clearly be seen in its manner of implementing processes and rituals in the prescribed and correct manner: adherence to an established process is an important task of this function, and it can be thought of, very broadly, as an inner accountant in this respect.

What follows now is a somewhat overdone ritual, but nevertheless I feel it may be helpful, so here is a rather broad burlesque of how each function might behave at a group meal. (To be clear, I am talking about *personified functions* rather than *people* with full personalities.)

Se might be experiencing the tastes, sounds, and sights of the event, while Ne might be looking for ways to improve it for next time; Te may be making sure everybody gets to the table on time, and explaining to everybody what each dish is, while Fe is making sure that the group harmony prevails by saying all the right things to help people feel welcome and taken care of. Fi could be tracking the many *faux pas* of value that occur in such situations, such as the words, behaviours, or appearances of others that they find offensive—which is not to simply cast Fi as a wet blanket, for this may also emanate as a sign of good taste and breeding, a poise which encourages every other attendee to behave better. Maybe Ti will be frustrated because nobody else seems to know the purpose and meaning of this dinner, or even be interested in what dinners really *are*. Ni may simply watch and weigh, noting the events and interactions as epiphenomena of much deeper movements taking place below the surface; if there is a fight to break out later in the evening, they may have become aware of this potentiality the moment they walked in the door. Si might be silently comparing a specific dish to every dish of that type that they have ever experienced, heard about, or somehow perceived the potential of in their lives.

The perception functions are sometimes called the irrational functions, and the judging functions are sometimes called the rational functions, because the former are oriented to gathering data without applying any rational criterion, whereas the latter constitute rational processes.

Intuiting

Sensing

} Perception (Irrational)

Feeling

Thinking

} Judging (Rational)

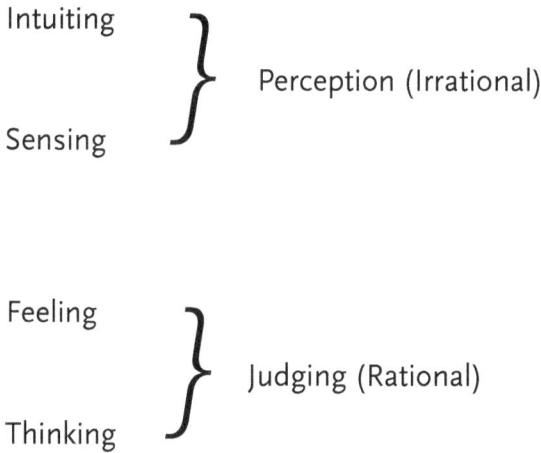

Figure 5.1 Four functions grouped into irrational/rational.

Jung had to say, on this point:

> If sensation or intuition wants to be reasonable [rational]. . . this will be a great mistake. If you adopt a 'reasonable' attitude when observing, you will not see the unexpected . . . The very essence of these two functions is to perceive what is there, however unexpected it may be.[70]

It is probably obvious enough why thinking is considered rational, but feeling is as well since it is adjusted in accord with values—whether those values are themselves reasonable, aesthetic, or ethical.[71]

Though these descriptions should serve as a useful touchstone, the clearest way to elucidate them will be in relationship to *Cymbeline*. As a given function comes up over the course of the discussion, I will reiterate and elaborate the function's individual qualities.

The *I Ching* has formed an important source of archetypal knowledge throughout this book, and it can aid us again when it comes to type. Chenghou Cai has made convincing associations between the eight trigrams of the *I Ching* and the eight functions,[72] which are as follows:

1. Ti with 巽, *Xùn*, the Gentle (Wind/Wood).
2. Te with 震, *Zhèn*, the Arousing (Thunder).
3. Fi with 艮, *Gèn*, Keeping Still (Mountain).
4. Fe with 兑, *Duì*, the Joyous (Lake).
5. Si with 坤, *Kūn*, the Receptive (Earth).
6. Se with 离, *Lí*, the Clinging (Fire).

7. Ni with 坎, *Kǎn*, the Abysmal (Water).
8. Ne with 乾, *Qián*, the Creative (Heaven).[73]

The following chart combines the axes, functions, function-attitudes, semantic fields, and associated trigrams.[74]

Axis	Function	Function-Attitude	Semantic Field	Trigram
Rational	Thinking	Introverted Thinking (Ti)	Naming—Defining—Understanding	巽, *Xùn*, the Gentle (Wind, Wood)
		Extraverted Thinking (Te)	Regulating—Planning—Enforcing	震, *Zhèn*, the Arousing (Thunder)
	Feeling	Introverted Feeling(Fi)	Judging—Appraising—Establishing the Value	艮, *Gèn*, Keeping Still (Mountain)
		Extraverted Feeling(Fe)	Validating—Affirming—Relating	兌, *Duì*, the Joyous (Lake)
Irrational	Sensing	Introverted Sensing (Si)	Implementing—Verifying—Accounting	坤, *K'un*, the Receptive (Earth)
		Extraverted Sensing (Se)	Engaging—Experiencing—Enjoying	離, *Lí*, the Clinging (Fire)
	Intuiting	Introverted Intuiting (Ni)	Imagining—Knowing—Divining	坎, *Kǎn*, the Abysmal (Water)
		Extraverted Intuiting (Ne)	Entertaining—Envisioning—Enabling	乾, *Qián*, the Creative (Heaven)

Figure 5.2 Axes, functions, semantic fields, and associated trigrams.

1, 2, 3, 4: Typology of the Persona

As mentioned, every person is considered to have all eight of these functions available to them, though typically the functions exist at radically different levels of development. A person's 'type' is identified by the combination of their most-preferred function (the *dominant* function) with their second-most-preferred function (the *auxiliary* function). In typological terms, I am an introverted thinking person with auxiliary extraverted intuition. My third function is introverted sensing, and my fourth function—the *inferior* function, as it is known—is extraverted feeling. Ti, then Ne, then Si, then Fe. The first four functions constitute the territory of the individual's persona; these ways of functioning are more ego-syntonic to the individual, and they tend to work more adaptively and with more positive purpose than the latter four, the back half, the shadow functions.

The functions themselves are seen as existing in pairs of opposites. On one axis live the rational functions, thinking and feeling. On the other axis live the irrational functions, sensing and intuiting. When visualized, these functions are typically shown in a cross shape or mandala, depicting the intersection of the two axes. This cross helps to represent the ways that functions at either ends of an axis tend to exclude, oppose, and compensate one another. Which of the rational/irrational axes is vertical, and which horizontal, depends on the individual's given type. For me, the two axes look like this:

1: Thinking

RATIONAL   2: Intuiting ——————————— 3: Sensing

4: Feeling

IRRATIONAL

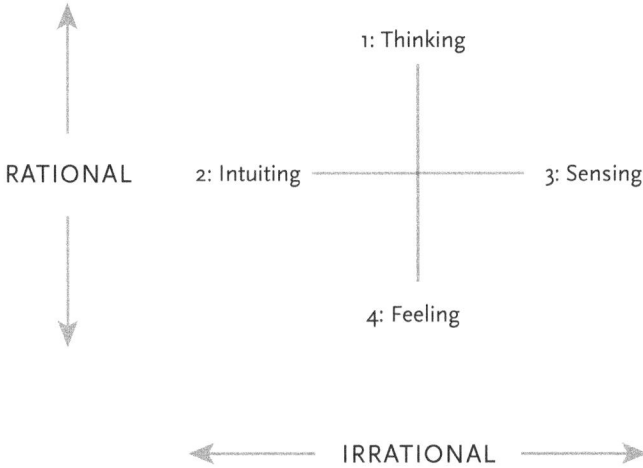

Figure 5.3 Joel Crichton's first four functions, arranged in mandala-format.

The balance of opposites also pertains to the level of the attitudes: when one function is introverted, the function on the opposite end of its axis is extraverted. To fill in the diagram of my own type with this attitudinal information looks like this: It will be observed that, in number order from one to four, the attitudes also alternate—the first is introverted, the second extraverted, the third introverted again, and the fourth extraverted. In MBTI terms, INTP.

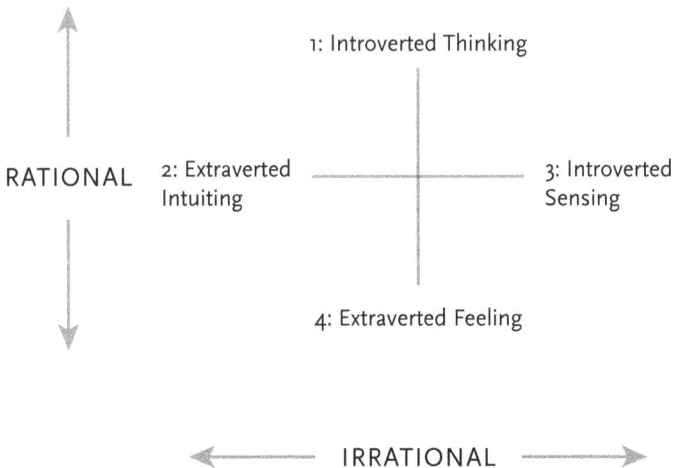

1: Introverted Thinking

RATIONAL   2: Extraverted   3: Introverted
            Intuiting ——————————   Sensing

4: Extraverted Feeling

IRRATIONAL

Figure 5.4 Joel Crichton's first four functions, with attitudes.

Let us leave my own type alone for now, in favour of some remarks on the psychological type of Shakespeare himself. Beebe's opinion is that Shakespeare's dominant function was extraverted feeling (Fe), with auxiliary introverted intuiting (Ni),[75] and I feel there is a very strong case to be made for this hypothesis. In itself, however, that is a subject which takes us a little too far afield from this chapter's theme to be elaborated in detail. Suffice it to say that "sweet" "friendly" "honey-tongued"[76] Shakespeare certainly had enough of an Fe function to be able to write several plays about Queen Elizabeth's ancestors without causing royal offence, while still wielding the dramatic edge necessary to keep audiences interested. He appears to have adeptly navigated the echelons of society well beyond his station, and thereby skirted many of the punishments, dishonours, and indignities into which his contemporaries seemed to blunder.

The primary four functions of Shakespeare's proposed typology, visualized, look like this: Extraverted feeling (Fe) in the first place, introverted intuiting (Ni) in the second place, extraverted sensing (Se) in the third place, and introverted thinking (Ti) in the fourth place. In MBTI terms, ENFJ.

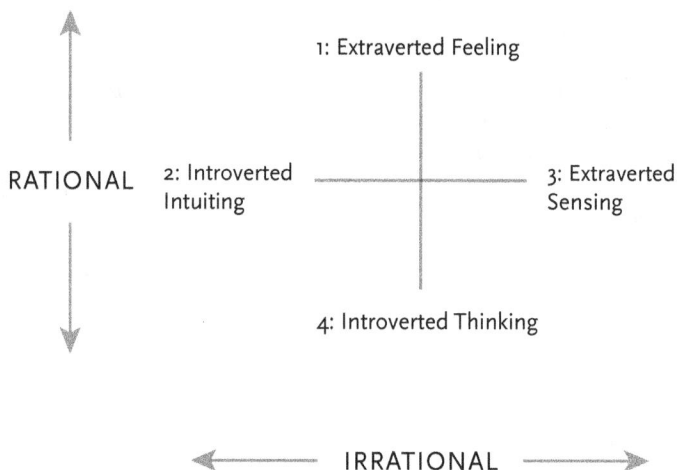

Figure 5.5 Proposed typology for Shakespeare, first four functions.

5, 6, 7, 8: Typology of the Shadow

The first four functions provide helpful but limited insight into a full personality. Certainly this is the case with *Cymbeline*, which has shadow written all over it. In particular, from a typological point of view, the first really remarkable thing about *Cymbeline* is that it seems to be written not from Shakespeare's dominant Fe, or even his auxiliary Ni, but rather from his Te—the function which is theoretically the furthest from his consciousness, 8th place out of 8 total functions. The fifth-through-eighth functions, or the shadow functions,[77] reflect the order established by the first four. Visually, this makes a second 'cross' diagram, with opposite attitudes from the first. Continuing with Shakespeare's typology, then, his fifth-through-eighth functions would be visualized like this:

Introverted feeling (Fi) in the fifth place, extraverted intuiting (Ne) in the sixth, introverted sensing (Si) in the seventh, and extraverted thinking (Te) in the eighth.

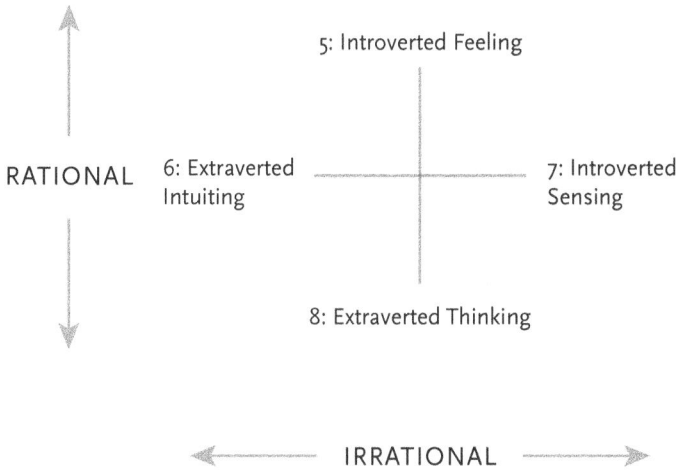

Figure 5.6 Proposed typology for Shakespeare, 5th-through-8th functions.

The Archetypal Constellation

An analogy: in astrological thought, the quality of a given planet is coloured by the constellation in which it falls—Venus in Scorpio is expressed differently from Venus in Capricorn, for example. Another: in the theatre, different actors may perform the same role—Harriet Walter and Judi Dench make very different Innogens, though they both begin with the same text. This is what the final level of this typological model is like. It concerns the qualities of the different positions in which the functions fall—e.g., Fe as 1st, or Te as 8th. The functions tend to express certain qualities based on the position which they hold in an individual's psyche. An extraverted thinking function in 1st position will behave very differently from one in 8th position, though they are still the same core process. Jung and von Franz had already firmly established that the superior and inferior function—the 1st and 4th of the 8, respectively—have particular qualities and key roles in the psyche.[78] Beebe's development is to have addressed the archetypal qualities of the remaining six.[79]

Here are the numbered positions along with their associated archetypal dominants:

1. Hero/Heroine
2. Father/Mother (Auxiliary or parental function)
3. Puer/Puella (Eternal or Divine Child)
4. Anima/Animus (Soul-image, and inferior function)
5. Opposing Personality
6. Senex/Witch (Senex means Old Man)
7. Trickster
8. Demon/Daimon

We will leave the first seven alone for now, and start with the 8th, which I have suggested is the place in Shakespeare's psyche from which *Cymbeline* is written. The 8th function in a person, according to this model, typically behaves with a *demonic* quality. This, in *Cymbeline,* can help us to understand its ruthless counter-orthodoxy and destruction of theatrical forms—it uses *convention,* which as a collectively-held idea is a Te 'object'—as a tool to undermine its audience's experience. This is Shakespeare's demonic extraverted thinking, Shakespeare at his most darkly-driven. The demonic function also has the potential to become *daimonic* at times,[80] having a diabolically inspired quality, a sort of *duende* that emerges from the dark depths of the psyche to tutor it. This helps us understand why it is that *Cymbeline,* despite all its difficulties, remains a powerful and transformative work.

In this chapter, the two levels of character interpretation used in this book up until now still pertain. The first is the level of psychological 'realism', in which the interiority of the characters is assumed, and they are imaginatively accorded the dignity of being full and individual persons. Therefore I will at times speak of an individual character's 'typology', as though he or she is a human being with a dominant function, inferior function, and all the rest.

On the second level, the characters are regarded structurally—as though they each personify a single function in the psyche, and thus take up a position on the cross-shaped mandalas. This second level is what I refer to as the 'typological riddle' of the play, and it affords us a unique method of exploring the creative work going on under the surface of *Cymbeline*—both in terms of what it means to itself, and what it might mean for Shakespeare's psyche.

I propose that *Cymbeline*'s typology is the same as that proposed for Shakespeare himself above. Therefore a visualization of the eight functions, and their associated archetypal dominants, in *Cymbeline* order, looks like this:

PERSONA

1: Heroic Fe

2: Parental Ni ———————————— 3: Puer/Puella Se

SHADOW

4: Inferior (Anima/Animus) Ti   5: Opposing Fi

6: Senex/Witch Ne ———————————— 7: Trickster Si

8: Demonic/Daimonic Te

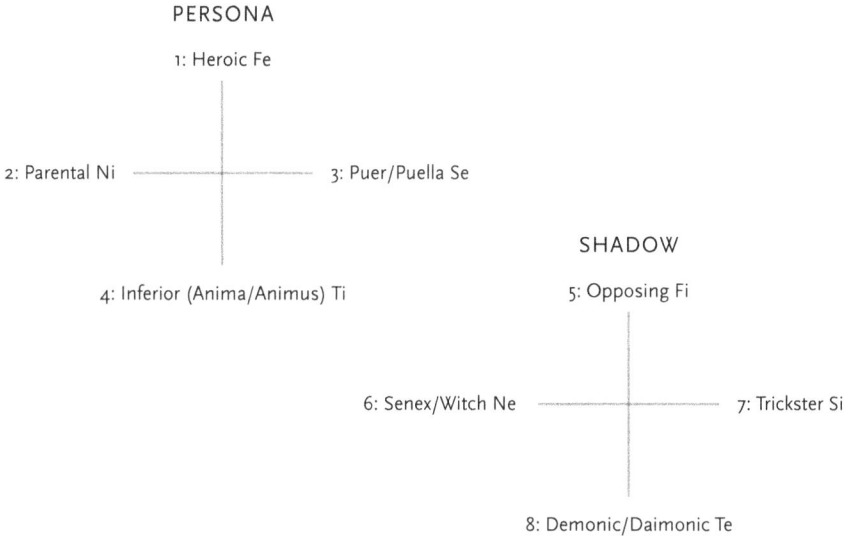

Figure 5.7 Proposed typology for *Cymbeline.*

Okay. We're ready to go.

Notes

1 I follow the contemporary Arden editors in using the name Innogen rather than Imogen (despite the latter being the more beautiful), assuming that they are correct that 'Imogen' was ultimately a printer's error mistaking 'nn' for 'm' (Wayne 2017, 71). When a citation uses the name "Imogen", I leave this intact.
2 Kirsch (1967, 294).
3 Landry (1982, 68).
4 Kirsch (1967, 286).
5 Granville-Barker (1947, 243).
6 Kermode (1963, 22).
7 Bloom (1999, 635).
8 Bloom (1999, 618).
9 Hazlitt (1908, 11).
10 Crumley (2001, 298).
11 Wilson Knight (1948, 129).
12 Chambers (1930, 338–9).
13 Chen (2015, 40).
14 Marcus (2013).
15 Hazlitt (1908, 11).
16 Beaumont & Fletcher (1908, 18).
17 Wayne (2017, 19–20).
18 Tanner (2010, 721).

19 Kawai (2006, 437; 445; 440).
20 Wayne (2017, 28).
21 Barton (2007a, 19).
22 Maley (1997, 88) suggests that "Shakespeare is our contemporary exactly because the British problem has the same currency, indeed, the same urgency, that it possessed when he grappled with it". I would say *Cymbeline*'s relevance extends far beyond 'just' Britain.
23 Jung (CW 6, 959).
24 Johnson (1989, 307).
25 Mowat (2003, 130).
26 Shaw (1961, 54).
27 Shaw (1946, 133).
28 Shaw (1946, 135–6).
29 Shaw (1946, 134).
30 Shaw (1946, 135).
31 Shaw (1946, 149).
32 Swander (1964, 266).
33 Swander (1964, 264).
34 Wayne (2003, 391).
35 For example, Lawrence (1931, 203).
36 Peter Hall also felt that his production missed that—"if we had done that double, we'd have the play" (Warren 1990, 90).
37 Landry (1982, 69).
38 Swander (1964, 260).
39 Carr (1978).
40 Wayne (2003, 398).
41 Wilson Knight (1948, 183; 166).
42 Hawkes (2002, 62).
43 Billington's review in *The Guardian* (2016).
44 King (2005, 2).
45 Chen (2015, xiii).
46 Chen (2015, 60).
47 Chen (2015, 51).
48 Chen (2015, 54).
49 Lerer (2018, 171).
50 Warren (1989; 1990).
51 Bate (2011, xii).
52 Nosworthy (1955, xlv); referencing Leavis (1942).
53 This is the order given by Bate (2011), though it is not *particularly* important to any of my argument whether *WT* comes before or afterward, as Wayne (2017) has it.
54 Bate (2011, xxviii). Wayne (2017, 30) puts it slightly later—as above, after *The Winter's Tale* rather than before.
55 Jones (1971, 254).
56 Chen (2015, 47).
57 Bate (2010, 321).
58 Jones (1971, 261).
59 Bate (2011, xxviii).
60 Bate (2011, xxviii); Wayne (2017, 94–109).
61 Beebe (2006, 130).
62 Jung (CW 6, Foreword to the Argentine Edition).
63 Jung (CW 6, Foreword to the Argentine Edition).
64 Beebe (2017, 153).

65 Jung (CW 6, 983).
66 Murphy (2021, 1075).
67 Jung (2022, 18).
68 Beebe (2022b, 27): "There's kind of a *jouissance* to the function that only comes at the level of what Jung calls the self, which is a genuine *relating* to the *unus mundus*[.]"
69 Clavell et al. (2024).
70 Jung (2022, 23).
71 Jung (2022, 23).
72 Cai (2021).
73 As each trigram, doubled, constitutes a hexagram, I will in the following chapter be exploring those 8 hexagrams' relationships with the 8 functions. The implication of these connections is profound, and even metaphysical—though as I understand Professor Cai to be developing his work further at present, I will refrain from unintentionally pre-empting him by saying more.
74 Semantic fields developed by Beebe (2017, 4).
75 John Beebe, personal communication, 5 April 2022.
76 Duncan-Jones (2010, 149; 206; 149fn).
77 Beebe (2017, 38–47).
78 Jung (CW 6); von Franz & Hillman (2020).
79 Beebe (2017, 44).
80 Beebe (2017, 44).

Chapter 6

The Achievement of Normality in *Cymbeline*

From *Cymbeline*'s very first line, we know we're in for trouble:

1 GENTLEMAN: You do not meet a man but frowns. Our bloods
No more obey the heavens than our courtiers
Still seem as does the King.

(1.1.1–3)

I mean not only that "you do not meet a man but frowns" seems to bode ill, but the line itself—what does it mean? It is syntactically two-faced—duplex—it refuses to lay flat. We may get the gist of it: our feelings (bloods) do not obey the heavens, and our courtiers are acting (seeming) like the frowning king, and therefore all are frowning. But why does the gentleman word it *this way?* It is virtually unactable. Editors' attempts to repunctuate the line and coax some sense out of it do little to help.[1]

But it's not as if Shakespeare doesn't know how to write a great opening line that sets the tone for the entire piece: "Now is the winter of our discontent" (*RIII* 1.1.1); "Two households, both alike in dignity" (*RJ* Pro.1); "O for a muse of fire" (*HV* Pro.1). This opening, by contrast, throws us before we've become situated, like an unbroken horse. It balks at its own rhetorical promise, in seeming to offer a straightforward comparison—'*X* is no more true than *Y*'—and then changing course midway. And so while the explanation above is the generally accepted meaning of the line, the line itself seems designed to elicit a sense of interference. The gentleman himself seems to be saying two things at once; his unconscious interferes and he says neither of them clearly.

The second implication might be that, in this kingdom, *seeming* has lost its meaning. Their frowns reflect the king's displeasure, yes, but these frowns are meaningless masks. And the typical good face—the Merry Olde England of Shakespeare's earlier days, as well as the stiff upper lip and the *Keep Calm and Carry On* which came to characterize Britain several centuries later—has been abandoned.

The rigidity of the kingdom extends to the dramatic structure of the play. *Cymbeline* is identified as a 'romance', not by Shakespeare but by his publishers, and its characters do often threaten to behave essentially as symbols. It may therefore seem to be technically incorrect for me to interpret them through a characterological

DOI: 10.4324/9781003596967-7

lens, but my reason is simply that they do not seem to me to be romance symbols. Chambers was sure they were even "puppets",[2] and by this I think he means to refer to the way in which they sometimes seem to be conscripted into an overly complex plot. Nosworthy's modulation is that *Cymbeline*'s characters are *supposed* to be romantic symbols, but Shakespeare has more-or-less fumbled the transition from literary romance tradition to stage romance, accidentally writing puppets that occasionally come to life.[3] He gives many examples of the characters straying beyond what 'should' be their limits, and at some point one begins to wonder if there are not too many exceptions for the rule to be valid at all. I suspect that the play itself is a try at something new: a romantic frame with human beings inside, striving to individuate.

Stein finds the playworld "paranoiac",[4] and Kott would have recognized the Stalinist-lite tones of the opening situation, in which we all must "wear [our] faces to the bent / Of the King's looks" (1.1.13–4) in a desperate attempt to save our own skins. Consider the anecdote from Solzhenitsyn's *Gulag Archipelago*:

> At the conclusion of the conference, a tribute to Comrade Stalin was called for. Of course, everyone stood up . . . The small hall echoed with "stormy applause, rising to an ovation." For three minutes, four minutes, five minutes . . . But palms were getting sore and raised arms were already aching. And the older people were panting from exhaustion. It was becoming insufferably silly even to those who really adored Stalin. However, who would dare be the first to stop?. . . After all, NKVD men were standing in the hall applauding and watching to see who quit first! And in that obscure, small hall, unknown to the Leader, the applause went on—six, seven, eight minutes! They were done for! Their goose was cooked! They couldn't stop now till they collapsed with heart attacks! At the rear of the hall, which was crowded, they could of course cheat a bit, clap less frequently, less vigorously, not so eagerly—but up there with the presidium where everyone could see them?. . . Nine minutes! Ten!. . . Insanity! To the last man! With make-believe enthusiasm on their faces, looking at each other with faint hope, the district leaders were just going to go on and on applauding till they fell where they stood, till they were carried out of the hall on stretchers! And even then those who were left would not falter . . . Then, after eleven minutes, the director of the paper factory assumed a businesslike expression and sat down in his seat. And, oh, a miracle took place! Where had the universal, uninhibited, indescribable enthusiasm gone? To a man, everyone else stopped dead and sat down. They had been saved! The squirrel had been smart enough to jump off his revolving wheel.

But there is peril in displaying the slightest individuality—the slightest awareness that *one is not a puppet*:

> That, however, was how they discovered who the independent people were. And that was how they went about eliminating them. That same night the factory

director was arrested. They easily pasted ten years on him on the pretext of something quite different. But after he had signed Form 206, the final document of the interrogation, his interrogator reminded him:

"Don't ever be the first to stop applauding!"[5]

A persona is maintained, but entirely devoid of any faith that persona can have real meaning anymore; now our faces participate in a cynical game of follow-the-leader. Cymbeline's kingdom is in just such a state of disorder. Don't ever be the first to stop frowning.

Puppet-characterization is not so much an unconscious convention of the play as it is an intentional theme; they are no more puppets than are Murakami's protagonists, or the men who applaud Stalin because their life depends on it. They may *feel* confined to their roles, but this is a significant difference from their having been written *as symbols*. By the final scene, our characters have all rather remarkably transcended their own marionette-strings; in its penultimate scene the play treats us to a mystifying revelation of the one who *pulls* said strings. My impression of the relationship of *Cymbeline* to other stage romances of the same period is that it represents a try at one-upping the genre, even commandeering it for Shakespeare's own needs, rather than anything like an attempt to create a genre-conforming piece.[6]

Cymbeline's characters inhabit the uncanny valley between romance symbols and the deeply human characterization for which Shakespeare is known. But look: don't we *all* feel the tension between the world's definitions of us, and our innermost being? Between what has come to be expected of us, and creative individuation? This tension forms one of the thematic threads of the piece, and it is part of the 'human condition' with which the characters themselves struggle. I may be over-credulous to see in Cymbeline's name an expression for this: 'symboline', a hidden neologism along the lines of 'crystalline'. The characters in the play are not symbols, but they *are* symboline.

Time

Over and above Jupiter, Diana, or Hecate, the god with which Shakespeare is most truly concerned is Kronos. The force to which Shakespeare refers most consistently—constantly, even—to evoke realness is Time, the word itself often capitalized as a proper noun. In Shakespeare's usage, Time is a law of the universe, an inevitable quality of being real, making itself felt in each moment of itself. But it is also something to which human beings are subjected, whether they will or no. Time is what makes us real—because Time is what makes us mortal, and human—but Time also makes puppets of us all, as one-after-another we submit to its flow, and fall to its scythe. Time renders us helpless and small in a vast cosmos.

Time may devour, but Time also heals, and this plays an especially notable part in the romances. Act 4 of *The Winter's Tale* begins with the remarkable stage direction, "*Enter Time, the Chorus*" (*WT* 4.1.0), and Time, here embodied, helps to "slide / o'er sixteen years" (*WT* 4.1.5–6) to move the plot forward, which allows baby daughter Perdita to grow up and old King Leontes to outgrow the jealousy that ruined everybody in Sicily's life. *Pericles* also jumps something like sixteen years to let baby daughter Marina grow up. *The Tempest*'s plot *begins* on the far side of such a caesura, twelve years after the exile of old Prospero and his baby daughter Miranda; twelve years which have allowed Prospero to perfect his art, as well as to prepare himself to abjure it in the miraculous act of healing forgiveness, and abdication of power, which he will perform at the end of his play.

Time is of the essence in *Cymbeline* just as in the other romances, and it remixes the logical uses of all three. First, as in *The Tempest,* we begin many years (twenty) after what would have provided material enough for another entire play. In the first scene, we are caught up on the birth of Posthumus Leonatus and the death of his parents, the theft of King Cymbeline's two sons, and Posthumus' adoption into the king's court, all twenty years' past. Second, the great leap forward of Time that is seen in *The Winter's Tale* and *Pericles* also shows up here, but less literally: rather than moving the entire world forward in time sixteen years, Shakespeare disappears Posthumus from the stage for two whole acts, nearly two hours of playing time, and in the meantime he develops sixteen years' worth of wisdom. Posthumus' development-while-absent is as remarkable as that of Leontes or Prospero.

A great leap forward is, I believe, what this play intends to make in Shakespeare's creative process. And this alludes to a third quality of Time in the play, which is the play's remarkable impatience. Cymbeline at one point interrupts an overlong story, saying "I stand on fire. / Come to the matter" (5.5.168–9), which may express our dominant impression of the first two acts. The haste with which Shakespeare runs through these acts is palpable—one has the sense repeatedly that the plot, character, and thematic developments are being assembled to build a structure from which the play can *then* begin, moving from the known into the unknown.[7] Little in these first two acts is of especial interest; they feel boilerplate, ironically and self-consciously so; however, aside from Innogen—a clarity amid grotesquerie—the irony seems to be the main thing keeping us involved.

The sense of boilerplate, of an over*known*ness in the play, is most clearly illustrated by the first scene, an exposition that hits the ground running; a blatant ironic comment on the nature of dramatic exposition itself. In it we, the audience, 'overhear' a conversation which is plainly meant for us, between two characters who exist solely to have it and whom we never see again; a tour guide to the cursed kingdom, and his tourist. One of them asks all the right questions, and the other answers him.

2 GENTLEMAN: But what's the matter?
1 GENTLEMAN: His daughter, and the heir of's kingdom, whom
He purposed to his wife's sole son—a widow
That late he married—hath referred herself
Unto a poor but worthy gentleman. She's wedded,
Her husband banished, she imprisoned. All
Is outward sorrow . . .

2 GENTLEMAN: And why so?
1 GENTLEMAN: He that hath missed the princess is a thing
Too bad for bad report; and he that hath her . . .
                          I do not think
So fair an outward and such stuff within
Endows a man but he . . .
2 GENTLEMAN: What's his name and birth?
                                        (1.1.1–27)

And so on. The exposition proceeds methodically and nearly artlessly—except that Shakespeare's apparent artlessness in this play often has the curiously postmodern quality of 'performatively low effort', and seems to emerge out of confidence with the form rather than lack of skill.[8] But, to return to the given circumstances: the kingdom is in sorrow. The reason? The king (Cymbeline) has banished his son-in-law (Posthumus), a good but poor man, as punishment for secretly wedding the princess (Innogen). For her husband, the king prefers his stepson (Cloten), who though preferred is foul. Some general valuations are established: the king and his stepson are badguys, and the lovers are goodguys. The king also has two long-lost sons—"mark it" (1.1.58) since you won't see them for a while and are liable to forget. With more self-conscious irony, Innogen charmingly and unnecessarily recaps this for us at the top of 1.6:

INNOGEN: A father cruel and a stepdame false,
A foolish suitor to a wedded lady
That hath her husband banished . . .
                . . . Had I been thief-stolen
As my two brothers, happy . . .
                          (1.6.1–6)

And the second Lord does it for us again at the end of 2.1:

2 LORD: . . . Alas, poor princess,
Thou divine Innogen, what thou endur'st
Betwixt a father by thy stepdame governed,
A mother hourly coining plots, a wooer
More hateful than the foul expulsion is
Of thy dear husband, than that horrid act
Of the divorce he'd make.
                          (2.1.55–64)

These recaps are actually rehearsals of the damsel-in-distress puppet-role which threatens to suffocate Innogen, and which she is forced to transcend as the play develops. This is one example of the way that throughout *Cymbeline,* we are repeatedly taken through an apparent boilerplate to the edge-point of previous narrative conventions, including Shakespeare's own. By foregrounding Innogen and Posthumus' illicit marriage in the first scene, we feel the play begins in the third act of *Romeo and Juliet*, with Cloten as a demented Paris—though we are quickly hustled on to situations reminiscent of many other plays. As Posthumus and Innogen have acted as dissidents within Cymbeline's decaying system, Shakespeare acts as a rogue element within his own established methods of exposition and narrative, beginning to undermine them from within. The first scene also introduces the audience to a sensation on the palate which will become very familiar by play's end, which is its continual incorporation of glancing, direct, or distorted references not only to many external sources but to many other of Shakespeare's works.

There is therefore a *fourth* dimension of Time in *Cymbeline*, and that is Shakespeare's "self conscious, critical re-use of themes, motifs and images, both verbal and theatrical, from his own previous work".[9] Throughout the play we are introduced to a critical mass of Shakespearean references. In a way reminiscent of *Macbeth's* witches who season their hell-broth with a fenny snake, eye of newt, and so on (*Mac.* 4.1.12–38), *Cymbeline's* pot is filled with partial ingredients:

> . . . an angry father, a possessively jealous husband, a wicked queen who manipulates her uxorious husband and later commits suicide, a laughable dolt, a dependent mother-son relationship, a villainous Italian, a wager, a misogynist invective, threatened or actualized rape, a slandered heroine, a young woman in male disguise, a redemptive daughter, a faithful servant who disobeys an unjust command, a severed head, a pensive jailor, a false poison, a cloth with blood-red markings, a catalogue of flowers, an illusory death, a misinterpreted letter, a soothsayer, a prophecy, a ring that changes hands, a mole that proves ancestry, a dumb show, a masque with a theophany, music and songs, shifts between court and country, legendary British history, Roman history, invasion, war, a surprise victory in battle and a concluding peace.[10]

This logic is referenced in Cloten's description of Innogen: "From every one / The best she hath, and she of all compounded / Outsells them all" (3.5.72–4); the Queen's work with "poisonous compounds" (1.5.8) provides a darker view of the same motif. Like the alchemist's creative process of *separatio, sublimatio, mortificatio*, Shakespeare in *Cymbeline* "reflects on, reimagines and parodies his previous work while making something distinctively new"[11]—like his characters do, he overhears and responds to himself.[12]

Even the conventions of theatrical speech are not safe from ironical reinvention: Iachimo in 1.6 repeatedly parodies the soliloquy by waxing philosophical to an unseen audience, in Innogen's full hearing. In 2.1, Cloten appears to *hear* the second Lord's derogatory 'aside' to the audience—a mechanic, I think, without precedent. In one moment of metatheatricality, Posthumus catches himself in couplets:

POSTHUMUS: 'Lack, to what end?
Who dares not stand his foe, I'll be his friend,

For if he'll do as he is made to do,
I know he'll quickly fly my friendship too.
You have put me into rhyme.

(5.3.59–63)

I submit that the Goldmanian Centre of *this* play—the fundamental holistic experience of *Cymbeline*—is in its very *un*wholesome fragmentariness; this is the experience that actors, characters, and audience must all go through together. In this early modern play about premodern times with a strong sense of our contemporary postmodern adriftancy, the actors must struggle to find coherence and wholeness in characters that seem (impossibly) to flirt with both unidimensionality and incoherent variety. This reflects the action of the characters, who also spend much of the play stripping away false and imposed layers, struggling to know *themselves*. This in turn mirrors the experience of the audience, who is given a tremendous amount of material to take in and digest; they too must rely on their own inclinations to determine what, in this play, is central or peripheral—style or substance—syntactical or semantic. We are all, together, de-centred and made itinerant by *Cymbeline*. Only in confronting this fragmentary quality, paradoxically, do we find any hope of cohesion in *Cymbeline*'s alienating style; in its constant self-consciousness; in its ironical over-plottedness, with a staggering number of reversals, contradictions, negations, about-faces, and threads all at once. Just as Innogen finds her lost family deep in the Welsh wilderness, *Cymbeline* is at home in its homelessness. It is no coincidence that many theatre practitioners and critics have found the play to be about *home* as such;[13] a patriotic masque in honour of Britain, the author and original audience's home.

The return home, to the place of origin, is fundamental in *Cymbeline*, and its great leap forward is therefore accomplished by going backward. As in Hexagram 6 of *I Ching*, Sòng (訟, Conflict):

Heaven and water go their opposite ways:
The image of CONFLICT.
Thus in all his transactions the superior man
Carefully considers the beginning.[14]

This hexagram resonates lightly with the first line of the play, earlier referenced, "Our bloods / No more obey the heavens" (1.1.1–2). Though we may not have completely understood the First Gentleman, we comprehend that blood does not obey the heavens—water and heaven go their opposite ways—the human feeling does not match the ideal one. This conflict between ideal and reality, between heaven and water, between report and experience, is the central interest of *Cymbeline*, and it is the breadth of this conflict that has us all constantly asking along with the second gentleman, "But *what's the matter?*" (1.1.3).[15]

Conflict of every kind is the theme, and consideration of the beginning its antidote. This takes many forms:

- The return to Wales, site of legendary British origin, in which the chief location is a cave, the imaginal origin of our species;
- The eternal return to old theatrical conventions, many of which are revivified and redeemed[16];
- Innogen, motherless herself, bearing the name of the legendary mother of the line of British kings, the wife of Brute;
- Belarius' practice of burial, and Innogen's smearing of blood upon her face, in a subtly graphic resurgence of the ancient Celtic psyche;[17]
- The separating of the play's characters, roughly, into three generations:

  - The parents—Cymbeline, the Queen, Belarius, and Caius "rather father thee than master thee" (4.2.394) Lucius;
  - The children—Innogen, Posthumus, Cloten, Guiderius, and Arviragus;
  - The forebears—Sicilius, Cassibelan and Julius Caesar;

- Mirroring the co-existence of parent and child on a national scale is the conflict between Britain and Ancient Rome, as well as the anachronistic co-existence both of Renaissance Italy and *its* forebear Ancient Rome;
- The play's opening with an immediate look back to the antecedent action of twenty years' past.

What is the dramatic purpose of all this backward-glancing, interrogating, and returning? Shakespeare, his characters, the playworld, and all the actors and audience too, are fragmented and fragmenting, and in search of something to hold together; in search of lost *value*, for in this play something is shattered in the state of value itself and value itself must be retrieved. As Spurgeon noted, the text is thick with images of "buying and selling, value and exchange, every kind of payments, debts, bills and wages."[18] This kind of language occurs so frequently that it begins to annoy, revealing its neurotic character; it feels like unconscious perseveration on a theme, a complex-indicator[19] coming not from one or two characters, but rather from the mouths of nearly every character in the play. It forms part of the fabric of the playworld: Cymbeline's Britain is a world in which everyone is constantly, neurotically, referring to value, worth, and worthiness—often in the basest way, by reducing people to price.

If 'Cymbeline's Britain' showed up in the consulting room, the analyst would soon begin to wonder what was behind this apparently obsessive assertion of value. When a person insists, to this degree, on adhering to simple rules about 'how the world works', we are liable to get the hunch that this represents a compensatory attempt to contain or fix something which, to them, feels threateningly fluid. So the obsession with value in *Cymbeline* seems compensatory; it seems to belong to a society that is trying to *locate* value, to remember how to identify what *matters* and what does not. The characters constantly assert value, compare value, try to establish worth with bizarre and often misguided certainty. Even where we generally agree with the characters' assertions of value, they seem to be lacking in nuance. The inadequacy of money as a heuristic for value is spoken reactively but plainly by Arviragus:

ARVIRAGUS: All gold and silver rather turn to dirt,
As 'tis no better reckoned but of those
Who worship dirty gods.

(3.6.51–3)

And here we can recognize the fundamentally idolatrous state of the playworld. Like the worshipers of the golden calf at the foot of Mount Sinai, the collective has lost faith in a *deus absconditus*—not only the psychologically absent king but the absent value system—and they have no recourse but to cling to the next best thing: price. *Cymbeline* is a portrait of a society in this conflict; early modern with a postmodern sensibility, written in post-Elizabethan, post-plague (and therefore post-apocalyptic) England.

The fairytale setup of *Cymbeline* allows us to recognize this archetypal theme with clarity: the king is sick, and remarried to a witchy second wife. Symbolically, the ruling principle—that is, the *extant value system*—has decayed and been joined with something corrosive. Naturally, this situation will see the children take to the field in search of some kind of redemption.[20]

But the secret discovery of *Cymbeline* is that not only must we redeem, revivify, or envaluate the past, but that the past redeems, revivifies, and envaluates *us*.

The last form of consideration of the beginning—or return to the origin—that Shakespeare enacts in *Cymbeline* is the next for the purposes of this paper, and that is a return to the fundament of the body and its immediate experience. Near the origin-point of Jung's psychology, this was called extraverted sensation, and he often spoke of it as the first of the eight psychic functions, the precondition for the other seven, because it represents the basic ability to perceive what *is*.

Innogen's Body

The very crown and flower of all her father's daughters,—I do not speak here of her human father, but her divine,—woman above all Shakespeare's women is Imogen. As in Cleopatra we found the incarnate sex, the woman everlasting, so in Imogen we find half-glorified already the immortal godhead of womanhood. I would fain have some honey in my words at parting . . . and am, therefore, something more than fain to close my book upon the name of the woman best beloved in all the world of song and all the tide of time; upon the name of Shakespeare's Imogen.[21]

These are the words of Algernon Charles Swinburne, and only the tip of the iceberg; Innogen has endured some centuries' worth of mad idealization. Her critics have been even more effusive than the men who actually encounter her in the play.

Innogen's journey from idealized heroine to regular woman forms an important thread of the play; her utterance "experience, O thou disprov'st report!" (4.2.34) reflects, on some level, her own ongoing discovery of herself. And ours—for our experience of her disproves the report too. It is only at the end of the story, when her report (i.e., her idealized princess persona) has been demolished and then partially restored, that we feel she might be able to rest in a persona which has more fidelity to her inner reality. It is possible to see the entire plot of *Cymbeline*—which begins with her secret marriage to Posthumus—as having been set in motion by Innogen's unconscious desire to blow up the story-report, that is, the situation which curtails her freedom and individuality, while imposing on her a burden of unnatural responsibility, being unwillingly made heir to the throne by her brothers' absences. I would remind those critics that see her eventual demotion from heir as a patriarchal wish-fulfilment that she envies those of lower status ("Blessed be those, / How mean soe'er, that have their honest wills", 1.6.7–8), and it is she herself who wishes her rank away ("Would I were / A neatherd's daughter, and my Leonatus / Our neighbour shepherd's son", 1.1.149–51). A wish, which, by the way, is shared by Henry VI (*3HIV* 2.5.21–54) as well as Prince Arthur: "So I were out of prison and kept sheep / I should be as merry as the day is long" (*KJ* 4.1.17–8). Some are born great, some achieve greatness, and some have greatness—*unwillingly*—thrust upon 'em. Innogen is sensibly glad to have the heavy weight of the crown taken off her shoulders at play's end:

CYMBELINE: O Innogen,
Thou hast lost by this a kingdom.
INNOGEN: No, my lord,
I have got two worlds by't.
                (5.5.371–3)

And she is always eager to divest herself of her persona, jumping with aplomb into the disguise of a farmer's wife, and then of a young page: "I see into thy end and am almost / A man already" (3.4.166–7). The sole times she seems to identify with her rank are in her brief combat with Iachimo ("The King my father shall be made acquainted / Of thy assault", 1.6.148–9), and in bitter extremity, as when using it to shame the absent Posthumus:

INNOGEN: And thou, Posthumus,
That didst set up my disobedience 'gainst the King
My father, and makes me put into contempt the suits
Of princely fellows, shalt hereafter find
It is no act of common passage but
A strain of rareness[.]
                (3.4.87–92)

And can it be any wonder at that point, having learned Posthumus intends her to be murdered for an adultery she did not commit, that she might look for some solace in her superiority? Superiority of this kind is the central collective attitude of the world that she finds herself in, and this moment finds Innogen at her most collective. Adelman sees sadism in the play's treatment of Innogen[22]—this misses the vital fact that throughout her sufferings, she is progressively being freed. She is enduring, to use the alchemical metaphor, a *mortificatio* which painfully necrotizes all that is unnecessary or false.

There is some debate as to whether Innogen and Posthumus' marriage has been consummated[23]—my feeling is that it seems to fit their relationship better if they *have* experienced sexual intimacy together. It somewhat accounts for the fact that their relationship, though apparently solemnized, in other respects seems to regress to pre-marriage stages of courtship,[24] such as the exchanging of love-tokens— essentially, they got married in a fever, and it is all still new, new, new. I agree with Adelman that Posthumus' line "me of my lawful pleasure she restrained / And prayed me oft forebearance" (2.5.9–10) implies moderation in sexual activity rather than abstinence,[25] and his knowledge of her birthmark certainly implies that he has some familiarity with her body.[26]

The ambiguity about her sex life would seem to be intentional, though with the opposite accent to *Twelfth Night*'s sexless wonderland. Wayne notes that the question of her virginity is misleading, ultimately deriving from the male gaze,[27] and this would be basically correct if it were the case of a real person (as in the moral panic of the early 2000s over whether Britney Spears was sexually active). But Innogen is a character whose subjectivity we are encouraged to plumb, and whom actors and actresses definitely have a prerogative to make decisions about. There is no *moral* question about her sexuality: young women may or may not be sexually active; that is a natural fact. But the question yet has bearing on how we understand her, and certainly on how we understand her relationship with Posthumus.

Iachimo penetrates her private quarters, in part, to learn the truth of her—but even here he is stymied by the symbolically conflicting imagery of her bedroom— the tapestry of "Cleopatra acquiring yet another Roman lover"[28] is counterpoised by the chimney-piece of "Chaste Dian bathing" (2.4.82).[29] Her ceiling is fretted with innocent cherubs, but her hearth is flanked by flirty Cupids (2.4.87–9). She herself is involved in the transitional conflict between innocence and experience— as Britney Spears sang, "Not a Girl, Not Yet a Woman"[30]—similarly to Viola, whose father could not survive her thirteenth birthday. And while some of the men around (and in the critical literature) may feel compelled to resolve her into virgin or coquette, this is merely an expression of their own lack of imagination. She is envisioned as a slave to virtue, an innocent Innogen ivory lady, but her reading material is rated 'R': Ovid's *Metamorphoses*, specifically Tereus' rape of Philomel. Experience, thou disprov'st report: what is heroic about Innogen is not her *chastity*—good heavens, the reddest of herrings—her heroism is clearly in that which is communicated by her choice of pseudonym: her *fidelity*. Shakespeare has written a heroine whose heroism is in the fact that she stays true to her own heart, and her own unfolding story, *no matter what*.

Innogen's fears about *Posthumus'* fidelity, however, as in "another wife" (1.1.113), "the shes of Italy" (1.3.29), "some jay of Italy, / Whose mother was her painting" (3.4.49–50), "some Roman courtesan" (3.4.123), and her prayer "that we two are asunder, let that grieve him" (3.2.32), hold that peculiar sexual anxiety belonging to the fragility of a relationship that has only *just* been consummated, while also pointing to her sense that her husband does not quite know himself well enough to be relied on. Harriet Walter, who played the role in 1987, agreed: "sexual knowledge opens the Pandora's box of jealousy, fear of loss, mistrust and ignorance of the opposite sex."[31] They are both adolescently anxious about the other's bodily faithfulness.

And is any body in Shakespeare subject to more attention than Innogen's? Certainly other bodies are submitted to more abuse—*King Lear* sees Gloucester lose his eyes, and *Titus Andronicus* takes Lavinia's hands and tongue. But Innogen, to whom "Helen" is but a handmaid (2.2.1), is vaunted quite as much as Helen of Troy is, and objectified as much too (Iachimo unironically calling her "this object" at 1.6.101). Both Helen (of Troy) and Innogen are idealized and then compensatorily objectified—Iachimo's drive to vulgarize Innogen is, psychologically, a necessary countermovement launched in response to Posthumus' idealization. It is true that her qualities of character are recognized and affirmed throughout the play as well, but in the theatre, where the primary experience of the play is the actors upon the stage,[32] the centrality of her body is unignorable. The two images which I feel to be most central to the play are both voyeuristic views of her body: first, lying asleep and partially exposed in 2.2 while Iachimo inventories her room and body; second, her awakening next to Cloten's corpse, both bodies strewn with flowers. Iachimo makes much of "all of her that is out of door" (1.6.15), her cheek (1.6.98), hand (1.6.99), skin (2.2.16), lips (2.2.17), breath (2.2.18), eyelids (2.2.20–3) and of course the underside of her left breast (2.2.37–9). It sounds like admiration but feels like dissection. This "inventory" (2.2.30) of Innogen recalls the droll "inventory" of Olivia's particles and utensils (*TN* 1.5.236–40)—which, through Innogen, is made uncomfortably literal. Two hints at the potential for Iachimo to rape her are made while she is most vulnerable: "Our Tarquin thus / Did softly press the rushes" (2.2.12–3), and his rather tendentious take on Philomel 'giving up' (2.2.46). Tarquin and Tereus are prominent rapists of antiquity and myth, respectively, and Iachimo's treatment of both is creepily companionate.[33] Later, Innogen's body is put through the rigors of long overland travel and sleeping on the ground (3.6.2–3). This physical ordeal added to her emotional strain, it is no wonder she becomes sick (4.2.5); then her attempt to medicine her ills is subverted by the sleeping dram which she finds "murd'rous to th' senses" (4.2.327). Her body awakes next to another body—only a body, with no head—in whose blood she covers herself. Her *mortificatio* journey from Britain's princess to "nothing" (4.2.367) is as physically degrading as it is emotional. At last, even when we may think she has gone through the worst of it, at the very moment that should be her loving reunion with Posthumus, she is struck in the face by him—her original persona totally unrecognized. Servant Pisanio catches the feeling of this final insult-on-top-of-injury, simultaneously giving voice to our satisfaction that so far there seems to be nothing this princess cannot endure: "O my lord Posthumus, / You ne'er killed Innogen till now" (5.5.230–1).

In this play, Shakespeare repeatedly emphasizes the role of present Time, of direct experience, and of the body as the instrument which registers both. In the language of Jungian typology, we might say that the function of extraverted sensing (Se) is a particular interest of *Cymbeline*, and furthermore that this function is largely centred in Innogen. Se is essentially sense-perception, focusing "on the current objective, external world to fully experience the details of the environment through the five senses."[34] Someone who leads with this function is oriented primarily towards the experiences of their five senses in the concrete physical world. The line "Experience, O thou disprov'st report!" (4.2.34), in addition to sounding a leitmotif of the entire play,[35] speaks to the heroic potential of the Se function, which is in its ability to dispense with everything that could interfere with present moment experiencing. The experience-report motif is recalled when affirming her perception of the corpse next to her, "not imagined, felt" (4.2.306). The same motif is reflected back to her by Lucius shortly after:

LUCIUS: The Roman Emperor's letters
Sent by a consul to me should not sooner
Than thine own worth prefer thee.
                    (4.2.383–5)

Se is "the only perception process that is not influenced by associations from the past, present, or future."[36] Consider, in this light, Innogen's exchange with Pisanio as she makes ready to depart for Wales:

PISANIO: Madam, you're best consider -
INNOGEN: I see before me, man. Nor here, nor here,
Nor what ensues but have a fog in them
That I cannot look through.
                    (3.2.77–80)

Walter found this line to be key to Innogen's "characteristic impetuosity."[37] Her father imperiously commands his Lords to "pen her up" (1.1.154), and he is, technically, onto something with this phrase. He does know his daughter, and she is a touch wild—the animal in the princess is not so far from the surface.

In situations of high tension, her diplomatic process characteristically involves an unvarnished statement of what is happening in the moment, no more, no less, as when trying to digest Iachimo's sudden about-face from seducer to devotee—"You make amends" (1.6.167)—or when making her own amends to the cave-dwellers for having invaded their home—"I see you're angry" (3.6.54).

On one level, Innogen's longer speeches do not contain much that is really deeply engaging; they do not plumb the depths of remarkable inner conflicts, or have revolutionary thoughts within them, or even much in the way of poetic imagery. In part this is because she is rarely conflicted: her greatest strength—except perhaps for her wit—is her singleness of purpose. Her speeches are therefore immediate, replete with the language of Se, moving from one immediate mental stimulus to another, whether focusing on the reality of travel between home and Milford Haven (3.3.48–67; 3.4.1–2; 3.6.2–8), tracking the moment-to-moment changes in Pisanio's countenance (3.3.4–14), or struggling to take in the nightmarish reality to which she awakens after her funeral (4.2.294–321), then searching for the missing piece of her husband—

INNOGEN: O Posthumus, alas,
Where is thy head? Where's that? Ay me, where's that?
                        (4.2.319–20)

She immerses herself in reading for three hours at once until "sleep hath seized [her] wholly" (2.2.7), one sensate experience displacing another. She has an indelible memory of Posthumus' handwriting (3.3.27–8),[38] and despite being royalty knows how to keep house, sauce broths and cut roots "in characters" (4.2.48–50). When she reads Posthumus' order to have her killed, her response is instantaneous: "The paper / Hath cut her throat already" (3.4.33–4). She demands Pisanio act it out with all haste, to transform her unbearable inner experience into an immediate sensate experience of the sword:

INNOGEN: Look,
I draw the sword myself.
[She draws Pisanio's sword and offers it to him.]
                Take it, and hit
The innocent mansion of my love, my heart.
                        (3.4.64–7)

She demands again—"Do his bidding, strike" (3.4.69)—and again—

                Come, here's my heart.
        Something's afore't. Soft, soft, we'll no defence,
        Obedient as the scabbard.
                        (3.4.77–9)

She takes a moment to perform her own concretized gesture of divorce, throwing her love-letters "Away, away" (3.24.82), before demanding the sword one more time:

                Where's thy knife?
        Thou art too slow to do thy master's bidding
        When I desire it too.
                        (3.4.95–7)

Here it may be helpful to remind the reader new to typology that *feeling,* as a function, is not the same as emotion, and so Innogen's obvious emotionality does not render her a feeling-type—rather I think that her emotions come to her hard and fast as immediate embodied experiences to which she is compelled to react.

Innogen's Se has a heroic quality, but with a particular impetuous, impulsive, youthful intensity. It flies ("O for a horse with wings!", 3.2.48); it is not particularly tempered by reality:

> I would have broke mine eye-strings, cracked them, but
> To look upon him till the diminution
> Of space had pointed him sharp as my needle[.]

> (1.3.17–9)

Cai associates Se with *I Ching* Hexagram 30, *Li* (離, The Clinging: Fire);[39] Innogen's Se presentation in particular recalls *Li*'s fourth line: "Its coming is sudden; / It flames up, dies down, is thrown away".[40] In Jungian terms, she has qualities with which we have become very familiar over the course of this book: those of the puer aeternus archetype, the divine or eternal child, or rather its feminine counterpart, puella aeterna. "O for a horse with wings!" (3.2.48) links her with one of the chief pueri of antiquity, Bellerophon, who tried to fly Pegasus to Mount Olympus. Further references to her high-spirited and un-grounded nature include the prophecy which ends the play, in which she is signified by "a piece of tender air" (5.5.445–51), as well as the birds and flight images which attend her ("th'Arabian bird", 1.6.27; "The bird is dead / That we have made so much on", 4.2.196–7). On the darker side, her quick crash to suicidality when reeling from Posthumus' betrayal is, of course, also puella.

The puella is not merely a puer translated into a female body. Schwartz's work has emphasized the performative, 'as if' quality of the puella archetype, in many ways dovetailing with what I have described in the last chapter as 'histrionic'. This can be seen as the foundation from which Innogen pushes off; the expectation to live "like a blueprint for a woman's fantasy based on male models"[41] is what she actively rebels against. In this way Innogen, as we so commonly find in Shakespeare, makes for a wonderful psychological analogy not for a pathology, but for a complex *that is being worked on.* Her heroic Se is also her own limiting factor, as the dominant function always is sooner or later—the puella suffers from lack of "sufficient connection to their individual ground of being", and it is perhaps this connection that Innogen seeks everywhere in the world except within, that is, until she has been reduced to "nothing" (4.2.366), consciously accessing her introversion at last.

But she also, notwithstanding her femininity, has qualities more associated with the masculine puer. Walter brought "fanatical ardour"[42] to the role, and Innogen's uncompromising energy is crucially important in deadlocked psychological situations such as we find in Britain in this play. The puer can, for better or worse, stand for something; a kind of to-thine-own-self-be-true-ness, which is not exactly the same as a grounded integrity but at least represents an internal congruency.

It would seem that puer and puella, like Sebastian and Viola, come together. The two archetypes seem to act as a syzygy, a union of opposites, and often show up as a pair rather than being limited by the sex of the person whose psyche is concerned.[43]

To continue moving to the level of considering Innogen as a whole person rather than as a part-personality representing a function: a person with dominant extra-verted sensing has 'inferior' introverted intuiting. 'Inferior' is the name given to the function that tends to have a particular vulnerability in the personality, being a way of engaging the world that is opposite to our preferred mode; in this way it offers a necessary balancing to the personality. Introverted intuiting requires going beyond the Se facts of the here-and-now and into the domain of possibilities and hunches, and here lies a particular weakness of Innogen's. For example: she may know Posthumus' *handwriting* as well as a learned astronomer knows the stars, but she perceives entirely the wrong meaning in his letter; Sanders writes that her "wish-fulfilment approach to interpretation guides Imogen to miss altogether what is negative".[44] She can be tragically naïve, as again in her conduct with Iachimo. She rebuffs his attempt to seduce her, but his quick about-face into 'only jok-ing!' is too easily accepted—a developed intuitive function might not know *why* this was wrong, but it *would* know it was wrong.[45] Ashcroft reflected on playing Innogen that her "only failing is to attribute to other people her own straightfor-wardness and integrity."[46] In this play, which is opened by lines that are exactly as meaning-obscuring as her lover's letters and his rival's technical-truths, naïveté is a very costly flaw.

Yet, naïve as she may be in situations of danger, her intuition elsewhere has a tendency toward paranoia in relation to the wrong things: she is tormented by the imagined "shes of Italy" (1.3.29) that may steal her husband, and she rashly assumes that Pisanio has betrayed her (4.2.310–28). She seems to be aware of this weakness, stating it as a general principle in "doubting things go ill often hurts

1: Heroic Se

4: Inferior Ni

Figure 6.1 Innogen's dominant and inferior functions, or "Spine of consciousness".[47]

more / Than to be sure they do" (1.6.94–5), and as a more personal vulnerability in "I have such a heart that both mine ears / Must not in haste abuse" (1.6.128–9), suggesting that anxieties of this type have at times caused her serious pain. "For every simple statement . . . Innogen provides a mythic over-reading."[48] She seems to recognize the fallibility of relying on her senses in "I do condemn mine ears that have / So long attended thee" (1.6.140–1).

Then again, she does have certain charming intuitive notions, and this may remind us of the fact that the inferior part of a person's functioning is where a great deal of life energy resides. To paraphrase Leonard Cohen, the cracks are where the light gets in.[49] When we see Innogen blessing the bees who make the sealing wax (3.2.35–6), or repeatedly including the divine in her thoughts, as in "You good gods, / Let what is here contained relish of love" (3.2.29–30), "though the gods hear, I hope / They'll pardon it" (4.2.377–8), or "O gods and goddesses!" (4.2.294), it is hard not to appreciate her depth. Her relation to the divine may be subtly childlike and overfamiliar—Wilson Knight felt that she "half speaks to 'Jove' as a companion",[50] as in "O Jove, I think / Foundations fly the wretched" (3.6.6–7). Perhaps this is indicative of the way that she needs to relate to the Ni realm "beyond beyond" (3.2.56): by drawing it into her Se function and relating to gods as though they are her invisible pals.[51]

It is no wonder that Innogen is so well-loved by the other characters and her audiences alike,[52] for she has a remarkably well-rounded and adaptive personality, especially considering the environment she's grown up in, and having lost her mother at an early age. As Wayne writes, "Cymbeline's absence enables Innogen's presence",[53] and Innogen's situation is, on some level, the archetypal situation of the orphaned hero(ine). She provides an example that illustrates just *why* the mythological hero or heroine is so often orphaned: he or she grows up in the lacunae left by the parents' personalities—the parents' unlived lives—perhaps contained not by the parents themselves but by their failings. On the collective level, the analogy would be that the heroic impulse comes precisely in the current blind spot of the prevailing culture, for that is both where it is needed as well as being the only place where it can be properly tolerated and borne.

The most innovative expression of Innogen's puella Se comes in her speech in 4.2, when she, awakening dazedly from a drug-induced and deathlike slumber, finds herself next to what she believes to be the headless body of her husband Posthumus—an amazing symbolic depiction of the *abaissement de niveau mental* (lowering of the mental level) that is concomitant with awakening into one's inferior function. Her inferior Ni prevails at first, given that her Se is extremely compromised both by the effects of the drug ("have I not found it / Murd'rous to th' senses?" 4.2.326–7) as well as by the horrifying situation—psychologically, she is in the antipodes, and she mistakenly identifies Cloten's body as Posthumus':

INNOGEN: A headless man? The garments of Posthumus?
I know the shape of 's leg; this is his hand,
His foot Mercurial, his Martial thigh,

The brawns of Hercules, but his Jovial face—
Murder in heaven? How? 'Tis gone.

(4.2.307–11)

It *sounds* like Se taking in the details—except that it is so very inaccurate. Her religious associations to various deities also suggest that it is her inferior Ni which is functioning at this moment: what she experiences is not factual reality but underlying archetype. Her inferior function then goes further into forming wild 'knowings' about what has happened—she does correctly pick up that she has been betrayed, but decides nonsensically that Pisanio has drugged her and murdered Posthumus, and laid them together. Sanders writes that "the tragicomic proportions of Imogen's capacity for misconstruction here reach their height."[54] This may remind us that though the Ni function may 'know', it is not necessarily *right.* Wilhelm helpfully noted that "intuition that contradicts logic is not truly intuition, but prejudice."[55]

Director Peter Hall "emphasized the element of theatrical virtuosity" in this scene, "as though Shakespeare had asked 'How can I invent the most horrible situation anyone could ever think of for a love scene?'"[56] The truly remarkable bit comes at the end of her speech, when extraverted sensing reasserts itself in what is surely the play's central image:

INNOGEN: O,
Give colour to my pale cheek with thy blood,
That we the horrider may seem to those
Which chance to find us. O, my lord, my lord!
[*She smears her face with blood and lies on the body.*]

(4.2.328–31)

There may be no more potent instance of the Se drive for hands-on experience in Shakespeare. I think it is totally likely that we (the audience) expect her to commit suicide here; we've all seen *Romeo and Juliet.* We know too well what can happen when a girl wakes up in a tomb with her dead husband. So Innogen's act of *amor fati,* a literal bodily embrace of her fate, is an epiphany on both the theatrical and the metatheatrical level. It transcends *noli me tangere* (do not embrace me) with a deeply human embrace. *This is the coagulatio which Twelfth Night sought in vain.*

The symbolic significance of bathing in the wounds of her would-be rapist is that this is very much an immersion in—and embrace *of*—the shadow. Recall that the shadow of puer/puella is trickster; the trickster in the scene's construction, those dramatic contrivances which have led her to awaken next to her husband's dead doppelgänger, initiates the puella. And afterward, in contrast to her previous flights of naïveté and paranoia, we do not see her naïve again. I know there are some who would disagree, finding her reunion with Posthumus in the last scene regressive, and that I will address later on. But my impression is that, with the body of Cloten, she integrates the lesson of one-sidedness, in the hardest way.

The symbolic significance of the Se function in the context of the play is that it is the beginning of the antidote to the problems infecting Cymbeline's court, which can be condensedly described as having to do with the failure to see what *is*. It seems impossible that one with eyes could miss the Queen's evil, and yet it is Cymbeline's senses that betray him in this respect:

CYMBELINE: Mine eyes
Were not in fault, for she was beautiful;
Mine ears that heard her flattery, nor my heart,
That thought her like her seeming. It had been vicious
To have mistrusted her . . .

(5.5.62–6)

"Who is't can read a woman?" (5.5.48) shows a terrible lack of perception, and the fact that this line usually produces a laugh[57] is evidence that *anybody* could have read *that* woman, except for him. It also seems that this lack of proper perception is not a new problem for him, for 20 years ago he banished the very worthy Belarius on a mere report of treason (3.3.65–9). The psychological poisoning of Posthumus occurs through the channel of sensation as well, as Iachimo describes his (memorized) account of Innogen's room and body, and the (invented) experience of his amorous night with her.

In a world where misvaluation runs rampant, and in which false report seems continually to eclipse experience, a dedicated extraverted sensation represents a return to the here-and-now of the situation, the *actual* facts, and the foundation of experience.

The first part of our typological mandala comes together, then, like this:

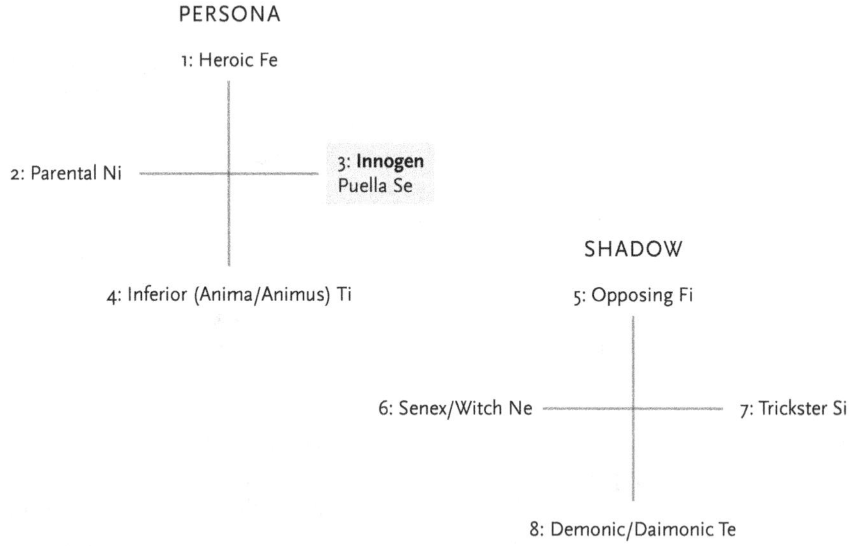

PERSONA

1: Heroic Fe

2: Parental Ni   3: **Innogen**
                        Puella Se

SHADOW

4: Inferior (Anima/Animus) Ti   5: Opposing Fi

6: Senex/Witch Ne   7: Trickster Si

8: Demonic/Daimonic Te

Figure 6.2 Innogen as Puella Se

Iachimo's Device

Next to the Queen, Iachimo is probably the character with whom it may be most tempting to make do with a stereotype. He is easy to dismiss as a plot device, though at times he has seemed "the chief character of the play",[58] being treated as the male lead and played by the famous actors of the day.[59] There is more to Iachimo than the scheming and boastful I-talian that could mark the start and end-point of his interpretation. This is critical—"an Innogen and Posthumus depend very much on the actor of [Iachimo] to provide them with something to react to".[60] He is inwardly nuanced, with a capacity to be unexpectedly endearing to the audience. His soliloquy in 2.2 leaves him effectively alone onstage with the audience for more than five minutes, and during this time he may unfold a personality that is curiously relatable.

He flirts with showing up as nothing but a hypomanic peacock. Through the typological lens, it therefore seems natural that he would be an extraverted intuitive braggart. Certainly he mobilizes certain Ne *tactics* in order to pursue his goals, otherwise he would not be able to perform the remarkable feats of faking out, deception, and infiltration that he does. The Ne function "almost instantaneously creates an entire realm of specific possibilities", and envisions "how situations, objects, and information can be used",[61] and this is surely active when manipulating Posthumus into the wager, and even more clearly when inventing, on the fly, his back-up plan to conceal himself in the trunk which gains him access to Innogen's chamber.

However, "observers cannot always judge a person's type by their actions. Most often the choice of behaviour depends on the motive for the behaviour".[62] If we look into the motive for Iachimo's behaviour, it seems not to be driven by an Ne vision, and though he takes "enormous risks because of his overpowering desire for [Innogen]",[63] to the point of kissing her while she sleeps, we can also safely write off the idea that he is primarily driven by lust, because he does restrain himself. His underlying motive, so far as I can tell, is compensatory: to balance the scales away from the over-idealization of Posthumus and Innogen. This aligns him with the goals of the play itself, which is one reason he can seem more puppet than individual. These two lovers, however—Britain's star-crossed 'it' couple—are thought of far too highly for anyone to bear, including themselves. Iachimo comes onto the scene by deflating Posthumus' image ("I could then have looked on him without the help of admiration" 1.4.4–5), and shortly locks horns with Posthumus' childish and competitive overvaluation of his wife. Posthumus' certainty galls Iachimo, as it galled the Frenchman at their previous meeting (1.4.35–63). Iachimo seems to know that all this overblown rumour can't be right. Functionally, Iachimo's drive is to *vet the claims*, and is therefore much more along the lines of the introverted sensing function. When we consider that the Si function in this play would seem to be associated with the *trickster*, this piece of the puzzle falls into place.

As noted, structurally speaking, the trickster is the shadow of the puella or puer, and the aspect of the psyche that is needed to transcend the double-bind that the eternal children always seem to find themselves in. The double-bind, of course,

PERSONA

1: Heroic Fe

2: Parental Ni ———————— 3: **Innogen**
Puella Se

SHADOW

4: Inferior (Anima/Animus) Ti   5: Opposing Fi

6: Senex/Witch Ne ————————— 7: **Iachimo**
Trickster Si

8: Demonic/Daimonic Te

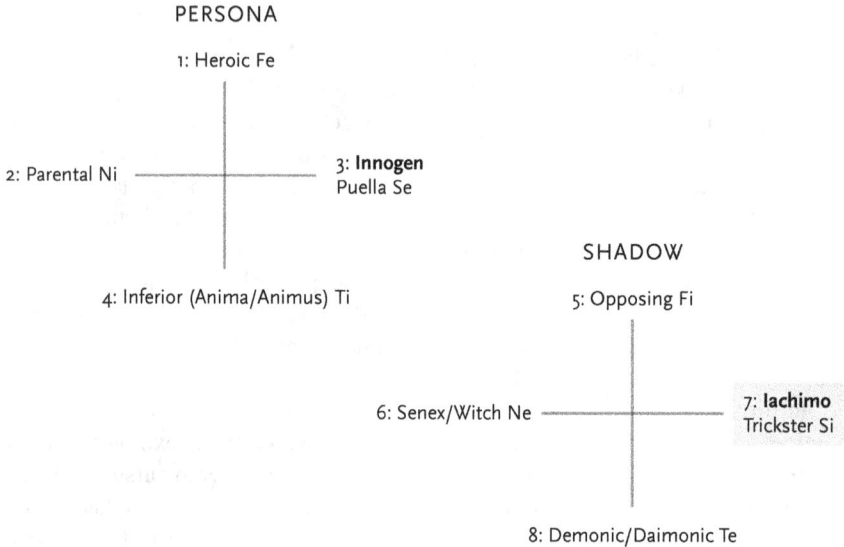

Figure 6.3 Iachimo as Trickster Si.

is Innogen's: marry Posthumus and forsake her father, or marry Cloten and for-sake herself? Or, more fundamentally: behave as expected and suffer the inner consequences, or behave 'badly' and suffer the outer consequences? Iachimo, as a psychological mechanism (*not as a literal bedroom-invading pervert*), does her a service by breaking the deadlock.

I would propose that a dominant Si also allows for Iachimo to be a far more interesting and nuanced character than an Ne interpretation would deliver. A qui-etly provocative Si self-assurance seems more likely to get under Posthumus' skin. It makes Iachimo a credible threat. The "revelry in physical restraint"[64] that Carr sees can allow him to be sexy rather than swaggering, creating the possibility of ambiguity in the encounter with Innogen, as Helen Mirren found, "showing her discovery . . . that she is corruptible, open to seduction."[65] For an Innogen to be so requires also a Iachimo that could conceivably seduce a woman rather than instantly giving her 'the ick'. At the same time, a basically introverted Iachimo gives the audience more credit, who does not need it to be telegraphed to them how he is to be evaluated. Donald Sumpter, seemingly playing him in an introverted way in 1987, had surveyed Innogen's room and body "with the cool fascination of a surgeon."[66] Colm Feore, in 1986, "erotically . . . seemed to be whispering over one actress' and a couple thousand audience members' shoulders all at once."[67]

Iachimo's Si puts to scrutiny the prevailing mythos around Posthumus and Inno-gen; he demystifies. His Si instinct says: prove it. He senses the falseness in the accounts and needs it clarified. He probably is somewhat sociopathic, except that the consequences of his actions actually pierce the shell and bring him literally, in Act 5, to his knees.

As noted earlier, he expresses a curiously sympathetic treatment of the great rapists Tereus and Tarquin, the latter of whom he even claims kinship with, as a Roman: "our" Tarquin (2.2.2). This may express his empathy for them, derived from his own unrestrained Si need to *make sure*—to *confirm* that a given phenomenon, even a woman's inaccessible body, has "such and such" (2.2.27) qualities. Then again, by evoking them he also is able to distance himself from them: "I have enough" (2.2.46). I think it is an Si-monomania—a kind of one-sidedness—rather than anything like sexual desire, which powers him. The fact that the woman's body is treated as a sacred precinct by others serves, for him, to intensify his trickster-identification; for the trickster, nothing is sacred until proven otherwise. The trickster must cross boundaries—this is his archetypal compulsion—and he crosses the boundaries of decency in Philario's salon, of Innogen's bedroom, of her body, and as he falls later on the battlefield, he blames it, in effect, on having crossed beyond his natural national borders:

IACHIMO: I have belied a lady,
The princess of this country, and the air on't
Revengingly enfeebles me[.]
                    (5.2.2–4)

The trickster always undoes himself.

Iachimo's Si becomes his chief tool in undoing Posthumus: "More particulars / Must justify my knowledge" (2.4.78–9). The ruse is built upon volumes of memorized sensate data: "Why should I write this down that's riveted, / Screwed to my memory?" (2.2.43–4).

Curious though it may be, Iachimo may be the only male in *Cymbeline* who has a coherent notion of what a woman 'is'—begging the reader's pardon for this potentially provocative statement. Though he obviously objectifies Innogen, Iachimo does at least seem interested in what women *are* as earthly beings rather than ideals. For Posthumus a woman is at first an untouchable goddess, and later an indescribable evil. Cloten has been reading the same magazines. For Cymbeline, a woman is a pretty face behind which lies an unfathomable mystery. Arviragus and Guiderius have probably never encountered a woman apart from their deceased nurse-mother. We can see why the play *requires* Iachimo to take up something like a middle position.

In his contrition, too, he depends on Si, to Cymbeline's irritation and impatience. Asked to "come to the matter", Iachimo insists that "All too soon I shall, / Unless thou wouldst grieve quickly" (5.5.168–70). He seems to feel it necessary to include the entire context of his story, not only to set the record straight, but to make it known with complete clarity what has transpired, and how and why Posthumus and Innogen were abused.

Cymbeline & Lucius

A new quality begins to emerge in the play in the third act: reverence. We have heard Innogen's pretty religious thoughts already; in fact, as Wilson Knight observed, *Cymbeline* "probably exceeds any other Shakespearian play in its fecundity of classical, and especially mythological, reference,"[68] but these references have fallen short of deep religious feeling, and have failed to pierce the veil of irony which shrouds the first two acts. In the third, however, another side begins to show itself. This act begins with Cymbeline's entrance "in state" (3.1.0), giving a sense of importance and centrality, which has until now been entirely absent. The remarkable civility with which Cymbeline and the Roman leader Caius Lucius conduct diplomacy in this scene begins to whisper of something deeper and more subtle in this world than we had been led to expect; it feels grounded even despite the provocations of Cloten and the Queen. At this point Cymbeline seems to begin regaining his strength, overcoming the "languishing death" (1.4.9) of his Queen, and functioning increasingly independently from her; it is as though his reconnection with his own Roman past reconnects the "lofty cedar" (5.5.452) with his life-giving roots; "Thy Caesar knighted me; my youth I spent / Much under him; of him I gathered honour" (3.1.69–70).

The lofty cedar itself, with branches lopped, which signifies King Cymbeline in Jupiter's final prophecy, would seem to be an image of excessive verticality: something like a pseudo-spirituality or ideological inflation which has lost its relationship with the external world. This helps to characterize Cymbeline's particular form of weakness as a detachment from reality and from matter.

The 'King', symbolically speaking, is multifaceted, just as the Shakespearean kings themselves are. Next to the child Henry VI, Cymbeline begins as probably the weakest of all of them. He seems brittle and half-living (at best). His is kingship at its most tenuous, a wraithlike grasp on a few small threads of power. A more modern literary comparison might be made with King Théoden of *The Lord of the Rings*:[69] they are both shadows of their former selves, and for similar reasons. Théoden has been parasitized by the witchy advisor Grima Wormtongue, and Cymbeline has been parasitized by his witchy Queen. The film version of *The Lord of the Rings: The Two Towers*[70] goes so far as to construe Théoden as magically possessed by an evil wizard, and I think this is not far from Cymbeline's truth. He may not be literally possessed by his Queen, but she is seeming-lovely and apparently beautiful, and this play clearly establishes that those things alone are more than enough to enthral many men, even those who should know better. To consider him as metaphorically possessed helps us to characterize his overall archetypal function in the play: he is something *demonic* in the playworld, acting primarily in a shadowy, unconscious, and undermining way,[71] seemingly not on his own behalf but on behalf of the witch who has enchanted him. Jung writes that the cultural phenomenon of demonism

> denotes a peculiar state of mind characterized by the fact that certain psychic contents, the so-called complexes, take over the control of the total personality

in place of the ego, at least temporarily, to such a degree that the free will of the ego is suspended.[72]

Typologically, I associate him with the demonic extraverted thinking function. Te is the function that "is driven to structure and organize the external world"[73] through regulating, planning, and enforcing.[74] Cai writes that "Te acts with the directness and authority that we might associate with thunder",[75] associating the function with hexagram 51, *Zhèn* (震, The Arousing: Shock, Thunder). Te is, at its best, "merely trying to ask human nature to honour the possibility of following rules that will curb its tendency to chaos", however with a compensatory tendency to assert itself "in an intrusive way without any regard for its effect on others". Cymbeline's characteristic rage ("like the tyrannous breathing of the north", 1.3.36) seems to come from the fact that what *is* does not accord with what *should* be ("You have done / Not after our command", 1.1.152–3). This is also the blind spot that allows him to overlook his Queen's wretched heart—she at least seems to be his ally, or she *should* be, based on a collective definition of what she 'is' as wife and Queen, and so she is generally exempt from his badgering.

Cymbeline's Te is not healthy. In regard to the hexagram *Zhèn*, he most closely evokes the fourth line: "Shock is mired". On this line, Wilhelm comments that "if there is neither a resistance that might be vigorously combated, nor yet a yielding that permits of victory—if instead, everything is tough and inert like mire— movement is crippled."[76] It seems to be a credible threat that his rage might overwhelm his body and kill him—Innogen rebelliously warns him against this possibility ("I beseech you, sir, / Harm not yourself with your vexation", 1.1.134–5), and the Queen hopes for it:

CLOTEN: Go in and cheer the King. He rages, none
Dare come about him.
QUEEN: [aside]   All the better. May
This night forestall him of the coming day.
(3.5.67–9)

Cymbeline seems to be *visibly* unhealthy, for the Queen tells Pisanio that her potion is "a thing I made which hath the King / Five times redeemed from death" (1.5.62–3)—of course she is lying about the potion, but Pisanio easily accepts the fact that the king has nearly died five times. All this taken together overdetermines the interpretation that the lofty cedar with no arms is an image which indicates a necessary reconnection with the horizontal plane, if it is to be brought into balance. A nameless Lord gives a surprisingly accurate diagnosis of the king, although consciously he is referring to military strength: "The want is but to put those powers in motion / That long to move" (4.3.31–2). Shock is mired.

Again, there is a loose link between the concept of the demon and the *daimon*, which is a much less malignant sort of spirit, though still potentially of untoward origin. The *daimon* can, rather than possess a person and drive them to evil and ruin, bequeath a sort of inspired genius. Diotima's definition of the *daimon* is given in Plato's *Symposium*:

> "What is the function of a spirit [daimon]?" I asked.
> "Interpreting and conveying all that passes between gods and humans: from humans, petitions and sacrificial offerings, and from gods, instructions and the favours they return."[77]

When "held to a standard of integrity," Beebe writes, there is "an opportunity for spirit to enter the psyche" through the 8th function.[78] This is what seems to emerge in 3.1, because Cymbeline's relation with Caius Lucius is inspirited, admirable, firm, and robust; prior to this we have only seen him function with petulant tyranny. We might not have thought this new behaviour to be possible of the old king. Often, however, a man can be emasculated by a poisonous relationship, and then seem to come to life again when in company which reminds him of his spine.

Considered as a full person with dominant Te, Cymbeline's inferior function would be introverted feeling, and I identify Caius Lucius as one of the two major carriers of this function in the play. In fact, even moreso than Lucius it is *Ancient Rome* that seems to carry this function. "Fundamental ideas, ideas like God, freedom, and immortality, are just as much feeling-values as they are significant ideas",[79] and I suspect there are few stronger feeling-values in human history than *Romanitas*. The conflict in the Britain-Rome plot is a Te-Fi conflict: Cymbeline wishes to inaugurate a new era for his nation, free from Roman influence. Such Roman virtues as duty, piety, clemency, and gratitude have decayed in Cymbeline's Britain. When Lucius readily adopts the disguised Innogen as his page, perhaps it doesn't hurt that her chosen name Fidele reflects a core Roman virtue: "Thy name well fits thy faith, thy faith thy name" (4.2.380).

The feeling-values of Rome cannot permit Cymbeline's disrespect, and so, war. But Lucius' presence seems to activate Cymbeline's relationship with his own Fi; I suspect that in Cymbeline's youth, his anima—that is, his experience of his own soul's aliveness within him—was directly linked with Rome. Contact with Lucius and the Romans begins to awaken Cymbeline's dormant integrity,[80] and by the end of the play he has reconnected these severed parts of his own personality and nation.

In the typology of the play as a whole, Fi is in the 5th position of the 'opposing personality', and it should be clear enough why the general of the enemy army suits the designation of 'opposing'. There are further nuances of this archetypal position of the opposing personality, however, which will be explored below.

Belarius & 'Morgan'

If 3.1 (the introduction of Ancient Rome) calls an all-but-forgotten vitality out of Cymbeline, 3.3 (the introduction of Wales) bursts with unexpected vitality in the context of the play. Warren found these scenes to be unfailingly successful in performance.[81] 3.3 shares a lot with 1.1—it feels again like a 'tour guide' scene, in

PERSONA

1: Heroic Fe

2: Parental Ni ----------+---------- 3: **Innogen**
Puella Se

SHADOW

4: Inferior (Anima/Animus) Ti

5: **Caius Lucius**
Opposing Fi

6: Senex/Witch Ne ----------+---------- 7: **Iachimo**
Trickster Si

8: **Cymbeline**
Demonic Te

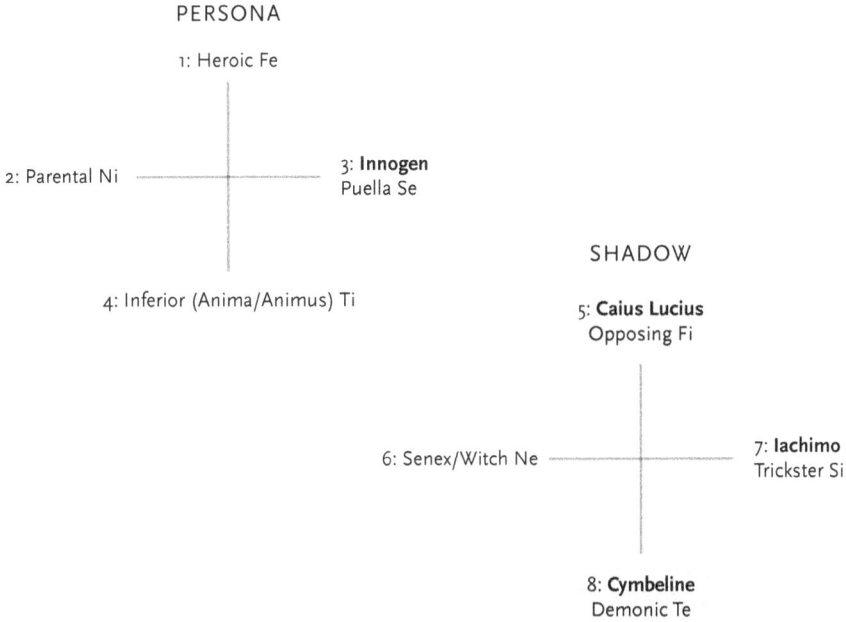

Figure 6.4 Cymbeline as Demonic/Daimonic Te, Caius Lucius as Opposing Fi.

which the characters speak far too plainly and conveniently for the audience to maintain a sense of naturalism—but whereas 1.1 is cold and grey, 3.3 is vigorous and verdant. Hall saw the transition, when staged, as a huge surprise, "like a jump-cut in a film".[82] It is my favourite moment. It is here that we are introduced to Belarius, the soldier who 20 years past was falsely accused of treason, and who in revenge stole Cymbeline's sons, "Thinking to bar [him] of succession" (3.3.102), raising the boys as his own in the Welsh wilds. Cymbeline's offense against Belarius' own introverted feeling is the genesis of the Belarius who we first meet in the play—or rather the 'Morgan', as his pseudonym would have it. Iachimo is often compared with *Othello*'s Iago, on the basis of their mutual lies which slander honest women and drive their husbands mad, as well as their names, Iachimo's suggesting that he is kind of a bootleg 'little Iago'. But Belarius carries some significant portion of Iago's epigenetic material forth as well, having gone to true extremes to punish a wrong done to his honour, in particular a wrong done to a soldier in despite of loyal service.

We can imagine the situation of Belarius, 20 years ago, as he sees his king becoming slowly corrupted, evoked by the second line of Hexagram 52, *Gèn* (艮, Keeping Still: Mountain), which is associated by Cai with Fi[83]:

Keeping his calves still.
He cannot rescue him whom he follows.
His heart is not glad.[84]

Wilhelm adds the commentary that this describes

> a man who serves a master stronger than himself. He is swept along, and even though he may himself halt on the path of wrongdoing, he can no longer check the other in his powerful movement. Where the master presses forward, the servant, no matter how good his intentions, cannot save him.

Noble disobedience is a recurrent theme of *Cymbeline*, centred in Pisanio—

PISANIO: How? That I should murder her
Upon the love and truth and vows which I
Have made to thy command? I, her? Her blood?
If it be so to do good service, never
Let me be counted serviceable.

(3.2.11–5)

—and echoed with dramatic irony later by Posthumus: "O Pisanio, / Every good servant does not all commands" (5.1.5–6). We might observe that the play ruled by Shakespeare's demonic Te is a story about what happens when a *kingdom* is ruled by demonic Te, and given this, we can see why disobedience in service of a higher morality comes up so often.

The third line of *Gèn* reads:

Keeping his hips still.
Making his sacrum stiff.
Dangerous. The heart suffocates.[85]

Wilhelm's commentary evokes the wrong done to Belarius, as well as the perceived wrong done to Iago, and their mutual outcomes: "this refers to enforced quiet. The restless heart is to be subdued by forcible means. But fire when it is smothered changes into acrid smoke that suffocates as it spreads." One insults the values of an introverted feeler at one's own peril.

However, that is Belarius, and this is *Morgan*. The distinction may at first seem spurious, but I think it holds. Much as Cesario seems to emphasize a particular side of Viola, Belarius' 20 years as Morgan has brought some very different aspects to the fore of his personality. Belarius acted out of an introverted feeling wound, yet Morgan seems to be working along the axis between introverted intuiting and introverted sensing. The quality of reverence, which was only hinted at in Cymbeline's conduct toward Lucius, is given even greater expression in Morgan's relationship with the divinity of the natural world:

BELARIUS: A goodly day not to keep house with such
Whose roof's as low as ours. Stoop, boys: this gate

Instructs you how t'adore the heavens and bows you
To a morning's holy office.

(3.3.1–4)

Belarius/Morgan is this play's good father, and the 2nd position is where his fatherly introverted intuition sits on our typological mandala. Perhaps it is precisely his fatherhood which has required him to develop this function; a particular relationship may call something heretofore unlived out of us. He definitely has his hands full with the boys, and one gets the sense that parenting them has stretched him.

The paternal feeling of Belarius/Morgan comes across largely in a religious attitude[86] that he seems to have developed during his time in Wales, and which he tries to impart to his 'sons'. A religious attitude can be thought of as comprising a bridge from an introverted *intuitive* perception of "what is real, fundamental, and of lasting importance"[87] to a distinctly introverted *sensate* attention to detail and scrupulosity toward proper observance of rituals and forms. Morgan's personal religiosity can be seen most clearly in his treatment of the dead in 4.2:

BELARIUS: He was a queen's son, boys,
And though he came our enemy, remember
He was paid for that. Though mean and mighty rotting
Together have one dust, yet reverence,
That angel of the world, doth make distinction
Of place 'tween high and low. Our foe was princely,
And though you took his life as being our foe,
Yet bury him as a prince.

(4.2.243–50)

And his diligence regarding the appropriate funeral rites:

BELARIUS: Here's a few flowers, but 'bout midnight more:
The herbs that have on them cold dew o'th'night
Are strewings fitt'st for graves.

(4.2.282–4)

Guiderius has picked up some of this attitude without yet understanding it himself: "Nay, Cadwal, we must lay his head to th' east. / My father hath a reason for't" (4.2.253–4).

Belarius/Morgan essentially furthers the religiosity—the sense of living in a cosmos ruled by invisible forces (archetypes), here personified as gods (Jupiter)—which is hinted at by many other characters, and grounds it in actual practice. Even so, his religious attitude feels nascent, not particularly developed—one does not feel that he has a serious mystic depth of wisdom within him—rather he seems to have only got as far as implementing certain rituals properly. It is for this reason also that I suspect that the Ni-Si axis which he expresses does not stem from his dominant function, which I again consider to be Fi.

The diagram below indicates a proposed typology for Belarius, highlighting the stretch from Si to Ni that underlies the religious attitude.[88]

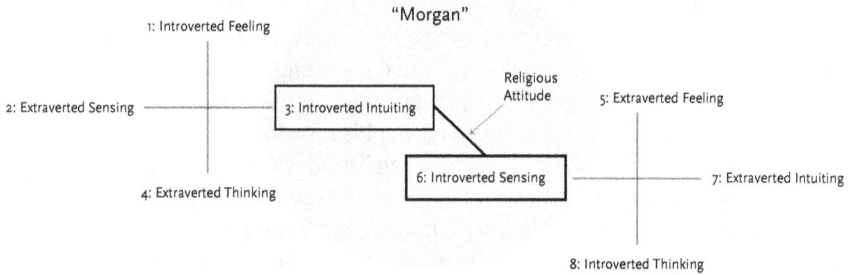

1: Introverted Feeling
"Morgan"
Religious Attitude
2: Extraverted Sensing
3: Introverted Intuiting
5: Extraverted Feeling
4: Extraverted Thinking
6: Introverted Sensing
7: Extraverted Intuiting
8: Introverted Thinking

Figure 6.5 Proposed typology for Belarius, with the two functions making up the religious attitude highlighted.

He feels like a man with a very concrete background who has come to his spirituality in the second half of life.[89] Despite having taken a new path and opening up an unexpected side of his personality, he still has the rationality and concretism of the soldier in him. He is no saint; rather, he is like the rest of his world: a descendant of a greater age. Unlike the rest of his world, however, he protects the exiled sacred in exile himself, although he may not understand it in much depth.

Belarius' religious attitude contrasts with that which we have seen in the first two acts, and through this we may realize here another dimension of the *symboline* in Cymbeline's kingdom: symbols have, all across Britain, lost their meaning, and are being acted out blindly. Though the gods are often referenced, true piety and discernment are absent, because they have been mistrusted and banished, just as Belarius has. It is surely no accident that it is in exile that he discovers that which has also been exiled from Britain. The play gives us few specifics about the nature of his banishment, but it had something to do with a trumped-up accusation of treason, *in particular* that he was "confederate with the Romans" (3.3.68). Indeed, both Rome and Belarius being holders of Fi, this accusation was true on a depth-psychological level if not in reality. Fi values have been vilified in Britain: the tribute to the king's soul is not being paid.

So long as Belarius and the boys are in the wilds, he unceasingly lectures his sons on how much better their life is than that lived in Cymbeline's court. Of course this has the effect that forbidding of fruit tends to have, and the boys are dying to visit the Big Apple (Lud's Town). I think that Belarius must have some intuitive hunch regarding the fact that his life with the boys is nearing its end. He is never seen without making reference to the court from which he has been absent 20 years, and though it is understood that this court represents an unhealed wound for him, the constancy with which it is at the front of his mind is nevertheless notable. He is nearly paranoid in his expectation that he will be found and punished, first in his assurance that Cloten has not come alone—although he *does* intuit correctly that the appearance of Cloten is the beginning of the end for their Welsh life—and later in his fear that joining the battle against the Romans will result in discovery (4.4.7–14). That this fear is absurd and uncharacteristic of him is affirmed by Guiderius—

GUIDERIUS: This is, sir, a doubt
In such a time nothing becoming you,
Nor satisfying us.

(4.4.14–6)

I suspect Belarius sees the Se hunger in his boys—they are unequivocal about their desire for broader experience (3.3.27–44)—and he intuits the writing on the wall—that he cannot keep them forever. He sees that,

BELARIUS: . . . though trained up thus meanly
I'th' cave wherein they bow, their thoughts do hit
The roofs of palaces[.]

(3.3.82–4)

Unlike Cymbeline, who tries to control his daughter's independence by fiat, Belarius seems to find it necessary to reiterate to his sons the value of their life and time together, consolidating in their final moments as family the many lessons he has striven to instil in them. This fatherly drive to cram them full of useful wisdom before they outgrow him may account for the respect he offers Cloten's rank in burial.

It is Belarius' coming to terms with the necessity of returning his sons to their 'true' father that allows him to do so with dignity in the final scene—and in this connection, consider another aspect of the hexagram *Gèn*, "True quiet means keeping still when the time has come to keep still and going forward when the time has come to go forward."[90] The admission Belarius makes here is one that he believes will save their lives and forfeit his own, perhaps arriving at this late moment to that "awakening [of] consciousness to that principle of Self to which the ego willingly submits" that characterizes a thorough religious attitude.[91] His speech is a long passage that is packed with love, paternal pride, and heartbreak:

BELARIUS: But, gracious sir,
Here are your sons again, and I must lose
Two of the sweet'st companions in the world.
The benediction of these covering heavens
Fall on their heads like dew, for they are worthy
To inlay heaven with stars.

(5.5.346–51)

Belarius' last line of this speech alludes, perhaps, to the origin of his piety—a quality which does, after all, beg the question: how exactly is it that the soldier who 20 years ago vengefully kidnapped two toddlers can evidence the humility that Belarius does? One answer could be that it comes simply from being free of the politics of the court and living in touch with nature. But I think it is not nature in general but two specific natures that have touched him, and am therefore more persuaded by the several times that Belarius gives voice to the innate value of his two boys: "How hard it is to hide the sparks of nature" (3.3.79); "O noble strain! / O worthiness of nature, breed of greatness!" (4.2.24–5). It seems to me that these wonderful children, who for him embody the goodness of nature, brought deep meaning and delight to his life; they did indeed "inlay heaven with stars" (5.5.351) for him, bringing the transcendent to life. He was able to *see* the wonder in them better than their own father could have; Cymbeline and his Queen certainly seem to be the only people in the known world who fail to appreciate the other child, Innogen. In the final scene's swell of reunion we scarcely pause to wonder at Cymbeline's apparently unmixed joy at receiving his sons back—is he not simultaneously being confronted with the man who *abducted and kept them for 20 years?*—but it nevertheless feels right, and I think this is why: their relocation saved them and Belarius both, and perhaps Cymbeline as well. Belarius has obviously raised them splendidly, and there is a psychological truth here that takes priority over the merely personal.

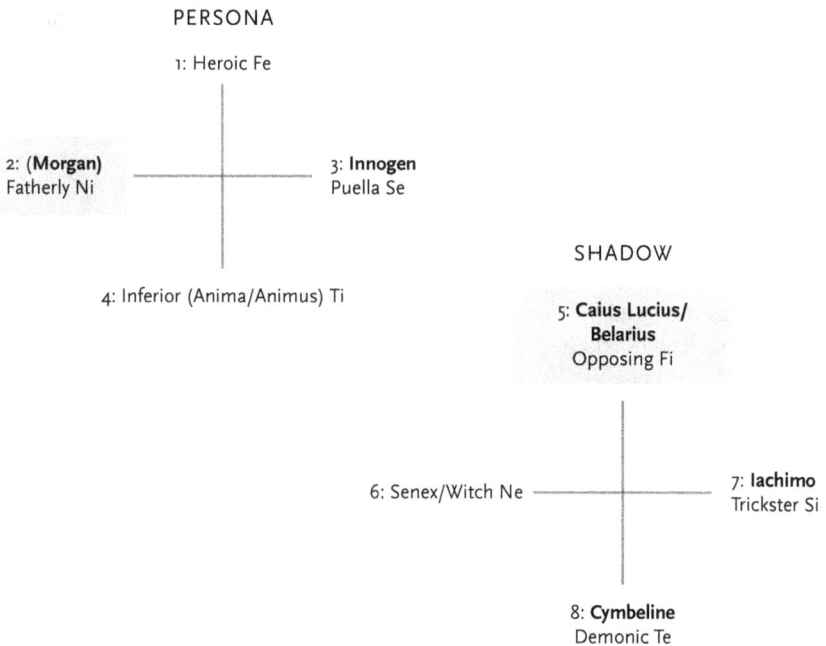

Figure 6.6 Caius Lucius and Belarius as Opposing Fi, "Morgan" as Fatherly Ni.

Sacrifice

Warren writes that "the language and rhythms" of Arviragus' response to the apparent death of Fidele/Innogen "convey a haunting impression that the body is itself becoming a part of the natural world":[92]

ARVIRAGUS: Thou shalt not lack
The flower that's like thy face, pale primrose, nor
The azured harebell, like thy veins; no, nor
The leaf of eglantine, whom not to slander,
Outsweetened not thy breath. The ruddock would
With charitable bill—O bill sore shaming
Those rich-left heirs that let their fathers lie
Without a monument—bring thee all this,
Yea, and furred moss besides, when flowers are none,
To winter-ground thy corpse.

(4.2.219–28)

In the redeeming and returning to balance of the playworld, Innogen largely functions as the sacrificial lamb, the locus in which the play's *mortificatio* is acted out, and which returns her to her base elements. Her persona is a burnt offering to the gods; persona as such is what needs to be sacrificed, as made clear by much of the play's concern with the deceptiveness of appearance, in plot and imagery alike: as a single representative example, Posthumus' "be not, as is our fangled world, a garment / Nobler than that it covers" (5.4.104–5). Let us again 'consider the beginning', returning to the trouble caused by the first line of the play which is borne out of trying to say two seemingly contradictory things about persona at once. The gentleman says:

1 GENTLEMAN: You do not meet a man but frowns. Our bloods
No more obey the heavens than our courtiers
Still seem as does the King.

(1.1.1–3)

He speaks to the paradox that there is both too much persona *and* too little. Either way you slice it, persona is out of joint.

Typologically, extraverted feeling is out of joint. In another situation, one in which the prevailing feeling is *objectively grim*, then "The weight of this sad time we must obey" (*KL* 5.3.322), and then certainly it is appropriate that "you do not meet a man but frowns". But the marriage of Innogen and Posthumus, which initiates the play, ought to be a cause for celebration. A king, by virtue of his central and archetypal position, has the power to establish a collective feeling,[93] and when he establishes feeling that is wholly inappropriate and out-of-*tao*, as Cymbeline's misery is, it becomes *bad* Fe to match this feeling; "If it be so to do good service, never / Let me be counted serviceable" (3.2.14–5).

This bastard Fe, which is merely identification with the current norm, must be sacrificed, and in the play Innogen leads the charge, shedding layer after layer of her persona, moving first from princess to wife, then losing her freedom and husband and becoming a royal prisoner, then flying the palace and becoming a fugitive dressed as "a Franklin's housewife" (3.2.77); after she learns of Posthumus' betrayal she divests herself of her sex ("You must forget to be a woman", 3.4.155) and becomes the boy Fidele, who after some days as a vagrant (3.6.2–3) is taken in by her cave-dwelling brothers, becoming "a cave-keeper / And cook to honest creatures" (4.2.297–8); she then loses her health and takes the sleeping dram, which loses her now her consciousness; awaking later, for all she can tell, in the underworld, as a corpse next to her husband's headless body. When Lucius discovers her, she defines herself in negation:

LUCIUS: What art thou?
INNOGEN: I am nothing; or if not,
Nothing to be were better.

(4.2.366–7)

Her *via negativa* intersects here with the *via Romana*, turning to a path upon which she can be reborn a Roman's page, eventually returning her to her royal place. Significantly, it is with Lucius that she connects with an introverted feeling that at last can touch ground.

Innogen's persona is restored by the end of the play, but with substantial psychological change.[94] Finally, the sacrifice that is made by her is the one that her name alludes to: innocence.[95]

But in the final scene's symphony of reunion, forgiveness, and reintegration, there are two characters who pointedly do not get to come home again: the Queen and her son Cloten. Where Innogen outlives her persona sacrifice, Cloten has nothing that could survive the transformation.

For her part, the Queen is generally unsympathetic, except for her stirring (if overdone) patriotic speech in 3.1:

QUEEN: Remember sir, my liege,
The kings your ancestors, together with
The natural bravery of your isle, which stands
As Neptune's park, ribbed and paled in
With oaks unscalable and roaring waters,
With sands that will not bear your enemies' boats,
But suck them up to th'topmast. A kind of conquest
Caesar made here, but made not here his brag
Of 'came and saw and overcame'. With shame –
The first that ever touched him – he was carried
From off our coast, twice beaten, and his shipping,
Poor ignorant baubles, on our terrible seas

Like eggshells moved upon their surges, cracked
As easily 'gainst our rocks.

(3.1.16–29)

This has puzzled some critics, who wonder at why Shakespeare assigns these inspiriting lines to the Queen, of all people.[96] The question, however, may be too metatheatrical in its reference to the author—it is rather more fruitful to ask, why does the Queen herself need to speak this way at this moment? I do not find these lines mystifying, for it is not at all unusual to find secret pockets of hidden sentimentality lurking within a woman so cold as her. She is delighted with the unassailability of her wicked ways, as in "I never do him wrong / But he does buy my injuries to be friends" (1.1.105–16), and she later echoes Edmund's bloodless calculation in *King Lear*: "Which of them shall I take? / Both? One? Or neither?" (*KL* 5.1.58–9):

QUEEN: Gone she is
To death or to dishonour, and my end
Can make good use of either.

(3.5.62–4)

It is a natural extension of this that against the Romans we find her similarly delighting in her perceived unassailability of her island home. Britain, for her, is a self-symbol. And this is the witchiest thing about her: that she considers herself basically invulnerable, above all the laws of cause and effect that other petty mortals are subject to. In the cited examples, as well as her imperious behaviour with the doctor Cornelius, we feel a consistently self-assured 'no one can touch me' within. This proves to be both as haughty and as fragile as one of her own dramatic forebears, the "fiend-like" Lady Macbeth (*Mac.* 5.8.82), as in the latter's "What need we fear who knows it, when none can call our power to account?" (*Mac.* 5.1.39–41[97]). These psychological touches aside, Shakespeare doesn't even bother to give this Queen a name, which leaves no doubt as to her fundamental emptiness. She is a collection of tactics surrounding an abyss; a body animated by a power drive. Typologically, she stands for a witchy extraverted intuition, obsessed with her great vision of power. True to one-sided Ne, the specifics of her vision do not seem to be terribly important: she is interested in ridding herself of Pisanio, Cymbeline, and Posthumus, as well as Innogen if and when it proves to be convenient. Her main interest in Innogen is as a path for her son to the throne, but it is pretty clear that the Queen would be just as happy for Innogen to be dead, leaving herself and Cloten to rule as king and queen. The Queen's vision, ultimately, is probably a return to the opening image of *King John*: Mother and son, Queen and King.

Cloten is something like the Queen's human exponent, and there are several moments of potential connection between the audience and him, notwithstanding the fact that he is almost entirely loathsome. Psychologically speaking, he barely exists in his own right. I do not mean by this that he is a failure as a character—merely a

PERSONA

1: Heroic Fe

2: **Arviragus/** **(Morgan)** Fatherly Ni

3: **Innogen** Puella Se

4: Inferior (Anima/Animus) Ti

SHADOW

5: **Belarius/** **Caius Lucius** Opposing Fi

6: **Queen** Witch Ne

7: **Iachimo/** **(Morgan)** Trickster Si

8: **Cymbeline** Demonic Te

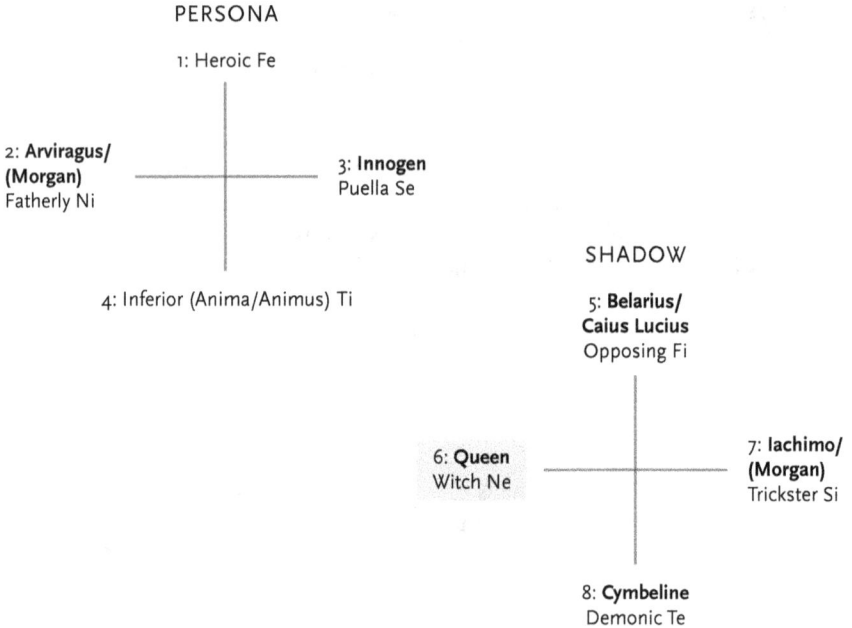

Figure 6.7 Queen as Witch Ne.

failure as a person. He is foregrounded as a kind of gaming and gambling addict, as so many other men trapped in their mother complexes wind up being, the game as such being a sort of perpetually stimulating and gratifying maternal womb. Games can serve the function of acting as a simulated reality in which one can play and play and win and win without ever having to face the consequences that challenge in external reality would come with[98]—except Cloten cannot win, not even for a moment. He fantasizes himself a capable warrior, athlete, and shark, but in his first appearance (1.2) he has just lost a duel, in his second (2.1) a game of bowls, and in his third (2.3) he has been up all night losing at dice. In 4.2, when Belarius instantly recognizes him after *twenty years*, it implies that *Cloten has not changed*. Indeed, Cloten reads as though he would be the same age as the other teenagers—Innogen, Posthumus, Guiderius, and Arviragus—but if one works out the play's chronology it appears that he is in his mid-thirties. He might be one of the most unlikeable characters in all of Shakespeare. And yet we may feel some pity for him, for he is son to one of Shakespeare's many suffocating mothers,[99] and *she* hardly even exists as a person.

Of course Cloten's name evokes the "clotpoll" (blockhead) to which Guiderius reduces him (4.2.183), but that is not the only resonance. In this play a recurrent implicit question is, 'where is value located?' and Cloten's name unites two of its most common answers: blood—clot—and dress—clothing. It of course places him on the negative end of both of these categories, for in a play in which children carry the blood and vivifying lifeforce of their parents,[100] Cloten is a clot, and in a world struggling to differentiate between surface appearance and inner worth, Cloten is little more than his clothing.

He takes Innogen's clothing-based insult absurdly concretely—

INNOGEN: His meanest garment
That ever hath but clipped his body is dearer
In my respect than all the hairs above thee,
Were they all made such men.
                    (2.3.133–6)

—and he becomes fixated on Posthumus' garment. He can do this not only because he is stupid, but because he really is shallow enough to completely mistake the appearance of value for value itself. He becomes hooked on the idea of the garment, the way Macbeth hooks on the prophecy about "none of woman born" (*Mac.* 4.1.79), and sadly for Cloten it does, similarly, turn out to be a riddle that spells his demise.

His concretistic attitude is quite consistent with his earlier remark about music: "If this penetrate, I will consider your music the better; if it do not, it is a vice in her ears" (2.3.24–5[101]). If she doesn't like it, she is *wrong.* His relationship to money betrays a similar anaemia of character, as he explains how he will buy his way into Innogen's confidence: "What can it not do and undo?" (2.3.72–3). To him, money, clothing, rank, and other such gross indicators of worth are all he has which might render value measurable and life comprehensible. The fantasy of value embedded throughout the play but centered in him might be articulated as: if we can have control over value by defining it (rather than *recognizing* it), we can control life itself.

What is Cloten's significance to the typological system of *Cymbeline?* It is difficult to discern, since he is so much the child of his parents. At his worst moment, which is when he develops his plan to murder Posthumus in front of Innogen and rape her while wearing Posthumus' clothes, he combines the psychopathy of his mother's Ne envisioning with the autocracy of his stepfather's Te enforcing. But where does Cloten himself, presuming there *is* such a thing as Cloten himself, really land in terms of type?

My proposal will at first seem perverse, but I suggest that he is this play's main carrier of extraverted feeling. Such a lovely function—what is *he* doing with it? Fe is supposed to be concerned with "the formation and maintenance of easy and harmonious emotional relationships";[102] Beebe names the highest level of Fe as "relating".[103] Possibly the reader who has thus far followed the typology in this chapter with interest may now feel I am trying to cram something in to fit my preferred model. However, as with many of the other character-function associations so far, we may discern Cloten's particular expression of Fe in the *shadow* of the function itself. This may be best illustrated by recourse to hexagram 58: *Duì*

(兑, The Joyous: Lake), which Cai associates with Fe.[104] This hexagram seems, at first, to be rather positive, as in its image:

> Lakes resting one on the other:
> The image of THE JOYOUS.
> Thus the superior man joins with his friends
> For discussion and practice.[105]

We do, early in the play, meet one representative of a more standard Fe in *Cymbeline*, and that would be Philario, Posthumus' host in Rome. In his salon we can see the very image described above, and Philario does his best to maintain the social atmosphere in this international melting pot. But he is powerless against Iachimo's determination to behave in an utterly antisocial manner. Philario's failure here in 1.4 is an early expression of the felt impotence of the Fe function in *Cymbeline* as a whole.

Duì, which may be read as consisting of logical moments within the functioning of Fe, is (aside from the main image) actually filled with admonition and warning. The third line reads "Coming joyousness. Misfortune." Wilhelm comments:

> . . . if one is empty within and wholly given over to the world, idle pleasures come streaming in from without. This is what many people welcome as diversion. Those who lack inner stability and therefore need amusement, will always find opportunity of indulgence. They attract external pleasures by the emptiness of their natures. Thus they lose themselves more and more, which of course has bad results.[106]

And about the sixth line, "Seductive joyousness", Wilhelm writes that

> A vain nature invites diverting pleasures and must suffer accordingly . . . If a man is unstable within, the pleasures of the world that he does not shun have so powerful an influence that he is swept along by them. Here it is no longer a question of danger, of good fortune or misfortune. He has given up direction of his own life, and what becomes of him depends upon chance and external influences.

By consulting these two lines I think we are permitted significant insight into Cloten himself, who is both empty and unstable within. He spends his energy on games of chance, a typical diversion for those who hope that life will happen *for* them; he hangs his future on achieving the love of Innogen, a similar 'moonshot' gamble that does not pay off, at which point he becomes utterly lost, both figuratively and literally (4.2.62–3). In some ways he would be more at home in the gamester's paradise of *The Merchant of Venice* than he is in Ancient Britain.

It is possible that his gaming has to do with an attempt to achieve the archetypal ideal of the hexagram—"the superior man joins with his friends / For discussion and practice."[107] We could imagine his games having an originally social intention, being an attempt at merrymaking that he cannot sustain. Perhaps he is trying to make friends, but is too poor a sport?

It is of interest that this hexagram should seem to be so riddled with danger. *Kǎn*, which is associated with Ni, is similar in this respect. They also both have to do with water, *Duì* with the Lake and *Kǎn* with the Abyss, or "water in motion".[108] These similarities seem to intimate that the hexagrams—and therefore the functions—have equal and opposite dangers. Ni, as an introverted function, runs the risk of being carried along with the flow of the *inner* world and drowned in it, whereas Fe, as an extraverted function, runs the risk of being submerged in the flow of the *outer* world and drowned in that.

We can see one of the risks of a more typical Fe by returning to Viola in *Twelfth Night*, who basically personifies some of Jung's early thoughts on the function:

> It can provide the aesthetic padding for a situation, but there it stops, and beyond that its effect is nil. It has become sterile. If this process goes any further, a curiously contradictory dissociation of feeling results: everything becomes an object of feeling valuations, and innumerable relationships are entered into which are all at variance with each other. As this situation would become quite impossible if the subject [i.e. Viola] received anything like due emphasis, even the last vestiges of a real personal standpoint are suppressed. The subject becomes so enmeshed in the network of individual feeling processes that to the observer it seems as though there were merely a feeling process and no longer a subject of feeling. Feeling in this state has lost all human warmth; it gives the impression of being put on, fickle, unreliable, and in the worst cases hysterical.[109]

As far as the heroic archetype that would be associated with Fe in the 8-function model, I think that if we ask what Cloten's image of himself would be, it cannot be anything other than the hero—in particular the collectively-identified romantic and heroic heir to the throne. Garber and Carr find him a hero-*parody*.[110] He thinks he is a Romeo or a Henry V—but he has missed the memo that he is not leading-man material, nor does he recognize that this play has no room for such a man. He attempts romantic courtship of Innogen (2.3), but has been pre-empted by the upstart Posthumus, who has already married her; he attempts to enter her chamber by force of will, but has been pre-empted in this by the slippery "Iach-in-the-box";[111] he expects the crown of Britain but is pre-empted by the existence of Guiderius and Arviragus, two legitimate heirs to the throne. His closest analogues are not other typical heroes or villains; rather, his kinsmen are the vainglorious blowhards like *Beauty and the Beast*'s Gaston or *Harry Potter*'s Gilderoy Lockhart.[112]

He is also Prince Arthur through-the-looking-glass and all-grown-up, without having ever developed any real autonomy from his mother. *King John*'s Constance is not the witch Queen, though we do not have to squint too hard to see their silhouettes align. They even both pass away offstage: "With horror, madly dying" (5.5.31) and "in a frenzy" (*KJ* 4.2.122) in connection with the miserable deaths of their miserable sons.

Cloten cannot be a complete dolt, or it becomes impossible that Cymbeline would miss his counsel when he is gone (4.3.27). There must be something valuable, and something even relatable in him.[113] He attempts to perform the heroic task of affirming and championing what seem to be the collective values of the time, though he is about as successful at this as Belarius is at being a mystic. There are very few opportunities for *Cymbeline*'s characters to put their best foot forward. We may recognize Cloten as our contemporary, however, through his vain attempt to establish objective value without any meaningful collective system of doing so.

Like *Twelfth Night*'s Andrew Aguecheek, he has been encouraged to discredit his own perception of his beloved's disposition toward him, as his mother tells him to "make denials / Increase your services" (2.3.48–9). Both men are taught that the way to a woman's heart is through ignoring her words and behaviour.

His ignorance about his own character is consistently reinforced by his flatterer, the first Lord, though the distance between this and a more objective view of him is repeatedly (and tediously) sounded by the difference between the first and second Lord. Given this, and given the general state of the nation in which nobody is willing to put on a good face and have a try at heroism anymore *save* for Cloten, and given Cloten's obsession with rank, surface, and even literal garments, it seems that Cloten stands for heroism in its absolute thinnest presentation: *seeming*. But even with this modicum, he is an anachronism in his own time, the last vestige of the hero in Britain.

Cloten is a heroic failure, or perhaps more antiheroic, as hinted at by the comparison to Thersites, Homer's antihero (4.2.251–2). But Cloten's sense of himself as the bearer of heroic Fe comes across best with his "famously beautiful" courtship song to Innogen, "as refined as a medieval French tapestry"[114] though often staged as a painfully saccharine ordeal:

MUSICIAN: Hark, hark, the lark at heaven's gate sings,
        And Phoebus 'gins arise,
    His steeds to water at those springs
        On chaliced flowers that lies,
    And winking Mary-buds begin to ope
     their golden eyes.
    With every thing that pretty is, my lady
     sweet, arise,
            Arise, arise.
          (2.3.20–6)[115]

His hunger for Innogen does betray a human desperation and vulnerability. He 'loves' her, as far as he can articulate, because of her inventory of qualities—

CLOTEN: From every one
The best she hath, and she of all compounded
Outsells them all. I love her, therefore . . .
        (3.5.72–4)

And shortly before his death he is still struggling to comprehend why Innogen loves Posthumus rather than him:

CLOTEN: . . . the lines of my body are as well drawn as his: no less young, more strong, not beneath him in fortunes, beyond him in the advantage of the time, above him in birth, alike conversant in general services, and more remarkable in single oppositions. Yet this imperseverant thing loves him in my despite. What mortality is!

(4.1.9–15)

As these two passages suggest, his fundamental issue with value is that he is fixated at the level of things being a sum of their parts; he does not understand that there is a whole that is greater.

I suspect that, deep down, Cloten's dysfunctional Fe antiheroism reflects not his real personality but a "falsification of type",[116] and here, once again, we have echoes of Arthur. Falsification of type comes about when a child, in an attempt to win the love and approval of a parent, has leaned into a function that would not naturally be their leading one; they live out of it *as if* it is, with increasingly neurotic results the longer the situation persists. There is a surprising corroboration of this idea in Belarius' observation that "his humour / Was nothing but mutation" (4.2.131–2). Cloten may unconsciously glance at it himself when he complains, "I had rather not be so noble as I am" (2.1.18), which is interestingly a similar sentiment to those expressed repeatedly by Innogen: they both want out of the box. It seems possible that young Cloten was subject to his mother's demand (conscious or unconscious) that he live up to her idea of a heroic princely son, which he very obviously is not capable of pulling off. I do not dare hazard a guess as to what his 'real' type is—I can't tell. Leave it to the actor.

Cloten's exclamation "what mortality is!" (4.1.15) is distinctive—it sounds like the interjection of a demigod—and at any rate it sums up his view that it is not he that is in error, but life itself. The only possible explanation that he and his sycophant attendant can accept for Innogen's choice requires them to denigrate her: "Her beauty and brain go not together. She's a good sign, but I have seen small reflection of her wit" (1.2.27–9). He remains the spokesperson for the romantic conventions which Shakespeare is obsoleting—a hero with "a conventionally tragic frame of mind dominated by violence and shaped, ultimately by the conviction that life is somehow at fault".[117]

His plan to murder Posthumus in front of Innogen and rape her while wearing Posthumus' clothes is obviously appalling,[118] even without the added kicker that he thinks this will be the foundation of a marriage between them. All in all, however, it fits, because unfortunately for Cloten, his mother is a living will-to-power, and the fruit does not fall far from the tree. He has no means to engage with a reality that does not conform to this view, save for denial, grandiosity, and combativeness; a combativeness which, despite his oft-averred eagerness to use his sword (1.2.21, 3.1.40–42; 3.5.84; 4.1.15–24, 4.2.96), gets him killed with comedic dispatch as soon as he encounters someone willing to face him down.

"What mortality is!" (4.1.15)—what *is* mortality in this play? Of course it is another word for Time, but mortality's end—death—is fickle and unpredictable for *Cymbeline*'s characters. It is not merely that ghosts walk about onstage in Act 5. The seeming-dead Innogen/Fidele and Posthumus also return to life. When Fidele seems to be visited by death early, Arviragus "had rather have / Skipped from sixteen years of age to sixty", (4.2.197–8), in effect fantasizing an exchange of his own Time for Fidele's; in contrast, Cymbeline would rather Iachimo "shouldst live while nature will / Than die ere I hear more" (5.5.151–2), imaginatively ceding his lawful power over a captive's Time to hear the story.

Mortality is something to be feared, and then to "fear no more" (4.2.257). It has matured beyond the Bastard's "thorns and dangers" (*KJ* 4.3.141), and Hamlet's "slings and arrows" (*Ham.* 3.1.37), simultaneously regressing to the elemental: "the heat o'th sun . . . the furious winter's rages" (4.2.257–8), the "lightning flash" and the "thunder stone" (4.2.269–70). Mortality is a place one visits, does one's "worldly task" (4.2.257), and once done, goes "home" again (4.2.260). Innogen's body does not just become part of the natural world, but the natural world is something we *return* to after life, from where we came *before* life. Our little life is rounded with nature.

Posthumus cannot find his own death when he seeks it; Lucius comes expecting victory in battle, but after their rout expects death, and then expects reprieve, and then again expects death, and in the end *is* reprieved along with all the other Romans. The war itself has such a sudden turnabout, for it seems to be the Britons' loss until the Welsh three turn the tide. Cloten's own death is sudden and shocking, though no less welcome for that. His mother the Queen's death happens offstage, and seems to be a direct result of seeing her power-play evaporate when her son vanishes; Time is waiting for her where power gives out. Mortality, like Time, the body, and value in this play, is *not* subject to human power. Nosworthy offers a convincing account of the audience's experience as the play unfolds, including their likely expectation that it ends in tragic death, certainly for Innogen, and probably Posthumus, Cymbeline and many others as well.[119] Just as *Cymbeline* constantly flirts with genre-conforming romantic choices and then changes course, it constantly flirts with tragedy and then changes course.

In a way, we might take the antecedent action summarized in the first scene as the 'tragedy' of twenty years' past. As in *The Tempest* and the second half of *The Winter's Tale*, this play takes place 'post-tragedy', in a world which seems to operate by slightly different rules, perhaps having learned something from past pain. Here, the choices that get people killed in tragedy can be pulled back from the brink and redeemed.[120] *Cymbeline* is set in a pre-Christian time, but its theology ultimately verges on New- rather than Old-Testament. "Pardon's the word to all" decrees Cymbeline (5.4.21), curmudgeon no more, and proto-Christian as well. The upshot is that mortality itself is a trope in this play, and Shakespeare plays with it and exploits it just like all the rest.

Innogen's belief is that the human "afflictions" that we suffer are either "A punishment or a trial" (3.6.9–11), and the "trial" part is more-or-less confirmed straight from the horse's mouth, when the secret divine prerogative that Jupiter himself reveals is "Whom best I love, I cross, to make my gift, / The more delayed, delighted" (5.4.71–2). This a far cry from Shakespeare's tragedy, which sees the most remarkable of human beings burned to ashes by their own magnitude. Of course, there is nobody in this play of that calibre; none so brilliant as Hamlet, so passionate as Othello, so imaginative as Macbeth, so suffering as Lear, so large as Antony or so impossible as Cleopatra, so embittered as Timon or so absolute as Coriolanus; there is no love quite so uncompromising as that of Romeo and Juliet. *Cymbeline*'s characters, by contrast with these, are normal, banal, mundane; human, all-too-human. Mortal. Hamlet lives on long after *Hamlet* in our hearts and minds. Nobody in *Cymbeline* has this immortality—Innogen is *very* interesting, but I must agree with Bloom that she would need to be in a different play than this one to truly show her worth.[121] There is simply no comparable effect, because even Innogen exists on a different plane of existence from the great tragic heroes. The magic, such as it is, has moved out of the individual characters and into the syntactical and stylistic level of the play itself. It is the *play* in which transcendence now lives, as it transcends its conventions with the regularity and ferocity that Hamlet once transcended his own thoughts. *Cymbeline,* for the most part, is a move away from plays about remarkable people, toward regular people in a remarkable play.[122] And the hard-won regularity, the normality—the inescapable mortality of these characters, most of whom survive the play (and so are denied the immortality of a tragic end), is of great consequence and can help us understand the play as a whole. More will be said on this below, when the discussion comes round to Posthumus.

For now, we have not done with Cloten: when he first appears onstage, a hint to his symbolic significance is dropped, as his toady unwittingly foreshadows his fate: "Sir, I would advise you to shift a shirt. The violence of action hath made you reek as a sacrifice" (1.2.1–2). In other words, Cloten has the smell of sacrifice about him from the beginning. If Innogen is the lamb, Cloten is the scapegoat. Sacrifice is where Cloten's story begins; sacrifice also happens to be where the play ends:

CYMBELINE: Laud we the gods,
And let our crooked smokes climb to their nostrils
From our blest altars.

(5.5.475–7)

In the dream-logic of the play, the sacrifices that take place are not only on the persona level, but include also the lives of Cloten and his mother. In this play that is so much about the reality of the body, Cloten's is the only corpse we see. But it is only through their deaths that the ending can be allowed to happen.

The etymology of 'sacrifice' has to do with making sacred; with releasing the sacrificed object from its physical form into a higher level of existence, as the crooked smokes climb up from the altar, up to the nostrils of the gods. And Cloten's death allows him to be, in some sense, made sacred. Belarius rather unexpectedly accords him the dignity in death that he expected in life. And once dead, and divested of that head which caused such trouble, he can at last receive Innogen's embrace—though of course it is only 'posthumously', and ironically it is given precisely due to the garment he wears—Cloten, finally, is reduced to clothing.

What do the sacrifices of him and the Queen represent, psychologically speaking? It cannot be anything but the will-to-power. And this reconnects us with another main theme, for the will-to-power is precisely what is sacrificed when taking the reality of the body seriously. The will-to-power is itself an attempt to conquer the body and Time both, by dissociating from their realities. It is, however, inevitably defeated. As Shakespeare was unable to forget, "that old common arbitrator, Time" (*TC* 4.5.225) cannot be dodged; with him there is no shuffling. The reality of the body, *Cymbeline* reminds us, is not only in its wonderful capacity to experience, but also in the terribly banal fragility of the material of which we are made. Characters are continually close to death, and can die at any moment. Cloten's years have left no inner or outer trace, yet he dies before Belarius, whose body is unrecognizable with age (4.4.33) though "marked / with Roman swords" (3.3.56–7) which tell tales of his youth.

Shakespeare's constant meditations on Time reach out and over the stage/page and into the audience/reader, reminding us that we too die; we age; and however we age, we die; our status as mere bodies provides hard limits to our 'power', in inverted commas here because in the light of Time it really does seem to be *so-called* 'power'.

Does any writer deal with death so fully as Shakespeare? Predeceased by his son, three brothers, his patron, many colleagues and rivals, his parents, his Queen . . . But had he some premonition of his own early death? He lived until only 52 but writes, at times, with the wisdom of a man twice that old.

Cymbeline seems to be on death's door; he may have been near-death five times. The Leonati are dead twenty years, and our story begins in the shadow of their past. One all-powerful Caesar has been assassinated, giving way to another. Parents and grandparents die; children grow up with them, or posthumously, without them. We see Cloten's premature death kill his mother, the only evidence that she had a heart; but Shakespeare's son, we recall, died long before he did.

The Briton people crawl forth from a Welsh cave in Time prehistoric. The generations pass. Rome invades; Rome departs. Cassibelan rules—Cymbeline rules—Guiderius rules. The young—no longer young—are left the inheritors of the kingdom. We all grow older, but at different speeds. Britain grows out from under Rome's shadow. Rome declines. Elizabeth I gives way to James I.

As Time passes, and as we pass through Time, our body—the instrument which registers Time—asserts increasing dominance over us. At every moment, the body has more Time behind it and less Time ahead of it. The body takes more of our Time away from other pursuits. Some pursuits take too long, and others become impossible. It takes much longer to get fit, and a tremendous amount of discipline and Time to *stay* fit; injuries become more likely and take longer to heal; sicknesses linger with more weight and leave deeper impacts, possibly never leaving at all. Other bodies—of friends, or partners, or parents, or children—begin to take up our Time as well, and if our bodies are not changing, theirs are. We may become more responsible for things in the physical world generally—rooms, homes, meals, clothing, transportation. Time itself becomes reality; it starts to matter and be inextricable *from* matter; we can say along with Cymbeline, "I am amazed with matter" (4.3.28). There is a famous lament among female actors, that by the time you are old enough to understand Juliet, you are too matronly to play her;[123] we might here repurpose the old trope, and instead observe that by the time you are old enough to begin to grasp what a body *is*, it's already beginning to degrade on you.

Bodies have been subjected to the will-to-power throughout *Cymbeline*. Posthumus tries to exert power over Innogen's wayward body by murdering it. Iachimo steals a view and a kiss with impunity. Cymbeline tries to "pen her up" (1.1.154). Belarius has escaped bearing the two boys' bodies. The Queen's experiments on the bodies of others have rotted her mind away; the body comes back to revenge itself on her in the end. Cloten and Innogen learn the limits of their bodies the hard way, that life is neither a game nor a story, but a field where risks have hard consequences. Yet the nature boys in Wales have an integrated respect for the exertions of the body, knowing that

BELARIUS: . . . our stomachs
Will make what's homely savoury. Weariness
Can snore upon the flint when resty sloth
Finds the down pillow hard.

(3.6.32–5)

Cloten is reduced to a body, but without his head he is as good as Posthumus, and Fidele as well ("Thersites' body is as good as Ajax' / When neither are alive" 4.2.251–2). Belarius brings dignity and respect to the bodies of Euriphile, Innogen, and Cloten—the mother, daughter, and son, though none to one another, united in burial. Once Cloten is only body, he is made good; being rendered a mere body is, paradoxically, what frees him. His mind, his 'big head' as it were, is what divorces him from reality—he is beholden to his own will-to-power.

With Cloten as antihero, we may wonder: where is the true hero? It would not be overstating to say that this is the biggest difficulty of the play—there is no obvious protagonist. Innogen and Posthumus both disappear from the stage for too long; Cymbeline is an absent bore; Cloten dies halfway, and we cannot possibly accept him as the lead. One way to think about it would be to recognize that Cloten and the Queen are the chief evils of the play—who then, is the hero who vanquishes them? It is the potentially forgettable Guiderius.

The Many Gifts of Guiderius

With closer investigation, we see that Guiderius' killing of Cloten is motivated precisely by a *healthy* extraverted feeling—rustic though it may be. There is an instinctive affirmation, on Guiderius' part, of the objective feeling situation: this

Cloten needs to be dealt with. This is why the sudden unexpected killing is among the most satisfying moments of the play, a grim delight. The antihero Cloten has, just at the point of growing to an insupportable size, been lanced, as a boil.

Guiderius' instinctive and unschooled-in-the-ways-of-the-world Fe is exactly what Britain cries out for at this moment. His rejoinders to Cloten are a breath of fresh air:

CLOTEN: I am son to th' Queen.
GUIDERIUS: I am sorry for't, not seeming
So worthy as thy birth.
CLOTEN: Art not afeard?
GUIDERIUS: Those that I reverence, those I fear, the wise.
At fools I laugh, not fear them.
                                        (4.2.93–6)

And he is entirely unflappable when defending his killing:

BELARIUS: What hast thou done?
GUIDERIUS: I am perfect what: cut off one Cloten's head,
Son to the Queen, after his own report,
Who called me traitor, mountaineer, and swore
With his own single hand he'd take us in . . .
BELARIUS: We are all undone.
GUIDERIUS: Why, worthy father, what have we to lose
But that he swore to take, our lives? The law
Protects not us, then why should we be tender
To let an arrogant piece of flesh threat us,
Play judge and executioner all himself,
For we do fear the law?
                                        (4.2.116–28)

His treatment of Cloten's head is unforgiving:

GUIDERIUS: With his own sword,
Which he did wave against my throat, I have ta'en
His head from him. I'll throw't into the creek
Behind our rock, and let it to the sea
And tell the fishes he's the Queen's son, Cloten.
That's all I reck.
                                        (4.2.148–53)

And though this is not the *typical* presentation of extraverted feeling, which is known for being 'nice', it is the heroic Fe that is deeply needed. Guiderius seems to act, in regard to Cloten, with the energy of the fifth (and perhaps most interesting) line of the hexagram *Duì*: "Sincerity towards disintegrating influences is danger-ous."[124] This is a lesson his father Cymbeline has yet to learn.

I think this is key to staging and playing Guiderius, who seems at risk of fad-ing out of the play as only half of a character, the other half being his brother Arviragus. He has been raised under the name Polydore, which means something like many virtues, and this seems to be accurate, for in addition to carrying the play's heroic Fe, he seems also to have a gift for Se and Te too. He is part giant, a slightly-superhuman boy who has outgrown his father and his cave, and operates with a straightforward confidence that would terrify were it not for his obvious goodness.[125] I sometimes feel he has been abducted into the past from *Seven Brides for Seven Brothers*.[126]

However he is played, it seems to me that Guiderius does the Fe job of affirm-ing the *objective* feeling situation, which, despite being at odds with the collective feeling established by King Cymbeline, is resonant with the collective feeling of the *audience*, and everyone else in Britain, as we learned in the first scene, when Cloten was established as "Too bad for bad report" (1.1.17). Guiderius' killing of him is the turning point from the initial mouldering situation of the kingdom toward renewal. The source of the objective feeling at the start of the play is syn-onymous with worldly power: it is in the possession of Cymbeline, the Queen, and Cloten. Here it begins to shift, and the 'objectivity' of the objective feeling begins more to belong to *us*, as the audience and readers! After the harrowing audience experiences of Shakespeare's tragedies, he has finally begun to give the audience the endings they want again.

If we are correct about the typology of Shakespeare himself, it makes perfect sense that Fe should be the function which needs to undergo the greatest transfor-mation throughout his work. In the development of one's personal typology, there is a process analogous to the life, death, and regeneration of the hero which needs to take place. A dominant function can be lived through almost exclusively, with relative success, for two, three, maybe even four decades—but at some point a personality needs *more*, and in order for this to happen the identification with the dominant function needs to be broken. The stronger it has been identified with up to this point, the more painful the separation from it. It may feel akin to having to operate without one's head, which is exactly what happens to Cloten. Jung writes,

> A collapse of the conscious attitude is no small matter. It always feels like the end of the world, as though everything had tumbled back into original chaos. One feels delivered up, disoriented, like a rudderless ship that is abandoned to the moods of the elements.[127]

It is here, when reflecting on Shakespeare's overall journey with Fe that we might recall that this seemingly post-everything play is also, significantly, post-*Timon of Athens* and post-*Coriolanus*. In *Timon* we are exposed to the bitterness of the failed one-sided Fe personality—an extreme version of the more-or-less typical case of one who gives himself away to others, and then horrifically discovers that his assumption that the arrangement would be mutual is wrong. And in *Coriolanus* we see a hero tragically and combatively opposed to using Fe at all; his performative self-sameness is carried to the point of utterly poisoning all his relationships. In *Cymbeline,* Shakespeare seems to have a hangover from those explorations, and Cloten is the bloody mess that is vomited up; he seems to be an extraverted feeling heroic type written by someone who had lost all faith in extraverted feeling, a character that could very well have been written by Timon of Athens.

Perhaps there is something that *Cymbeline* can teach us here about individuation, and the development of personal typology. The prevailing myth in Jungian typology is that the heroic function must, at some point, be *sacrificed*, leaving another function to step up to carry the load. *Cymbeline* tells a more nuanced story. The heroic function here is in decay from the beginning—"You do not meet a man but frowns" (1.1.1) is a bottoming-out of Fe in the kingdom—but *sacrifice* of this function, strictly speaking, is not what takes place. In the rigidified initial situation, the burden does fall upon another function to create some movement—and the obvious choice might seem to be the auxiliary, but that one is usually oriented more towards taking care of others than it is toward pursuing one's own development; thus it falls to the third function: the puella/puer. The puella/puer is a limited expression of the hero archetype, and it makes sense that this function would be the one to have the heroic energy to inject some drive into the overall psychological situation, linked as it is with the energy of youthful and renewing creativity.

This is acted out in *Cymbeline*, and we may imagine, one last time, that the play itself is an analysand. We can see the initial situation of this analysand as a psychological deadlock, in danger of falling into total catastrophe. Innogen is the psyche's 'Hail Mary pass': a *symptom*. She represents a sudden and insistent emergent emphasis on immediacy and experience, which has the effect of precipitating a crisis in the psyche. Her sudden marriage does the same thing that a psychological symptom may do in an individual, which is to force a reorganization. The puella Innogen is, as symptoms usually are, turned against by the rest of the system who want little more than to pen her in and shut her up. Were it not for Pisanio, she would be erased. Pisanio, as the servant, may represent the most humble of psychological processes, perhaps symbolic of humility itself—his name evoking (Italian) *paesano,* a word meaning something like 'fellow countryman', but also, essentially, 'peasant'. It is very fortunate for Innogen that Pisanio recognizes her value even in the face of her demonization by his master.

In an analysis, a discerning humility of the Pisanio variety may allow the inherent *positive* value in an analysand's symptom the chance of being understood. If this happens, the flow of defensive and repressive energy against the symptom may be reversed, and it becomes possible to recognize the symptom as a rare "gift of the gods" (1.4.88). Here, naturally, I reference one of Jung's most oft-quoted insights,

The gods have become diseases; Zeus no longer rules Olympus but rather the solar plexus, and produces curious specimens for the doctor's consulting room, or disorders the brains of politicians and journalists who unwittingly let loose psychic epidemics on the world.[128]

For the symptom to be recognized in this way is to recognize what, for me, is the most important insight of psychoanalysis bar none: that the psychological issue which bedevils us may be our own psyche's best attempt at helping us; the seeming beggar at the door may be an angel in disguise. *The Tempest* is not a focus of this book, but its most remarkable psychological achievement would seem to be the final acceptance of *its* monstrous and hideous 'symptom', Caliban: "this thing of darkness I / Acknowledge mine" (*Tem.* 5.1.275–6).

For her part, Innogen the puella symptom needs to escape the hostile system first, which constitutes the setting up of a second centre of consciousness, in the area of the third function. Since the rigid psyche will not allow the disidentification which would be required for transformation, *she* disidentifies with *it*. Sometimes this is seen in an analysis—a person begins to express thoughts, feelings, and behaviours of a new and excitingly creative cast, which are not integrated into the dominant attitude; the dominant attitude continues to dominate as ever, and two seemingly parallel streams continue for some time, as if the left hand doesn't know what the right is doing.

It is Innogen who connects at last with the three true exiles, including a new bearer of Fe in Guiderius. That is the key point: Fe is not sacrificed out-and-out—it is *rejuvenated and surpassed* by a superior version of itself. Guiderius' Fe is simultaneously revolutionary *and* a return to 'first principles' of the function. Cloten's beheading represents not a total disidentification with the dominant function, but rather the replacement of a deranged version of the function with a more suitable one.

The miracle of Innogen is that she can find a way to love even the mutilated and misshapen form of Cloten's corpse: she truly experiences and mourns the loss, as her own, and does not shrink from the encounter. This is the moment that the transcendent capacity of the puella shines through her, even as she herself transcends her puella identification; the moment itself is a moment of transcendent functioning which includes and outgrows the former complex.

The dethroning of Cloten's rotten Fe by the robust Fe of Guiderius bears fruit in the final scene when Guiderius is reintegrated as heir. It is at *this* point that Cymbeline can finally find it in his heart to operate with his *own* functional extraverted feeling, taking unbelievable care for the entire assembled cast, and conducting the dissonant players into harmony. Cymbeline at last makes the stretch from extraverted thinking to extraverted feeling.[129] And as Guiderius ends the play in the position of the future king of Britain, we can see that *Cymbeline*, psychologically, looks forward to the re-establishing of heroic feeling value after its obliteration in *Timon of Athens*, enantiodromia in *Coriolanus,* and perversion in Cloten.

PERSONA

1: **Guiderius/**
Philario/
Cloten
Heroic Fe

2: **Arviragus/**
(Morgan)
Fatherly Ni

3: **Innogen**
Puella Se

SHADOW

5: **Caius Lucius/**
Belarius
Opposing Fi

4: Inferior (Anima/Animus) Ti

6: **Queen**
Witch Ne

7: **Iachimo/**
(Morgan)
Trickster Si

8: **Cymbeline**
Demonic Te

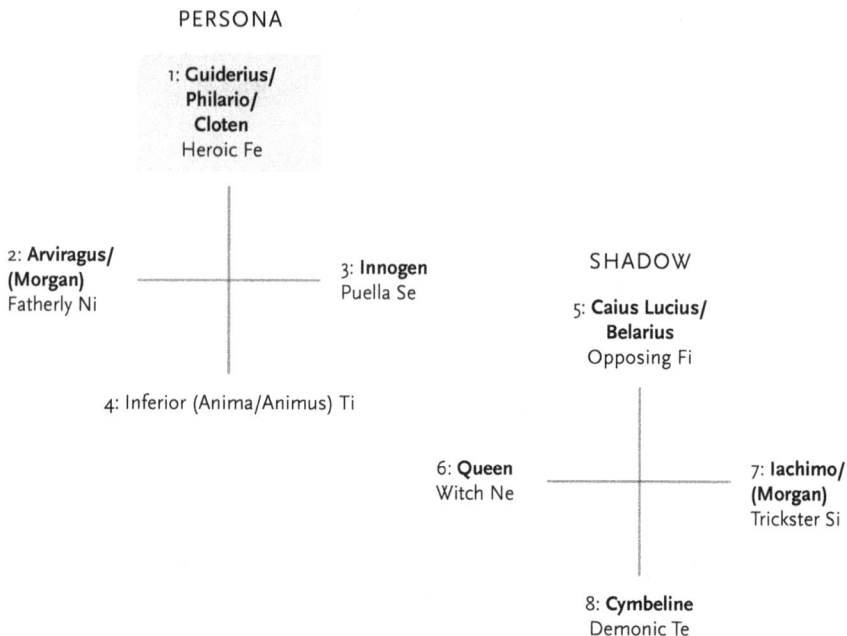

Figure 6.8 Guiderius, Philario, and Cloten as Heroic Fe.

Posthumus

Posthumus Leonatus has a great big mother-shaped hole in his psyche, and critics of him can forget that he was orphaned at birth, despite the ghosts of his parents showing up to remind everyone. He was taken in and brought up in Cymbeline's court, but Posthumus has never lost the sense of being the cuckoo in the robin's nest. His own name never lets him (or us) forget that he is living in an aftermath, a posthumous extension of his absent good father and mother. He fits into Britain, quite well in fact, but he comes up against the reality of his class situation in heartbreaking fashion when he dares to marry Britain's princess in secret. He is, naturally, banished as a punishment for usurping the rule of law. We may inwardly protest, along with the rest of the nation, that he is a far more appropriate man for Innogen to marry, characterologically speaking, than Cloten—but really, given the circumstances, nobody should be surprised that their wedding is received as a catastrophe rather than as an event to be celebrated. If they are shocked by the king's response, it speaks as much to their naïveté as it does to his intransigence.

Posthumus' social inferiority is constantly at front of mind, kept there especially by Cymbeline and Cloten, though their fixation on it seems unnecessary as he has internalized it himself—the imagined circumstances of his birth are precisely where his mind first goes when he believes himself betrayed ("We are all bastards",

2.5.2). He idealizes Innogen beyond reason, likely in compensation for his inferior sense of himself—as though winning the heart of the most perfect lady in all the world could ever make up for having no home or family. It is this idealization that provokes the attack from Iachimo, for something about Posthumus' exalted vision of Innogen is intolerable to the Italian, as well as the Frenchman present, and to us as well if we are honest. Iachimo may disgust us, but in his way he acts as a deflating mechanism on behalf of the overall system. He cannot tolerate a perfect Innogen any more than she can tolerate being perfect herself.

Posthumus, almost instantly when in male society, defaults to the lowest common denominator of proclaiming Innogen's worth as an object: "I praised her as I rated her: so do I my stone" (1.4.76). Attempting to define her as 'priceless' back-fires; he seems to sense this, and tries unsuccessfully to talk his way out of it:

POSTHUMUS: You are mistaken: the one [the diamond] may be sold or given, or if there were wealth enough for the purchase or merit for the gift; the other [Innogen] is not a thing for sale, and only the gift of the gods.

(1.4.85–8)

The other is not a "thing for sale", and Posthumus seems to be trying to back-pedal on defining her as a "thing", but Iachimo smells uncertainty and presses his advantage:

IACHIMO: Which the gods have given you?
POSTHUMUS: Which by their graces I will keep.
(1.4.89–90)

Posthumus skirts away from speaking of Innogen explicitly as a "thing", but is still seduced into objectifying her *honour* (1.4.98). And by the conclusion of the scene, he has laid the unpardonable wager: 10,000 ducats says you can't f— my wife. Iachimo gets under his skin so thoroughly in 130 lines that the Posthumus we have heard about—

1 GENTLEMAN: . . . a creature such
As, to seek through the regions of the earth
For one his like, there would be something failing
In him that should compare.
(1.1.19–22)

—disintegrates before our very eyes; his must be the first instance in the play in which "experience, O thou disprov'st report!" (4.2.34) is acted out.

Posthumus' quick fall can only be possible as a result of his terrible cuckoo-inferiority complex and consequent need to prove himself, in combination with his voidlike mother complex. Having grown up with, at best, a nurse to mother him, he has only the most abstract and wildly conflicting ideas about what a grown woman is. He has had nobody to properly mediate the mother archetype for him; one does not imagine the Queen stepping in, and Cymbeline himself is at best a father-figure of the benevolent-neglect school. And so in the place of a formed mother complex, Posthumus has only a primal chaos. To Posthumus, Iachimo's cynicism looks like the surety of an accomplished knower-of-women, and allows Iachimo to slide right into this vulnerability—though Iachimo has no clue how vulnerable Posthumus really is.

Both Posthumus and Innogen feel some adolescent anxiety regarding the other's faithfulness. While Innogen manages her anxiety by projecting it onto wily Italian *donne*, Posthumus manages his by disavowing his knowledge of Innogen's sexuality and redefining her as unavailable even to him ("I profess myself her adorer, not her friend", 1.4.70; "I thought her / As chaste as unsunned snow", 2.5.13). Roger Rees, who played him in 1979, finds Posthumus' vows on departing Britain "too adamant and brittle to be trusted";[130] when swearing "I will remain the loyal'st husband that did e'er plight troth" (1.1.95–6), he sounds much like the foolish Troilus, who Cressida acerbically (and rightly) punctures:

CRESSIDA: They say all lovers swear more performance than they are able, and yet reserve an ability that they never perform, vowing more than the perfection of ten and discharging less than the tenth part of one. They that have the voice of lions and the act of hares, are they not monsters?

(*TC* 3.2.82–7)

Innogen has not learned any of Cressida's cynicism about love, however, and so the necessity of bringing Posthumus down to earth falls not to her but to Iachimo, who responds with sanguine gusto to the challenge.

The compensatory nature of Posthumus' overstated view of Innogen is expressed at first by his surprising unconscious predisposition, as Butler notes, "to attribute whoredom to Innogen."[131] And when the conscious idealized image is lost, the gaping maw of the unmediated negative mother complex hidden within him explodes in a spiral dive from idealization to devaluation worthy of borderline pathology, his unconscious erupting with graphic imagery of his betrayal, framed by psychotic misogyny that outdoes every other character in Shakespeare:

POSTHUMUS: Could I find out
The woman's part in me—for there's no motion
That tends to vice in man but I affirm
It is the woman's part: be it lying, note it,
The woman's; flattering, hers; deceiving, hers;
Lust and rank thoughts, hers, hers; revenges, hers;
Ambitions, covetings, change of prides, disdain,
Nice-longing, slanders, mutability,
All faults that name—nay, that hell knows—why hers
In part or all, but rather all, for even to vice
They are not constant but are changing still,

One vice but of a minute old for one
Not half so old as that.

                         (2.5.19–31)

The proper response to this is uttered by Innogen two acts later: "O Posthumus, alas, / Where is thy head? Where's that? Ay me, where's that?" (4.2.319–20).

Posthumus carries many of the qualities typically associated with the inferior function—in particular, an inferior introverted thinking function. For one thing, introverted thinking never knows when to stop,[132] and this rant illustrates that with clarity. Continuing to not stop, Posthumus follows up his litany of grievances against women (a reversal of the previous gushing 'inventories' of Innogen) with a bizarre intent to "write against them" (2.5.31)[133]—and then he goes even further and instructs Pisanio to murder Innogen. And as pertains to the content of his rant, has anybody ever heard more thoughtless thinking than this? The poor fellow is struggling to contain the terrible emotion with which he is confronted by naming and defining what has happened, but is so unequal to the task that these mad boilerplate generalizations are all he can come up with. "We are all bastards" (2.5.2), actually, is probably wishful thinking. Bastardy in Shakespeare, as we saw in *King John*, is a social inferiority but a strategic advantage. To fantasize himself a bastard is for Posthumus to try and claim his autonomy; to be "As if a man were author of himself" (*Cor.* 5.3.36).

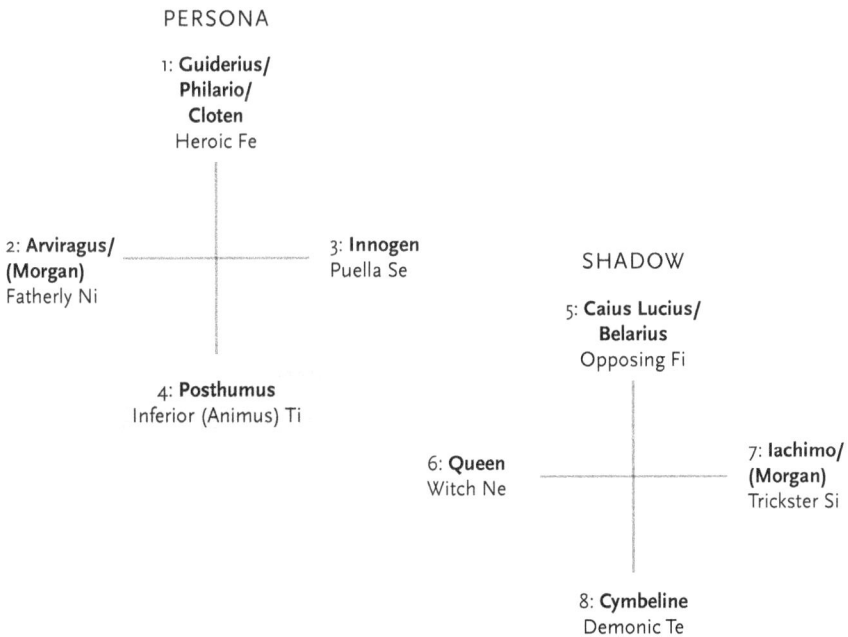

PERSONA

1: **Guiderius/**
    Philario/
    Cloten
    Heroic Fe

2: **Arviragus/**   3: **Innogen**   SHADOW
(Morgan)   Puella Se
Fatherly Ni   5: **Caius Lucius/**
                                                         Belarius
                                                         Opposing Fi
    4: **Posthumus**
    Inferior (Animus) Ti

                        6: **Queen**   7: **Iachimo/**
                        Witch Ne   **(Morgan)**
                                                  Trickster Si

                                  8: **Cymbeline**
                                  Demonic Te

Figure 6.9 Posthumus as Inferior (Animus) Ti.

The inferior function, according to von Franz, is "generally slow . . . infantile and tyrannical"[134]; unadapted, primitive, and touchy, and connected with "a tremendous charge of emotion."[135] Beebe adds that "each of us usually has an inferiority complex around that particular area of our conscious functioning,"[136] which pretty much points to Posthumus, *Cymbeline*'s socially inferior inferiority complex.

On the other hand, the inferior function also has "a great concentration of life"[137] in it; the potential to render the world "exciting, dramatic, full of positive and negative possibilities", which helps to comprehend Posthumus' remarkable turn from heel to face in the fifth act. The inferior function is said to be "the door through which all the figures of the unconscious come into consciousness,"[138] and there are a couple of interesting points in this connection. First, he is exiled to Renaissance Italy—which functions in this play as one domain of Britain's unconscious, the other two being Wales and Ancient Rome—and it is his unadapted behaviour there which calls forth the challenges from the Frenchman and Iachimo. In this way, we could consider those two characters as unconscious compensations for Posthumus' inferior attitude—as though they come into being purely for the purpose of correcting him.[139] The other point, which for now I will simply gesture toward, is the fact that it is to Posthumus that the deep unconscious of the play makes itself manifest, first in the form of his deceased ancestors, and then in the collective unconscious form of the god Jupiter. More will be said on Posthumus' Vision below.

Posthumus' thinking is not beyond redemption, and against Iachimo it puts on a good show. With the help of Philario,[140] he defends himself far longer against *his* scheming Italian than Othello (one of his spiritual predecessors) defended against the insinuations of Iago. He is more challenging to crack than Malvolio, who as we saw did all the work himself. Posthumus manages to dispense with *most* of Iachimo's spurious proofs, but Iachimo's volumes of sensate data eventually overwhelm him.

After his hideous rant, it is no wonder he disappears for two acts—he, the play, and the audience all need some space. As this passage shows, Posthumus has little creativity even in soliloquy. Even in rant he remains banal. Rees saw him as "Britain and virtue personified . . . everything the world has come to expect of the true-born Englishman";[141] and Wilson Knight wrote that Posthumus represents "British manhood",[142] neither of which reflect very well on British manhood, but both of which catch the scent of Posthumus' striking normalness, his transcendent mediocrity, a quality that is key both to his character as well as to his holding down of the inferior function.

When he returns in Act 5, he brings with him a personal development with a collective significance that represents "a moral transformation without parallel on the early modern stage":[143]

POSTHUMUS: You married ones,
If each of you should take this course, how many
Must murder wives much better than themselves
For wrying but a little.

(5.1.2–5)

In the tiny phrase "wrying but a little" lies a revolution in Shakespeare's male-female relations. With it, Posthumus surpasses all of his jealous and vengeful predecessors—Othello, Claudio, Leontes, the Poet of the Sonnets—by repenting *while he still believes Innogen to be 'guilty'*. Shaw approved: "after being theatrically conventional to the extent of ordering his wife to be murdered, he begins to criticise . . . the slavery to an inhuman ideal of marital fidelity which led him to this villainous extremity."[144] Othello, Claudio and Leontes repent their cruel overreactions, yes, but they only do so after they learn that they were mistaken, and that their wives were innocent of the accusation. Posthumus here forgives Innogen's supposed sexuality; he accepts the reality of her body, and of her autonomy, in a way that no other man in Shakespeare does. He accepts, at least in theory, that Innogen is *real*.

(Actually, *one* Shakespearean character has beaten Posthumus to the punch with this: the Bastard! In embracing his mother's age-old infidelity, *KJ* 1.1.261–76.[145])

Posthumus now even gets to utter the capstone to the play's thematic arc of surface-versus-substance: "To shame the guise o'th' world, I will begin / The fashion: less without and more within" (5.1.32–3). And he does begin the fashion. Contrary to the earlier man who was desperate to prove his value, this one keeps his light under a bushel. When recounting the battle, he does not reveal his participation in it, and only acknowledges his heroics in the end so that he may also lay out his sins.

Finally, however, the man himself is ordinary as common clay. Wilson Knight observed that throughout the play he is praised, but in notably reserved language:

> The words selected [to describe Posthumus] are quite colourless; and the language gets . . . involved in the attempt to define an extreme worth without committing itself to the high-sounding phrase . . . he is *pitied*, with an attendant loss of glamour.[146]

This pitying praise, which Chen finds to be virtually empty of content,[147] occasionally has a patronizing and hopeful tone, as when we blind ourselves to a friend's poor character and instead construe them as 'just *such* a good guy'. Posthumus himself "has, as a man, no such impact on us as Othello and Leontes; he is a colourless person . . . with no core to his personality."[148]

For Bloom, "the wonder again is why Shakespeare so consistently labors to make Posthumus so dubious a protagonist."[149] I think the answer to this is hiding in plain sight: Posthumus' terrible normality. He is one of "that large company of Shakespearean husbands and lovers totally unworthy of their women",[150] and I suspect that for once that may be the point.[151] Swander writes that Shakespeare exposes "an essential meanness in the man", implying "that he is not worthy of his marriage" until the final act.[152] I wonder if Posthumus, of all Shakespeare's men, might be the one who can make the leap to acceptance of his wife's humanity precisely *because* of how much a schmo he is. He has nothing of the gigantic personae of Othello, Leontes, or even Claudio, to live up to. He earlier convinced himself that he *deserved* "th'Arabian bird" (1.6.17) but he comes to know that, deep down, what he deserves (if anyone will have him at this point), is someone normal like him.

Regarding normality on a broader scale: the historical impetus for the *Cymbeline* story comes from what seems to be the limpest chronicle in Holinshed, "at best, a confused account of a reign so uneventful that it had defeated the inventive powers of generations of quite imaginative chroniclers."[153] This play, apparently inspired by a history distinctly uninspiring, takes place in the aftermath of the great struggle between Cassibelan and Julius Caesar; in the aftermath of Sicilius Leonatus and the rest of Posthumus' family's noble careers; it also takes place in a post-tragic and post-heroic age, which leaves little for young orphaned men to do with themselves; it is a fairytale-esque time, but one where magic has deserted the kingdom.

Illo tempore[154]—Mircea Eliade's term for 'those days', the mythical time-before-time—is a critically important archetypal idea for Shakespeare, and many plays deal in one way or another with the world 'after the fall', or the reality of life after legend. *Cymbeline,* perhaps more than any other of his plays, navigates the transition from *illo tempore* into this real, profane time. Posthumus, therefore, is terribly mundane, but so is Iachimo, as are Cymbeline, Cloten, Belarius and even, ultimately, Innogen. The witch Queen has no magic about her, involved in her black mass of poison experiments on cats and dogs (1.5.38). The boys Arviragus and Guiderius have some seeming-magical sparks, and grew up in a land of fairies (3.6.41; 4.2.216) and turbaned giants (3.3.5–6), but it is after all they who represent a connection with the kingdom's lost magic, its survival in strictly limited form. Many characters experience archetypal inflations, but these come to nothing. All through the play, the extraordinary gives way to the regular. Experience disproves report. Characters fail to be symbols, instead they are merely symboline. This is best expressed by, fittingly, Cloten, in the initial negotiations with Lucius, commenting on the pale comparison Augustus Caesar makes with his predecessor: "There be many Caesars / Ere such another Julius" (3.1.11–2); "as I said, there is no more such Caesars" (3.1.35–6); and more colourfully,

CLOTEN: Why should we pay tribute? If Caesar can hide the sun from us with a blanket, or put the moon in his pocket, we will pay him tribute for light; else, sir, no more tribute, pray you now.

(3.1.42–5)

The age when gods and god-men such as Julius Caesar walked the earth is, in *Cymbeline,* over—they absconded along with the value system, and those human beings left behind have to live in their absence. For Cloten, Julius Caesar represents *illo tempore*; in *King John* it was the reign of Richard Lionheart, and in *Twelfth Night* it seems to be the carnival which refuses to end; for Shakespeare my impression is that the time of Henry V constituted 'those days', though perhaps by the

Jacobean years in which *Cymbeline* was written, even the days of Queen Elizabeth felt like a mythical past.

Even the patriotic defence of Britain against Rome gives way, in the end, to a measured resumption of the old norm:

CYMBELINE: My peace we will begin. And Caius Lucius,
Although the victor, we submit to Caesar,
And to the Roman empire, promising
To pay our wonted tribute, from the which
We were dissuaded by our wicked Queen[.]

(5.5.458–62)

Cymbeline is, in many ways, a drama which charts the disappointment, disillusionment, and humble coming-to-terms that is part and parcel with growing older; Cymbeline recognizes that unending hostility with Rome simply isn't worth it, his first individuated value-judgment in the play (and therefore relationship with his anima Fi). At the end of the nigh-unbelievable explosion of plot that has taken place, we are left with idealism's transformation into sense and sensibility.

King Cymbeline's description of the "crooked" smokes (5.5.476) which his sacrifices will raise is, I suppose, best amplified by *Henry V*, which is begun by the Chorus telling us that the company of players is going to do their best, but our best simply isn't going to be good enough, and so please would the audience forgive us in advance?

CHORUS: But pardon, gentles all,
The flat unraised spirits that hath dared
On this unworthy scaffold to bring forth
So great an object . . .
O pardon, since *a crooked figure* may
Attest in little place a million,
And let us, ciphers to this great account,
On your imaginary forces work.

(*HV*, PRO.8–18)

"Crooked smokes" seems to be an acknowledgment of the naked frailties of all those who make said sacrificial smokes, kings though they may be. In *Henry V* we hear the player's entreaty for forbearance from his *de facto* god, the audience, and I suppose a little touch of this survives all the way to King Cymbeline, at the conclusion of his play, amazed with matter, expressing his pious wonder at the way things *are*. Things appear to be coming into harmony in Britain—but after all, we are merely crooked figures making crooked smokes, and would the gods please bear with our human weakness, and understand that we're all just doing our human best?

Till the Tree Die

I think that an accepting attitude toward the very-imperfect-but-normal ways of the profane world may be best illustrated in one of the most typically controversial moments of the play: Innogen's return to Posthumus at the end. This is, admittedly, a difficult moment, and it does not explain itself—it shuts us out from its interiority. I think that, with careful attention, however, it does yield itself to an interpretation that does not betray either the text or our credulity.

Some, considering the moment to be Shakespeare's half-hearted method of patching up the play's ending, find the reunion nigh-unforgiveable. Shaw, with characteristic dryness, writes that "Imogen is so dutiful that she accepts her husband's attempt to have her murdered with affectionate docility."[155] For Adelman, "Posthumus's gain requires Imogen's loss".[156] Adelman is half-correct, for in a relationship as initially imbalanced as Innogen and Posthumus', a move in the direction of equal status does seem to be indicated, if the relationship is going to have any chance. This 'loss' of Innogen's, however, is one she desires. As far as her rank goes, her position as sole heir is entirely unnatural, due only to the kidnapping of her older brothers, as well as unstable, judging by the fact that it is Innogen herself who initiates the chaos that begins the play. Adelman leaves out, I think, that in Shakespeare it is typically only maniacs who *want* the crown,[157] and Innogen very sanely does not. In *Cymbeline* especially, the overall arc of redemption is achieved through willing submission to a lower place, most obviously in Cymbeline's acquiescence to Rome—Innogen is not a woman singled out by this.[158]

Criticism that tends in this direction seems to want an Innogen that serves as a didactic prop, the Liberated Heroine; a symbol of 'a strong female character'—*something* at least to tell the audience what they are supposed to think about Posthumus at the end. In effect such critics commit the same folly as Posthumus does—demanding Innogen live up to their projections. Gratification of this would render her basically unchanged from the beginning of the play. Geraldine James found her "wiser and steadier, less reckless and volatile",[159] from her funeral onward. This is an incredibly valuable transformation, and it is our loss if we let idealization of her earlier self seduce us into refusing to let her change.

Some have seen Shakespeare's treatment of Innogen as sadistic. She is "robbed of her own powerful selfhood, put entirely under male command",[160] subject to "cruel and pointless . . . mean tricks that Shakespeare deliberately seems to be perpetrating on his heroine",[161] or dealt "death-blows" through which only a "simulacrum" survives.[162] I just think this misses the point, comes from an egoic view of suffering and power, and underestimates a person's resiliency. The point is not that Innogen suffers but that she survives—"Thou divine Innogen, what thou endur'st" (2.1.56)—there is something indestructible in her, and she has made it through the underworld experience, as Juliet (for example) did not. We also must not think that Jupiter's theology applies only to Posthumus.

Consider her willingness to dive into disguise as a Franklin's housewife, to "change command into obedience" (3.4.154–5) as Fidele, her apparent satisfaction while playing cave-keeper to the three Welsh wild men, saucing broths and cutting roots—do not these suggest an unlived side to her royal personality? Despite being politically unpopular in the 21st century, it may be that *her* desire is more as wife and mother than as ruler and adventurer. Has she not discovered that "a man's life is a tedious one" (3.6.1)? If we take Innogen as a symbol of general womanhood and a predestined return to the hearth, we are of course furious, but if we take Innogen as one woman on her own path of individuation, the ideological quarrel fades into irrelevance.

The reunion between her and Posthumus *is*, however, deeply ambivalent and perhaps uncomfortably ordinary. He has *really* hurt her, and he has really hurt himself too. Their relationship has been traumatized. And yet she returns to him. I'd like to make a closer examination of these lines, to see what can be found:

INNOGEN: Why did you throw your wedded lady from you?
[She embraces him.]
Think that you are upon a rock, and now
Throw me again.
POSTHUMUS: Hang there like fruit, my soul,
Till the tree die.

(5.5.260–3)

These were the lines held open by Tennyson in the final moments of his life; he had asked for a copy of *Cymbeline* on his deathbed.[163] There seems to be something exquisite here that a cynical transactional criticism misses. What is the context? The lines themselves come after some delay: Innogen has approached Posthumus while he laments her supposed death and proclaims his guilt—

POSTHUMUS: Spit and throw stones, cast mire upon me, set
The dogs o'th' street to bay me. Every villain
Be called Posthumus Leonatus, and
Be villainy less than 'twas. O Innogen!
My queen, my life, my wife. O Innogen,
Innogen, Innogen.

(5.5.222–7)

—He is a bit histrionic here, but as his feeling of guilt is probably the first germ of an actual experience of self for him, maybe we can forgive him for overdoing it. When approached by Innogen, he mistakes her for a Roman page—which, technically, she *is*—and strikes her to the ground. 'Do not embrace me' indeed. Then follow another 30 lines during which Innogen, Pisanio, and Cornelius work out the details of her poisoning, and Posthumus is silent. I think the fact that he does not take priority in this sequence, coming after his servant, the deserving and true-hearted Pisanio, and even being delayed until after the joke—Cornelius' very funny "O gods! I left out one thing" (5.5.242)—is of dramatic significance. He must stand there, somewhat in shock, but more importantly like a bump on a log, being collectively ignored after striking his wife in front of everybody and showing himself once and for all to be an idiot.

She then initiates the moment with him—"Why did you throw your wedded lady from you?" (5.5.260)—a line that communicates her heartbreak and disillusionment with him, with an overtone of recrimination. The phrase "your wedded lady" distances her; it dissociates the "wedded lady" from the speaker, and therefore seems to come from outside of her, perhaps from the status of the princess calling the man to account.[164]

Perhaps she just cannot bring herself to say 'me' yet. The phrase itself has to do specifically with his broken wedding vow, more than with the individual lady: a "wedded lady" is not something to be thrown from you.[165] This question comes after Innogen has heard Posthumus' story, and Iachimo's, about how it all came to pass; *she still asks why*, and her point would seem to be that, *despite* Posthumus being misled as to her faithfulness, and *despite* his being murderously angry with her, she is still *his wedded lady* to whom he had made a vow in Jupiter's temple (5.4.76).[166]

"Your wedded lady": does such a vow not mean anything anymore? Do souls not guide vows, are vows not sanctimonious? (*TC* 5.3.145–8) This brings the religious attitude home again, in the form of reverence with respect to their sacred bond. The implication is that, during a wedding, *something happens* that is not to be insolently thrown away.[167] I think *Cymbeline* (and our postmodern egalitarian aspiration) often tempts us to dismiss the class difference between Innogen and Posthumus as superficial trumpery, but here, more than anywhere else, do we really feel that gap. He has acted utterly without class.

He does not answer, yet she embraces him. What is communicated without words there? It is *something*—the two have known each other since infancy, and I do not think it is overgenerous to interpret an unspoken understanding passing between them which is expressed in their embrace. It need not be complicated: I think Posthumus' deep sense of shame does enough. It seems to me that the power differential is much more complex at this moment than Adelman and Shaw allow; rather than submitting to him, she very well may *pity* him in this moment. And her fire has, contrary to Shaw's reading, *not* deserted her, for she then *dares* him: "Think that you are upon a rock, and now / Throw me again" (5.5.261–2). Mischievous with a touch of poignancy, this line is one of the only opportunities we have in the play for a sense of what their normal relational dynamic might look like.

Of the 31 words in this exchange, 28 are monosyllabic. John Barton's advice on such lines was that

> Shakespeare loves to use monosyllables for particularly charged or heightened moments. They need air, they need to go more slowly than other lines, and they tend to do so naturally . . . Monosyllabic lines and words are packed with thoughts and feelings.[168]

In Posthumus' response, "Hang there like fruit, my soul, / Till the tree die" (5.5.262–3) I feel a heavy penitence; shame for the crime he committed not only against Innogen but also against his own soul. Perhaps there is also a disbelieving gratitude that he has been afforded a second chance. "Till the tree die" seems to promise to never wry again. The imagery is not poetically clean—she is like a fruit, but she *is* his soul, and he is a tree—it has the slightly inarticulate nature of something expressed directly from the heart, through difficult-to-contain emotion. This might be the first line of his in the play where we can actually feel something valuable emanating from him, that we can actually feel someone is there. Not to dismiss his entire fifth-act redemption arc, but this line has a unique significance: he has his soul back.[169]

Overall, there seems to be love here, with no requirement that Innogen debase herself. She is dignified, with a very human vulnerability. We can imagine that there are some major issues to be overcome between them, but at the moment the objective feeling tends toward forgiveness rather than to evening the score—in this way, the play may subtly dispense with the previously dominant logic of price. Posthumus tried earlier to barter with the gods: "For Innogen's dear life, take mine, and though / 'Tis not so dear, yet 'tis a life; you coined it" (5.4.22–3). The answer given here is not zero-sum. Posthumus was not allowed the 'easy way out' of paying his life for Innogen's; he has now to atone; he *gets* to atone.

And then Cymbeline finishes the verse-line Posthumus began:

POSTHUMUS: Hang there like fruit, my soul,
Till the tree die.
CYMBELINE: How now, my flesh, my child?
                              (5.5.262–3)

Their moment is situated in a much bigger picture which Cymbeline, the surprisingly virtuoso conductor, continues encouraging towards its finale. The lovers have little opportunity to linger; the ending moves on apace. This is not dramatically intuitive, especially in an age used to 'Hollywood' storytelling, but the practical future of their damaged relationship is not the concern of *Cymbeline*'s ending as such, any more than the ending is concerned with punishment for Belarius' 20 year-old crime. Whatever scene Innogen and Posthumus need to have together is not foreclosed on but seemingly remains between them *in potentia*—and it cannot happen with nine other people (minimum) standing about onstage. I think these two have learned quite shockingly what 'love' can really mean outside of the nice containment of the childhood palace. Posthumus in particular has had a terrible reality check with his own capacity for evil. But despite our immense interest in them, there are bigger things moving in Britain which need our attention, and the play—quite *maturely*—situates the lovers not front and centre but as part of the overall context. This moment is, in a way, a belated confirmation of Cloten's remarks about music; the ending may not do what we think we want it to do, but maybe the fault is in our ears; the areas where it dodges our expectations are hints of where to look for its inner coherence and integrity.

Jupiter, the Ghosts, and Redemption by the Past

The final scene has such gravity that the discussion keeps drawing to it, despite not yet having addressed its leadup. To step back by one scene to 5.4, before the ending comes the literal *deus ex machina*. This is a complicated scene, which Wilson Knight attempted a valiant aesthetic defence of,[170] and which Bloom regarded as deliberately awful.[171] I think the Vision is a great joke—not a funny one, mind you, but a great one, and a symbolically necessary one. Shakespeare is having it both ways: he forces absurdity, but through this very nearly attains sublimity.

Posthumus, in prison after being unable to find his own death in battle (like a reverse-Macbeth), is visited in his sleep by the ghosts of his ancestors, staging an intervention on his behalf, protesting that Jupiter's treatment of his life has been unfair. They speak in rhyming 'fourteeners', a verse form generally un-Shakespearean but popular during his earlier career in the 1590s[172]—so, like the Leonati, about 20 years out of date. The lines feel antiquated, even clumsy.[173] But the most salient point is that the verse cannot fail to be recognized by anyone who has read Ovid's *Metamorphoses,* in the translation that Shakespeare had grown up with. The Golding *Metamorphoses* was surely one of Shakespeare's favourite books,[174] and to evoke them is again to 'consider the beginning'. For him, to use fourteeners is to return to *illo tempore,* those ancient days in which all the great transformations took place—when Actaeon became a stag, Narcissus a flower and Echo a voice, Icarus a cautionary tale, when Pyramus and Thisbe lost their lives and Adonis spurned Venus, when Jupiter ran amok through the woods and bedrooms of the ancient world—but also Shakespeare's own younger days, immersed in this book and its verse, perhaps a time when great transformation came more readily. To solve the unsolvable problems that this play has engendered, he reaches back to the simplicity of myth and antiquity; *il recule pour mieux sauter*—he steps back to better leap forward. To evoke *Metamorphoses*, the Roman Book of Changes, is to subtly prepare his audience for the transformative turning point. We have seen Arthur in prison, and we have seen Malvolio in prison, but Posthumus' time in prison is to have a decidedly different transformative outcome.

Dramatically, it sets these spirits apart from the world of the play, coming as they do from a realm beyond, and speaking as they do to a realm beyond beyond—Craig writes that perhaps "gods and those who speak to gods, especially if they themselves are spirits, must speak differently from creatures of this world".[175]

SICILIUS: No more, thou thunder-master, show thy spite on mortal flies.
With Mars fall out, with Juno chide, that thy adulteries
Rates and revenges.

(5.4.30–2)

In other words, 'pick on someone your own size, you bully'. "No more" is quite a bold way to open a plea to a powerful deity.

The verse is especially interesting in comparison with the rest of the play, in which the standard blank verse, or iambic pentameter, is thoroughly unregular. This is a hallmark of Shakespeare's later work,[176] and in *Cymbeline* it is part of the overall disintegrative tone; even the verse is losing its mind and stretching itself to find new form. As the verse structure implicitly guides both the reader in reading and the actor in acting, this has a significant though usually unconscious effect. And then the fourteeners arrive, and they are (with two exceptions, 5.4.32;47) as regular and rhythmic as anything.

$$\cup \quad / \quad \cup \quad / \quad \cup \quad / \quad \cup \quad / \quad \cup \quad / \quad \cup \quad / \quad \cup \quad /$$
1 BROTHER: Like hardiment Posthumus hath to Cymbeline performed.
$$\cup \quad / \cup / \quad \cup \quad / \quad \cup \quad / \quad \cup \quad / \quad \cup \quad /$$
Then Jupiter, thou king of gods, why hast thou thus adjourned
$$\cup \quad / \quad \cup \quad / \cup / \cup \quad / \quad \cup \quad / \cup \quad / \quad \cup \quad /$$
The graces for his merits due, being all to dolours turned?

(5.4.54-6)

The change in verse being as striking as it is, this very difficult-to-stage sequence might benefit from leaning rather unsubtly into its rhythm. This gives it the otherworldly, ritualistic tone that it asks for; it is an invocation of a god and it seems appropriate for it to have a conscious semi-musical thrum beneath it.

Another rhythmic anomaly earlier in the play anticipates this, and if observed can prepare the way for a more integrated Vision. That would be the song which earlier Guiderius and Arviragus sang—or, more to the point, did *not* sing—to the seeming-dead Fidele. There is a most curious moment in this part of the play, in which Arviragus has suggested they sing, and Guiderius responds:

GUIDERIUS: Cadwal,
I cannot sing. I'll weep, and word it with thee,
For notes of sorrow out of tune are worse
Than priests and fanes that lie.
ARVIRAGUS:
                We'll speak it then.

(4.2.238–41).

Like *Twelfth Night*'s "do not embrace me" (*TN* .1.247), this is one of those things which productions may simply ignore or cut, finding the temptation to include a musical number too great. But to do what the text says, and let it be treated as a spoken-song, which is to say remaining in rhythm without any melody, gives it a tremendous sombreness. It feels like the recitation of a funeral prayer.[177] This is what was found in Hall's staging of this moment, which discovered that "emotions are expressed through the linear structure and the rhythmic formality."[178] I include here only one stanza, though in my estimation its sheer length helps impart the effect of a Catholic Mass or Buddhist chant.

```
  /  U  /  U  /  U   /
Fear no more the heat o'th' sun,
  /  U  /  U  / U   / U
Nor the furious winter's rages,
  /  U  /  U  /  U   /
Thou thy worldly task hast done,
  /  U  /  U  /  U  /U
Home art gone and ta'en thy wages.
  /  U  /  U  /  U  /
Golden lads and girls all must,
  U  /  U  /  U   /  U  /
As chimney-sweepers, come to dust.
```

(4.2.259–65)

The repeated "and come to dust" is especially chantlike, a quality that may be lost if the text is sung.

If the earlier song is presented in this way, then the ghosts' rhythm and appearance feels more to be within the circle of what the play has already established as convention. The ghosts' appearance, and Jupiter's epiphany, can be a *coup de théâtre* without the unhappy sense that a different show has accidentally walked onstage.[179]

Typologically, this would seem to be the moment where the inferior function (Posthumus as introverted thinking) really comes into its own as "the door through which all the figures of the unconscious come into consciousness."[180] The appeal that these particular figures of the unconscious make, however, leaves something wanting, in their portrayal of Posthumus as an innocent victim of Cymbeline, of Iachimo, and indeed, of Jupiter. Posthumus himself has recognized his culpability, and perhaps here he has surpassed his own family, who from beyond the grave seem to have a narrow view of things—

SICILIUS: Why did you suffer Iachimo, slight thing of Italy,
To taint his nobler heart and brain with needless jealousy,
And to become the geck and scorn o'th' other's villainy?

(5.4.48–50)

—conveniently leaving out Posthumus' active participation in his own tainting. Never mind—the dead may be as imperfect as the living,[181] and their concern is Posthumus' unfair treatment and hard life. They make a case for this, portraying him, Job-like, suffering at the whims of a sadistic god.[182] And—marvel upon marvel—Jupiter now descends from the sky, also reminiscent of the Book of Job, although he rides an eagle rather than speaking from the whirlwind. Sicilius' "no more" (5.4.30) is served back to him:

JUPITER: No more, you petty spirits of region low,
Offend our hearing. Hush! How dare you ghosts
Accuse the thunderer, whose bolt, you know,
Sky-planted, batters all rebelling coasts.

(5.4.63–6)

Compare with Yahweh's speech in Job:

Who is this that darkeneth counsel by words without knowledge?[183]
Canst thou send the lightnings that they may walk, and say unto thee, Lo, here we are?[184]

If there is a meaning to the Job connection in this parody of a theophany, perhaps it is to ironically underscore Posthumus' definite blameworthiness in contrast with Job's blamelessness, emphasizing Posthumus' ultimate human, all-too-human-ness. When Jupiter cites his divine prerogative: "Whom best I love, I cross, to make my gift, / The more delayed, delighted" (5.4.71–2), it also recalls the Book of Job, in which Yahweh's wager with Satan is over the incorruptibility of a similarly beloved creation:

Hast thou not considered my servant Job, how none is like him in the earth? An upright and just man, one that feareth God, and escheweth evil?[185]

So boasts Yahweh, prompting Satan's challenge. This in turn recalls our story's own wager, which, in retrospect, is precisely the kind of wager two divine beings would make as to the quality of an apparently peerless mortal, illustrating just how inflated Posthumus and Iachimo were at the time.

In some ways, the Jovian revelation of this scene ("whom best I love, I cross", 5.4.71) seems theologically thin—"it does not fill a couplet—as if the rather trite notion it offers cannot quite sustain the whole of two lines" says Lyne[186]—yet we can find similar metaphysical conclusions in a study of the *I Ching*: some of Wilhelm's extended commentary on the first line of 48: 井, *Jǐng*, The Well, reads that

The person whom God intends to be great and whom he entrusts with a mission is first thoroughly tormented. God opposes him and obstructs his plans. God tires out his body and persecutes him with sickness and with pain. And because of this a man's spirit becomes pliable and his nerves strong.[187]

He adds that our task is "not to permit the effort to vex us. No matter how often we are disappointed, we must try to start again."

Earlier we saw hints of the *daimonic* potential in King Cymbeline's demonic Te; here Jupiter effects the same metamorphosis, but of the *play's* dominant Te, as he lays out his infallible divine plan:

JUPITER: Your low-laid son our godhead will uplift;
His comforts thrive, his trials well are spent . . .
He shall be lord of Lady Innogen,
And happier much by his affliction made.
      [He gives a tablet to the ghosts.]
This tablet lay upon his breast, wherein
Our pleasure his full fortune doth confine.

(5.4.73–80)

And now the stage is set for things to be made right again in Britain. Te has been rehabilitated in the play, by repatriating it to the patriarch *par excellence*: a function which was originally arrogated to the ego of one inflated king is now seen to be the rightful property of the king of the gods.

Overall, what is the meaning and purpose of the Vision? Bloom more-or-less rejects an aesthetic defence of it: "something buffoonish breaks loose in Shakespeare", he writes. "There is no way that Shakespeare, keenest of ears, does not apprehend the absurdity of this . . . we are expected to sustain it as travesty."[188] It is a parody of a theophany; it is a parody of Job; it is a parody of itself. One wonders, as it progresses, whether Shakespeare himself could even believe it was happening.

Jupiter's plan, if it does not *redeem* all the mad events of the play by contextualizing them, at least offers a justification for them. It also seems to mark a transformation of the Shakespearean god-image.[189] Though we cannot naïvely take the statements of individual characters to represent Shakespeare's (or an individual play's) relationship with the divine, Gloucester in *King Lear* does seem to find words for that play's view of divinity: "As flies to wanton boys are we to the gods, / They kill us for their sport" (*KL* 4.1.38–9). This is not so far from how Jupiter actually appears in much of the *Metamorphoses*: he is wildly, divinely amoral. How different, then, is *Cymbeline*, where Sicilius' ghost intervenes on behalf of these "mortal flies" (5.4.30), and in which we even get a reply from the top god himself, telling us that misfortune is a mark not of his indifference but of his *love*. I find it rather provocative to 'think' this backwards in the Shakespearean canon, and imagine that this refers to all of Shakespeare's greatest sufferers. Bradley felt that the thing that linked such characters as Othello, Hamlet, Macbeth, and Lear was something like intensity of personality[190]—maybe *that* is what Jupiter loves, and the 'reason' for their suffering? It is not a totally clean way of thinking about it—yet perhaps we can sense here an implicit affinity with Jung's concept of individuation as the flower of human life: the realized individual, we learn in this late play, tested and developed through hardship, is what God loves.

It still leaves us with the problem of defining what there could possibly be for Jupiter to find so lovable about *Posthumus*, but there I think we have to throw up our hands and say that God has mysterious ways, and Jupiter mysterious preferences—as *Metamorphoses* continually demonstrates. We never really see the Posthumus that many of the other characters seem to admire and love.

After the Vision, something has changed in him; even as he is still intent on dying, certain that he is bound for hell, he is in a bizarrely convivial mood, riffing away with his jailer—

JAILER: Come, sir, are you ready for death?
POSTHUMUS: Over-roasted rather; ready long ago.
JAILER: Hanging is the word, sir. If you be ready for that, you are well cooked.
POSTHUMUS: So if I prove a good repast to the spectators, the dish pays the shot.
(5.4.122–7)

He says "I am merrier to die than thou art to live" (5.4.142), and then seems to be just as merry to live as to die when he is given reprieve. Bloom found him unrecognizable in this scene,[191] but I think Posthumus rather has the feeling of sudden lightness that accompanies someone for whom a long-held complex has finally dissolved.

The ultimate dramaturgical meaning of the Vision may be as a recognition that there are some situations from which man cannot untangle himself; it brings forth the mystery of what it means for Posthumus to be redeemed by the past—why is a confrontation with his ancestors *necessary*? I do not mean 'necessary' merely in terms of his own personal journey. Recall the hexagram *Sòng*, Conflict: in times of conflict, the sage "carefully considers the beginning."[192] Skura interpreted that,

The child can leave his family behind, but he cannot escape its influence, and in some sense he cannot know who he is until he knows where he has come from—until he knows his roots . . . there is no way for him to find himself as husband until he finds himself as son, as part of the family he was torn from long ago.[193]

Posthumus' full name is, after all, Posthumus Leonatus: Just as his first name points to the *loss* of the past in the present (*Post-Humus*: Post-Burial), his surname points to the past's *ongoing* presence through his origin (*Leo-Natus*: Lion-Born).

The redemptive power of the beginning has been hinted at earlier in the play, obliquely, by the Queen's heavy-handed patriotism, and her exhortations to Cymbeline to "Remember sir, my liege, / The kings your ancestors" (3.1.16–7). Yet these are but petty forms of what I think the play is saying on a larger scale.

Cymbeline's redemption requires the death of his Queen and son-in-law. However, by the point at which they perish, he has already changed from his first appearance. Throughout the play, he does gradually find it in himself to "put those powers in motion / That long to move" (4.3.31–2), and this ultimately seems to spring from the humility of his relationship to his past, beginning with the respect he feels for Lucius, and for Rome, the land of his youth, and ending in the eventual *rapprochement* between the two powers. When Cymbeline says,

CYMBELINE: Although the victor, we submit to Caesar,
And to the Roman empire, promising
To pay our wonted tribute[.]

(5.5.459–61)

I imagine that, in the word "tribute"—a word which has been a tremendous subject of contention throughout the play, in its sense of 'a payment demanded'—he recognizes the other meaning, an expression of gratitude and respect, and in his utterance recognizes that his leadership skill, and indeed his nation, *do* owe tribute to Rome.[194] Like a maturing young adult, Britain comes to appreciate the parenting it *had* rather than remaining fixated on its parent's shortcomings.[195] Our parents wound us; our wounds also parent us.

So too does redemption come from the past in the form of the exiled Belarius, who returns the children who emerged from the Welsh cave—the origin of them, Britain, and humanity. Even the technically superfluous plot device of Guiderius' identifying mole contains a nod to the logic of the returning past redeeming the present: "It was wise nature's end in the donation / To be his evidence now" (5.5.366–7).

Redemption by the past in this play relates not mainly to cynically political (or even genuinely patriotic) appeals to *reinstate* the past, nor even to *doing right* by the past, though these are all aspects of the whole. Part of *Cymbeline*'s method is a ruthless attack on the past, in the form of audience expectation and theatrical convention, part of an alchemical *calcinatio* that burns away everything false to try to arrive at what remains. And thanks to this ruthless irreverence, in the end *Cymbeline* is able to speak, explicitly as well as in its deep subtext, of a humble, even awed relation with the past, without being beholden to it; this understanding of the past includes and transcends the chain of events that has led to the present; it cherishes relationship with the successes, failings, and sacrifices made in the past that bring us where we are today; it achieves the sense of embeddedness in a meaningful fabric, the fabric of Time, stretching back and up to us and forward past us; it imparts a real living knowledge that, for better or worse, we stand on the shoulders of giants just as Cymbeline was knighted by Julius Caesar.

The individuation process, Jung's concept for the central goal of psychological life, involves confrontation of one's

. . . instinctive foundations, given him from the beginning, which he cannot make disappear, however much he would like to. His beginnings are not by any means mere pasts; they live with him as the constant substratum of his existence, and this consciousness is as much molded by them as by the physical world around him.[196]

The recognition of one's historical continuity is one thing that can allow the will-to-power to subside, for this can allow the inflated and narcissistic ideals of personal destiny to relativize and rest in the great container of context.

Elsewhere, Jung wrote,

> I became aware of the fateful link between me and my ancestors. I feel very strongly that I am under the influence of things or questions which were left incomplete and unanswered by my parents and grandparents and more distant ancestors . . . It has always seemed to me that I had to answer questions which fate had posed to my forefathers, and which had not yet been answered, or as if I had to complete, or perhaps continue, things which previous ages had left unfinished.[197]

This is what 'coming home' does—it grounds. And to the extent that *Cymbeline* comes home to British origin and British history, it situates its English audience in the fabric of history, perhaps just at a time when they were in need of it, after the plague and in the early post-Elizabethan years; the first of James' reign, and the beginning of the "century of revolution".[198]

Time, Body, Power, and Value

Cymbeline is far more than British. It illustrates a kingdom in conflict, and it reaches back years, generations, and eras, to Time immemorial, to develop a response to conflict that can endure. Its integration of the past into the present culminates in a conclusion that is triumphantly humble—a paradox which is, however, only one of its many paradoxes.

Its expansive View reminds us that our Bodies are subject to Time; that our Power games are infantile rebellions against Time; that Value can only exist in the presence of Time, and can only be recognized through the surrendering of Power.

Written in post-Elizabethan, post-plague, post 16th-century England, it neverthe-less resonates anew in present Times, themselves disturbingly post—: Post-millennial, post-9/11, post-COVID, post-truth, post-modern, and post-apocalyptic; it reminds us that all our lives are post-something, and that the world of our previous century is as gone as 'Merry Olde England' was for Shakespeare.

Cymbeline, however, looks backward not to get mired in cause, but in order to look forward.

Shakespeare's abstract and sometimes dissociative sense of irony in this play reflects our own post-modern aesthetic, characterized by "surface and self-reflection without content".[199] He succeeds (as we too must, if we are to re-locate Value) in taking the irony to its own growing edge and allowing it to develop past itself. Irony is too intellectual a pleasure to sustain long onstage, and too cold a comfort to sustain society or life. Ethically, irony demands to be transcended, and *Cymbeline* tracks the conflict-ridden transformation of idealism into irony and then past it, at last, into modesty.

Cymbeline's title character is largely inert, "a vacuity that others fill".[200] And yet who but he could conduct the symphony of *anagnorisis* (recognition) that is Act 5, Scene 5? The conductor, like the theatre director and the psychoanalyst, benefits from a capacity to stand back and let the music happen, directing where necessary but not interfering. King Cymbeline is a model conductor in this scene, bringing about a series of concentric revelations unparalleled in Shakespeare. He then identifies the objective feeling in the psychological field and sacrifices his previous stance of Power to affirm it: "Pardon's the word to all" (5.5.421). The conclusion of the play's typological riddle is that once Cymbeline's extraverted thinking has been freed from the demonic archetype by which it was possessed, he can make the stretch to heroic extraverted feeling, forging at last an effective *social attitude*, which is precisely what is needed to run the newly crystallized society.[201]

The archetypal identifications formerly associated with each character have, by play's end, been transcended. We therefore have reason to hope that Cymbeline (Te) and his son Guiderius (Fe) will be able to bring the world back into order without being locked in a battle between the heroic and the demonic. We feel good about the possibility of them leading with justice and integrity thanks to the reintegration of Belarius and the alliance with Lucius and Rome (all carrying Fi, no

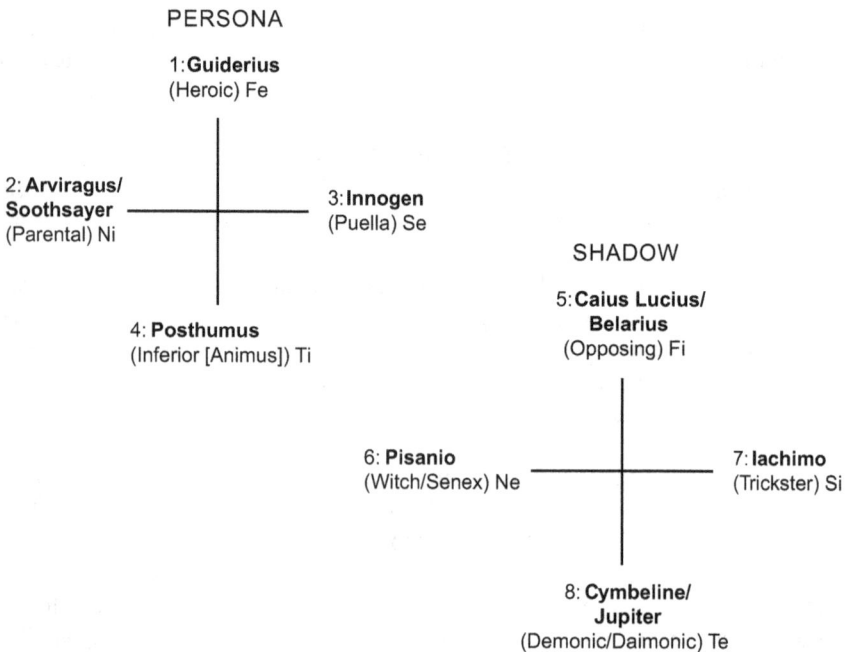

Figure 6.10 The final typological situation of *Cymbeline*.

longer opposing). Innogen (Se), no longer heir to the throne, is freed from the necessity of puella heroicism and can live her life, whatever that may now entail. Posthumus (Ti) is back in the fold, suitably chastened and ready to develop as a man after his brush with psychosis; inspired by Innogen's forgiveness of him,[202] he then expresses an unexpected quality of the 'superior man' in sentencing Iachimo not to die but to atone. Iachimo (Si) has repented his trickster ways and set the record straight; he can now seek his own redemption.[203] Rome has its wise sage in Philharmonus, and Britain has its philosopher-prince-in-the-making with Arviragus (both Ni). There would almost seem to be a hole in the final typological mandala left by the Queen's absence, and this hole would not be unacceptable, yet I suspect that the vacant Ne spot is where we find the as-yet-unidentified Pisanio, whose vision and ability to find a way through a tight spot did tremendous service in saving the life of Innogen.

Most significantly of all, Britain has solved its false double-bind, falling neither for subjugation nor forever-war, and found a transcendent third way to earn her independence from Rome with no need for further strife, and honour Rome without loss of dignity. Cymbeline himself may well be "the least distinguished and colourful of Shakespeare's titular heroes,"[204] but as with so much in this play, what seems accidental or haphazard is not. For Cymbeline, at the end of *Cymbeline,* is exactly the king Britain needs.

Notes

1 Chen (2015, 64–8).
2 Chambers (1925, 221).
3 Nosworthy (1955, li).
4 Stein (1970, 221).
5 Solzhenitsyn (1985, 27–8), as told to Solzhenitsyn by N. G—ko.
6 Kirsch (1967, 297): "Beginning with a traditional story and traditional moral attitudes, he works from within to expose and destroy their rationale." Swander (1964, 269) offers a concrete example of how this is done with regard to Posthumus and the "blameless hero" trope. Duncan-Jones (2010) also suggests several instances of competition and one-upping that may have occurred between Shakespeare and his contemporaries.
7 Hughes (1992, 335): "The familiar features hurry past, as he squeezes this rehabilitated plot into two and a half acts, with a geometry of motivation so stark it seems perfunctory."
8 See Granville-Barker (1971).
9 Gibbons (1993, 14).
10 Wayne (2017, 28).
11 Wayne (2017, 30).
12 Bloom (1999, xvii).
13 See Lander (2008).
14 Wilhelm (1984, 29).
15 Emphasis added, obviously.
16 Wilson Knight (1948, 146) felt that some of Shakespeare's recurring dynamics achieved purest expression in *Cymbeline*.
17 For the burial practice, Wayne (2017, 301fn), for the blood, Kerrigan (2013, xxxv-xxxvi).

18 Spurgeon (1935, 296).
19 Jung (CW2, 100). See also Kast (1980); O'Brien & O'Brien (2024).
20 As in the Grimms' tale "The Water of Life".
21 Swinburne (1880).
22 Adelman (1992, 211).
23 Wayne (2017, 82–3); Adelman (1992, 351); Barton (2007a).
24 See Barton (2007a, 20).
25 An interpretation with which Harriet Walter also agrees (1993, 203): "we know the marriage was consummated, but that she sometimes had a headache." Anne Barton (2007a, 24), on the other hand, sees an explicit biological reference to Innogen's continued virginity at 2.5.16–19; Wayne disagrees with this (2017, 82–3).
26 It could be that the submerged implication is that they have 'bundled'—"the custom which allowed contracted couples in the period to spend the night together . . . and to engage in a good deal of sexual play so long as actual intercourse did not occur" (Barton 2007a, 28). This is in part an interesting interpretation because it allows everybody to be right.
27 Wayne (2017, 83).
28 Barton (2007a, 3) observes these and other "blurred and contradictory" sexual signals.
29 Re-casting Iachimo as another Actaeon.
30 Spears (2001).
31 Walter (1993, 206).
32 See Skura (1993, 20–1).
33 Sanders (2000, 58–62) expands the sense that Iachimo's invasion and notation *is* a kind of rape.
34 Haas & Hunziker (2006, 33).
35 Hill (1984, 64).
36 Haas & Hunziker (2006, 34).
37 Walter (1993, 204).
38 Though, weirdly, so does Cloten (3.5.108).
39 Cai (2021, 1062).
40 Wilhelm (1984, 121). Earlier in this book the same line was related to King John.
41 Schwartz (2009, 112). See also Schwartz (2024).
42 Irving Wardle, *The Times* (London), 14 November 1987. In Bate (2011, 180).
43 This would be consonant with the contemporary view that anima and animus archetypes—the archetype of life, and the archetype of meaning, respectively—also come together, as a syzygy (Kast 2006).
44 Sanders (2000, 64).
45 On the other hand, Judi Dench apparently played this scene with "icy civility" (Warren 1989, 39), so perhaps the text does allow for more shrewdness on Innogen's part.
46 Warren (1989, 38).
47 "Spine of consciousness" is Beebe's phrase (2017, 27).
48 Lerer (2018, 147).
49 Leonard Cohen (1992), "Anthem".
50 Wilson Knight (1948, 180).
51 Von Franz (2020, 22): "the superior function, like an eagle seizing a mouse, tries to get hold of the inferior function and bring it over into its own realm."
52 Lander (2008).
53 Wayne (2017, 70).
54 Sanders (2000, 66).
55 Wilhelm (1995, 168).
56 Warren (1990, 69).
57 Wayne (2017, 349fn).
58 "An unidentified review" of Macready as Iachimo, at Covent Garden, 1820; cited by Rees (1989, 145); see also Wayne (2017, 114).

59 e.g., Macready as above, or Irving in 1896.
60 Warren (1989, 48).
61 Haas and Hunziker (2006, 54).
62 Murphy (2021, 1080).
63 Warren (1990, 43).
64 Carr (1978, 327).
65 Sean Day-Lewis *Daily Telegraph*, 11 July 1983. Review of the film directed by Elijah Moshinsky (1982).
66 Bate & Rasmussen (2011). For a more in-depth description of this performance, see Warren (1989, 103–6).
67 Ewert (2012, 52).
68 Wilson Knight (1948, 183).
69 Tolkien (1991).
70 Jackson (2002).
71 Beebe (2017, 43; 132).
72 Jung (CW 18, 1473).
73 Haas & Hunziker (2006, 74).
74 Beebe (2017, 5).
75 Cai (2021, 1067).
76 Wilhelm (1984, 199).
77 Given by Socrates; Plato (2008, 202e).
78 Beebe (2017, 107).
79 Jung (CW 6, 639).
80 Beebe (2017, 129); see also Beebe (1992, 106) regarding the relationship between integrity and the inferior function.
81 Warren (1989, 44).
82 Warren (1990, 57).
83 Cai (2021, 1068).
84 Wilhelm (1984, 202).
85 Wilhelm (1984, 202–3).
86 Henderson (1984, 27).
87 Beebe (2017, 102).
88 The four "attitudes" identified by Henderson (1984) are associated by Beebe (2017, 97–113) with similar "stretches" between types. The Ti-Fi stretch is associated with the *philosophic* attitude; the Te-Fe stretch is associated with the *social* attitude; and the Ne-Se stretch is associated with the *aesthetic* attitude.
89 The concept of the second half of life is one developed by Jung, particularly in his essay *The Stages of Life* (CW 8, 749–95).
90 Wilhelm (1984, 201).
91 Henderson (1984, 27). 'Self' with a capital-S is a Jungian term referring to the archetype of wholeness (and therefore the 'whole' personality).
92 In Wayne (2017, 298fn)—citing Warren (1989, 24), but the quote does not actually appear to be in Warren, though the idea itself is present.
93 See the St. Crispin's Day speech in *Henry V* (*HV* 4.3.20–70) for an excellent example of the objective feeling being transformed by the King, with constructive rather than deleterious results.
94 Hers is not a "regressive restoration of the persona" (Jung CW 7, 254–9).
95 In *Frederyke of Jennen*, one of the play's apparent sources, the heroine's murder is feigned by the killing of her pet lamb—a hard-to-miss symbol of the sacrifice of innocence—her clothes then soaked in the lamb's blood and sent to her husband (Nosworthy 1955, xxiii). *Cymbeline* leaves out the lamb but keeps the "bloody cloth" (5.1.1).
96 Wayne (2003, 396); Curran (1997, 288); Redmond (1999, 311).
97 These citations from the Folger edition (Mowat & Werstine 2013).
98 Crichton (2018).

99 Adelman (1992, 216).
100 Doty (2022).
101 *New Cambridge* edition (Butler 2005).
102 Myers (1980, 79).
103 Beebe (2017, 5).
104 Cai (2021, 1066).
105 Wilhelm (1984, 224).
106 Wilhelm (1984, 225).
107 Wilhelm (1984, 224).
108 Wilhelm (1995, 160).
109 Jung (CW 6, 596). Technically, my impression is that it is *Cesario* rather than Viola who carries the Fe of *Twelfth Night*. I would designate Viola's personal type as Ni with auxiliary Fe–it is her parental Fe that is most apparent through Cesario, but *fundamentally* her approach to life seems to be to trust to the unfolding of time, which seems to me to be a characteristic of heroic Ni.
110 Garber (2004, 802); Carr (1978, 320).
111 Ewert (2012, 52).
112 Trousdale & Wise (1991); Rowling (1998).
113 See Warren (1989, 30–1) for a very good description of Clive Revill in the role in 1957.
114 Lerer (2018, 152); Carr (1978, 320).
115 Lindley (2006, 173) notes that it is unclear in the text whether Cloten or the Musician sings the song—but suggests that it is disastrous (for the effect of the scene) to give it to Cloten.
116 Jung (CW 6, 560).
117 Swander (1964, 269).
118 Echoing also the much earlier Chiron from *Titus Andronicus*, 2.2.130: "Drag hence her husband to some secret hole / And make his dead trunk pillow to our lust."
119 Nosworthy (1955, lxxiv–lxxvi).
120 Quiller-Couch's opinion was that Shakespeare "had come to realize that forgiveness is nobler than revenge and, accordingly, sought now to reach something better than tragedy." In Nosworthy (1955, xliii).
121 Bloom (1999, 638).
122 Shapiro (1994, 175): "[tragicomic romance] involved complexity of plot over complexity of character and high-lighted the dramatist's dexterity rather than the play-boy's."
123 Rees (1989, 142).
124 Wilhelm (1984, 226).
125 Carr (1978, 322–3) calls the boys "demigods" with an "aura of superhuman strength and freedom".
126 Donen (1954).
127 Jung (CW 7, 254).
128 Jung (CW 13, 54).
129 Te-Fe is the combination of functions that can create the *social* attitude (Beebe 2017, 102).
130 Rees (1989, 148).
131 Butler (2005, 135fn).
132 Beebe (2017, 150).
133 Given this along with the fact that his handwriting is easily recognizable (by Innogen and Cloten), I wonder if he is meant to be a habitual note-taker like Hamlet (*Ham.* 1.5.107)—who is himself a far superior representative of introverted thinking.
134 Von Franz (2020, 17).
135 Von Franz (2020, 21).
136 Beebe (2017, 26).

137 Von Franz (2020, 21).
138 Von Franz (2020, 72).
139 For Carr (1978, 327), Iachimo "acts as an instrument of Posthumus' will".
140 Philario, an extraverted feeling type, may have auxiliary introverted sensation to be able to take care of Posthumus in this way against Iachimo. In the language of the MBTI, this would make Philario an ESFJ type.
141 Rees (1989, 141).
142 Wilson Knight (1948, 138).
143 Miola (2014, 188). See also Swander (1964, 267): "This soliloquy destroys the whole conventional pattern." See also Carr (321–2).
144 Shaw (1946, 135).
145 It has also been anticipated, though not fulfilled, in *Much Ado About Nothing*, 4.1.224–34.
146 Wilson Knight (1948, 141).
147 Chen (2015, 70).
148 Wilson Knight (1948, 140).
149 Bloom (1999, 632).
150 Bloom (1999, 619).
151 Carr (1978, 328): "[Posthumus'] inadequacy is part of the play's nexus of meaning."
152 Swander (1964, 260).
153 Nosworthy (1955, xviii).
154 Eliade (1958, 395).
155 Shaw (1946, 136).
156 Adelman (1992, 209).
157 This is a sentiment nearly as old as Shakespeare's career, as in one of his first written plays, King Henry VI sadly muses, "Was never subject longed to be a king / As I do long and wish to be a subject" (2HIV 4.9.5–6).
158 Carr (1978, 330): "the play's peaceful conclusion depends on . . . willingness to accept the limits of being human".
159 Warren (1990, 71).
160 Adelman (1992, 211).
161 Carr (1978, 317–26).
162 Granville-Barker (1984, 88).
163 Wayne (2017, 131).
164 Or perhaps from Fidele—in light of the fact that Viola also, at first, speaks in third person, as Cesario, when she is reunited with her other half ("that day when Viola from her birth / Had numbered thirteen years" *TN* 5.1.240). These protean moments of transition from one identity to another can apparently give a temporary perspective from outside the situation. Penuel (2010, 75) finds these moments of third-person self-objectifying.
165 Jordan (1994, 34): "when Posthumus loses faith in and hence is unfaithful to Imogen, he violates the promises he made at his betrothal."
166 The fact that this is a strange location, given Jupiter's habit of adultery, is noted by Barton (2007a, 24–5).
167 Though the validity of the marriage is questioned by Cymbeline and Cloten, and obliquely by Posthumus, the fact that *something happened* is evidently true at least for Innogen and Jupiter. See Barton (2007a).
168 Barton (1984, 247); a practice also communicated by Peter Hall (Warren 1990, 29).
169 Posthumus' tree anticipates the "stately cedar" (5.5.436–7) that stands for Cymbeline in Jupiter's prophecy. The tree in this moment is Posthumus, but the tree is also the King, and therefore Britain, and in the collective unconscious the tree of life as well: "Till the tree die" is a way of saying 'eternally'. Carr (1978, 329) sees the tree as,

instead, the "mortal and transient . . . a tree that will not live forever", and that may be, though I would still insist that in this play, the acceptance of "mortal" is itself an achievement.

170 Wilson Knight (1948, 168–202).
171 Bloom (1999, 633).
172 Nosworthy (1955, xxxvi).
173 Lerer (2018, 172): "such metrical affiliations place them firmly in the past: as if the ghosts of the last generation of actors and playwrights had taken the stage."
174 Bate (2000).
175 Craig (1948, 55).
176 McDonald (2006).
177 Lerer (2018, 167): "the poem's imagery recalls the language of the Elizabethan *Book of Common Prayer*, that moment in the Order for the Burial of the Dead when repetition becomes rite: 'earth to earth, ashes to ashes, dust to dust'."
178 Warren (1990, 63).
179 Wilson Knight (1948, 168) painstakingly substantiated the Vision as a dramaturgically inevitable moment in the play. Some productions (i.e., Stratford Festival in 2024, the RSC in 2016) try to anticipate the Vision by including the ghosts earlier in the play, lurking around the fringes, as though they are 'always watching'. I don't think this works. It is confusing; it also undermines the essential *coup de théâtre* of the Vision, by preparing the audience to expect something supernatural.
180 Von Franz (2020, 72).
181 Jung (1963, 308): "If there were to be a conscious existence after death, it would, so it seems to me, have to continue on the level of consciousness attained by humanity, which in any age has an upper though variable limit."
182 Carr (1978, 323) found Posthumus "an Everyman figure . . . the battlefield on which God and the Devil are fighting."
183 Job 38:2, GNV.
184 Job 38:35, GNV.
185 Job 1:8, GNV.
186 Lyne (2007, 45).
187 Wilhelm (1995, 249).
188 Bloom (1999, 633–4).
189 See Edinger (2015). Jung documented a transformation of the God-image in *Answer to Job* (CW 11, 560–758); perhaps this scene is Shakespeare's own answer to Job.
190 Bradley (1904).
191 Bloom (1999, 635).
192 Wilhelm (1984, 29).
193 Skura (1980, 207–8).
194 See Python (1979).
195 Porterfield (1994, 73–98) explores a related (yet more fraught) development in *Hamlet*, which she calls "the universal disappointment of imperfect parents".
196 Jung (1963, 341).
197 Jung (1963, 233).
198 Hill (1961).
199 Kawai (2006, 437).
200 Wayne (2017, 70).
201 Beebe (2017, 102). For Cymbeline's personal typology, Fe would be his own *daimonic* function.
202 Carr (1978, 328).

203 In one of Shakespeare's apparent sources, Boccaccio's *Decameron,* the Iachimo figure Ambrogiuolo is "tied to a stake, his naked body smeared with honey, and is left to hang until he shall drop to pieces" (Nosworthy 1955, xxi–xxii). I mention this mainly to glance at what Posthumus does *not* do to Iachimo—perhaps because he feels himself to be equally culpable.

204 Hadfield (2004, 164).

Chapter 7

Postlude

Good (Enough) Ground

ARTHUR: The wall is high, and yet I will leap down.
Good ground be pitiful and hurt me not!

(KJ 4.3.1-2)

FESTE: Youth's a stuff t'will not endure.

(TN 2.3.51)

GUIDERIUS: Golden lads and girls all must,
As chimney-sweepers, come to dust.

(Cym. 4.2.261-2)

It is not possible to end this book other than with humility, a word which means being close to the ground. There is no small sadness that comes with leaving behind golden time. Perhaps the writing of this book has been a golden time in my own life.

But the hardest lesson for the airy spirit to learn is that golden time is not the end; life goes on, and while it may glitter less dazzlingly, there are times even richer than gold, and pleasures deeper than flight. But that downward leap of faith cannot be forced; it is born out of inmost necessity. This book is not an instruction manual, but rather more like *Cymbeline*'s funeral spoke-song, an elegy for the puer and puella, the golden lads and girls.

The Tempest's Prospero is often casually paraphrased into having said 'We are such stuff as dreams are made of'. But that's wrong. We are not such stuff as dreams are made *of*—"we are such stuff as dreams are made *on*" (*Tem.* 4.1.156–7[1]).

Just like that. The Jungian point is that we are not myth-ingredients, little abstracts of gods, but people. We do not encounter *archetypes* in our lives. We encounter the *archetypal*. The theory of archetypes only makes any sense through paying scrupulous attention to the archetypal, the *real*. When we insist that we are living *an archetype,* we inflate everything about ourselves, and about reality. Prospero's very subtle point is correct. We are not living the dream. *We are living the stuff.* And what wonderful stuff it can be if we allow it. What amazing matter.

Throughout this book we have followed the development of that human spirit which confuses itself with a dream. The puer and the puella mistake height for their

DOI: 10.4324/9781003596967-8

great achievement. But height comes naturally. The great achievement for them is not height. The great achievement for them is humility.

In *King John* we saw the fate of a world broken by abstraction, a nearly nihilistic tale held together, first, by the preponderating grief of a mother who will lose her son, but who has already lost her ground of being, and second, by the most unlikely person imaginable, the fool and trickster who has become wise through his own folly and trickery, discovering the degree to which a trickster fool needs a coherent world to survive in. Without any kings to fool or straight-men to trick, those energies will be lost in the void of the devouring flood.

Twelfth Night, or, What You Will begins with surviving the flood, and attempting to secure lasting happiness. In context, the attempt looks as naïve as those who described the Great War as the war to end all wars. Apparently, peace and stability are harder won than that. There is no shuffling. The price must be paid.

This book has passed over, in relative silence, the period of the great cost—Shakespeare's tragedies, in which the psyche seems increasingly intent on passing through the fire, no matter the pain and the toil. The facile escape of golden time is finally laid to rest in *King Lear*, with scenes so painful that certain notable critics have been unable even to reread them.

This whole process is condensed in Innogen, and her fidelity to her own individuation. She expresses the determination of the entire Shakespearean canon, by refusing to back down from herself. She is not the immortal godhead of womanhood, as Swinburne anointed her, yet she does carry the psychological function of femininity through to fruition, a function which Wilhelm describes expertly in relation to *Duì* 兌 (The Joyous: Lake), in its aspect of the youngest daughter:

> We are not talking about woman as only an empirical phenomenon, as part of humanity, but rather of the eternally feminine, which is a part of all of us. *The effects of this eternally feminine aspect are precisely such that by attracting us, we are led into depth and led out into clarity.*[2]

That is the significance of Innogen, as a metaphor. The expression of this aspect allows, in *Cymbeline*, for the great achievement of mundanity.

Every book is, unavoidably, a psychological confession of its author. I honour that in my choice of closing words, a maxim for the falling and fallen, borrowed from Caius Lucius, that is far more truth than cliché:

> Be cheerful, wipe thine eyes:
> Some falls are means the happier to arise.
> (*Cym.* 4.3.400–1)

Notes

1 Emphasis added.
2 Wilhelm (1995, 266; emphasis added). I know of no better definition of this aspect of anima.

Acknowledgments

I find myself more likely to read a book's acknowledgments if they come at the end, rather than the beginning. Particularly if I have enjoyed the book, I like the chance to stay with it a little longer. With that hopeful thought in mind, there are thanks to be made and credit to be given.

Dear Imogen, your name came before I began to pay any serious attention to the princess from whom you got it. It is surely no coincidence that work on this book began little more than a month after your arrival. You've provided a grounding motive that I did not know I needed. I did not know this would be a book when it began, and I can only imagine what you will be that I could never have planned.

And dear Mareike, take no offense at coming second in this list. This writing would have been utterly impossible without your astonishingly good-natured and willing sacrifices. You've done at least as much as I have in helping this work to be done.

I must also thank John Beebe for his time, care, advice, and willingness to get into the trenches of this work, virtually every step along the way.

I understand that my name will appear on this book's cover, but I am not sure I have really written it. At any rate there are a vast number of contributors, which can be perused in the bibliography in the coming pages. But more than that I have been fortunate to be working with a virtual co-author, that is William Shakespeare, who after all shaped the liquid magma of the creative unconscious into the plays that I here have had the opportunity to wonder about and 'analyse'.

The Kristine Mann Library of New York City was kind enough to give their 2023 Research Award to this project. This was very helpful in providing some financial support, but perhaps more importantly some professional encouragement to continue pursuing what eventually led to this book. So thank you to the KML board and staff: Jay Sherry, Bob McCullough, Farzad Mahootian, Carol Cooper, Beth Darlington, Stephen Moskovitz, Heidi Boyson, and Matthew.

Evangeline Rand, through many hours of searching talks, teas, and supervision, helped me very much to come in touch with my own ground, and my relationship to psyche.

John Hoedl was responsible for many years of mentorship, getting me off the ground as a Jungian, and helping develop the foundation of my relationship to soul.

Later, Mark Winborn and Ursula Brasch helped me to understand what it meant to put it all into clinical practice.

Speaking of which, there are many patients who I cannot name, but who, through the sharing of time and psychological energy, have made themselves invisibly, implicitly present beneath the surface of this work.

Thank you to Ronald Bugge who oversaw an earlier version of the *Cymbeline* chapter, which formed my thesis for the C. G. Jung Institute of Zürich, and Jeeyoun Kim and Susan Rowland for acting as co-advisors and offering their invaluable feedback.

Thank you to Craig Stephenson, who was willing to read an earlier draft of the book at lightning-speed and give some much-needed words of encouragement and affirmation, along with some necessary challenges.

To those others who agreed to be advance readers, thank you for your time and willingness to participate: Edmund Stapleton, Jan Selman, Peter Hinton-Davis, Kevin Kerr, Michael Hadley, and Peter Hinton.

Thank you to Tynan Boyd for helping my little diagrams look clean, professional, and properly spaced.

Thank you to Manon Berset and Katie Randall at Routledge for facilitating (and discussing) the publication process with me, from proposal to deadline.

Thank you to LeeAnn Pickrell who edited and cleared up an earlier version of the chapter on *King John* which was published in Jung Journal.

I would like also to acknowledge those who were most significant in my development as a theatre practitioner, and taught me what theatre is and why: Rhonda McCarthy, John Peck, Mark Knowles, Mary Bleier, Tanya Ryga, Lynda Adams, Thomas Usher, Danica Clark, Kevin McKendrick, Larry Reese, David Ley, Don Hannah, Sandy Nicholls, Kate Weiss, J. P. Fournier, Beau Coleman, Kim Mattice-Wanat, Mike Kennard, Marie Nychka, Jon Lachlan Stewart, Vincent Forcier, Amy Shostak, Adam Meggido, Martin Dockery, Leigh Rivenbark, Steve Pirot, Joe Slabe, Kelly Reay, Kory Mathewson, Jen Rider-Shaw, Clinton Carew, Matt Grue, and Dustin Clark.

Bibliography

Abt, T. (2005). *Introduction to picture interpretation according to C. G. Jung*. Zurich: Living Human Heritage Publications.

Adelman, J. (1992). *Suffocating mothers: Fantasies of maternal origin in Shakespeare's plays, Hamlet to The Tempest*. New York: Routledge.

Arlidge, A. (2000). *Shakespeare and the prince of love: The feast of misrule in the Middle Temple*. London: Giles de la Mare.

Armstrong, P. (2001). *Shakespeare in psychoanalysis*. London: Routledge.

Aronson, A. (1970). Shakespeare and the ocular proof. *Shakespeare Quarterly*, 21(4), 411–29.

Aronson, A. (1972). *Psyche & symbol in Shakespeare*. Bloomington, IN: Indiana University Press.

Astington, J. (1993). Malvolio and the Eunuchs: Texts and revels in Twelfth Night. In S. Wells (Ed.), *Shakespeare Survey* (Shakespeare Survey, pp. 23–34). Cambridge: Cambridge University Press.

Avrich, B. (Director). (2015). *King John* (T. Carroll, Stage Director). Stratford: Stratford Festival.

Baker, H. S., & Baker, M. N. (1987). Heinz Kohut's self psychology: An overview. *The American Journal of Psychiatry*, 144(1), 1–9.

Bakhtin, M. (1968). *Rabelais and his world* (H. Iswolsky, Trans.). Cambridge, MA: MIT Press.

Bakhtin, M. (1973). *Problems of Dostoevsky's poetics* (R. W. Rotsel, Trans.). Ann Arbor, MI: Ardis.

Barber, C. L. (1959). *Shakespeare's festive comedy: A study of dramatic form and its relation to social custom*. New York: Meridian Books.

Barrie, J. M. (1904). *Peter Pan; or, the boy who wouldn't grow up* [Stage Play]. New York: Charles Scribner's Sons.

Barton, A. (2007a). 'Wrying but a little': Marriage, law and sexuality in the plays of Shakespeare. In *Essays, mainly Shakespearean* (pp. 3–30). Cambridge: Cambridge University Press.

Barton, A. (2007b). *As You Like It* and *Twelfth Night:* Shakespeare's 'sense of an ending' (1972). In *Essays, mainly Shakespearean* (pp. 91–112). Cambridge: Cambridge University Press.

Barton, J. (1984). *Playing Shakespeare: An actor's guide*. New York: Anchor Books.

Bate, J. (2000). Shakespeare's Ovid. In *Ovid's Metamorphosis* (A. Golding, Trans., pp. xli–l). Philadelphia, PA: Paul Dry Books.

Bate, J. (2010). *Soul of the age: A biography of the mind of William Shakespeare*. New York: Random House.

Bate, J. (2011). Introduction. In J. Bate & E. Rasmussen (Eds.), *Cymbeline* (RSC Shakespeare). New York: Modern Library.

Bate, J., & Rasmussen, E. (Eds.) (2011). *Cymbeline (RSC Shakespeare)*. New York: Modern Library.

Beatles. (1970). *Hey Jude* [Audio Recording]. London: Apple.

Beaumont, F., & Fletcher, J. (1908). *The works of Francis Beaumont and John Fletcher* (A. H. Bullen, Ed.). London: George Bell & Sons.

Bednarz, J. (2001). *Shakespeare and the Poets' War.* New York: Columbia University Press.

Beebe, J. (1992). *Integrity in depth.* College Station, TX: Texas A&M University Press.

Beebe, J. (1997). He must have wept when he made you: The homoerotic *Pothos* in the movie version of *Interview with the Vampire.* In K. Ramsland (Ed.), *The Anne Rice reader* (pp. 196–211). New York: Ballantyne Books.

Beebe, J. (2006). Psychological types. In R. Papadopoulous (Ed.), *The handbook of Jungian psychology: Theory, practice and applications* (pp. 130–52). New York: Routledge.

Beebe, J. (2017). *Energies and patterns in psychological type: The reservoir of consciousness.* London: Routledge.

Beebe, J. (2022a). The trickster in the arts. In S. Carpani (Ed.), *Anthology of contemporary clinical classics in analytical psychology: The new ancestors* (pp. 17–48). London: Routledge.

Beebe, J. (2022b). Why is this real? In R. A. Segal, I. Błocian, & A. Kuzmicki (Eds.), *Collective structures of imagination in Jungian interpretation* (pp. 17–31). Leiden: Brill.

Beier, B. V. (2014). The art of persuasion and Shakespeare's two Iagos. *Studies in Philology,* 111(Winter, 1), 34–64.

Belsey, C. (1993). *Twelfth Night:* A modern perspective. In B. A. Mowat & P. Werstine (Eds.), *Twelfth Night, the New Folger Library Shakespeare* (pp. 197–207). New York: Washington Square Press.

Bentham, J. (1995). *The panopticon writings.* London: Verso.

Berne, E. (2004). *Games people play: The basic handbook of transactional analysis.* New York: Ballantine Books.

Berry, C. (Performer), & Bartholomew, D. (Songwriter). (1972). *My ding-A-ling* [Musical Recording]. Chess Records.

Berry, R. (1981). *Changing styles in Shakespeare.* London: George Allen & Unwin.

Billington, M. (2016, May 11). Cymbeline review—the RSC's bizarre romance comes straight from the heart. *The Guardian.* https://www.theguardian.com/stage/2016/may/11/cymbeline-review-rsc-royal-shakespeare-theatre

Bloom, H. (1994). *The Western canon: The books and school of the ages.* New York: Harcourt, Brace & Co.

Bloom, H. (1999). *Shakespeare: The invention of the human.* New York: Riverhead Books.

Boas, F. S. (1900). *Shakespere and his predecessors.* New York: Charles Scribner's Sons.

Bodkin, M. (1934). *Archetypal patterns in poetry: Psychological studies of imagination.* London: Oxford University Press.

Bonjour, A. (1951). The road to Swinstead Abbey: A study of the sense and structure of *King John. ELH,* 18(4), 253–74.

Bradley, A. C. (1904). *Shakespearean tragedy.* London: Macmillan.

Breuer, J., & Freud, S. (1957). *Studies on hysteria* (J. Strachey, Trans.). New York: Basic Books.

Bromberg, P. M. (1996). Hysteria, dissociation, and cure: Emmy von N revisited. In *Standing in the spaces: Essays on clinical process, trauma, and dissociation* (pp. 223–37). Hillsdale, NJ: Analytic Press.

Brubaker, E. S. (1989). Staging *King John:* A director's observations. In D. T. Curren-Aquino (Ed.), *King John: New perspectives* (pp. 165–72). Newark, NJ: University of Delaware Press.

Bruster, D. (2007). The materiality of Shakespearean form. In S. Cohen (Ed.), *Shakespeare and historical formalism* (pp. 31–48). Aldershot: Ashgate.

Burckhardt, S. (1968). *Shakespearean meanings*. Princeton, NJ: Princeton University Press.

Butler, J. (1999). *Gender trouble: Feminism and the subversion of identity*. New York: Routledge.

Butler, M. (2005). *Cymbeline (New Cambridge Shakespeare)*. Cambridge: Cambridge University Press.

Cai, C. (2021). The current situation and the cultural background of psychological type theory in China. *Journal of Analytical Psychology*, 66(5), 1048–73.

Campana, J. (2007). Killing Shakespeare's children: The cases of *Richard III* and *King John*. *Shakespeare*, 3(1), 18–39.

Campbell, L. B. (1958). *Shakespeare's 'histories': Mirrors of Elizabethan policy*. San Marino: Huntington Library Press (1947; repr. 1958).

Candido, J. (2022). Introduction. In J. Candido (Ed.), *Shakespeare: The critical tradition: King John* (pp. 1–30). London: Bloomsbury.

Caputi, A. (1978). *Buffo: The genius of vulgar comedy*. Detroit: Wayne State University Press.

Carlisle, C. J. (1989). Constance: A theatrical trinity. In D. T. Curren-Aquino (Ed.), *King John: New perspectives* (pp. 144–64). London and Toronto: Associated University Presses.

Carnegie, D. (2001). "Maluolio within": Performance perspectives on the dark house. *Shakespeare Quarterly*, 52(3), 393–414. http://www.jstor.org/stable/3648686

Carr, J. (1978). "Cymbeline" and the validity of myth. *Studies in Philology*, 75(3), 316–30.

Chambers, E. K. (1925). *Shakespeare: A survey*. New York: Penguin Books.

Chambers, E. K. (1930). *William Shakespeare: A study of facts and problems* (Vol. 2). Oxford: Oxford University Press.

Champion, L. S. (1989). The "Un-end" of *King John*: Shakespeare's demystification of closure. In D. T. Curren-Aquino (Ed.), *King John: New perspectives* (pp. 173–85). London & Toronto: Associated University Presses.

Chen, X. (2015). *Reconsidering Shakespeare's 'lateness': Studies in the late plays*. Newcastle upon Tyne: Cambridge Scholars Publishing.

Clarke, C. (Producer), & Sichel, J. (Director). (1970). *Twelfth Night* [Motion Picture]. London: ITV Sunday Night Theatre.

Clavell, J., Kondo, R., Marks, J. (Writers), & Toye, F. E. O. (Director). (2024). *Shogun*, Season 1, Episode 10, "A Dream of a Dream". Aired April 23, 2024. FX Productions.

Cobb, N. (1990). *Prospero's island: The secret alchemy at the heart of The Tempest*. London: Coventure.

Cohen, L. (1992). "Anthem", on *The Future* [Music Recording]. New York: Columbia Records.

Coursen, H. R. (1986). *The compensatory psyche: A Jungian approach to Shakespeare*. Lanham, MD: University Press of America.

Craig, H. (1948). Shakespeare's bad poetry. In A. Nicoll (Ed.), *Shakespeare survey* (Shakespeare Survey, pp. 51–56). Cambridge: Cambridge University Press. https://doi.org/10.1017/CCOL0521064147.006

Crichton, J. (2018). The magic circle: Phenomenology of gaming. *Jung Journal: Culture & Psyche*, 13(4), 35–52.

Crumley, J. C. (2001). Questioning history in *Cymbeline*. *Studies in English Literature, 1500–1900*, 41, 297–315.

Curran, J. E. (1997). Royalty unlearned, honor untaught: British savages and historiographical change in *Cymbeline*. *Comparative Drama*, 31, 277–303.

Curren-Aquino, D. T. (1989). Introduction: *King John* resurgent. In D. T. Curren-Aquino (Ed.), *King John: New perspectives* (pp. 11–28). London and Toronto: Associated University Presses.

Debord, G. (2021). *Society of the spectacle* (F. Perlman & K. Knabb, Trans.). Critical Editions.

Donen, S. (Director). (1954). *Seven brides for seven brothers* [Motion Picture]. Hollywood, CA: Metro-Goldwyn-Mayer.

Doty, J. S. (2022). Blood, virtue, and romance in *Cymbeline. Shakespeare Quarterly*, 72(3), 203–28.

Dover Wilson, J. (2009). *Introduction to The Cambridge Dover Wilson Shakespeare: King John* (J. D. Wilson, Ed.). Cambridge: Cambridge University Press.

Dover Wilson, J., & Quiller-Couch, A. (Eds.) (1930). *Twelfth Night or what you will.* Cambridge: Cambridge University Press.

Driscoll, J. (2019a). *Shakespeare and Jung: The god in time.* Washington, DC: Academica Press.

Driscoll, J. (2019b). *Shakespeare's identities: Psychological, mythic, and existentialist perspectives.* Washington, DC: Academica Press.

Duncan-Jones, K. (2010). *Shakespeare: An ungentle life.* London: Methuen Drama.

Dusinberre, J. (1990). *King John* and embarrassing women. *Shakespeare Survey*, 42, 37–52.

Edinger, E. F. (1991). *Anatomy of the psyche: Alchemical symbolism in psychotherapy.* Chicago, IL: La Salle.

Edinger, E. F. (1995). *The mysterium lectures: A journey through C. G. Jung's Mysterium Coniunctionis.* Toronto: Inner City.

Edinger, E. F. (2001). *The psyche on stage: Individuation motifs in Shakespeare and Sophocles.* Toronto: Inner City Books.

Edinger, E. F. (2015). *The new god-image: A study of Jung's key letters concerning the evolution of the Western god-image.* Wilmette, IL: Chiron Publications.

Elam, K. (1984). *Shakespeare's universe of discourse: Language-games in the comedies.* New York: Cambridge University Press.

Elam, K. (2008). Introduction. In Arden Shakespeare (Third Series), *Twelfth Night.* London: Bloomsbury.

Eliade, M. (1958). *Patterns in comparative religion* (R. Sheed, Trans.). New York: Meridian Books.

Emerson, R. W. (1940). *Selected writings of Ralph Waldo Emerson.* New York: Random House.

Ewert, K. (2012). Colm Feore. In J. R. Brown (Ed.), *The Routledge companion to actors' Shakespeare.* London and New York: Routledge.

Fabricius, J. (1997). *Shakespeare's hidden world: A study of his unconscious.* Bicester: Karnac Books.

Fiedler, L. A. (1972). *The stranger in Shakespeare.* New York: Stein and Day.

Fike, M. A. (2009). *A Jungian study of Shakespeare: The visionary mode.* New York: Palgrave Macmillan.

Fineman, J. (1980). Fratricide and cuckoldry: Shakespeare's doubles. In M. M. Schwartz & C. Kahn (Eds.), *Representing Shakespeare: New psychoanalytic essays* (pp. 70–109). Baltimore, MD and London: Johns Hopkins University Press.

Fisher, S., & Fisher, R. (1981). *Pretend the world is funny and forever: A psychological analysis of comedians, clowns, and actors.* Hillside, NJ: Lawrence Erlbaum Associates Publications.

Freebury-Jones, D. (2024). *Shakespeare's borrowed feathers: How early modern playwrights shaped the world's greatest writer.* Manchester: Manchester University Press.

Freud, S. (1955). The 'Uncanny' [1919]. In *The complete psychological works, Vol. XVII* (pp. 217–56, 1955 & Edns.). London: Hogarth Press.

Freud, S. (2020). Some character types met with in psycho-analytic work (1915). In J. Riviere (Trans.), *Sigmund Freud: Essays and papers* (pp. 351–81). London: Riverrun.

Frye, N. (1957). *Anatomy of criticism: Four essays.* Princeton, NJ: Princeton University Press.

Frye, N. (1965). *A natural perspective: The development of Shakespearean comedy and romance.* New York: Columbia University Press.

Frye, N. (1986). *Northrop Frye on Shakespeare.* Markham, ON: Fitzhenry & Whitside.

Gabbard, G. O. (2005). *Psychodynamic psychiatry in clinical practice* (4th ed.). Washington, DC: American Psychiatric Publishing.

Garber, M. (1981). *Coming of age in Shakespeare.* New York: Routledge.

Garber, M. (1992). *Vested interests: Cross-dressing and cultural anxiety.* New York: Routledge.

Garber, M. (2004). *Shakespeare all along.* New York: Knopf Doubleday.

Gay, P. (1985). Introduction. In E. S. Donno (Ed.), *Twelfth Night* (pp. 1–53). Cambridge: Cambridge University Press.

Gibbons, B. (1993). *Shakespeare and multiplicity.* Cambridge: Cambridge University Press.

Gittings, C. (1984). *Death, burial, and the individual in early modern England.* London: Croom Helm.

Goldman, M. (1972). *Shakespeare and the energies of drama.* Princeton, NJ: Princeton University Press.

Goldman, M. (1985). *Acting and action in Shakespearean tragedy.* Princeton, NJ: Princeton University Press.

Granville-Barker, H. (1947). *Prefaces to Shakespeare, second series.* Bungay: Richard Clay & Co.

Granville-Barker, H. (1971). The artlessness of *Cymbeline.* In D. J. Palmer (Ed.), *Shakespeare's later comedies* (pp. 225–33). Harmondsworth: Penguin Books.

Granville-Barker, H. (1984). *Prefaces to Shakespeare: Cymbeline, the winter's tale.* London: B. T. Batsford.

Greenblatt, S. (2004). *Will in the world: How Shakespeare became Shakespeare.* New York: Norton.

Greif, K. (1988). A star is born: Feste on the modern stage. *Shakespeare Quarterly,* 39(1), 61–78.

Grennan, E. (1978). Shakespeare's satirical history: A reading of *King John. Shakespeare Studies,* 11.

Grudin, R. (1979). *Mighty opposites: Shakespeare and renaissance contrariety.* Berkeley, CA: University of California Press.

Haas, L., & Hunziker, M. (2006). *Building blocks of personality type.* Eltanin Publishing.

Hadfield, A. (2004). *Shakespeare, Spenser, and the matter of Britain.* Basingstoke: Palgrave Macmillan.

Hawkes, T. (2002). *Shakespeare in the present.* London: Routledge.

Hayles, N. (1980). Sexual disguise in *As You Like It* and *Twelfth Night. Shakespeare Survey,* 32, 63–72.

Hazlitt, W. (1908). *Characters of Shakespeare's plays* (J. H. Lobban, Ed.). Cambridge: Cambridge University Press.

Heberle, M. A. (1994). "Innocent Prate": *King John* and Shakespeare's children (E. Goodenough, M. A. Heberle, & N. Sokoloff, Eds.). *Infant Tongues,* 28–43.

Henderson, J. L. (1984). *Cultural attitudes in psychological perspective.* Toronto: Inner City Books.

Henderson, J. L. (1990). Ancient myths and modern man. In C. G. Jung (Ed.), *Man and his symbols.* London: Arkana.

Henry, G. (2004). King John. In R. Smallwood (Ed.), *Players of Shakespeare 6* (pp. 37–49). Cambridge: Cambridge University Press.

Hill, C. (1961). *The century of revolution: 1603–1714.* London: W. W. Norton & Co.

Hill, G. (1984). "The True Conduct of Human Judgment": Some observations on *Cymbeline.* In G. Hill (Ed.), *The lords of limit: Essays on literature and ideas.* Oxford: Oxford University Press.

Hillman, J. (1975). *Loose ends: Primary papers in archetypal psychology.* Dallas: Spring Publications.

Hillman, J. (1979a). Senex and Puer. In J. Hillman (Ed.), *Puer papers* (pp. 3–53). Dallas: Spring Publications.

Hillman, J. (1979b). Puer wounds and Ulysses' scar. In J. Hillman (Ed.), *Puer papers* (pp. 100–29). Dallas: Spring Publications.

Hillman, J. (Ed.). (1979c). *Puer papers.* Dallas: Spring Publications.

Holinshed, R. (1577). *The Holinshed project* (Vol. 4) [Website]. https://english.nsms.ox.ac.uk/holinshed/texts.php?text1=1577_5316

Honigmann, E. A. J. (Ed.) (1954). Introduction. In Arden Shakespeare (Second Series), *King John* (pp. xi–lxxv). London: Bloomsbury.

Hotson, L. (1955). *The first night of Twelfth Night.* London: Rupert Hart-Davis.

Hoveden, R. (1853). *The annals of Roger of Hoveden: Comprising the history of England and of other countries of Europe from A.D. 732 to A.D. 1201* (H. T. Riley, Trans.). London: H. G. Bohn.

Howard, J. E., & Rackin, P. (1968). *Engendering a nation: A feminist account of Shakespeare's English histories.* London: Routledge.

Huang, F. (2010). *The complete I Ching: 10th anniversary edition.* Rochester: Inner Traditions.

Hughes, T. (1992). *Shakespeare and the goddess of complete being.* London: Faber & Faber.

Hunter, K. (2004). Constance. In R. Smallwood (Ed.), *Players of Shakespeare 6* (pp. 37–49). Cambridge: Cambridge University Press.

Hutton, R. (1994). *The rise and fall of merry England: The ritual year 1400–1700.* Oxford: Oxford University Press.

Jackson, P. (Director). (2002). *The lord of the rings: The two towers* [Motion Picture]. Los Angeles, CA: New Line.

Jing-Nuan, W. (Trans.) (1991). *Yi Jing.* Washington, DC: The Taoist Center.

Johnson, S. (1989). *Samuel Johnson on Shakespeare* (H. R. Woudhuysun, Ed.). London: Penguin Books.

Jones, E. (1971). Stuart *Cymbeline*. In D. J. Palmer (Ed.), *Shakespeare's later comedies* (pp. 248–63). Harmondsworth: Penguin Books.

Jordan, C. (1994). Contract and conscience in "Cymbeline". *Renaissance Drama*, 25, 33–58.

Jordan-Finnegan, R. (2006). *Individuation and the power of evil on the nature of the human psyche in C. G. Jung, Arthur Miller, and Shakespeare.* Bicester: Karnac Books.

Jung, C. G. (1933). *Modern man in search of a soul.* Orlando: Harcourt.

Jung, C. G. (1957). The associations of normal subjects. In M. Fordham (Ed.) & R. F. C. Hull (Trans.), *The collected works of C. G. Jung* (Vol. 2, 2nd ed.). Princeton, NJ: Princeton University Press.

Jung, C. G. (1958). Aion: Researches into the phenomenology of the self. *CW*, 9ii.

Jung, C. G. (1960). The stages of life. *CW*, 8, 749–95.

Jung, C. G. (1963). Memories, dreams, reflections. In A. Jaffé (Ed.), R. Winston & C. Winston (Trans.). New York: Pantheon Books.

Jung, C. G. (1967a). On the psychology of the unconscious. In M. Fordham (Ed.) & R. F. C. Hull (Trans.), *The collected works of C. G. Jung* (Vol. 7, 2nd ed.). Princeton, NJ: Princeton University Press.

Jung, C. G. (1967b). The relations between the ego and the unconscious. In M. Fordham (Ed.) & R. F. C. Hull (Trans.), *The collected works of C. G. Jung* (Vol. 7, 2nd ed.). Princeton, NJ: Princeton University Press.

Jung, C. G. (1969a). Answer to Job. In M. Fordham (Ed.) & R. F. C. Hull (Trans.), *The collected works of C. G. Jung* (Vol. 11), 560–758. Princeton, NJ: Princeton University Press.

Jung, C. G. (1969b). Psychological commentary on "The Tibetan Book of the Great Liberation". *CW*, 11, 759–858.

Jung, C. G. (1970). The transcendent function. In M. Fordham (Ed.) & R. F. C. Hull (Trans.), *The collected works of C. G. Jung* (Vol. 8, 2nd ed.). Princeton, NJ: Princeton University Press.

Jung, C. G. (1971). Psychological types. In M. Fordham (Ed.) & R. F. C. Hull (Trans.), *The collected works of C. G. Jung* (Vol. 6, 2nd ed.). Princeton, NJ: Princeton University Press.

Jung, C. G. (1973). *Letters, Vol. 1, 1906–1951.* London: Routledge & Kegan Paul.

Jung, C. G. (1976). *Letters, Vol. 2, 1951–1961.* London: Routledge & Kegan Paul.

Jung, C. G. (1977a). Mysterium coniunctionis. *CW*, 14.

Jung, C. G. (1977b). The definition of demonism. In M. Fordham (Ed.) & R. F. C. Hull (Trans.), *The collected works of C. G. Jung* (Vol. 18, 2nd ed., pp. 1473–74). Princeton, NJ: Princeton University Press.

Jung, C. G. (1980). Archetypes and the collective unconscious. In M. Fordham (Ed.) & R. F. C. Hull (Trans.), *The collected works of C. G. Jung* (Vol. 91). Princeton, NJ: Princeton University Press.

Jung, C. G. (2022). *Consciousness and the unconscious: Lectures delivered at ETH Zurich, Volume 2: 1934* (E. Falzeder, Ed., M. Kyburz, J. Peck, & E. Falzeder, Trans.). Princeton, NJ: Princeton University Press.

Juric, L. P. (2019). *Illyria in Shakespeare's England.* Vancouver, BC: Fairleigh Dickinson University Press.

Kamps, I. (2011). Madness and social mobility in *Twelfth Night.* In *Twelfth Night: New critical essays.* New York: Routledge.

Kander, J. (Music), Ebb, F. (Lyrics), & Masteroff, J. (Book). (1966). *Cabaret* [Musical Theatre Production].

Kast, V. (1980). *The association experiment in the therapeutic practice.* Stuttgart: Bonz Verlag.

Kast, V. (2006). Anima/animus. In R. K. Papadopoulos (Ed.), *The handbook of Jungian psychology: Theory, practice and applications.* Hove: Routledge.

Kastan, D. S. (1983). "To set a form upon that indigest": Shakespeare's fictions of history. *Comparative Drama*, 17(1), 1–16.

Kawai, T. (2006). Postmodern consciousness in psychotherapy. *Journal of Analytical Psychology*, 51(3), 437–50.

Kermode, F. (1963). *Shakespeare: The final plays.* London: Macmillan.

Kerrigan, J. (2013). Prologue: *Dionbrollach:* How Celtic was Shakespeare? In W. Maley & R. Loughnane (Eds.), *Celtic Shakespeare.* Farnham: Ashgate Publishing.

Kietzman, M. J. (2012). Will personified: Viola as actor-author in "Twelfth Night." *Criticism*, 54(2), 257–89.

King, R. (2005). *Cymbeline: Constructions of Britain.* London: Routledge.

Kirsch, A. (1967). *Cymbeline* and coterie dramaturgy. *ELH*, 34(3), 285–306.

Kirsch, J. (1966). *Shakespeare's royal self.* New York: G. P. Putnam's Sons.

K'Naan. (2012, December 8). Censoring myself for success. *The New York Times.* https://www.nytimes.com/2012/12/09/opinion/sunday/knaan-on-censoring-himself-for-success.html

Knowles, K. (2007). "This little abstract": Inscribing history upon the child in Shakespeare's *King John. eSharp*, 10, 1–24.

Ko, Y. J. (1997). The comic close of *Twelfth Night* and Viola's *Noli me tangere. Shakespeare Quarterly*, 48(4), 391–405.

Kott, J. (1964). *Shakespeare our contemporary* (B. Taborski, Trans.). New York: W. W. Norton.

Laing, R. D. (1962). *The self and others.* Chicago, IL: Quadrangle.

Lamb, C. (1986). On some of the old actors. In S. Wells (Ed.), *Twelfth Night: Critical essays* (pp. 49–60). New York and London: Garland.

Lander, B. (2008). Interpreting the person: Tradition, conflict, and *Cymbeline's* Imogen. *Shakespeare Quarterly*, 59(2), 156–84.

Lander, J. M., & Tobin, J. J. M. (2018). Introduction. In Arden Shakespeare (Third Series), *King John* (pp. 1–133). London: Bloomsbury.

Landry, D. E. (1982). Dreams as history: The strange unity of *Cymbeline. Shakespeare Quarterly*, 33(1), 68–79.

Lawrence, W. W. (1931). *Shakespeare's problem comedies.* New York: Macmillan.

Leavis, F. R. (1942). A criticism of Shakespeare's late plays. *Scrutiny*, 10, 339–45.

Leggatt, A. (1977). Dramatic perspective in *King John. English Studies in Canada*, 3, 1–17.

Lerer, S. (2018). *Shakespeare's lyric stage: Myth, music, and poetry in the last plays.* Chicago, IL: University of Chicago Press.

Levin, H. (1986). The underplot of *Twelfth Night.* In S. Wells (Ed.), *Twelfth Night critical essays* (pp. 161–9). New York: Garland.

Lewis, C. (2011). Whodunit? Plot, plotting, and detection in *Twelfth Night.* In *Twelfth Night: New critical essays* (pp. 258–72). New York: Routledge.

Lindley, D. (2006). *Shakespeare and music.* London: Bloomsbury.

Lisak, C. (2011). Domesticating strangeness in *Twelfth Night.* In J. Schiffer (Ed.), *Twelfth Night: New critical essays* (pp. 167–83). New York: Routledge.

Lloyd Webber, A. (1970). *Jesus Christ superstar: A rock opera.* New York: Decca.

Lothian, J. M., & Craik, T. W. (Eds.) (1975). Introduction. In Arden Shakespeare (Second Series), *Twelfth Night.* London: Methuen & Co.

Lyne, R. (2007). *Shakespeare's late work.* Oxford: Oxford University Press.

Maley, W. (1997). "This sceptered isle": Shakespeare and the British problem. In J. J. Joughin (Ed.), *Shakespeare and national culture* (pp. 83–108). Manchester: Manchester University Press.

Manheim, M. (1989). The four voices of the bastard. In D. T. Curren-Aquino (Ed.), *King John: New perspectives* (pp. 126–35). Newark, NJ: University of Delaware Press.

Manningham, J. (1976). *The diary of John Manningham of the Middle Temple 1602–1603* (R. P. Sorlien, Ed.). Hanover: University Press of New England.

Marcus, L. (2013). *Cymbeline* and the Unease of Topicality. In K. Ryan (Ed.), *Shakespeare: The last plays* (pp. 134–68). London and New York: Routledge.

Maslen, R. W. (2006). "*Twelfth Night*, gender, and comedy," from *Early Modern English Drama: A Critical Companion.* In H. Bloom (Ed.), *Bloom's Shakespeare through the ages: Twelfth Night* (pp. 203–14). New York: Bloom's Literary Criticism.

McDonald, R. (2006). *Shakespeare's late style.* Cambridge: Cambridge University Press.

McWilliams, N. (2011). *Psychoanalytic diagnosis* (2nd ed.). New York and London: Guilford Press.

Micklem, N. (1996). *The nature of hysteria.* London: Routledge.

Miller, G. (2016). "Many a time and oft had I broken my Neck for their amusement": The corpse, the child, and the aestheticization of death in Shakespeare's "Richard III" and "King John." *Comparative Drama*, 50(2/3), 209–32.

Milton, J. (1886). *Milton's paradise lost* (R. Vaughan, Ed.). Chicago, IL and New York: Belford, Clarke & Co.

Minton, E. (2017). *Shakespeare's hot 40: Ranking the bard's plays by stage popularity.* https://www.shakespeareances.com/dialogues/commentary/Bard_Board_Popularity-171012.html

Miola, R. S. (2014). "Wrying but a little?" Marriage, punishment and forgiveness in *Cymbeline.* In P. Gray & J. D. Cox (Eds.), *Shakespeare and renaissance ethics* (pp. 172–85). Cambridge: University of Cambridge Press.

Morse, R. (2004). What city, friends, is this? In D. Mehl, A. Stock, & A.-J. Zwierlein (Eds.), *Plotting early modern London: New essays on Jacobean city comedy* (pp. 177–91). Burlington: Ashgate.

Moshinsky, E. (Director) (1982). *Cymbeline* [Motion Picture]. BBCTV.

Mowat, B. (2003). 'What's in a name?' Tragicomedy, romance, or late comedy. In R. Dutton & J. E. Howard (Eds.), *A companion to Shakespeare's works, Vol. 4* (pp. 129–49). Oxford: Oxford University Press.

Mowat, B., & Werstine, P. (2013). *Macbeth (Folger Shakespeare).* New York: Simon & Schuster.

Mowat, B., & Werstine, P. (Eds.) (2004). *Julius Caesar (Folger Shakespeare).* New York: Simon & Schuster.

Murphy, E. (2021). Type development in childhood and beyond. *Journal of Analytical Psychology*, 66(5), 1074–93.

Murray, H. A. (1979). American Icarus. In J. Hillman (Ed.), *Puer papers* (pp. 77–99). Dallas: Spring Publications.

Myers, I. B. (1980). *Gifts differing: Understanding personality type*. Mountain View, CA: Consulting Psychologists Press.

Nosworthy, J. M. (1955). Introduction. In Arden Shakespeare (Second Series), *Cymbeline*. London: Methuen Drama.

Novais, F., Araújo, A., & Godinho, P. (2015). Historical roots of histrionic personality disorder. *Frontiers in Psychology*, 6, 1463. https://doi.org/10.3389/fpsyg.2015.01463

O'Brien, J., & O'Brien, N. (2024). *Jung's word association experiment: Manual for training and practice*. London: Routledge.

O'Hara, J. (2014). *The appointment in Samarra*. London: Penguin Classics.

Orgel, S. (1996). *Impersonations: The performance of gender in Shakespeare's England*. Cambridge: Cambridge University Press.

Ornstein, R. (1972). *A kingdom for a stage: The achievement of Shakespeare's history plays* (pp. 96–101). Cambridge: Harvard University Press.

Osborne, L. E. (1996). *The trick of singularity: Twelfth Night and the performance editions*. Iowa City: University of Iowa Press.

Paster, G. K. (2004). *Humouring the body: Emotions and the Shakespearean stage*. Chicago, IL: University of Chicago Press.

Pentland, E. (2011). Beyond the "lyric" in Illyricum: Some early modern backgrounds to *Twelfth Night*. In J. Schiffer (Ed.), *Twelfth Night: New critical essays* (pp. 149–68). New York: Routledge.

Penuel, S. (2010). Missing fathers: *Twelfth Night* and the reformation of mourning. *Studies in Philology*, 107(1), 74–96.

Pequigney, J. (1992). The two Antonios and same-sex love in *Twelfth Night* and *The Merchant of Venice*. *English Literary Renaissance*, 22, 201–21.

Piesse, A. J. (2002). *King John*: Changing perspectives. In M. Hattaway (Ed.), *The Cambridge companion to Shakespeare's history plays* (pp. 126–40). Cambridge: Cambridge University Press.

Plato. (2008). *Symposium* (M. C. Howatson & F. C. C. Sheffield, Eds. & M. C. Howatson, Trans.). Cambridge: Cambridge University Press.

Porterfield, S. (1994). *Jung's advice to the players: A Jungian reading of Shakespeare's problem plays*. Westport, CT: Praeger.

Python, M. (1979). *'What have the Romans ever done for us?' from Life of Brian* [Video Recording]. https://youtube.com/watch?v=9foi342LXQE

Radin, P. (1956). *The trickster: A study in American Indian mythology*. New York: Philosophical Library.

Redmond, M. J. (1999). "My lord, I fear, has forgot Britain": Rome, Italy, and the (Re)construction of British National Identity. In H. Klein & M. Marrapodi (Eds.), *Shakespeare and Italy* (*Shakespeare Yearbook* 10, pp. 297–316). Lewiston, ME: Edwin Mellon Press.

Rees, R. (1989). Posthumus in *Cymbeline*. In P. Brockbank (Ed.), *Players of Shakespeare 1* (pp. 139–52). Cambridge: Cambridge University Press.

Riemann, F. (2009). *Anxiety* (G. Dunn, Trans.). München, DE: Ernst Reinhardt Verlag.

Roesler, C. (2023). *Development of a reconceptualization of archetype theory: Report to the IAAP*. Freiburg: Katholische Hoschschule. https://iaap.org/wp-content/uploads/2023/04/Report-Archetype-Theory-Roesler-1-3.pdf

Rogers-Gardner, B. (1996). *Jung and Shakespeare: Hamlet, Othello, and The Tempest*. Wilmette, IL: Chiron Publications.

Rowland, S. (1999). *C. G. Jung and literary theory: The challenge from fiction.* London: Palgrave Macmillan.

Rowland, S. (2005). *Jung as a writer.* London: Routledge.

Rowland, S. (2010). Shakespeare and the Jungian Symbol: A case of war and marriage. *Jung Journal: Culture & Psyche*, 5(1), 31–46.

Rowland, S. (2016). The demonic and Narcissistic power of the media in Shakespeare's *Macbeth.* In L. Cruz & S. Buser (Eds.), *A clear and present danger: Narcissism in the era of Donald Trump* (pp. 213–24). Asheville, NC: Chiron Publications.

Rowland, S. (2019). *Jungian literary criticism: The essential guide.* London: Routledge.

Rowland, S. (2020). *Jungian arts-based research and 'The nuclear enchantment of New Mexico'.* London: Routledge.

Rowling, J. K. (1998). *Harry Potter and the chamber of secrets.* London: Bloomsbury.

Samuels, A. (1998). Will the Post-Jungians survive? In A. Casement (Ed.), *Post-Jungians today* (pp. 15–32). London: Routledge.

Samuels, A. (2004). Foreword. In J. S. Baumlin, T. F. Baumlin, & G. H. Jensen (Eds.), *Post-Jungian criticism: Theory and practice* (pp. vii–xv). Albany: State University of New York Press.

Samuels, A. (2008). New developments in the post-Jungian field. In P. Young-Eisendrath & T. Dawson (Eds.), *The Cambridge companion to Jung* (pp. 1–18). Cambridge: Cambridge University Press.

Sanders, E. R. (2000). Interiority and the letter in "Cymbeline." *Critical Survey*, 12(2), 49–70.

Schalkwyk, D. (2005). Love and service in "Twelfth Night" and the sonnets. *Shakespeare Quarterly*, 56(1), 76–100.

Schalkwyk, D. (2011). Music, food, and love in the affective landscapes of *Twelfth Night.* In J. Schiffer (Ed.), *Twelfth Night: New critical essays* (pp. 81–98). New York: Routledge.

Schiffer, J. (Ed.) (2011). *Twelfth Night:* Taking the long view: *Twelfth Night* criticism and performance. In *Twelfth Night: New critical essays* (pp. 1–44). New York: Routledge.

Schwartz, S. E. (2009). Puella's shadow. *International Journal of Jungian Studies*, 1(2), 111–22.

Schwartz, S. E. (2024). *A Jungian exploration of the puella archetype: Girl unfolding.* London: Routledge.

Shapiro, M. (1994). *Gender in play on the Shakespearean stage.* Ann Arbor: University of Michigan Press.

Shaw, G. B. (1924). *Saint Joan.* London: Constable & Company.

Shaw, G. B. (1946). *Geneva, Cymbeline refinished, & good King Charles.* London: Constable & Co.

Shaw, G. B. (1961). *Shaw on Shakespeare* (E. Wilson, Ed.). New York: E. P. Dutton & Co.

Sinden, D. (1985). Malvolio in *Twelfth Night.* In P. Brockbank (Ed.), *Players of Shakespeare 1* (pp. 41–66). Cambridge: Cambridge University Press.

Skea, A. (2021). *Ann Skea considers the development and legacy of Hughes's mythic Shakespearean study.* The Ted Hughes Society. https://thetedhughessociety.org/shakespeare

Skura, M. A. (1980). Interpreting Posthumus' dream from above and below. In M. M. Schwartz & C. Kahn (Eds.), *Representing Shakespeare* (pp. 203–16). Baltimore, MD: Johns Hopkins University Press.

Skura, M. A. (1993). *Shakespeare the actor and the purposes of playing.* Chicago, IL: University of Chicago Press.

Slights, C. (2009). When Is a Bastard Not a Bastard? Character and Conscience in *King John.* In P. Yachnin & J. Slights (Eds.), *Shakespeare and character: Theory, history, performance, and theatrical persons.* Basingstoke: Palgrave Macmillan.

Smallwood, R. (2004). Introduction to *Players of Shakespeare 6* (R. Smallwood, Ed., pp. 1–21). Cambridge: Cambridge University Press.

Smith, B. R. (2011). "His fancy's queen": Sensing sexual strangeness in *Twelfth Night*. In J. Schiffer (Ed.). *Twelfth Night: New critical essays* (pp. 65–80). New York: Routledge.

Solzhenitsyn, A. (1985). *The gulag archipelago. 1918–1956: An experiment in literary investigation* (T. P. Whitney & H. Willetts, Trans.). New York: Perennial Classics.

Spears, B. (2001). *"I'm not a girl, not yet a woman".* On *Britney* [Audio Recording]. New York: Jive Records.

Sprague, A. C., & Trewin, J. C. (1970). *Shakespeare's plays today: Customs and conventions of the stage.* Columbia: University of South Carolina Press.

Spurgeon, C. F. (1935). *Shakespeare's imagery and what it tells us.* Cambridge: Macmillan.

Stein, M. (1970). Between fantasy and imagination: A psychological exploration of *Cymbeline.* In F. Crews (Ed.), *Psychoanalysis and literary process* (pp. 219–83). Cambridge, MA: Winthrop.

Stewart, M. (1984). Carnival and *Don Quixote:* The folk tradition of comedy. In L. Cowan (Ed.), *The terrain of comedy* (pp. 143–62). Dallas: Dallas Institute of Humanities and Culture.

Stone-Fewings, J. (2004). The bastard. In R. Smallwood (Ed.), *Players of Shakespeare 6* (pp. 50–67). Cambridge: Cambridge University Press.

Swander, H. (1964). *Cymbeline* and the "Blameless Hero." *ELH*, 31(3), 259–70.

Swinburne, A. C. (1880). *A study of Shakespeare.* London: Chatto & Windus.

Tanner, T. (2010). *Prefaces to Shakespeare.* Cambridge, MA: Harvard University Press.

Taylor, M. (2001). *Shakespeare criticism in the twentieth century.* Oxford: Oxford University Press.

Thweatt, J. (2021). Excerpt from *Hitler as Puer. Jung Journal: Culture & Psyche*, 15(4), 55–70. https://doi.org/10.1080/19342039.2021.1979364.

Tolkien, J. R. R. (1991). *The lord of the rings.* HarperCollins.

Tree, H. B. (1901). The Saturday review, 9 February 1901, Preface to the Souvenir Program for *Twelfth Night*, 5 February 1901, His Majesty's Theatre. Harvard Theatre Collection.

Trewin, J. C. (1978). *Going to Shakespeare.* London: George Allen & Unwin.

Trousdale, G., & Wise, K. (Directors). (1991). *Beauty and the beast* [Motion Picture]. Walt Disney Feature Animation.

Tucker, K. (2003). *Shakespeare and Jungian typology: A reading of the plays.* Jefferson, NC: McFarland & Company.

UKParliament (2024). *Magna Carta* [Website]. https://www.parliament.uk/about/living-heritage/evolutionofparliament/originsofparliament/birthofparliament/overview/magnacarta/

Upton, J. (1748). *Critical observations on Shakespeare* (2nd ed.). London: G. Hawkins.

Vaughan, V. M. (1984). Between tetralogies: *King John* as transition. *Shakespeare Quarterly*, 35(4), 407–20.

Vaughan, V. M. (1989). *King John:* A study in subversion and containment. In D. T. Curren-Aquino (Ed.), *King John: New perspectives* (pp. 62–75). Newark, NJ: University of Delaware Press.

Vaughan, V. M. (2003). *King John.* In R. Dutton & J. E. Howard (Eds.), *A companion to Shakespeare's works, Vol. 2: The histories* (pp. 379–94). Oxford: Blackwell Publishing.

Von Franz, M.-L. (1981). *Puer Aeternus.* Santa Monica, CA: Sigo Press.

Von Franz, M.-L., & Hillman, J. (2020). *Lectures on Jung's typology.* Thompson, CT: Spring Publications.

Vujovic, A. (2021). *The Jungian art: The Jungian persona in Shakespeare's works: "Thou must be thyself": A Jungian Shakespeare.* Munich: GRIN Verlag.

Waith, E. (1978). *King John* and the drama of history. *Shakespeare Quarterly*, 29, 192–211.

Wali, M. I. (2011). *A midsummer night's dream: Shakespeare's syzygy of meaning.* Pittsburgh, PA: RoseDog Books.

Walter, H. (1993). Imogen in *Cymbeline.* In R. Jackson & R. Smallwood (Eds.), *Players of Shakespeare 3* (pp. 201–19). Cambridge: Cambridge University Press.

Wanamaker, Z. (1988). Viola in *Twelfth Night.* In R. Jackson & R. Smallwood (Eds.), *Players of Shakespeare 2* (pp. 81–92). Cambridge: Cambridge University Press.

Warren, R. (1989). *Shakespeare in performance: Cymbeline.* Manchester: Manchester University Press.

Warren, R. (1990). *Staging Shakespeare's late plays.* Oxford: Clarendon Press.

Wayne, V. (2003). *Cymbeline*: Patriotism and performance. In R. Dutton & J. E. Howard (Eds.), *A companion to Shakespeare's works, vol. IV: The poems, problem comedies, late plays* (pp. 389–407). Malden, MA: Blackwell Publishing.

Wayne, V. (2017). Introduction. In Arden Shakespeare (Third Series), *Cymbeline.* London: Bloomsbury.

Wells, S. (1977). *Royal Shakespeare: Four major productions at Stratford-upon-Avon.* Manchester: Manchester University Press.

Wells, S. (2016). *Shakespeare on page and stage: Selected essays* (P. Edmondson, Ed.). Oxford: Oxford University Press.

Welsford, E. (1935). *The fool: His social and literary history.* New York: Farrar and Rinehart.

Wheeler, R. P. (2000). Deaths in the family: The loss of a son and the rise of Shakespearean comedy. *Shakespeare Quarterly, 51*(2), 127–53.

Wilhelm, H. (1995). Change: Eight lectures on the *I Ching* (C. F. Baynes, Trans.). In H. Wilhelm & R. Wilhelm (Eds.), *Understand the I Ching: The Wilhelm lectures of the book of changes* (pp. 3–138). Princeton, NJ: Princeton University Press.

Wilhelm, R. (1984). *I Ching, or book of changes* (C. F. Baynes, Trans.). London: Routledge & Kegan Paul.

Wilhelm, R. (1995). Constancy and change (I. Eber, Trans.). In H. Wilhelm & R. Wilhelm (Eds.), *Understand the I Ching: The Wilhelm lectures of the Book of Changes* (pp. 139–316). Princeton, NJ: Princeton University Press.

Wilson, E. O. (1998). *Consilience: The unity of knowledge.* New York: Alfred A. Knopf.

Wilson Knight, G. (1948). *The crown of life: Essays in interpretation of Shakespeare's final plays.* London: Methuen & Co.

Winnicott, D. W. (2018). Ego distortion in terms of true and false self. In D. W. Winnicott (Ed.), *The maturational processes and the facilitating environment* (pp. 140–52). Oxon: Routledge.

Wood, J. O. (1973). Intimations of Actaeon in *Julius Caesar. Shakespeare Quarterly, 24*(1), 85–88.

Woodeson, N. (1993). King John. In R. Jackson & R. Smallwood (Eds.), *Players of Shakespeare 3.* Cambridge: Cambridge University Press.

Yachnin, P. (2023). Shame and solidarity in the Sonnets. *Shakespeare Quarterly, 74*(1), 37–48.

Yearling, E. M. (1982). Language, theme, and character in *Twelfth Night. Shakespeare Survey, 35*, 79–86.

Yeats, W. B. (1920). *The second coming.* https://www.poetryfoundation.org/poems/43290/the-second-coming

Index

Note: Numbers in *italics* indicate a figure.

Abt, T. 101
Actaeon 97–100, 107, 224, 234n29
Adam: Second Adam 49
Adelman, J. 174, 220n155, 222; *Suffocating mothers* 8, 17
Adonis 224; "Venus and Adonis" (Shakespeare) 17, 52
adultery 174, 237n166
Aguecheek *see* Andrew Aguecheek
alchemical tradition and metaphors 3, 17, 57–8, 68–9, 146–7, 169, 174; *calcinatio* of 89, 132, 230
All's Well That End's Well (AW) (Shakespeare) 80, 132
amor 104
amorality 40
amor fati 181
amplification 7, 10, 17, 98
Andrew Aguecheek 78, 94, 105, 112, 202
Angiers 22, 26, 39, 47; Citizen of Angiers 24
anima/animus 2, 139n60, *161, 182, 184, 189, 194, 198, 212, 215*
Antony and Cleopatra (AC)(Shakespeare) 80, 132
archetypal: anger 32; constellation 159–61; criticism 16; dominant(s) 33, 159, 160; energy 9; ether 14; experience 133; forces 153; functions 118, 186; idea 218; ideal 200; identifications 232; image 51; knowledge 155; material 154; motifs 14, 84; night-sea journey 138n54; order 23; patterns 2, 10, 11, 14; perspectives 60; pose 119; position 188, 195; qualities 159; resonances 6; situations 5, 6, 10, 42, 180; themes 172;

theory 16; View 49; wisdom 57, 73; wounding 35
archetype 2; anecdote-story-legend-fairytale-myth-archetype 6; concept of 7–9; defining 8, 9; the finalistic and 11; hero 12; heuristic of 10; Jungian 13–14, 17; literary uses of 14; mother 8; primeval 13; *puer aeternus* 30, 33, 178; trickster 9, 17, 30, 93; *see also* puer aeternus; trickster
Arlecchino 36
Arlidge, A. 86n8
Armstrong, P. 13–14
Aronson, A. 16–17, 76n101, 84 "Ocular Proof" 17; *Psyche & Symbol in Shakespeare* 17
Arthur (*King John*) 22–3, 25–6, 30, 102; absence of father of 57; bad taste of the treatment of 80; 'child subjectivity' moment in literary criticism and 28; death/killing of 41–2, 47, 62–9; Hubert's attempt to kill 23; as John's rival 33; Kanye/dream-Kanye and 65–70; as "little prince" 75; "nobody cares about" 52, 54, 58; 'Prince Arthur complex' 112, 125; Prince Arthur through-the-looking-glass 201; Shakespeare's Boys and 50–5; "poor eyes" of 55–6; in prison 56–60; as puer 36–7, 52, 69–70; as true king 25, 45; unconscious father-hunger of 126; unconscious wish of 173
Astington, J. 120
As You Like It (AY)(Shakespeare) 79, 136; Jaques 81, 130
AW *see* All's Well That End's Well

Babylonian Talmud 139n70
Bakhtin, M. 117, 119
Barber, C. L. 80, 110, 113, 121
Barrie, J. M. *see* Peter Pan
Barton, A. 86n29, 234n25, 237n166
Barton, J. 5, 83, 86n29, 98, 139n62, 222
bastards and bastardy in Shakespeare
    212, 215
Bastard, the (*King John*) 22–8, 36–45,
    49–50, 58–61, 65, 69, 71–2, 217;
    the Bastard Heart 38–44; inheriting
    of the kingdom by 118; integration
    into the Grand Mechanism of 84; as
    participant-observer 26; as a person 28;
    self-reinvention by 25; soliloquys by 73;
    "staying out of it" stance of 24; survival
    of 73; "thorns and dangers" of 204
Bate, J. 150, 162n53
Beatles: *Hey Jude* [Audio Recording] 126
Beauty and the Beast (animated film) 201
beauty and brains 203
Bednarz, J. 86n13
Beebe, J. 150, 158–60, 188; 8-function
    model of 18; on inferiority complexes
    215; on integrity and the inferior
    function 235n80; on Fe 199; on the puer
    64, 75n62; on the spine of consciousness
    179, 234n47; "The trickster in the arts"
    16, 64
Beier, B. V. 140n88
Belarius 142–3, 171, 182, 188–94, 218;
    Cloten and 203, 205–8; crime of 223;
    exiled 230; 'Morgan' and 188–94; as
    mystic 202; as opposing Fi *189, 194,*
    198, 212, 215, 232; proposed typology
    for *192*; reintegration of 232
Belch *see* Toby Belch
'belching whale' 111
Bellerophon 37, 49, 59, 76n111, 178
Belsey, C. 104
Bentham, J. 66
Berry, C. 127; *My ding-a-ling* [Musical
    Recording] 127
Bevan, Gilliam 148
Biden, Joe 71
Billington, M. 162n43
blame: concept of 35, 53; seeking targets to
    blame 64
blameless hero *see* heroes
blindness 17, 76n101
Bloom, H. 28, 38, 102, 120, 141n148, 144,
    205, 217, 224

Boas, F. S. 137n26
Bonjour, A. 29, 41, 50, 75n65
Book of Changes see I Ching
Book of Common Prayer 238n177
Book of Job (biblical) 227
Bradley, A. C. 141n148, 228
Brexit 70, 148
Bromberg, P. M. 91, 137n12
Brubaker, E. S. 73n6
Bruster, D. 94
Burckhardt, S. 23, 29, 72
burning bush, the (Biblical) 9
burning glare of the audience 97, 108
burning at the stake 126; *see also* heresy
Bush, George W. 26, 71
Butler, J. 137n8
Butler, M. 214

Cabaret (musical) 121
Cai, C. 155, 163n73, 178, 187, 200
Caius Lucius 171, 186, 188, 219, 241;
    as opposing Fi *189, 194, 198, 212,*
    215, 232
calcinatio 89, 132, 230
Campana, J. 76n125
Campbell, L. B. 74n36
Candido, J. 29
Capulet 53
Carlisle, C. J. 53
carnival 85, 89, 99; communality of 117;
    death of God and 114; Feste and 126;
    laughter of 117; Malvolio and 117–20;
    myths of or associated with 94, 117;
    ritual of 118–19; *Twelfth Night* and
    110–11, 113–14, 137, 218; twelfth
    night of 109, 113; utopian 120
Carnival King 117
Carr, J. 184, 201, 237n139
CE *see Comedy of Errors* (Shakespeare)
cedar tree 186–7, 237n169
celibacy 81
'censor' concept 92
Chambers, E. K. 51, 165
Champion, L. S. 26
Chen, X. 144, 148, 217
Cibber, Colley 27
Clavell, J. *see Shogun* (TV series)
Cleopatra 172
cliffhangers, narrative 71
Cloten 171, 184–7, 193, 196–211;
    beheading of 143, 211; burial of 193;
    corpse of 175, 180–1; foulness of 168;

as Heroic Fe *212, 215*; heroic self-image of 201; Innogen described by 169; Innogen's as love object of 142, 184; mundanity of 218; Orpheus referenced by 148; perversion in 211; Posthumus as shadow of 147; remarks on music by 223

Cobb, N. 16, 17

Cohen, L. 180

collective psyche 70

collective unconscious 2, 13, 33, 216, 237n169

Comedy of Errors (CE)(Shakespeare) 81

consilience 10

conspiracies 71, 86

conspiracy theories 26

Constance (*King John*) 22–2, 25, 27–8, 32, 36, 51–5, 60–3, 70, 83, 102, 135, 291; as widow 57

Cor *see Coriolanus* (Shakespeare)

Cordelion 36, 64–5

Coriolanus (Cor) (Shakespeare) 80, 116, 124, 205, 209–11

Coursen, H. R. 16, 18

COVID-19 26

Craig, H. 224

Curren-Aquino, D. T. 29, 70

Cymbeline (Shakespeare) 2, 134; achievement of normality in 164–233; Acteon archetype in 97; archetypical constellation in 159–61; Belarius and 'Morgan' 188–94; critics of 146–9; Cymbeline 144–6; Cymbeline & Lucius 186–8; final typological situation of *232*; Guiderius 207–11; Iachimo's device in 183–5; Innogen's body in 172–82; introduction to 18, 142–61; as kingdom in conflict 231; origin and first staging of 149–50; Posthumus 212–19; Posthumus in prison visited by ghosts 224–31; puer in 30; sacrifice in 195–207; sensation in 76n132; sidelining of title character in 28; synopsis of 142–4; 'till the tree die' (Innogen's return to Posthumus) 220–24, 237n169; Time in 166–72; typological riddles in 150–6; typology of the persona in 156–8; typology of the shadow in 158–9; unconscious structure of the play as a whole 3; *see also* Cloten; Demonic/Daimonic Te; Innogen

daimon: demon and 187; Diotima's definition of 188

Daimonic Fe 238n201

Daimonic Te 190, 228; *see also* Demonic/Daimonic Te

death-blows 220

death-mother 53, 61–2

demon: daimon and 187

demonic, the 160, 232

Demonic/Daimonic Te *161, 182, 184*; Cymbeline as *189, 194, 198, 212, 215, 228, 232*

demonism 186

Dench, J. 159, 234n55

deus absconditus 64, 172

deus ex machina 224

devouring flood 73, 241

devouring mother 30, 53

Diana (Roman goddess) 166

Diotima 188

dogs 97, 120, 218

"dogs, licking, candy, melting" cluster 115–16

double, the: death and 84; soul as the body's double 87n36

double act 114

double-agent 109

double-binds, double-bindedness 24, 183–4; Britain's false double-bind 233; dilemma of 30; puer/*King John* and 30, 35, 37, 39, 63–4, 69; trickster and 64, 91

double casting 147, 162n36

double dealing 87

double-entendres 144

doubleness 80, 84, 114

double-performance 107

doubles-back 71

Dover Wilson, J. 44, 86n8

Driscoll, J. 16

duende 160

Duì 兌 the Joyous: Lake 155, 156, 199–201, 209, 241

Duncan-Jones, K. 20n10, 135, 140n92, 141n156, 233n7

duplicity 80

Dusinberre, J. 36

Edinger, E. F. 16–17, 90

Elam, K. 81–2, 86n16, 107, 138n47, 140n100

Eliade, M. 218

Elizabeth I 30, 81, 86n5, 219; death of 133; James I as successor of 206; plays about 158
Elizabethan English: 'Hamnet' and 'Hamlet' in 141n154
Elizabethans and Elizabethan era 18, 23, 52, 66, 71, 73, 80–2, 139n72; loss of mourning of 135; post-Elizabethan England 172, 231
Emerson, R. W. 90
Empedocles 67
enantiodromia 116, 211
eros (in *King John*): ambivalent 57; faithful 43; faithless 25, 33–73; Shakespeare's own 63
eros (in *Twelfth Night*): unambivalent 110
existential: crisis 70; dilemma 124; imprisonment 60; problems 53
extraverted feeling (Fe) 152, 153, *156, 157, 158, 192*, 195, 199, 207–11; healthy 207; heroic 232; type 237n140; *see also* Heroic Fe
extraverted intuiting (Ne) 152, *156, 157, 158*, 159, 183; witchy 197; *see also* Senex/Witch Ne
extraverted sensing (Se) 152, *156, 158*, 181, *192*; *see also* Puella Se
extraverted thinking (Te) 152, *156, 159, 192*; Cymbeline's 232; demonic 160, 187; *see also* Demonic/Daimonic Te

fabric of history 231
Fabricius, J. 16
False Self 85, 125, 131
Falstaff (*Henry IV*) 8, 39, 40, 81, 112, 123, 145
fate 53, 71, 72, 90, 138n54, 205, 231, 241; *amor fati* (embrace of) 181
fathers 34, 60; absent 57, 64, 172; dead 64, 102; good 64, 191, 212; would-be 57
fathers and daughters 84
fathers and sons 8
Fe *see* extraverted feeling
Feore, Colm 184
Fi *see* introverted feeling
Fike, M. A. 16; *A Jungian study of Shakespeare: The visionary mode* 17
finalistic perspective 11
Fisherman (*Pericles*) 111
Fisher, S., & Fisher, R. 141n130
fool, the 39, 79, 89, 123; co-fools 84

forefathers 231
Freud, S. 92, 95, 97; on the double 84, 87n36; Jung and 1; on the latency period 139n64; on the 'navel' of the dream 127
Freudian(s) 15
Freudian stream 14
Freudian techniques and approaches 11–12; 'censor' concept of 92
Frye, N. 13–18, 84, 129–30
functions *see* psychic functions

gadfly 59
Garber, M. 50, 201
Garrick, David 147
Gaston (*Beauty and the Beast*) 201
Gay, P. 82
Gèn 艮 Keeping Still (Mountain) 155, *156*, 189, 193
Gilderoy Lockhart *(Harry Potter)* 201
God 9, 23–4, 58, 63, 65, 114, 118, 125, 227–9; the Devil and 238n182
God-image 228, 238n189
Goldmanian Centre 3, 33, 36, 88, 170
Goldman, M. 3, 137n29
Gore, Al 26, 71
Grand Mechanism, the 53, 75n94, 84
Granville-Barker, H. 121, 144
Greenblatt, S. 14
Greif, K. 125
Grennan, E. 35
Grima Wormtongue 186
Grudin, R. 137n7

Hal (Prince) 4, 13, 112
Hamlet (Ham)(Shakespeare) 7, 13, 16, 134, 141n154, 205, 228; everybody dies in 79; Hamlet as writer of (thought experiment) 132; Hamlet Senior 64; sexless and disgusting bodies of 100; "slings and arrows" of 204; Toby Belch and 111, 120; *Twelfth Night* as successor to 138n54; violets in 102; writing of 85, 101, 136
Hamnet (child of Shakespeare): death of 8, 51–2, 134–7, 141n156
Hamnet see Hamlet
Harry Potter and the Chamber of Secrets (Rowling) 201
Hawkes, T. 148
Hayles, N. 141n143
Hazlitt, W. 82, 144–5, 147

Heberle, M. A. 33, 50
Hecate 166
Hector 111
Helen of Troy 132, 175
Henderson, J. L. 43, 235n88
Henry V (HV) (Shakespeare) 44, 164,
    218–19, 235n93
Henry VI (1HVI, 2HVI, 3HVI)
    (Shakespeare) 4, 10, 39–40, 96, 173,
    237n157; *see also* Falstaff
Heraud, J. A. 27
heresy 126
hero archetype 12, 201, 210
heroes: antihero 202, 208; blameless 227,
    233n6; Cloten as 203; Cymbeline as
    233; Guiderius as 207; mythological
    180; Posthumous-as-hero 147;
    Shakespearean 233; tragic 205
heroic failure 202
heroic feeling 211
Heroic Fe *182, 184, 189, 194, 198*; Cloten
    as 202; Guiderius as 209; Guiderius/
    Cloten/Philario as *212, 215*; need
    for 208
Heroic Se *see* Se
heroine 14, 180; Viola 103
hero myth 43
hero's journey 209
Hexagram 6 170
Hexagram 7 107, 112
Hexagram 17 69
Hexagram 20 3
Hexagram 23 25
Hexagram 25 91
Hexagram 30 48, 178
Hexagram 51 187
Hexagram 52 189, 193
Hexagram 58 199–201, 209
Hillman, J. 34, 43, 46, 49–50, 54, 75n96
histrio (actor) 93
histrionic dysphoria 131
histrionic pattern (*Twelfth Night*) 2, 82,
    88–137
histrionic personality 2, 95, 97
histrionic, the 91, 93; histrionic Self 85
Hitler 44, 49
Holinshed, R. 46, 52; *Chronicles* 150, 218
Holocaust, the 70
Holocaust denialism 26
Hotson, L. 81
Hotspur 48
Howard, J. E. 24

Huang, F. 91
Hughes, T. 6, 15–17, 21n59, 233n7
humour (comedic): wit as distinct from
    20n43, 140n97
humours (bodily) and humouralism
    75n67, 94
hunter and hunted 97; *see also* Actaeon
Hunter, K. 63
Hutton, R. 140n82
hysteria 91–3, 137n16, 137n17

Iachimo 142–4, 169, 173–6, 179, 182,
    213–16; Iago compared to 189; Innogen
    and 212–13; mundanity of 218; as
    persuader 140n88; Posthumus as victim
    of 226; 'rape' by 234n33; stealing of a
    kiss by 207; as Trickster Si *184, 189,
    194, 198, 212, 215, 232*, 233; women
    and 185
Iachimo's Device 183–5
"Iach-in-the-box" 201
Iago 115, 132, 190, 216; Iachimo compared
    to189; as persuader 140n88
Iago–Roderigo 112
Icarus 37, 50, 65, 224
I Ching 3, 5, 10, 25, 35, 48, 69, 91, 107,
    170, 178, 227; as source of archetypal
    knowledge 155; tao of 73; *see also*
    Hexagram
ick, the 184
individuation 7, 11, 17, 85, 151, 221, 230
Inferior (Anima/Animus) Ti *161, 182, 184,
    189, 194, 198, 212, 215*
Innogen 128, 170–1; bedroom of 185;
    body of 172–82; Britian (the country)
    identified with 148; clarity of 167;
    disguising of herself as Fidele (a young
    man) 128, 142–3, 148, 188, 195–6,
    204, 207, 220; *see also* Puella Se;
    Iachimo and 183; Imogen vs. 161n1;
    plotline of *Cymbeline* involving 142–3,
    147; religiousness of 186; sacrifice of
    195; spine of consciousness of *179*;
    Walter and Dench's versions of 159;
    wedding of 168–9; *see also* Cloten;
    Puella Se
intrapsychic complexes 54
introverted feeling (Fi) 152, 153, *156, 159*,
    159; Belarius 188–90, *192*; Innogen 196
introverted intuiting (Ni) 152, 153–4, *156,
    158*, 158, *159*; 'inferior' 179; Morgan
    190, *192*

introverted sensing (Si) 152, 154, *156, 157, 159*, 159; Morgan 190, *192*; *see also* Trickster Si

introverted thinking (Ti) 152, 153, *156, 157, 158, 159*, 159; Belarius *192*; Hamlet 236n133; Posthumus *215*, 226; *see also* Inferior (Animus) Ti

Jackson, P. *see Lord of the Rings*

James I 145, 149, 206

JC *see Julius Caesar* (Shakespeare)

Jesus Christ Superstar (musical) 72

Jing-Nuan, W. 25

Job (biblical) 238n189

John (King) *see* King John

John Lackland (King John) 44–50

Johnson, S. (Dr.) 27, 146

Jonson, B. 81–2, 133; *Every Man Out of His Humor* 82, 117

Jordan, C. 237n165

Jordan-Finnegan, R. 16

Jove 180; *see also* Jupiter

Julius Caesar (JC)(Shakespeare) 69, 72, 116, 138n40, 171; Augustus Caesar 218; Brutus 5, 56; Cassibelian 218; Cassius 56, 119; 'Ceasario' and 103; conspiracy against Caesar in 81; Cymbeline knighted by 230; death of Caesar 41; Julius Caesar 41, 72, 81; Mark Antony 41, 44

Jung, C. G. 13; Answer to Job 238n189; *Psychological Types* 151; The Stages of Life 235n89; *see also* amplification; archetype; finalistic perspective; individuation; psyche; shadow; unconscious, the

Jungian: approach 5, 12–17, 28; archetype 10; concepts 2; criticism 13; key concepts 7; post-Jungian 148

Jungians 13–16

Jupiter (Roman god) 143, 216, 237n166

Juric, L. P. 138n32

Kamps, I. 137n8

Kanye *see* West, K.

Kastan, D. S. 24

Kawai, T. 145

Kerrigan, J. 233n17

Kietzman, M. J. 86n13

Kirsch, A. 17, 143, 233n6

King John (KJ) (Shakespeare) 135–6, 241; Arthur's attempt to break out of prison in 56–60; Arthur's blinding in 54–6; Arthur and Shakespeare's boys in 50–4; Arthur's treatment in bad taste in 80; bastardy in 215; the Bastard/Bastard Heart of 38–44, 118; Cibber's adaption of 27; Constance 83, 201; the Constant Mother archetype in 60–4; criticism of 27–9; faithless eros of 32–73; introduction to and overview of 22–30; John Lackland in 44–50; "Kanye on the Tower" dream imagery of 65–9; modern and postmodern 23–27; myth structures in 110; opening image of 197; origin of play 29–30; plot synopsis of 22–3; *puer aeternus* of 2, 33–8, 69–73; Puer King of 44–50; puer problem in 89; Richard Lionheart in 218; as tragedy of the *puer aeternus* 31; truth and legitimacy in 26; the "two sons" problem of 64–5; *see also* Bastard; Constance; Malvolio; *puer aeternus*

King Lear (KL)(Shakespeare) 80, 134, 138n40, 150, 241; Edmund 197; Gloucester/Gloucester's blinding in 55, 57, 175, 228

KJ *see King John*

KL *see King Lear*

Knowles, K. 51

Kott, J. 75n94, 96, 165

Ko, Y. J. 95, 99, 128, 165

Kronos 166

Kūn 坤 the Receptive (Earth) 155, *156*

Laing, R. D. 137n12

Lamb, C. 83

lamb: Innogen as 205; lost 58; pet, killing of 235n95; sacrificial 195, 235n95

Lander, J. M. 76 n100

Landry, D. E. 143, 147

Lawrence, W. W. 162n35

Leavis, F. R. 162n52

Leggatt, A. 74n35

Levin, H. 83

Lewis (*King John*) 22–23 39, 41, 63

Lewis, C. 84, 137n13, 140n87

Li 离 the Clinging (Fire) 48–9, 155, *156*, 178

Lindley, D. 236n115

Lisak, C. 138n32

LLL *see Love's Labour's Lost* (Shakespeare)

Lloyd Webber, A. *see Jesus Christ Superstar*

Lord of the Rings (film) 186
Love's Labour's Lost (LLL)(Shakespeare) 56, 81
Lucrece 17, 107
Lyne, R. 13–14, 227

MA *see Much Ado About Nothing*
Macbeth (Mac) 13, 80, 138n40, 150; Banquo 56; Lady Macbeth 197; Macbeth 55–6, 72, 199, 205, 228; prophecy in 199
madness (insanity) 51, 55, 62, 100, 126
Magna Carta 46, 71
male gaze 108, 174
Maley, W. 162n22
Malvolio 98, 112–20, 132; audiences' sympathy for 82–3; Barton's interpretation of 83, 87n32; as Carnival King 117–18; early critical interest in 82; Feste and 122–6; imprisonment of 79; Luciferian 129; madness of 100; metaphoric castration of138n47; Olivia pursued by 106; originality in Shakespeare's oeuvre of 81; plotline collapse of 128; puritanism of 114; revenge plot against 78; scapegoating of 130; Sinden's performance as 120; toadying behavior of 104
mandala 14, 67, 156; Crichton's four functions in shape of *157*, 160; typological 182, *182*, 191, 233
Manheim, M. 38, 51
manhood: British 216; Viola's 128
Manningham, J. 80–2
Maria Columbina (*Twelfth Night*) 114–20
Marlowe, Christopher: murder of 133
Masefield, J. E. 27, 49
mask 91; actor's (professional) 126; carnival and 113; comedian who cannot take off his mask 120; defensive 125; dropping of 127; false face as 107; meaningless 164; persona as 85, 125, 128; Viola 128–9, 131
masking: unmasking of masked performers 128–9
Maslen, R. W. 126, 140n86
Maugham, W. Somerset 139n70
May, Theresa 148
MBTI *see* Meyers-Briggs Type Indicator
McCamus, Tom 48
Measure for Measure (MM) (Shakespeare) 17, 80, 100, 132, 134

Merchant of Venice (MV) (Shakespeare) 18, 81, 130, 200; Lancelot Giobbe 123; Shylock 83
merrymaking 201
Merry Olde England 113, 164, 231
Merry Wives of Windsor (MWW) (Shakespeare) 97, 136, 139n80
Metamorphoses (Ovid) 224
Meyers-Briggs Type Indicator (MBTI) 150
Micklem, N. 91
Midsummer Night's Dream (MND) (Shakespeare) 9, 18, 29, 79, 81, 89
Milton, J. 48–9
Minton, E. 31n48
Mirren, Helen 184
mirror-hunger 91, 126, 137n9
mirrors and mirroring 22, 53, 72, 88; accurate 108; affirming 103–4, 106; audience as 170; histrionic/hysteria as mirror in search of 92–3; parents and countries as 171; Viola and 103–4, 106, 122
MM *see Measure for Measure* (Shakespeare)
MND *see Midsummer Night's Dream* (Shakespeare)
Morgan: Belarius and 188–94; Fatherly Ni *194, 198, 212, 215*; introverted intuiting 190, *192*; introverted sensing 190, *192*; Trickster Si *198, 212, 215*
Moses 9
mother: constant 60–4; death-mother 53, 61–2; devouring 30, 53; narcissistic 125
Mount Olympus 59, 178
Much Ado About Nothing (MA) (Shakespeare) 71, 79, 136, 237n145
Murakami, Haruki 145, 166
Murphy, E. 18
Murray, H. A. 75n56
MV *see Merchant of Venice*
MWW *see Merry Wives of Windsor*
myth 6, 13–14; Actaeon 97, 100; blinding theme in 55; carnival 94, 110–11, 113, 117; hero 43; heroic 210; Paradise 136; puer 34, 59; pueri of 37, 59; religious 129; Tarquin and Tereus 175; validity of, challenging of 148
myth-forms 13, 16, 110–11, 114
mythical time-before 218
myth-ingredients, humans as 240
mythological: properties 90; tricksters 93, 114

mythologization 46, 97, 100
mythology 10
mythos 184

narcissistic: ideals 231; mother 125;
    wounding 1, 91
Narcissus 224
Ne *see* extraverted intuiting
Ni *see* introverted intuiting
Nosworthy, J. M. 165, 204

Oth *see Othello* (Shakespeare)
Othello (Oth)(Shakespeare) 41, 80, 115,
    144, 205, 216–17; Desdemona 111,
    132; Emilia 111; *see also* Iago
otter 145
Oxberry, W. 27

panopticon 66
Paster, G. K. 75n67
Pegasus 59, 178
Pentland, E. 86n11, 138n32
Penuel, S. 99, 110, 135
Per *see Pericles, Prince of Tyre*
    (Shakespeare)
Pericles, Prince of Tyre (Per)(Shakespeare):
    belching whale in 111; family in
    80; happiness in 133; Marina (baby
    daughter) 58, 167
persona 50, 84–5, 104, 108, *161, 182,
    184, 189, 194, 198*; alternate 123;
    Cymbeline 161, 166, 173, 175;
    hypokrit 116; Innogen's 195–6; opaque
    122; performative 85; political 116;
    self-presentation of 14; typology of
    156–8
personal data harvesting 66
personality(ies) 2, 33–4; basic 151; the
    Bastard's 38; coherent 12; conscious
    8; coreless 217; failed Fe 209; Feste's
    114; full 158; histrionic 2, 82, 91,
    95, 97; male 34; opposing 160, 188;
    part-personality 179; puer 34–5; real 99,
    203; relatable 183; royal 221; theatre or
    theatrical 85, 135; total 186; unexpected
    192; Viola's 102–3; vulnerability in 179
personality disorder 93
personal mother 61
perversion 211
Peter Pan 32, 64; *see also puer aeternus*
*Peter Pan, or the Boy Who Wouldn't Grow
    Up* (Barrie) 131

Phaëthon 50
Plato 9, 92, 136; *Symposium* 188
Porterfield, S. 12, 16–17, 238n195
Posthumus *215; see also Cymbeline*
post-Jungian 148
postmodern aesthetic and/or sensibility
    145–6, 168, 170, 172, 222
postmodern *King John see King John*
postmoderns 24, 71, 73
presentism 145
prison 66
privacy 67
problem-play 94, 137n26
projective identification 74n18
pseudohistory 150
psyche 4, 8, 10; Aronson on 17; Arthur's
    57; author's 13; characters' own 36;
    collective 70; Edinger on 17; feeling
    as a reaction of 153; finalistic 11;
    'functions' of 150; histrionic 91, 93;
    Illyrian 99; one's own 15; paradox of 5;
    part-psyche 7; a play as/play's own 32,
    37; Posthumus' 148; puer and 34; Self
    and 17; Shakespearean/Shakespeare's
    own 89–90, 135; splinter 7;
    Viola's 105
psychedelic trips 121
psychic functions: eight 152–4; eight
    I Ching 155–6, *156*; irrational/rational
    155; perception 154; personified 154;
    see also extraverted feeling (Fe);
    extraverted intuiting (Ne); extraverted
    sensing (Se); extraverted thinking (Te);
    introverted feeling (Fi); introverted
    intuiting (Ni); introverted sensing (Si);
    introverted thinking (Ti)
puella 76n106
Puella Se: Innogen as 178, *182, 184, 189,
    194, 198, 212, 215, 232*
Puer/Puella Se 160, *161,* 180; *see also*
    Puella Se
puer (*pueri*) 43–54, 56–7, 59–69, 89, 131,
    133–134; *Cymbeline 161*; death-mother
    in lives of 61; latent suicidality of
    60; *see also* Bellerophon; Icarus;
    Phaëthon; senex
puer aeternus 2, 12, 33–8, 74n50, 75,
    62; cure of 136; death of the puer/long
    live the puer (King John) 69–73, 134;
    demise of 67; King John as 30, 33–8;
    Peter Pan as 32
puerility 112

puer/puella: elegy for 240–1; as expression of hero archetype 210; Se 159, *161*; synergy 76n106; syzygy 179; the trickster as shadow of 181, 183, *184*
puer–senex polarity 51–2
Pyramus and Thisbe 224

Quiller-Couch, A. 86n8

Rackin, P. 24
Radin, P. 93
Rees, R. 216
remorse 68, 119
Reville, Clive 236n113
Richard II (RII)(Shakespeare) 37, 44, 47, 109
Richard III (RIII) (Shakespeare) 29, 44, 51–2, 55; "winter of our discontent" 164
riddles 78, 118, 140n87; typological (Cymbeline) 150–6
Riemann, F. 95, 109
RII *see Richard II*
RIII *see Richard III*
RJ *see Romeo and Juliet* (Shakespeare)
Rogers-Gardner, B. 16
Romeo type 201
Romeo and Juliet (RJ)(Shakespeare) 17, 52, 79, 169, 181, 201; Capulets 53; love between Romeo and Juliet in 205; "two households. . ." 164
Rowland, S. 15–18
Rowling, J. K. *see Harry Potter and the Chamber of Secrets*
Royal Shakespeare Company (RSC) 114, 148–9
RSC *see* Royal Shakespeare Company

Saint-Exupéry, Antoine de 45, 62
Saint Crispin's Day speech (*Henry V*) 235n93
Saint Sebastien 109–110; feast day of 139n73
Samuels, A. 14–15
Sanders, E. R. 179, 181, 234n33
satire 33
Schalkwyk, D. 97
Schiffer, J. 83, 86n12
Schwartz, S. E. 76n106, 178
Se (extraverted sensing) 176–82; Cai on 178; heroic 178, *179*; Innogen's 178; *puer/puella* 159, *161*; *see also* Puella Se
senex 12, 30, 50–2, 141n126
Senex/Witch 160, *161*

Senex/Witch Ne *184, 189, 194, 198, 212, 215*; Pisanio as *232*
sex life 174
shadow *161, 182, 184, 189, 194, 198*; concept of 7, 11; Jungian 2; France as England's shadow 26; Malvolio as scapegoat and 113, 116, 126; persona and 17; puer's refusal to engage 63; trickster as puer's shadow 36, 64, 69, 93, 181, 183; typology of 158–9
shadow functions 156, 160, 199
Shakespeare, Hamnet *see* Hamnet
Shakespeare, John 141n154
Shakespeare, William *see* [plays by name]
shame 33, 61, 68, 73, 123, 128, 139n71, 173, 196, 217, 222–3
Shapiro, M. 236n122
Shavian commentary 24, 147
Shaw, G. B. 6, 42, 146–7, 217, 220, 222
Sher, Antony 8
Shogun (TV series) 154
Si *see* introverted sensing
Sinden, D. 83, 120, 130
Skura, M. A. 13, 91, 97, 116, 125, 137n9, 229n192
slander 169, 189, 195, 214
Smallwood, R. 38
Smith, B. R. 140n85
Spears, B. 174
spine of consciousness *179*, 234n47
Spurgeon, C. F. 16, 57–8, 96, 115–16
Stalin 44, 165, 166
Stein, M. 165
Stewart, M. 113
Stravinsky, Igor 145
Sumpter, Donald 184
Swander, H. 148, 217, 233n6
Swinburne, A. C. 147, 172–3, 241
syzygy 179, 234n43; anima/animus 139n60; puer/puella 76n106

TA *see Titus Andronicus*
Talmud *see* Babylonian Talmud
Taming of the Shrew (TS) 105
Tanner, T. 145
Tarquin and Tereus 175, 185
TC *see Troilus and Cressida*
Te *see* extraverted thinking
Tempest, The (Tem) (Shakespeare) 18, 149; Caliban 211; "past is prologue" 102; plot of 167; post-tragedy world of 204; Prospero 134, 167, 240; Time in 167

Tennyson 147, 221
TGV *see* Two Gentlemen of Verona
Théoden 186
Thweatt, J. 46, 74n50; *Hitler as Puer* 49
Ti *see* introverted thinking
Tim *see* Timon of Athens
Timon of Athens (Tim) 80, 116, 205,
    209–211
Titus Andronicus (TA) 52, 58, 97; Chiron
    236n118; Lavinia 175
Tobin, J. J. M. 76n100
Toby Belch (*Twelfth Night*) 78, 81, 94,
    111–14, 135
Tolkien, J. R. R. *see* Lord of the Rings
tree: 'Till the tree die' (Posthumus) 220–4,
    238n169
Troilus and Cressida (TC)(Shakespeare)
    80, 85, 89, 111, 132, 134
Trousdale, G., & Wise, K. *see* Beauty and
    the Beast
trickster 160; the Bastard as 39, 42;
    boundary-crossing by 185; Coyote
    93; female 114, 140n86; fool and 241;
    healing by 113; hero 37; histrionic
    91; Jung's view of 43; Loki 93;
    mythological 93; puer allied with 69,
    134; as puer's shadow 36, 64, 69,
    93, 181, 183; silence used by 115; as
    victims of own tricksterdom 105
trickster archetype 9, 17, 30, 93
Trickster Si *161*, *182*, 183; Iachimo *184*,
    189, *194*, *198*, *212*, *215*, *232*, 233
transcendent function 13, 38, 42–3, 211
Trump, D. 70–1
trumpery 222
TS *see* Taming of the Shrew
Tucker, K. 16, 18, 28, 76n110
Turing Test 93
Twelfth Night (TN)(Shakespeare): Andrew
    Aguecheek 78, 94, 106, 112, 202;
    coagulatio and *calcinatatio* in 88–90,
    181; criticism of 82–4; as farewell
    to childish things 133; Feste 120–5;
    Feste's False Self in 125–7; as hinge
    in Shakespeare's oeuvre 79–80;
    histrionic pattern in 2, 82, 88–137;
    histrionism in 90–3; Illyria in 96; Maria
    Columbina 114–20; Noli me Tangere
    (Sebastian and Viola) in 127–31, 225;
    Olivia 106–9; Ordinary Time in 88;
    origins of play 80–2; Orsino 97–100;
    performance and authenticity in 2;

persona in 84–6; Sebastian & Antonio
    109–10; self-performance in 69;
    sexlessness of 174; 'smiling at grief'
    in 78–86; survival themes in 241;
    synopsis and overview of 78–9; Toby &
    Andrew 110–14; Toby Belch 78, 81,
    94, 111–14, 135; the twelfth night of
    94–5; Viola 100–6, 201; . . . What You
    Will 96–7
two faced 164
Two Gentlemen of Verona (TGV) 81, 129
'Two Kings' struggle 26
two-person beings 136
typological mandala 182, *182*, 191, 233;
    see also mandala
typological riddles: Cymbeline 150–6;
    see also riddles
typology of the persona 156–8; *see also*
    persona
typology of the shadow 158–9; *see also*
    shadow

UKParliament *see* Magna Carta
uncanny valley 166
unconscious, the 7–9, 85, 102, 138n54,
    216, 226

Vaughn, V. M. 23, 26–7, 29, 71
Venus (the goddess) 224; astrological 159;
    "Venus and Adonis" (Shakespeare)
    17, 52
virginity 174, 234n25
Von Franz, M.-L. 18, 34–5, 45, 50, 60, 62,
    75n71, 158
Vujovic, A. 28

Walter, H. 159, 175–6, 178, 234n25
Wanamaker, Z. 96, 103, 105
Warren, R. 149, 188, 195, 236n133
Wayne, V. 145, 162n53, 162n54, 174, 180
Well, The 井, *Jing* 227
Wells, S. 74n27
West, K., and dream-Kanye 65–9, 98
Wheeler, R. P. 51, 103, 134
Wilhelm, H. 241
Wilhelm, R. 4, 48–9, 181, 187, 190, 200
Wilson Knight, G. 144, 148, 180, 186, 216,
    217, 224, 233n16, 238n179
Winnicott, D. W. 85, 125
Winter's Tale (WT) (Shakespeare) 149,
    162n54; post-tragedy of 204; Time in
    166–7

wish-fulfilment 179
womanhood 128, 147–8; Innogen as
    symbol of 172, 221
wood 155, *156*
Wood, J. O. 138n40
Woodeson, N. 35
woods, the 224
WT *see Winter's Tale*

Xùn 巽 the Gentle (Wind/Wood) 155, *156*

Yachnin, P. 139n71
Yorick (*Hamlet*) 123

Zeus 59, 211; *see also* Jupiter
Zhèn 震 the Arousing (Thunder) 155,
    156, 176

For Product Safety Concerns and Information please contact our EU
representative GPSR@taylorandfrancis.com
Taylor & Francis Verlag GmbH, Kaufingerstraße 24, 80331 München, Germany

* 9 7 8 1 0 3 2 9 8 0 8 3 6 *